The 'Wired' MNC

The Role of Information Systems for Structural Change in Complex Organizations

INSTITUTE OF INTERNATIONAL BUSINESS (IIB)
STOCKHOLM SCHOOL OF ECONOMICS

Address: Holländargatan 32, P.O. Box 6501, S-113 83 Stockholm, Sweden.
Telephone: +46 (0)8 736 9000; Telefax: +46 (0)8 319927; Telex: 16514 HHS S

- Founded in 1975.
- Is a research institute at the Stockholm School of Economics.
- Conducts theoretical and empirical research within the area of Business Administration with emphasis on International Business.
- Arranges seminars for businessmen, researchers and key people in the civil services.
- Is in charge of undergraduate and graduate courses in International Business at the Stockholm School of Economics.
- Publishes its research findings and results in a series of research papers, and in articles and books.

IIB BOARD

Further information about current research at the Institute and its publications ca be found in a brochure, which will be mailed on request.

The 'Wired' MNC

The Role of Information Systems for Structural Change in Complex Organizations

Peter Hagström

A Dissertation for the
Doctor's Degree in
Business Administration

Stockholm School of Economics 1991

ISBN 91-971730-0-2
gotab 94593, Stockholm 1991

Key words: Information Systems
Telecommunications
Computers
Multinational Companies
Organization Theory
Firm Strategy and Structure
Firm (Theory of)
Economic Geography; Corporate Geography

Cover illustration courtesy of SKF/IMIT.

Distributed by:
Institute of International Business,
Stockholm School of Economics,
P.O. Box 6501, S-113 83 Stockholm, Sweden.
Tel + 46 (0) 8-736 90 00
Fax + 46 (0) 8-31 99 27

To the Reader,

Acknowledgements

The working title of this volume has been "Synthesis or Confusion". I remain deeply grateful to all who have provided support in times of confusion and inspiration in my pursuit of knowledge. Synthesis, however, remains elusive.

The then Head of the Research Secretariat at the Swedish National Board of Trade, Per Magnus Wijkman, very generously released me from our 'suicide pact' when I was invited back to academic life. The warm welcome afforded me at the Institute of International Business will, likewise, never be forgotten. Professor Jan-Erik Vahlne took me on as a doctoral student and has remained as an important source of encouragement. The institute has continued to provide a most stimulating environment, both for research and socially. Thanks are due in rich measure to my past and present colleagues and to other members of the institute.

My thesis committee has been exceptionally supportive throughout the arduous process of completing this study. Professor Gunnar Hedlund introduced me to new questions and issues and has always been able to widen my horizons, something for which I am most grateful. His insightful comments have provided much inspiration for my work. Professor Claes-Fredrik Claeson's unfailing interest has been invaluable. Docent Lars Håkanson has spent much time reviewing my drafts and has always been ready to offer constructive comments. My warmest thanks. I am also indebted to Professor Claes-Robert Julander, especially for long discussions on the basics of doing research.

Professors Bruce Kogut, Ikujiro Nonaka, Charles Perrow, and Bengt Stymne have also contributed valuable comments at different points in the course of the study.

Dr. Jessie Lokrantz read the whole manuscript and came with useful suggestions for improving the language.

I want to thank General Electric Information Services in Sweden for providing seed money for the project. Generous research funding has been provided by the Swedish Council for Research in the Humanities and Social Sciences (HSFR), and by the Information Technology Research Program of the Institute for Management of Innovation and Technology (IMIT). I am most grateful.

SKF deserves special thanks for making the empirical phase of the research possible. In particular, I want to acknowledge Håkan Landahl, Director, Group Information Systems for the assistance given me during various stages of the process.

Without the generous and competent help of Robert Nobel and Vanja Ekberg this volume would never have seen the light of day. Computer and administrative support can be cruicial.

Finally, I want to thank my family for being there. Oliver and Andrea have a natural way of making sure that I have my priorities right.

Stockholm in October, 1991.

Peter Hagström

Contents

1. INTRODUCTION AND OVERVIEW

This is a study of changing complex organization. Our overriding interest concerns both the manifestations of complexity in organizations and the process of change.

Organizational complexity is a distinguishing hallmark of the multinational corporation (MNC) among the population of organizations. In addition, the MNC, arguably, represents one of the most important organizational forms in the contemporary world.

Organizational change is an elusive concept. A - perhaps the - key aspect of the functioning of organizations is the organizational information flows. Recent advances in micro-electronics technology have dramatically altered the ways in which information can be handled. In turn, the question of how, and if, organizations change with the arrival, and use of modern information technology clearly becomes pertinent.

This introductory chapter first clarifies the research issue further and indicates what the whole excercise has led to. Second, the chosen structure of the whole study is described together with a brief summary of its contents. Specifics concerning presentation and some guidance for the reader are given in the last main section.

1.1 Research Scope

The existence and spread of multinational corporations (MNCs) are a poignant manifestation of the rapid internationalization of the world economy in the 20th century. This development has been closely associated with the coming of modern methods of transportation and communication. The most recent example is the application of new information technology to international communications. The combination of telecommunications with electronic computing, in effect, constitutes a novel method for transport of information.

Although MNCs and new information systems have prompted much attention and research separately, the intersecting set of the two has attracted surprisingly little scholarly interest. If the past is anything to go by, this state of affairs appears somewhat curious. Considering that new means of communication give new meaning to concepts of distance, this would then be especially relevant for (large) multinational corporations, where both geographical and hierarchical distances are great.

More specifically, the advent of global (near)on-line-real-time information systems that involve the non-tangible transmission of machine-readable data for processing, storage and/or retrieval should alter the opportunity set of ways for firms to organize their activities. Thus, we find scope for discussing changes in the location of activities in MNCs in particular, subsequent to the introduction of international data communications and attendant computer-based systems.

Two main types of locational change are especially relevant:

I. geographical location (spatial distribution of activities), and

II. 'organizational location' (internal distribution of activities and their location in relation to the organizational boundary).

Whereas geographical location is a well-established concept, 'organizational location' is not. Moreover, 'organizational location' has two dimensions:

a) 'hierarchical location' (where inside the organization activities are performed), and

b) 'institutional location' (whether related activities are external or internal to the organization).

In consequence, control and coordination of firm activities in the face of locational change are key concerns for this study.

A motivating assumption for elevating location of activities as a focus of analysis is a view of the organization, or firm, as being a bundle of more or less loosely-coupled activities. That allows a more consistent treatment of organizational change as it is manifested in space and in organizational terms. For instance, 'hierarchical location' relates well to the established issue of centralization vs. decentralization, and 'institutional location' to externalization vs. internalization. An activities-view of the organization also achieves close congruence with the enabling characteristics of new information systems, in turn following from the improved transportability, especially of information-based services.

Our main purpose has been to investigate organizational change conceptually along the above dimensions, while still keeping our nose close to the ground, so as to ensure the practical relevance of the discussion. To this end, existing theoretical and empirical literature from various academic disciplines are discussed critically. The breadth of scope in terms of antecedents carries with it a cost of a commensurate lack of depth regarding each discipline. The troublesome trade-off is handled with recourse to instrumentalism, and thus to pronounced selectivity; only the directly relevant contributions, as argued, from the fields of geography, economics, business administration, organization theory, and computer science are considered.

The overwhelming part of the new empirical evidence gathered in the course of the present inquiry comes from one MNC: SKF. The company sports impeccable MNC-credentials, and was selected on the basis of having an excellent track record in usage of international data communications-cum-computer systems.

Several salient tendencies emerge from the present study.

New possibilities for firms to subdivide, or fragment activities open opportunities for specialization and subsequent recombination. On both counts, the MNC's opportunity set for geographical and 'organizational' (re-)location widens. Standardization imposed by the efficient use of the communication channels facilitates control and coordination of increasingly more fragmented and dispersed activities in the MNC.

In turn, the set of very different activities performed by the firm and their reciprocal linkages needs to be reconsidered. Information systems can provide an alternative to ownership through improved control, leading to selective vertical disintegration. The MNC can more easily exploit very activity-specific locational advantages also of a temporary nature. The very notion of a 'center' in the MNC is undermined, casting doubt on the usefulness of a familiar term like centralization.

If some conjecture may be allowed, we can discern traits of a slightly idealized generic MNC; a shorthand for which is the 'wired' MNC, where information systems are a key aspect of organization structure.

The 'wired' MNC clearly becomes more opaque as the organizational boundary is blurred. The tolerance for deviation from (formal) organizational orthodoxy increases with information systems, making control and coordination along multiple dimensions much more of a viable proposition. Some coordination can be 'automated', e.g. with embedded decision-rules for interfacing order-entry and production scheduling systems. The very likely deepening internal differentiation among organizational subunits tends to go hand-in-hand with organizational change becoming more of a continuous process.

With an extensive communications infrastructure in place, spontaneous lateral communication opens new avenues for coordination in MNCs. For example, we have found instances of various internal markets appearing, of lateral information exchange short-circuiting the traditional chain of command, and of demand-propelled knowledge-sharing (particularly as pertains to remote access to databases and specific technical computer applications). Finely tailored roles for subsidiaries are not only assigned; they are assumed, perhaps making it more appropriate to speak of 'auxiliaries' than subsidiaries. Finally, even the information systems themselves can be seen to fill an integrative role, being a cohesive influence in a less stable, more dispersed MNC.

1.2 Summary Presentational Structure

The whole study is collectively reported in the present text and in five separate papers, two of which are appended and three which are only published elsewhere.

The main text of the present volume is meant to be a 'covering note' in relation to the other papers. The latter should be thought of as self-contained contributions, but from different angles, to the core subject of usage of international information systems in MNCs. The purpose of the covering note is twofold: first, to articulate more exhaustively the theoretical and empirical underpinnings of the total research effort, and second, to provide a comprehensive framework for the collected research as presented in this volume.

Chapter 2 of the main text provides a critical review and systematization of a very limited field, viz. the empirical and theoretical antecedents in the intersecting set of research that focus on effects of computer-based information systems usage in organizations and of research that address issues of the structural characteristics of MNCs. Admittedly, the criteria for inclusion had to be applied with some generosity. The remaining relative paucity of the thus identified previous research probably explains why no rival surveys could be found. At least, the need for further research can be established.

Consequently, in Chapter 3 the net is cast wider primarily in order to bolster the theoretical (but also to some extent the empirical) base for defining the relevant research issues. First, information systems under study are investigated and a rather unconventional view is developed; a perspective where the interplay between communications networks and computer-based systems takes center stage.

Second, the broad issue of MNC structure is addressed. Again, the subject is treated in a somewhat unusual manner, largely due to a wish for maintaining at least a semblance of consistency. Previous research on MNC structure is categorized and discussed along the two main dimensions of whether it is found to be concerned with the structural form of the MNC or with the 'functioning' of the same (rather than according to traditional academic demarcation lines).

Third, the idiosyncracies of the proposed research are brought to the fore by developing a perspective of the research problem, by defining appropriate concepts, and by identifying salient limitations to the present inquiry. In the process, some issues concerning information systems in organizations in general are evaluated.

It should be reemphasized that Chapter 3 does not provide exhaustive reviews of any well-established research tradition. Choice of relevant antecedents, and the use to which they are put, are predicated on the unifying focus on activities and their location, which is intended to usefully link the studied MNC structure and information systems.

Having thrashed out the research problem, Chapter 4 turns to methodological issues following from a clearer specification of the research purpose. The development of a research strategy, and its subsequent operationalization, for the empirical investigation yield a methodological 'package' that involves a two-phased design of a longitudinal case study. The phases differ in type (arm's length vs. some afforded access); in degree of detail and scope; and in degree of comprehensive analysis (due to the accumulation of knowledge inherent in sequential designs). The 'insistent' approach represents a significant deviation from standard case study practice and, as such, brings out a neglected topic in the literature on case studies. Denial of access after very careful case selection, prompted a systematic exploitation of 'information leakage' from an initially quite recalcitrant object of inquiry, ultimately rewarded by relative success.

The somewhat loosely defined objective of 'trying out theory', which is explained and employed, hinges on an assumption of the chosen case - SKF - having forerunner experience of information systems usage in an MNC context. In turn, that explains the heavy emphasis placed on relevant selection criteria, and the subsequent perseverance during data collection.

The final part of the covering note, Chapter 5, contains an attempt at putting the main theoretical and empirical findings emanating from the whole research effort in relief against previous research. Some new light is thrown on some existing, outstanding research issues and some general characteristics of an emerging 'wired MNC' are sketched, as briefly indicated in the previous Section (Section 1.1). The conceptualization of a 'wired MNC' invites competing comparisons and further research; both of which are afforded mention in the concluding chapter.

The accompanying papers fall in two categories; empirical study and developing perspective, respectively. Hagström (1987a)[1] and Appendix 1[2] report the results of the empirical study of SKF. Although the two studies constitute different stages in the research process[3], cover somewhat different material[4], and manifest methodological points associated with the combination of the studies[5], only the latter study is reproduced in this volume. Apart from reasons of sheer volume, Appendix 1 'usurps' the prior study. Appendix 1 provides the greatest descriptive detail and the most extensive attempts at judging the effects of information systems usage in SKF. Both quantitative and qualitative data are scrutinized and interpreted. In concluding, the identified effects are put in the context of SKF strategic and structural change. The analysis seeks to specify the role of international information systems for the key organizational capabilities of SKF; a complex and important role, much underestimated both inside and outside SKF.

In Hagström (1990a)[6] a first analysis of the sequence of international information

---

[1] The full reference is: Hagström, P. (1987), "Linking New Information Systems to Corporate Strategy and Structure: The SKF Experience", Research Paper 87/11, **Institute of International Business**, Stockholm School of Economics, Stockholm. [Reprints are available directly from the author or from the Institute of International Business.]

[2] Appendix 1, "The Role of New Information Systems in the MNC: A(nother) Case Study of SKF", has not been released previously.

[3] Hagström (1990a, 1990b, and 1991; see further below) rely in no small part on the parallel empirical work on SKF. The inspirational relationships between Hagström (1987) and Hagström (1990a), on the one hand, and Hagström (1991) and Appendix 1, on the other, are close. Appendix 2 (i.e. Hagström, 1990b) falls somewhere between, having been written before the data from the second empirical study had been systematized.

[4] One main difference is that Hagström (1987b) provides greater detail on the historical evolution of SKF's strategy and organizational structure.

[5] However, the methodological issues are raised in Chapter 4 of this 'covering note'. It is worth mentioning, though, that more specifics on the 'how to' of conducting an 'insistent' case study are contained in Hagström (1987b).

[6] The full reference is: Hagström, P. (1990), "New Information Systems and the Changing Structure of MNCs" in Bartlett, C. A., Doz, Y. L. and Hedlund, G., eds., **Managing the Global Firm**. London: Routledge, pp. 164-185 (revised version of a paper with the same title presented at the European Institute

systems usage in MNCs is carried out. A sequential action pattern is generated, where the fate of MNC activities, information links, and scope of standardization are traced through three idealized phases. An MNC is argued to have the emphasis of international information systems usage shift from an initial concern with cutting costs of the given organization; via a phase of revenue generation associated with redeployment of firm resources geographically and organizationally; through to an 'integrative' phase, where activities are rebundled, the organizational boundaries blurred, and the information flows seek new ways.

Appendix 2[7] focuses almost exclusively on the theory of geographical location. More specifically, an argument is developed for extending the theory of "corporate geography" and is given some empirical support from MNC usage of international information systems. The view of the firm as a bundle of many different activities (and of information systems as a transport system for information-based services) leads to a rejection of the traditional, but only hitherto implicit, assumption of 'automatic' agglomeration advantages accruing to activities if only carried out within a firm. Instead, geographical location of firm-activities is found to be more of a continuous process. Activities are dynamically relocated in response to location factors operating on several levels of geographic aggregation; location factors which attract and repel activities; and in response to internal as well as the traditionally recognized, external location factors. The advantages of simultaneous optimization of the spatial location of activities are indicated. This Hagström (1990b) is reproduced in this volume primarily because it covers research beyond the scope of the present text.

---

for Advanced Studies in Management, Brussels in June, 1987). [Reprints are available directly from the author or from the Institute of International Business.]

[7] Reprint of Hagström, P. (1990b), "Unshackling Corporate Geography", **Geografiska Annaler**, Series B, Human Geography, Vol. 72 B, No. 1, pp. 3-12.

In Hagström (1991)[8] internal MNC relationships are discussed in conjunction with international information systems usage. Traditional headquarters-subsidiary relationships are examined in that light, drawing on illustrations from ten Swedish MNCs (incl. SKF). An expository distinction is made between vertical and non-vertical (in a hierarchical sense) use of international data communications-cum-systems. Vertical applications tend to allow more differentiated internal relationships among organizational units while fostering greater integration of firm activities. Improved control possibilities make a more complex organizational structure easier to live with for the MNC. Non-vertical applications exhibit significant unanticipated, or spontaneous, uses of corporate data communications networks. These later developments improve the coordination of activities among more disparate subsidiaries, not uncommonly without involving headquarters at any level in the MNC. In short, the main internal characteristics of the 'wired' MNC show up here.

1.3 Reading Practicalities

As can be deduced from above, one logical sequence of going through the present volume is to first turn to Chapters 2-4 of the covering text, then to read the accompanying papers, and to conclude with the final Chapter 5 in this text. Alternatively, the reader can follow the covering text straight through, picking up on the other five papers as they are referred to in the following. Each of the six texts can also be read separately from the other ones.

It has been impossible to avoid some overlap between texts, since it is a collection of related writings that is presented. However, the strong desire to minimize repetition without impairing comprehension has brought at times perhaps a somewhat tedious cross-

[8] The full reference is: Hagström, P. (1991), "Inside the 'Wired' MNC" forthcoming in Antonelli, C., ed., **The Economics of Information Networks**. Amsterdam: North Holland/Elsevier Science Publishers, (provisionally) pp. 305-325. [Reprints are available directly from the author or from the Institute of International Business.]

referencing of texts in this volume. It is also worth noting that the bibliographic material pertaining to each text will differ, and dramatically so, for the three texts included in this volume.

The writing style exhibits some variation; in particular the case studies have been held in a more personally narrative tone in order to improve the readability of great amounts of descriptive material.

Much effort has been spent on making the covering main text coherent to the reader without him or her necessarily having to refer to the extensive footnotes. The annotated material merits its considerable claim to page space primarily as a function of the variation in the sources referenced. Spanning different academic disciplines, however superficially, at times warrants elaboration.

Finally, a point on notation is that single quotation marks (' ') are used for the author's idiosyncratic terminology, and double quotation marks (" ") for the specific terms of others.

2. PREVIOUS RESEARCH, NARROWLY DEFINED

Our area of research interest lies in the confluence of the wider traditions which focus on effects of computer-based information systems usage on organizations, and on the structural characteristics of MNCs, respectively. However, research regarding MNC structure typically glosses over any role for data communications, and research on information systems in organizations, as a rule, stops before the systems cross a national border. Before attempting to straddle these broader perspectives (which is a recurrent theme in the following chapters), we turn to the directly relevant research, which explicitly - and substantially - addresses the possible impact of international data communications on MNC structure.

The present chapter first provides a fairly detailed overview of each of the empirical studies found, and, second, looks at some specific conceptualizations of data communications in MNCs. In a brief, final section the implications for our research question are discussed.

2.1 Empirical Studies

Limiting our search to contributions that link usage of international data communications and/or international information systems to over-all MNC structure immediately yields some hallmark characteristics of the resultant population:

- existing empirical such studies are remarkably few;
- the studies are almost exclusively explorative and inductive;
- the all-pervasive approach takes its cue from telecommunications-related research; and
- directly relevant studies are very likely to reflect concerns of multilateral organizations and their members, viz. nation states.

Most of the more comprehensive work in the area has taken place under the auspices of the OECD[9], or subsequently built on those efforts. Although primarily focussing on policy issues (cf. OECD, 1980), some OECD-generated studies have dealt specifically with users, notably MNCs[10]. The object of use is termed "transborder data flows" (TDF or TBDF)[11], or, lately, information networks[12]. - A parallel, but much more modest, repository of active interest in MNC usage of international information systems is the United Nations Centre on Transnational Corporations (UNCTC). Again, the prime concern is within the realm of telecommunications policy[13].

A - arguably the - leading example of this research is a pilot study by Antonelli (1981) on the effects of computer communications systems on the structure and performance of MNCs[14]. Concentrating on information retrieval[15], Antonelli identified three main types of international data flows: for control functions, for logistics coordination, and for financial management. Their relative importance varied across firms but, without exception, significant economies of scale in coordination through an international

---

[9] More specifically, a special Committee for Information, Computer and Communications Policy (ICCP) under the Directorate for Science, Technology and Industry (DSTI) within OECD.

[10] This line of inquiry has typically been supported actively by users themselves through the OECD Business and Industry Advisory Committee (BIAC).

[11] The body most closely associated with these studies has aptly been designated the Expert Group on Transborder Data Flows under ICCP.

[12] The de facto suppressed qualification is 'telecommunications' networks.

[13] UNCTC is formally directed to provide background policy studies with the objective of supporting developing countries vis-à-vis MNCs. In our context, the issues are also framed in terms of TBDF (see UNCTC, 1982).

[14] Antonelli surveyed the experience of 24 MNCs with operations in Italy by questionnaires and interviews (all carried out locally). The results are presented in the form of general conclusions and six anonymous case studies.

[15] A distinction is made between using TBDF for data processing and for information retrieval, respectively. Separating these two uses reflects common computer-science practice (e.g. Martin, 1981a; see further Section 3.1). Subsequently, Antonelli (1981) also found that processing is of minor - and diminishing - importance as a result of the spread of distributed data processing capabilities. That conclusion contradicts the very early, seminal study on important international data networks in Europe, commissioned by OECD and carried out by Logica Ltd. in 1977 (reported in, for instance, Hughes and Sasson, 1980; and Freese, 1979). Six public and 24 private data networks were investigated. The most important reason for using networks was found to be sharing expensive resources, notably data processing equipment.

information network were attained in the firms[16]; benefits that vastly exceeded transmission costs[17].

In terms of MNC structure, Antonelli traced an overriding effect of international data communications bringing about strong centralization of decision-making, particularly strategic decision-making. Reiterating his findings and conclusions, Antonelli (1987) identified the then present stage of international data communications usage as being associated with MNCs employing a matrix structure based on "...the old product and regional divisions, where functional and centralized activities play an increasingly important role." (Antonelli, 1987:44).

But the story does not end there. From a later vantage point, Antonelli (1987) talks of a new, emerging structure where organizational units are increasingly specialized, either with a global mandate (product divisions and functional units) or with a very local scope of activities (sales units). Strategic management and control then come to rest with a central staff, "...responsible for overall planning and the electronic network of TDF." (Antonelli, 1987:44)[18].

---

[16] The most substantial gains were judged to result from internal financial arbitrage and firm-level coordination of activities across a broad range of external financial markets. Other important uses improving what Antonelli (1981) terms "performance" were reductions in working capital through improved logistics, exploitation of technical economies of scale, possibilities for intra-corporate transfer of production, and purchasing economies of scale.

[17] In a later study of 40 MNCs (overlapping the 1981 sample), Antonelli (1985) specifies this observation as one of 'international data telecommunications' being a process innovation for utilization in the coordination process in MNCs. However, the study concentrates on the diffusion of this innovation within and among MNCs, an issue which is less relevant here.

[18] Foreshadowing this concept of an emerging structure, Antonelli (1981) identified an ongoing "silent revolution" in the future yielding a more complex organizational pattern of MNCs. Condensed, the pattern would be one of global product divisions (with limited autonomy for specialized production affiliates), domestic sales subsidiaries (maintaining only commercial activities), and new global functional affiliates (primarily financial and purchasing centers). Further, "...commercial affiliates will be located in rich countries, production affiliates in export-oriented countries, and these will be centrally coordinated by financial and trading companies, with global product divisions playing a broad, supervisory role." (Antonelli, 1981:52).

A related, significant study[19] (OECD, 1983a and 1983c) took a somewhat different view, stressing that international data communications do not cause changes in MNCs, but are a response to, and at most, a reinforcement of changes already in motion. A case in point is the considerable evidence found regarding the implementation of a more integrated structure in MNCs, where TBDF use had been instrumental; but in no case did the availability of TBDF in itself result in structural change. The conclusion was that the role of international data flows is one of being a means for reconciliation of operational flexibility with organizational integration, and for provision of accurate and immediate information[20].

Drawing on a wealth of secondary sources for circumstantial pieces of information (and to a much lesser degree on its own research[21]), UNCTC (1982) develops an argument echoing the importance of TBDF as a means for achieving integration of the complex MNC and the increasing dependence of the MNC on cheap and reliable TBDF. However, UNCTC (1982)[22] goes one step further as use of TBDF is interpreted to be associated with a trend towards greater specialization of MNC subsidiaries and a concomitant loss of subsidiary autonomy. TBDF stimulates the "upward movement of control", ultimately to corporate headquarters.

Mention should also be made of an attitudinal survey by Business International (1983). Close to nine out of ten firms reported that TBDF was important or very important for

---

[19] The, so called, BIAC Report was based on a mail-survey, which drew questionnaire responses from 133 MNCs in eleven countries and on follow-up by interviews with more than 50 companies in ten countries.

[20] The OECD studies prompted activity also at the national, member state, level. The most comprehensive work was carried out in Sweden. The purpose here was more of preliminary and descriptive fact-finding and any conclusions, as they pertain to MNCs, parallel those of the OECD studies (cf. Civildepartementet, 1984; and Dykert, 1984).

[21] Most UNCTC-issued original research on TBDF pursues related, but quite different, topics such as national studies (e.g. UNCTC, 1983), geographical hard- and software markets (e.g. UNCTC, 1988a), and the activities of MNCs in one product or service market (e.g. UNCTC, 1984).

[22] This view reappears in the similar UNCTC (1984) and in Schumann (1984; a wider and more programmatic example of UNCTC research).

at least one corporate function[23]. A case is made for TBDF being a principal tool for bringing greater cohesion to the management of MNC operations.

A third leading study very much constitutes the state-of-the-art. It is a voluminous comparative inquiry into the impact of information networks on business strategies for firms in seven major countries (OECD-BRIE, 1989)[24]. Concentrating on large MNCs, the report identifies a two-phase process of adopting information networking technologies, and a four-item typology of use derived from common strategic goals of the firms surveyed. Starting with the latter, MNCs use telecommunications as:

1. "a utility", wanting to reduce communications costs;
2. "a productive force", seeking to improve the production process;
3. "a market interface", helping to monitor demand fluctuations and to attach services to its products; and
4. "an integrating force", trying to better coordinate operations from procurement to sales (Bar and Borrus, 1989:17ff).

The above four major ways of use are seen as coupled with a two-step learning cycle, during which firms first "automate" existing procedures by employing information networks, then master the art to "re-organize", whereby telecommunications become an integral part in devising more efficient and effective work processes[25]. In short, "automation" is not seen as changing the existing MNC organization, whereas "re-organization" means that new MNC structures evolve around new networking technologies.

---

[23] The survey covered 89 MNCs out of which 52 were US firms and 26 West European ones (see also the review in the CTC Reporter, 1984).

[24] The different national studies each contains a) an overview of the local market for telecommunications services (i.e. of the opportunities and constraints for users), and, b) a series of case studies of users for an assessment in terms of how usage is creating competitive advantage for the firms. In this way, the report provides some 30 detailed case studies of mostly large, and mostly international, firms in the US, the UK, France, Germany, Italy, Japan, and Spain. [The research was a joint project by OECD (i.e. ICCP) and the Berkeley Roundtable on the International Economy (BRIE) on competitiveness and telecommunications policy. In its preliminary, mimeographed form available to us, the report is 573 pages, incl. general conclusions and appendices.]

[25] Since the "re-organized" firm can be "automated", there is an underlying feed-back loop with successive iterations implying successive learning (cf. Bar and Borrus, 1989:20).

The transition involves dramatically revamping the corporate network. The crucial aspect is to achieve network flexibility, not only "applications flexibility", but even more so "configuration flexibility"[26]. The ideal becomes one of a "seamless interweaving" of telecommunications capabilities and business activities; of the network and corporate strategy (Bar and Borrus, 1989:3ff). Competitive advantage thus comes to hinge critically on the firm's telecommunications capabilities, in the long-term to continuously reallocate network resources (e.g. bandwidth) and reconfigure the network (cf. Bar and Borrus, 1989:19ff).

Within this framework, the process is driven by MNCs pursuing very similar strategic objectives and implementing them through more or less advanced use of telecommunications (cf. the four-way typology above). The competitive environment is seen to exert basically uniform pressures on firms, and industry differences are strongly downplayed. Differences in firm competitiveness are instead clearly viewed as increasingly reflecting

a) national availability of network resources, and the relative freedom afforded firms in using those resources (Bar and Borrus, 1989:19)[27];

and, related to this,

b) firms' own telecommunications capabilities[28].

The empirical support presented for the proposed framework is scant, however. The selected firms are still in the "automation" stage, and very few, indeed, have begun to enter the "re-organization" stage (cf. Bar and Borrus, 1989:3 and 19ff)[29]. Instead, the

---

[26] The simpler form of network flexibility is the ability to accommodate different applications on the same network, whereas "configuration flexibility" involves the capability to simultaneously reconfigure the corporate telecommunications network to handle a variety of application mixes and to create new applications that exploit the new configuration opportunities (Bar and Borrus, 1989:4ff).

[27] Presumably in the home country, since cross-national variations are stressed.

[28] However, if firms fail to go through the learning cycle and to master network flexibility, that can possibly be compensated by the public telecommunications operator [sic!] understanding and fulfilling firm requirements (cf. Bar and Borrus, 1989:20).

[29] Since national variation in the availability of telecommunications network resources is found to be a key explanatory variable, US firms are, on average, the most accomplished users. Specifically, Hewlett Packard and Xerox are seen as the most advanced, pioneering firms over-all. Japanese and UK firms are

framework is generated inductively, through piecing together vanguard uses found in the national studies, and through subsequent extrapolation.

A careful reading of the report (viz. OECD-BRIE, 1989) casts doubt over the use of information networks having had much effect on MNC structure so far. Admittedly, however, there is some disjointed and illustrative evidence of (and a forceful argument for) dramatic impacts being in the process of unfolding.

Other existing case studies of MNCs and their use of telecommunications tend to have a much more narrow focus: a specific application (a system), a particular functional activity and/or a limited geographical area. One exception is a long-running study of IBM and its internal use of telecommunications (Bakis, 1980 and 1987). The study is explorative and does not suffer from any excess theoretical baggage. What is lacking in focus is amply compensated for by wide-ranging discussion of impacts and by empirical detail. The clearest statements of any summary findings are encountered in Bakis (1987). He sees "telecommunications and teleprocessing" as being intimately associated with an MNC being able to maintain two parallel hierarchies[30], while also achieving global cohesion of activities (Bakis, 1987:158).

On closer inspection, Bakis (1987) actually, but very implicitly, argues for IBM actively using telecommunications for coordinating and controlling activities along multiple dimensions. More stable dimensions appear to be: by function, by product, and by geographical market. Temporary project organization is also hinted at. Moreover, telecommunications are seen to facilitate the physical relocation of activities. In particular, Bakis (1987) identifies a "geographical decentralization"[31], but coupled with

runners-up; a result of the more recent liberalization of the domestic telecommunications markets. French and German firms fall in an intermediate category, with the public telecommunications providers offering restricted, but fairly sophisticated, services (which is more of an advantage for small firms). Italian (and, by implication, Spanish) large users are the most constrained. (cf. Bar and Borrus, 1989)

[30] In IBM's case "functional" and "territorial" hierarchies.

[31] The term, in effect, refers to IBM France's observed propensity to expand operations primarily at provincial sites since the early 1960s (cf. Bakis, 1987:156-158), i.e. before any significant "teleprocessing" was viable.

less local autonomy due to tighter administrative control by headquarters (with special reference here to IBM France). The issue of causality vis-à-vis corporate structure is left in limbo as the discussion fans out to embrace French regional policy. However, a point is made of "teleprocessing" bringing about productivity increases in administrative activities, presumably meaning rationalization of a given structure.

Another line of inquiry ostensibly fitting our narrow definition relates to the particular impact of telecommunications regulation on TBDF and, in turn, on MNC structure. The problem got its most commonly employed formulation in an influential article by Buss (1984).

Based on company examples and national TBDF regulations in place, Buss (1984) argues for the regulatory threats being an underestimated key strategic issue for MNCs. The argument builds on the generally underestimated extent of existing and proposed privacy laws, taxation of foreign processing services, and local content rules[32]. The recommendations are for a comprehensive risk assessment with possible resultant shifting of vulnerable activities to 'safer' locations and for intensive lobbying of national governments and international bodies to change, or prevent, regulation[33]. Subsequent empirical investigations have, however, not found TBDF regulation to have had any significant impact on MNC activities so far, but suggest that it has the potential to become a major problem (for two recent examples, and reviews of previous studies, see Kane and Ricks, 1989; and Sambharya and Phatak, 1990[34]). One of the few more theoretical discussions (Samiee, 1984) echoes the same, rather dismal, conclusions[35].

---

32 Privacy laws are seen as the most restrictive and most important, especially since personalized information in MNCs is argued to be more common than generally perceived; Buss (1984) mentions payroll systems, client accounts, and employee skills data bases.

33 The concerns regarding regulation are, of course, closely linked to those of the OECD (and are directly referred to by Buss, 1984).

34 Kane and Ricks (1989) based their findings on a survey of 370 large US MNCs with a 41 percent usable responses, and on substantial follow-up interviews. Sambharya and Phatak (1990) chalked up a 17 percent response rate from the 455 largest US MNCs with a more dubious design (only attitudinal measures on a four-point Likert scale).

35 Samiee's (1984) main argument is that companies which need to communicate a lot internationally (particularly centralized MNCs) are the most threatened by possible TBDF regulations.

Before straying any further from our core area of interest, we now turn to conceptual discussions, concomitant to the reviewed empirical studies.

2.2 "The Multinational Computer"

The above title is borrowed from the earliest comprehensive statement on changing MNC characteristics linked to the use of international information systems: a seminal article by Nanus (1969). Now rarely acknowledged, it did set the stage for much of the early ensuing research efforts.

In Nanus's (1969) bold conception[36], the use of computer power as multinational in scope as the MNC itself would decisively strengthen the MNC as a pervasive institution in economic life, ultimately accelerating the international convergence of tastes, attitudes, product preferences and behavioral patterns. Corporate-wide use of information systems could then counteract the common excessive decentralization of MNC operations. Instead of having a "disjointed composite of small businesses", the MNC should build on its main competitive advantage; "...its ability to consider opportunities throughout the world." (Nanus, 1969:9)[37].

In particular, large-scale computer-based information systems would, in Nanus's (1969) vision, offer the advantages of economies of scale and better decision-making by improving the amount and quality of information available to the organization and its

[36] A significant Conference Board (1972) report alerting US business to the challenges of evolving information technology can provide some context to the pioneering nature of Nanus's (1969) vision. Particularly relevant are the judgments that information technology "communication channels **will** cross international boundaries" [emphasis added] and that (US) corporate headquarters risks losing control over international operations when international expertise then increases (in the international division; Kozmetsky and Ruefli, 1972:74).

[37] Nanus (1969) here (unknowingly?) closely parallels the evolutionary sequence postulated by Perlmutter (1969, earlier issue from same volume of the same journal, but originally unveiled in French in 1965), where MNCs move from a "polycentric" to a "geocentric" orientation. However, Nanus's (1969) preferred state clearly predates another influential conception of emerging MNC structure, viz. Vernon's (1979) "global scanner" (see further Section 3.2).

subsequent corporate-wide exploitation. Consequently, the centralized computer would bring about some centralization of decision-making authority. However, the centralized computer would also furnish local units with better information, thereby strengthening their ability to effectively respond to local conditions. But on both counts, the more important coordination of decision-making at all levels in the MNC would improve significantly[38].

Nanus (1969) is less specific on other structural repercussions. Some activities, like payroll, would be automated (and thus could be said to 'disappear'). Otherwise, the notion is, by implication, essentially one of a more efficient and flexible utilization of a given MNC structure and set of resources.

Moreover, Nanus (1969) reflects the general perception at the time that the technological development of the computer was following an inexorable path towards ever more powerful central processing units. In effect, centralized use of processing was then generally held to be the only viable option, technologically and economically. That 'shortcoming' was redressed in a later article (Nanus, 1978). The vision remains the same, but more emphasis is placed on communications, and the location of processing is here rendered largely unimportant[39].

Perhaps surprisingly, there are few homologous conceptualizations. The closest matches to "the multinational computer" are the empirical studies already reviewed. Companion statements and, to a lesser extent, discussions on telecommunications policy exhaust the list.

---

[38] With a terminology that gained acceptance in the late 1970s, Nanus (1969) thus can be said to have envisaged the multinational computer as allowing simultaneous achievement of "local responsiveness" and "global coordination" in the MNC. The terms represent a classic strategic trade-off with organizational repercussions (it was Prahalad, 1975, who first adapted the Lawrence and Lorsch, 1969, differentiation/integration dilemma to MNCs). Bartlett (1986) later identified a similar simultaneity in emerging MNC structures, but as a response to changing environmental demands on the MNC (and without reference to computers).

[39] However, the threat of government regulation of communications is introduced by Nanus (1978) as a very important consideration. It is done very early, since the issue did not really become an important concern for research until the 1980s (cf. Section 2.1).

Parry (1983) puts the OECD conclusions in the context of over-all developments of MNC structure. The pressures for change derive from the environment and TBDF is a critical means for effective MNC response to these challenges. Parry (1983) focuses on the scope of MNC activities, pointing to the major choices associated with integration and diversification strategies. In particular, new communications technology is seen to bring new opportunities for MNCs to integrate along non-production activities and to diversify into new markets based on functions and services.

The basic contention is that, although to some extent interdependent, developments in communications technology have preceded developments in MNC corporate strategy and, by implication, MNC structure. Thus induced "integration" and "diversification" responses by MNCs lead Parry (1983) to deduce that MNCs are likely to exhibit a trend towards greater centralization and tighter corporate control, increased internal specialization (particularly by function), limited (by activity) entry into geographical markets, and more entry into service markets. In short, Antonelli's (1981 and 1987) speculations receive additional support.

Views emanating from the telecommunications policy tradition tend to be less specific on MNC structure. Typically, they start from the notion of TBDF increasingly becoming more important. They grow as a share of total, continuously growing telecommunications traffic, and the MNCs are identified as the main users of TBDF. Again, increased MNC centralization, internal specialization, and corporate control are seen to follow. Through TBDF, MNCs gain an enhanced information advantage over domestic firms, and the existing international division of labor is exacerbated (cf. Sauvant, 1983 and 1986; UNCTAD, 1984; and Jussawallah and Cheah, 1983)[40].

[40] The losers, par excellence, are the LDCs, LDC indigenous firms, and MNC subsidiaries in LDCs. A more recent extension of the same argument is that information technology allows automation of many assembly operations, allowing them to be performed economically in high-wage countries (cf. UNCTC, 1988b). The implication is that even some of the activities traditionally located according to (LDC) comparative advantage may move 'on-shore', thus further reducing the scope of activities carried out at a local MNC subsidiary.

In concluding the review[41] of research on the impact of TBDF in one form or another on MNC structure, we can take heart regarding brevity from Snow (1988). He identifies only two sources specifically addressing the role of MNCs in global communications (Snow, 1988:158, n. 10)[42] in a very extensive and authoritative review of the literature on the economic, technological and public policy issues regarding telecommunications. The dearth of relevant sources is indirectly confirmed by Whitaker and Miles (1989)[43].

Looking even further afield, major reviews of the literature on information systems and organizations (e.g. Huber, 1990; Andersson, 1989; Tavakolian, 1989; Markus and Robey, 1988; Swanson, 1987; Mohrman and Lawler, 1984; Scott Morton, 1984; Robey, 1986 and 1977; and Kling, 1980) are conspicuously silent on any particularities associated with MNCs and, indeed, on MNCs at all. Conversely, the most comprehensive sources on the organizational structure of MNCs (e.g. Hedlund, 1991b; Bartlett and Ghoshal, 1989; Martínez and Jarillo 1989; Buckley, 1988; Egelhoff, 1988a and 1982; Martínez, 1987; Brooke, 1986; Caves, 1982; and Brooke and Remmers, 1970/1978) do not bring up international computer-based information systems other than in passing[44].

---

[41] No rival reviews have been found. The sources quoted above are also remarkably short on, even remotely relevant, antecedents.

[42] The two are Antonelli (1984) and Varis (1976). On closer inspection, however, we find that the former deals with the correlation between MNC activities and national demand for telecommunications services, whereas the latter concerns the influence of MNCs in the international (mass) media industry.

[43] In their bibliographic work on the wider concept "information technology", Whitaker and Miles (1989) has six entries on MNCs. Apart from Schumann (1984; see above), the references concern the telecommunications equipment industry, mass media, and employment impacts of new technology on LDCs.

[44] The single exception here is Hedlund (1991b), who goes beyond merely mentioning their existence by advocating that the consequences of modern information technology for changing MNC structures is one of the important avenues for future research in the area of organization and management of the MNC.

2.3 Implications of the State-of-the-Art

A perhaps worrisome aspect of the identified dearth of previous research, empirical as well as conceptual, is that our area of inquiry is uninteresting, wrongly defined, and/or not possible to investigate.

The other side of the coin holds some hope, however. First, some explicit pleas for more research into the use and effects of international (data) communications in MNCs can be found (e.g. Hedlund, 1991b; Bakis, 1987; Sauvant, 1983 and 1986; Jussawalla and Cheah, 1983; OECD 1983a and 1983c; UNCTC, 1982; and Gassman, 1980;). Second, each of the broader lines of study (viz. information systems and organizations, and organizational structure of MNCs) abound with exhortations for continued efforts within the respective traditions. Third, there is the distinct possibility that our approach to MNC structure has hitherto not received the attention it merits (on the grounds of fruitfulness)[45].

Given that we persist, at least two major problems remain outstanding. First, the terminology used so far has been less than unambiguous. 'Transborder data flows', 'international information systems', 'international communication networks', 'MNC organization' and 'MNC structure' need clearer interpretation for a more succinct statement of a research framework. That is the subject of the following chapter.

The second unresolved issue concerns the appropriate method for an empirical endeavor. That question is addressed in Chapter 4.

---

[45] This last, admittedly speculative, point does gain some credence from the fact that the two wider research traditions are of relatively recent origins themselves. Arguably, academic interest in the role of computer-based information systems in organizations dates from Leavitt and Whisler's (1958) seminal article on the subject. Likewise, the study of MNCs as a recognized separate area of economic research can be traced back to Hymer's (1960/1976) original statement. The upshot of this argument is that the probability of un(der)explored approaches existing, even mundane but potentially fruitful such, is rather high.

Some ideas stay with us from the review in the present chapter, though. Starting with the smallest common denominators, there is little disagreement in the literature as to international data communications being well suited for substantially improving control and coordination of MNC activities. Centralization of decision-making and concomitant reduction of subsidiary autonomy are frequently recurring conclusions[46].

There is also a consensus on international data communications first and foremost being used for non-technical or non-production purposes, such as financial management or logistics. Increased specialization by function, or by service activity, is seen to follow. A corollary point is that MNCs then are better equipped to exploit the international division of labor.

Albeit less clearly articulated, another common contention is the greater flexibility accruing to MNCs as a result of using international data communications networks. The argument concerns the related enhanced abilities to seize on opportunities arising anywhere in the world and to temporally adjust MNC activities[47].

A natural consequence of the exploratory nature of research to date is that there is less agreement concerning whether international data communications is a driving force in itself (e.g. Bar and Borrus, 1989; and Parry, 1983) or an instrument (e.g. OECD, 1983a and 1983c) for structural change. Does the advent of international data communications cause change in organizations or is the use of international data communications one of many means at managers' disposal when activities are reorganized? Actually, there is also little to go on regarding the nature of change beyond the above general statements. Should we expect a much more efficient, but essentially unchanged MNC (e.g. UNCTC, 1982; and Nanus, 1969) or a totally revamped MNC (e.g. Antonelli, 1981 and 1987)?

---

[46] Recall, however, that Nanus (1969) represents a significant qualification regarding the status of subsidiaries. He sees greater central control and centralization being associated also with greater, and better informed, local discretion, presumably regarding the (fewer) activities remaining locally.

[47] Temporal adjustment should be interpreted as more efficient dynamic exploitation of resources both internal and external to the firm.

The suspicion at this stage is that the observed shortcomings regarding precision can be alleviated by being more specific as to what in effect constitutes the new means of communication and which attendant characteristics of MNC structure to focus on.

3. PROBLEM SURVEYED AND DEFINED

Three tasks remain outstanding: defining the network and systems for subsequent empirical investigation; critically taking stock of the state-of-the-art research on MNC structure with an eye to its applicability to the later discussion on the role of international data communications; and specifying the perspective arising from the intersecting set of the two first tasks and of research on information systems and organizations.

The first main section addresses network from a somewhat unusual angle by singling out the network from the wider information systems. The second section broaches the issue of MNC structure in a slightly disrespectful manner, categorizing previous research across traditions for better correspondence with the defined usage of international information systems. A view of MNC activities and their location, as well as of the opportunity set of MNC structural choice is developed. The third section attempts to bring the discussion together (with some widening of the issue again), highlighting the fundamentals of information systems and identifying the organizational perspective chosen. Concurrently, the topic of inquiry is specified.

3.1 Networks and Systems

So far, we have used the terms 'network', 'communications', 'information systems' etc. quite generously, reflecting various uses that have gained currency. We need clearer distinctions that meet the broad criteria of user functionality (since we are interested in MNC structure) and existing usage (since we aim at an empirical investigation). Although our focus on international data communications and systems is a seemingly specific category, it is by no means uncomplicated but rather more akin to the mythological Pandora's box.

Our first major problem is the dual one of too much detail and/or too much generality in existing interpretations.

Somewhat bewildering detail is a common feature of approaches that take their cue from more recent technical advances in the computer and telecommunications fields[48]. Given our interest in communications, there is an explicit technical tradition to be acknowledged (e.g. Tar baum, 1989; and Doll, 1978).

Technical developments naturally also figure prominently in much policy-oriented telecommunications research (cf. Snow, 1988), and studies often extensively enumerate new technologies and services (e.g. as in Ungerer, 1986; and OECD, 1981). Technology-induced changing economies outpace the adaptive capacity of regulatory regimes raising basic issues of how to treat the de facto proliferation of new information/communications services (succinct discussions are Cleevely and Cawdell, 1986; and Dordick et al., 1979). The intuitively appealing distinction between communication and processing is argued as being possible to uphold (e.g. Trauth, 1986; and Seitz, 1980) or to be unworkable for practical reasons (e.g. Eckelman, 1983; OECD, 1983b; and Pool and Solomon, 1980)[49].

The main reason for this conundrum seems to be that technical and policy approaches work from the supply side of telecommunications services, where technical features, rather than functionality for the user, become the critical dimension in order to determine which equipment and software to use, and also if and how to regulate new telecommunications services.

With an eye to implications for organizational structure, one could expect to find solace in related managerial literature or, indeed, in the studies reviewed in the previous chapter. However, usage in the general management literature of terms like information

---

[48] A good illustration is the particularly condensed presentation of the sumptuous smorgasbord of technology-driven issues found in CSTD (1986).

[49] This debate primarily stems from the wish to separate simple carriage from value-added telecommunications services. For clarity, we come to side with the latter view but not on the grounds of regulatory impracticality advanced here. Rather, a user-end vantage point yields somewhat different distinctions (see Sections 3.1.1 and 3.1.2 below).

technology, information systems and information management is far from precise. An extensive survey[50] by Boaden and Lockett (1990) identified notable exceptions to the affliction of excessive generality only in some uses of "information systems", but they would then denote very specific systems. Tellingly, the terms 'data communications' or 'telecommunications' were not investigated at all by Boaden and Lockett (1990).

Still, there is a significant strand of writing stimulated by the influential statement of "three islands of technology" merging and having important implications for management (McKenney and McFarlan, 1982; and McFarlan, McKenney and Pyburn, 1983). The "three islands" are taken as a starting point, however, and the authors do not go any further than identifying them as office automation, telecommunications, and data processing.

Discussions on transborder data flows also yield rather broad definitions. The standard formulation is one of TBDF being "movements across national boundaries of machine-readable data for processing, storage, or retrieval" (Sauvant, 1983, n. 1; UNCTC, 1982:8; and Kirsch, 1983:3[51])[52].

In short, wanting to go further than looking at a particular computer application or telecommunications service, but stopping short of considering all telecommunications transmissions (or even physically carried "machine-readable data") , we get little guidance for empirical research from the above approaches as they stand. Therefore, we need to develop a workable framework, viz. striking a balance between lack of precision and excessive detail.

---

[50] A database with about 210 000 article references (incl. abstracts) to journals in business management and administration was searched yielding more than 12 000 articles with references to "information systems", "information technology", "information management", "management information systems", "data processing", and/or "decision support systems".

[51] For UNCTC (1982:8), add only two commas. For Kirsch (1983:3), add "electronic or [machine-readable data for] the purpose of", and "in computer systems" at the end.

[52] The related, more recent term "information networks" remains undefined, but its usage implies it referring to a collective of ways in which telecommunications technology, or more specifically, telecommunications network technology, is exploited (cf. OECD-BRIE, 1989).

That ambition leads to the second major problem; the one of disentangling what can loosely be called the 'computer' and 'telecommunications' perspectives. The former is typically closely associated with 'information systems' and the latter with 'communications networks'. However, "computer networks" is also used in the former tradition (e.g. Kiesler, 1986) and "information networks" in the latter (e.g. Bar and Borrus, 1989).

Arguably, the source of this terminological confusion simply mirrors the technological one. With converging technologies, communications networks and computer systems overlap, and so do the terminologies of the respective perspectives. In turn, with the blurred boundaries of computer systems and telecommunications, it is also easy to understand why we observe such little middle ground between detail and breadth within either of the two perspectives. New, and, in this case, also obfuscated, areas of study are naturally short on practical concepts suitable for empirical inquiry.

Even the modest intention to improve on the precision of previous, directly relevant research (cf. Chapter 2) then requires being more specific about the level of aggregation and finding a practical solution to the networks/systems overlap[53]. But rather than attempting the daunting task of putting substance to generality, we choose to build from detail.

3.1.1 Networks

Good overviews of data communications as primarily a technical phenomenon are Tanenbaum, 1989; Martin 1981a; Eaton and Smithers, 1982; and Doll, 1978. That tradition is followed, but as a point of departure only.

[53] The same concerns expressed in conjunction with the identified paucity of kindred research (cf. Section 2.3), of course, apply here as well.

A physical telecommunications network can be said to be comprised of different transmission media (twisted-pair cables, coaxial cables, fiber optic cables, microwave links, and satellites) and different repeater equipment along the links.

Logical networks operate on the physical telecommunications network but are kept logically separate by idiosyncratic equipment. For instance, telephone switches, telex stations, (data) concentrators, (data) packet-assembler/disassemblers, (data) cluster controllers, and data switches are parts of the different logical telephone, telex, packet-switched data, and circuit-switched data networks.

Different telecommunications transmission services use the physical network and one of the logical networks. An added complication is that several services are available on the same logical network. For example, the common (voice) telephone service, telefacsimile, and data transmission via modem (leased line or dial-up) are all offered via the logical telephone network. Conversely, data transmission can be effectuated on different logical networks.

A final distinction is that there are interfaces between logical networks allowing some services to interact, like telex and some types of data transmission.

With this terminology in place, we can view a corporate data communications network as, in essence, a bundle of data communications services. The main point for our purposes is that the firm has control over the network, in the sense that it decides over access to the network. Thus we define the data communications network from the user end[54].

The firm purchases data communications services or provides them fully in-house. In practice, a firm rarely builds physical telecommunications links other than within a site or between adjacent sites. These Local Area Networks (LANs) are not really considered further since we are not concerned with intra-site or intra-unit communications. But there

[54] In consequence, other dimensions of network control - like routing, physical networks, and method of transmission (analogue or digital) - do not have any import on our definition (see also Hagström, 1988).

are two caveats: first, when the same site houses different organizational units linked by a LAN, it is implicitly treated as any other inter-unit communications link; and, second, when local data interchange between terminals or computers is not possible (viz. when an organizational unit has separate, non-interfacing connections into data communications networks) the absence of LAN functions is made explicit[55].

Corporate data communications networks are largely private networks. The firm can 'build' a proprietary network by leasing lines from telecommunications carriers. An alternative is to use public networks, leaving switching and transmission control to a service provider. The main reason for choosing the former is that firms often find that their communications needs outstrip what services are offered publicly. Some value-added service providers can compensate for this lack of performance in common carrier networks, offering an additional alternative to own leasing of lines[56].

In the end, what in our parlance constitutes a typical corporate communications network are elements drawn from all the above categories. Private leased lines, dial-up connections, common public packet- and circuit-switched links, and value-added communications services more often than not coexist in a corporate data communications network. Exactly how the different users are tied is of little or no consequence when defining the extent of a corporate data communications network. What is important is that they <u>are</u> linked, viz. that a user perceives that he is connected to the corporate network.

---

[55] The converse of LAN, viz. non-local networks, are sometimes termed Wide Area Networks (WANs). We are primarily interested in the latter but this distinction is of less importance for our purposes.

[56] 'Value-added services' imply that more than mere transmission, or simple carriage, is offered. The value addition can be extremely limited (such as aggregation, forwarding and encryptation of data), involve a complete application (like a reporting system) or, indeed, management of the whole corporate network (a so-called virtual private network) with or without more specific applications. The reason for value-added networks (VANs) being singled out and having received much attention is that the different geographical markets for telecommunications transmission have been, and in most countries the market still is, highly regulated (see, for instance, OECD-BRIE, 1989; OECD, 1987; and OECD, 1980 for overviews).

By taking the vantage point of the user, our definition of a corporate data communications network then basically overrides all the distinctions so painstakingly made above. The reason for establishing the taxonomy nevertheless is twofold:

a) it makes it possible to relate our definition to mainstream literature on data communications;

and, more importantly,

b) that there are qualitative differences concerning usage, depending on what type of link is chosen in a particular case.

As a rule, using leased lines is more reliable, is faster, gives higher capacity, is more secure, and offers better temporal availability than using a dial-up connection. It is also considerably more expensive and demands more network management by the using firm. Consequently, the choice of communications link from a particular site into the network is an indication of the communications requirement. In a geographically dispersed firm, different organizational units will have qualitatively different types of links and this configuration of the network is likely to change over time.

Naturally, the choice of links is not only a question of weighing price against performance, but is also subject to availability. The relevant range of options for a specific site at a specific time varies and has to be taken into consideration. For a given communications requirement, availability has a bearing on if, and when, a site is connected to the network. For instance, the existence of a public circuit-switched data network in the Nordic countries makes local connections technically simple and very attractive on a price/performance basis. In South America, the range of options is not only much more limited but the alternatives are also more expensive and more cumbersome to implement. The 'threshold value' of a communications requirement for being connected to the corporate network will then tend to be higher in South America than in the Nordic countries.

In sum, our view of corporate data communications networks will differ from standard, technically-oriented definitions (e.g. Martin, 1981a; and Tanenbaum, 1989) in that we focus on the user-function of the network[57]. Our approach yields a wider concept, since the whole range of electronic data transmission alternatives is seen to be part of the same network. Hence, the ability and need to communicate are more important here than exactly how it is done technically.

Unfortunately, this is not our whole network story.

A physical connection is not a sufficient condition for allowing a terminal user to transmit data throughout the network in a coherent format and to access application programs located in different computers connected to the network. Some other, 'basic' communications services are required for a network to function as a data communications network. In consequence, a distinction between communications and information systems does not appear to hold up as neatly as one would hope.

For analytical purposes we maintain the distinction, but we include the basic communications services[58] in 'communications'. The main such services, which are intimately associated with a network, are interactive traffic, remote job entry, file transfer, different (technically determined) gateways, and connections to external systems and networks.

Remote job entry is a way to access processing power. A user enters a job to be processed at any of the computer centers connected to the network.

---

[57] We have also avoided the additional complication of different technical architectures in data communications networks. When a gateway exists between, say, an IBM SNA network and DEC's DECNET network, we regard them as parts of the same corporate network.

[58] Our concept of 'basic' services is not as indistinct as it may seem. It corresponds quite well to the International Standards Organization's (ISO) Open Systems Interconnection (OSI) model for data communication, although that model was developed for technical and regulatory purposes (cf. ISO, 1986; and Tanenbaum, 1989). The services we include relate to the three top layers of the model (i.e. session, presentation, and application). For instance, file transfer is specified in the top layer. The excluded services, to be discussed in the following section, go beyond the OSI-model in that they constitute more complex applications.

Interactive traffic simply means that a user with the proper authorization can access a particular on-line application program located in a computer connected to the data communications network.

Files can be transmitted between computers over the network. The requested file is copied and sent to the receiving computer. An important use of file transfers is for transmitting information between (and within) standardized common systems.

External connections often go via one point in the network. For instance, external databases can be utilized through one connection instead of users spread around the world having their own, separate connections. Access to other logical networks, e.g. telefacsimile, voice telephone, and telex, can be similarly handled.

With the network finally in place, the missing link is what more specific uses the network can be put to. These uses are embodied in the more specific (by application) systems operating on the network.

3.1.2 The Systems-Network Relationship

Conceptually, the standard argument explaining why a data communications network is established is twofold:

a) utilization of distant computer processing power,

and

b) the need to access data located elsewhere (cf. Martin, 1981a:24).

The first reason springs from a need to overcome local insufficient processing power and the second from data being collected and stored in different locations, notably, different from the locations where they may be needed. The advent of relatively cheap and more powerful small computers means that the second reason has come to dominate, especially since commercial transactions are "the bread and butter of data processing", and since these transactions do not require much in the way of computer power (Martin, 1981a:24).

The traditional argument can readily be extended by deduction in order to conform more closely to our user perspective of the previous section.

First, recall that computer processing is not just a matter of place, but also of time. Local power per se may well be sufficient for a transaction, but the sheer number of simultaneous uses may cause temporary congestion. Other processing units can then handle the 'overflow' from time to time. Further, and if designed for this to occur regularly, a data communications network can be motivated for reasons of efficient capacity utilization (in addition to the straight access to superior capacity needed for a particular type of transaction).

Second, and more importantly, not only data, but also applications are normally found at different locations. In order to highlight the point, we can construct an example: a user in one location may fetch data from another location to feed to an application in a third location. (The actual processing can, in turn, 'overflow' to a fourth location.) However, the gist of the illustration is that access to applications - as opposed to data - can conceivably be an important rationale for establishing a data communications network.

Third, the important function of being a system for communication needs to be given its due weight. This function can be perceived as divorced from what is commonly called "obtaining data for computer processing" (as in Martin, 1981a), unless the latter is given such a wide domain as to render it virtually meaningless. Consider, for instance, electronic mail. True, processing is involved, but it is minute and largely confined to enabling transmission. True, data are transmitted, but not really for local machine processing at the receiving end. Rather, we can typically conceive of electronic mail primarily as a delivery system; a message is sent to be received unchanged for subsequent human 'processing'[59]. Another example bringing out the point is remote systems

[59] The gist of our argument remains, although electronic mail messages frequently have attached files, or contain other information, which eventually is processed by a computer.

maintenance. It has less to do with processing at either end, or with transmission of data, than with providing a means for 'hands-on' maintenance of a computer system in a distant location. In short, the idea of enhanced communications - without reference to the twins 'processing' and 'data' - is an additional motivation for having a data communications network.

Our extended version of the rationale for data communications networks demonstrates the need to move beyond the, now, restrictive focus of the previous section. Especially access to dispersed data and to applications and use of communications systems shift the question more toward what the network is used for.

We choose to use the term information systems as the wider concept[60]. Databases are subsumed under the same heading.

The network of the previous section essentially constitutes the infrastructure for making information systems (and therewith associated data) available at geographically dispersed locations. The information systems also determine the type of data that can be handled within the data communications network, subject to the restrictions set by the communications hard- and software (and, in exceptional cases, by government regulations[61]). The implied communications network, plus the set of systems and pattern of availability or access make up the information systems infrastructure of the organization.

---

[60] The Boaden and Lockett (1990) survey gives us ex post (cf. Hagström, 1987) support for our choice of term if established usage is anything to go by. "Information systems" was both the most common, and fastest growing, of the surveyed terms. However, two observations are in order: first, recall that Boaden and Lockett (1990) do not concern themselves overly with telecommunications; and, second, they, themselves, suggest "information systems management" as a new and better term in order to bring out the subsumed social aspect of information systems.

[61] The regulations pertaining particularly to systems (or 'processing') primarily refer to different national privacy laws (see, for instance, Aronson and Cowhey, 1988; Feketekuty and Aronson, 1984; and Kirsch, 1983), but recall that there is little empirical support for these regulations being of more than limited relevance for MNCs (cf. Section 2.1). In fact, there is a case for MNC de facto usage of telecommunications now driving policy changes in the direction of deregulation (see, for instance, Mansell, Holmes and Morgan, 1990).

The existence of a communications link is a necessary, but not sufficient, condition for access to information systems, in principle available through the communications network. Control over access is thus a relevant issue also at the system level[62]. The details of access to a system can be an extremely complicated affair. It can be linked to a person, a position, an organizational unit, a site or specific hardware, or to combinations thereof. It is also a matter of degree, defining which transactions can be processed, which data are available for entry, and when the system can be used. None of these classifications is confined to internal use of a system. External parties may enter at any point.

Here, we are primarily concerned with the larger, organizational perspective as opposed to the individual or particular information system. Consequently, access tied to organizational unit and geographical site, as well as degree of access afforded these categories in terms of transactions permitted and data availability, will take the center stage. We now turn to this organizational correspondence objective.

3.2 MNC Structure

As has been discussed above, any clear link between our information systems and MNC structure is tenuous, at best. However, the technological bent, and stress on communications, of the previous section offer an avenue to approach the role of information systems in MNC structure.

Historically, it was technical developments in transportation and communications (notably the railroad and the telegraph) that made large and geographically dispersed corporations a viable proposition (Chandler, 1977; Caves, 1980; and Williamson, 1981). The argument is extended à fortiori to the advent of the first industrial multinational corporations at the turn of the century (Chandler, 1986).

---

[62] Similarly to the case of communications links, ownership of a system is not really an issue. A system may be housed in an external computer and maintained by an external party, without that impinging on the control of access to that system by the user organization (see also Hagström, 1988).

The related, early conceptions of (corporate) structure focussed on organization design for administrative purposes, encompassing both the lines of communication and the information that flow through them (Chandler, 1962:14). Structural change was found to be a response to loss of managerial control as the firm grows[63]. Organizational innovation, and its subsequent diffusion, allow the process to continue. The successive organizational archetypes that can be observed have been the unifunctional, the functional, and the divisional structures[64].

Control as a key facet of structure is particularly relevant in our context in two ways: first, computer and telecommunications technology is particularly well suited for control purposes[65], and, second, control figures prominently in later extensions of the concept of structure, as it has come to be used in approaches grounded in organization theory[66]. The reason for adopting an organization theory bias when pursuing MNC structure is straight-forward in that we need a rich concept of structure in order to trace organizational repercussions of information systems usage, and in the paramount role given to information flows in much of organization theory.

---

[63] The intervening variable between exogenous environmental change and required structural adaptation is the successive growth strategies pursued by the firm (volume, geographical dispersion, vertical integration, and product diversification; cf. Chandler, 1962:13).

[64] It should be noted that Chandler's (1962) original work constituted an observation and historical interpretation of the evolution of U.S. large business from the mid-19th to the mid-20th centuries. It carried no explicit normative implications. - A particularly clear statement of the broad, evolutionary interplay between new transport and communication capabilities, on the one hand, and growth strategies, on the other, leading to organizational innovation is found in the much neglected Chandler (1965).

[65] That maintenance, or increase, of control of economic activity in organizations is the prime function of information technology is argued, inter alia, by Ackoff (1967), Beniger (1986), Boddy and Buchanan (1986), and Francis (1985 and 1986). Beniger (1986) goes the farthest, viewing the much vaunted 'information society' as nothing more than a part of the continuing "Control Revolution". It was set in motion by the acceleration of industrialization into the 19th century with its increasing speed of material processing and flows in the economy. The "Control Revolution" was the technological and economic response to the threat of loss of control ("crisis of control"). - Note that Beniger's (1986) argument bears some resemblance with Chandler's (1962), but with the important caveat that the former sees technological development as endogenous, and extends his argument to all aspects of human society.

[66] As, for instance, in the influential statement by Child (1972), who defined structure in terms of allocation of work roles, and mechanisms for control and integration of work activity (see also Galbraith and Nathanson, 1978).

The translation of the requirements of richness and of focus on information properties to MNC structure is by no means uncomplicated, however. Current main strands of research on the organizational structure of MNCs can be seen to put different emphasis on the form and on the functioning of MNCs, respectively. Stretching the argument, the difference in perspective, in turn, mirrors a division in allied viewpoints in economic theories of the MNC and in theories regarding the strategic behavior of MNCs. Our somewhat unorthodox juxtaposing of two broad perspectives across disciplines is a concession to achieve better correspondence with the network/systems relationship, which was framed very much as an issue of form and content. Also, an extensive review of the literature on MNCs would lead too far in the present context, wherefore a simplified taxonomy of the field(s) is economical[67].

Briefly, structural form of the MNC is the dependent variable in organizational research that can claim direct descent from Chandler's (1962) original statements. Recent proponents of the view that MNC organizational form is an outcome of the balance between the MNC's information processing requirements and the information processing capabilities of different organizational forms are Egelhoff (1982 and 1988a), and Gates and Egelhoff (1986). Here the information processing requirements are determined jointly by the external environment and the firm's strategy (indeed, they are in practice seen as two sides of the same coin, cf. Egelhoff, 1988a:11), whereas the chosen strategy assumes prime importance in closely related approaches (e.g. Daniels et al., 1984 and 1985; and Lemak and Bracker, 1988). A common key point, though, is that the derived structural form consequently should exhibit some "fit" with the strategy and/or environment in order to ensure survival[68].

Not too dissimilarly, internalization (extensive exposés in Buckley, 1989; Buckley and Casson, 1976 and 1985; and Casson, 1987) and transaction cost (particularly Teece, 1985

---

[67] Consequently, preference is given below to major and/or synthesizing references, and to more recent contributions. However, some influential contributions transcending the employed taxonomy (notably Dunning, 1981; Rugman, 1982; and Toyne, 1989) are excluded for expository purposes.

[68] For a particularly incisive, critical review of how the links between environment, strategy and structure have been used in research related to MNCs, see Hedlund and Rolander (1990).

and 1986; and Williamson, 1985) explanations of the existence of MNCs see the MNC as an efficient institutional response to information constraints (including those posed by potentially opportunistic behavior). The MNC economizes on transaction costs, and does so internationally, thus being an MNC (as opposed to 'just' a firm)[69]. 'Form' is, however, here more a question of extent of the firm (as opposed to markets), than of the internal structure of the firm.

Different strategic growth theories of the evolution of MNCs highlight the successively increased geographical reach of the MNC or as strategic rivalry in oligopolistic industries spills over national boundaries[70], as foreign demand and (lower) production costs are exploited[71], or as uncertainty about foreign markets is reduced[72].

Where more weight is put on the functioning of the MNC, the MNC is taken as a given, and research worry more about how it is maintained and about what possible advantages

---

[69] Both the internalization and transaction cost approaches draw their inspiration from Coase's (1937) original hypothesis about firms as the most efficient response to contractual - as opposed to production - constraints in order to effectuate exchange. The transaction cost view (in the formulation of Williamson, 1975, 1985 and 1989) restates this insight in terms of the firm as a governance structure; as internalizing long run exchange relationships, which otherwise cannot be adequately enforced through arm's-length contracting (cf. the hazards of cheating and the difficulty in pricing technology). In the end, hierarchy is an instrument of control. Internalization theory of the MNC add the twin, related propositions of industry market structure (Casson, 1987) and the possibility to create internal markets (e.g. Buckley, 1988; and Hennart, 1982 and 1986). Whereas the transaction cost approach assumes centralization of decision-making following from internalization, the internalization theory explicitly allows for decentralized pricing decisions (when different national markets offer idiosyncratic competition), and the creation of internal markets using shadow pricing (enforcing control through incentives rather than the more costly hierarchical control).

[70] Arguably, Hymer's (1976/1960) seminal work with the telling title: "The International Operations of National Firms" is the original exponent of placing prime importance on competition in different industries prompting internationalization. Other early, significant contributions are Knickerbocker (1973) and Graham (1978). Present day proponents of the primacy of industry structure typically rely on Porter (1985, 1986a, and 1986b). For an exhaustive overview of this line of argument, see Sölvell (1987).

[71] For the sequential expansion of MNCs dovetailing the life cycle of their products see Vernon (1966) and, i.a., the contributions in Wells (1972).

[72] This incremental internationalization is closely associated with the growth of the firm. This type of internationalization model is well represented by, and summarized in, Johanson and Vahlne (1977 and 1990; see also Buckley, 1990). In the same vein, the "network" approach sees the firm as operating within a set of specific inter-firm relationships (viz. with buyers and suppliers). Consequently, different parts of the internationalized organization, for instance subsidiaries, also operate within different such networks (comprehensive statements of this view relating to the MNC are found in Forsgren, 1990; and Johansson and Mattson, 1988).

possibly accrue to an existing, internationally dispersed firm. Dynamic coordination of a complex network of resources becomes relatively much more important.

In the organizational vein, form is here much less important as an element of structure than are the more elusive informal methods of coordination such as management systems, staffing, normative values, and modes and patterns of internal communication. Recent, comprehensive conceptions of this kind, which explicitly distance themselves from MNC structure as a question of organizational form, are Bartlett (1986), Hedlund (1986), Bartlett and Ghoshal (1988) and White and Poynter (1990)[73]. Any structural "fit" with the environment or strategy then becomes a multidimensional issue, and, indeed, only coincidental, since the relationship between strategy, structure and the organization's environment is seen as being symbiotic[74].

Kindred views put forth by economists stress the sequential advantages of being, as opposed to becoming multinational (Kogut, 1983 and 1990[75]) and the inherent ability of MNCs to arbitrage across imperfect (financial) markets (Lessard, 1986; and Lessard and Nohria, 1990; see also Kogut, 1989). Also, Vernon's (1979) conjecture of an MNC as a "global scanner", picking up on commercial ideas and opportunities wherever they arise in the world for subsequent exploitation globally, shows kinship with those later contributions.

A corresponding view of MNC strategy as being inherently different, especially in terms of its qualitatively greater complexity, is argued, in particular, by Doz and Prahalad (1986

---

[73] These contributions explicitly (Hedlund, 1986; and Bartlett and Ghoshal, 1988) or implicitly resuscitate Perlmutter's (1969) original conception of MNCs ultimately having to adopt a "geocentric", or world-oriented, attitude of management in order to achieve corporate integration and coordination across markets. The renewed academic interest in elaborating the required 'world-orientation' was predicated on the identified qualitative change in the way MNC business practices evolved in conjunction with global market segments appearing, more rapid diffusion of technology and radically improved access to multiple geographical markets (cf. Bartlett, Doz and Hedlund, 1990).

[74] Perlmutter (1984) and Hedlund (1986) bring out the symbiotic nature, in a wide sense, of the firm-environment relationship.

[75] The identified advantages are economies of scale and scope, operating flexibility, and successive learning about varying local conditions. They accrue to the already internationalized firm, which can exploit its geographically dispersed network of organizational units.

and 1987), and Prahalad and Doz (1987). Main tasks of management in MNCs are to maintain cohesion while allowing for strategic variety (between countries, businesses, and modes of market participation), and to be able to effectuate periodic strategic redirection as a process intervowen with organizational change.

Control and coordination are clearly key concerns when discussing the structure of MNCs. In the following, the terms will be used in very much of a common-sensical way, picking up on relevant particularities as the need arises so as to avoid being immersed in intricate discussions on the nature of the concepts. That usage very much follows that of the 'form' and 'functioning' research traditions, as well as the 'rational' interpretation given by Scott (1987). As to organizational structure, formal and informal structures are commonly contrasted. However, two reasons militate against us drawing battle lines at this stage. First, we need to explore several aspects of structure, be they formal or informal. Second, the informal structure is exceedingly difficult to define, and no attempt will be made here (for overviews of the role of informal structures, see Mintzberg, 1979; and Scott, 1987). More importantly, we have chosen the terms 'form' and 'functioning' of MNCs since that distinction is seen as more fruitful when discussing changes in location of activities and the issues connected to controlling and coordinating those activities.

In line with the focus on the functioning of the MNC, we do not need to explain why MNCs arose, but rather to see how they possibly change; in our case with the advent of new information systems. On the other hand, we need an understanding of the choice of MNC structure and of the distribution of MNC resources, i.e. the geographical and organizational configuration of MNC (organizational) units. These issues overlap, but will be discussed separately with reference to the 'form' and 'functioning' main strands. In order not to stray too far we maintain a rather high level of abstraction in the following, only very selectively bringing out the aspects we need for the framing of our problem. Moreover, to avoid definitional questions as to what exactly constitutes an MNC, we concentrate on highly internationalized MNCs (i.e. with proportionally large foreign operations and presence).

3.2.1 Choice of Structure

As a general proposition, the still dominating approaches tied to the form of the firm leave little room for managerial discretion when designing firm structure. When 'erroneo' ' choices are made, the iron-law of (economic) efficiency weeds out such firms and does so reasonably quickly. A corollary of this point is that similar firms, in terms of scope of activity, in similar environments should exhibit similar structures.

In terms of large firms, and large MNCs in particular, the internal structural hall-mark is the multi-divisional form. The internalization and transaction cost approaches has little to say beyond that point. The divisions are quasi-firms, bound together by an internal miniature capital market (Williamson, 1975:143ff), since the corporate head-office has superior abilities to audit, advise, and plan for its divisions compared to the external capital market, wherefore corporate allocation of resources among the division is also commensurably superior. Although the firm itself is still very much of a black box, recall that the limit of the firm is all the much clearer. The firm interface with the market is then primarily an efficiency issue, relating to the end-points of the sequence of activities performed by the firm[76]. Degree of vertical integration and additional forms of contractual relationships (viz. joint ventures, franchising, subcontracting, and licensing) consequently become the most pertinent questions (cf. Casson, 1987; and Williamson, 1985).

Strategy-grounded approaches frame the latter issue for MNCs more in terms of form of entry into new geographical markets and successive change of market presence[77] (viz. agents and sales subsidiaries, green-field investments and acquisitions etc.). Similarly to internalization theory (cf. Buckley, 1988), MNC subsidiaries are seen as more or less

[76] This sequentiality of activities parallels the conceptualization of the firm in strategic terms as a "value-chain" (as popularized by Porter, 1985).

[77] For a recent review along these lines, see Ågren (1990).

closely tied to the head-office depending on external conditions (the most important from a strategy point of view being local market structure and nature of competition in the industry internationally) within a multi-divisional form of sorts, but typically global product divisions (e.g. Hout, Porter and Rudden, 1982). The "network" approach adds the embeddedness of subsidiaries in their local environment (e.g. Forsgren, 1990), by implication further limiting managerial discretion at the enterprise level of choice of form[78].

Traditional, organizationally-inclined research on MNC structure also, on the whole, assigns supremacy to external factors determining MNC form, again with reference to economic efficiency[79]. Two, closely related issues are of particular importance here: what organizational form is found most relevant for MNCs, and what restrictions "fit" places on choice of MNC structure.

First, the concept of "fit" is intuitively appealing (who would want to wear size 9 or 11 shoes when having size 10 feet?), but difficult to operationalize and to uphold empirically[80]. The more recent applications of the concept to MNCs have instead come to talk about several "fits"; viz. between elements of strategy and structure (e.g. Galbraith

---

[78] Somewhat surprisingly, Ghoshal and Bartlett (1990) subscribe to the same view apparently in contradiction to the much wider scope of intervention afforded the managers of the "transnational" MNC (e.g. Bartlett and Ghoshal, 1989 and 1987).

[79] According to Chandler (1962) this is clear, since a strategy "required" (1962:151) a particular structural form, in turn, since a lack of alignment would lead to inefficiency (1962:314). Lately, however, "effectiveness" has come to be used instead (notably by Egelhoff, 1988a). Its meaning is less clear, since it is a function of several "fits" and should be evaluated over a longer term (1988a:265ff). In the aggregate, it is a question of one structural form being better at exploiting environmental resources than another (1988a:13), as reflected in higher probability of survival and growth (1988a:267).

[80] For instance, considerable national variation, on the one hand, and no established superior performance of large corporations with "fits", on the other hand, cast doubt over the concept (a celebrated series of national cross-sectional studies are reviewed in Scott, 1973, and in Dyas and Tanheiser, 1976; Franko, 1976, in a widely acclaimed study, showed a distinctly different evolutionary pattern for organizational structures in European - as opposed to US - MNCs). Egelhoff (1988a) rejects both arguments, claiming a "culture-free" model (1988a:258) and sampling only "successful" (1988a:45) MNCs.

and Nathanson, 1978; and Egelhoff, 1988a[81]), thereby de facto recognizing the overriding complexity of MNC activity.

Although not appreciated, that insight is evident already in the influential work of Thompson (1967), who indicated that crossing international boundaries probably is the most dramatic source of complexity for organizations to deal with (1967:70). In this version of contingency theory, it is logical that different parts of the organization would exhibit different structures (and "fits"), since they face different environments[82].

But 'fit with what?', remains a problem. Contingency theory has been unclear on the separation and relative influence of technology and environment (Schoonhoven, 1981; and Pennings, 1975)[83]. The confusion has an added dimension in that the view of strategy as essentially technology-determined (McGee and Thomas, 1988; Ergas, 1984; Hayes and Abernathy, 1980; and Kantrow, 1980) has gained credence in traditional strategy approaches. The main point here, however, is that a primary function of management is to design the organization so as to conform rather passively to externally determined conditions while maintaining internal control[84].

Second, what form of organization is then 'best' for the MNC? The seminal study by Stopford and Wells (1972) showed a development towards global divisional forms; by product when foreign product diversity was high, and by area when the share of foreign sales was high. But the form became largely indeterminate (some form of matrix or

[81] One source of inspiration here is the identified interdependence between the concepts of strategy and environment (e.g. Child, 1972; and Mintzberg, 1979). More subtle requirements of "fit" (also in internal relationships) follow. (Leksell, 1981, represents an early attempt at exploring complicated alignments in a few MNCs.)

[82] However, the internal rationality of the organization is set by norms of the employed technology in Thompson's (1967) world, wherefore competition is not what propels "organizations in action" (see further Astley and Van de Ven, 1983, who compare Thompson, Chandler and Williamson on this score).

[83] This confusion is mirrored as far back as in the forerunners of contingency theory, where Burns and Stalker (1961) focussed on markets, and Woodward (1965) on production technology, as determining organization structures.

[84] Recall, however, the element of choice when selecting a type of environment to be in (cf. Child, 1972; and Mintzberg, 1979).

mixed structure) when both product diversity and share of foreign sales were high. Adding a high share of foreign manufacturing, a product/area matrix seemed to follow (Egelhoff, 1988b). Although widely predicted to come with increased internationalization (e.g. by Stopford and Wells, 1972; Prahalad, 1976; Davis and Lawrence, 1977; and Brooke and Remmers 1970/1978), matrices have remained the exception and not the rule (cf. Egelhoff, 1988a; Lemak and Bracker, 1988; Daniels et al. 1984 and 1985; and Pitts and Daniels, 1984). The same scarcity has been found regarding the final dimension of divisionalization generally considered, viz. by function. An explanation is that functional divisions are seen to be the most communications intensive (Egelhoff, 1982), and thus likely to be less well suited for geographically highly dispersed MNCs[85].

In spite of the refinements of the "fit"-requirement(s), the concept of the firm itself has remained quite undeveloped in the organizational stream of research. In the references cited above (with the exception of Brooke and Remmers, 1970/1978), only two levels in the organization are considered in practice: headquarters (corporate-cum-divisional) and subsidiaries and relationships are framed in this dyadic context[86]. Although "lateral relations" are a prominent feature of influential theoretical antecedents[87], they do not recur in relation to subsidiaries of MNCs. In consequence, subsidiaries are assumed to have little to do with one another, except through a head-office of sorts.

A rather early spate of writings could, however, establish a very extensive, qualitative variety in headquarters-subsidiary relationships also within the same firm (for instance, Brooke and Remmers, 1970/1978; Barlett, 1979 and 1982; Robinson, 1978; Hedlund, 1980 and 1981; Kagono, 1981; Prahalad and Doz, 1981; Welge, 1981; and Hedlund and Åman, 1983 - see also Otterbeck, 1981). From there, the step to identifying different roles for different subsidiaries in combination with emphasizing informal means of coordination

[85] The degree of internationalization commonly regarded as "high" tends to reflect U.S. standards. For instance, Daniels et al. (1984 and 1985) use the epithet "heavily involved abroad" (e.g. 1985:223) for MNCs with more than 20 percent sales abroad, and Egelhoff (1988a) used 15 percent as a cut-off when selecting successful MNCs (see further Hagström, 1991).

[86] See further Hagström (1991).

[87] Specifically in the information-processing view of organizations, see Galbraith (1973 and 1977), Tushman (1978 and 1979), and Tushman and Nadler (1978).

and control (cf. in particular Bartlett and Ghoshal 1986 and 1987; Doz and Prahalad, 1986; Hedlund, 1986; Hedlund and Rolander, 1990; and Jarillo and Martínez, 1990[88]) is logical, but represents a clear departure from the traditional focus on organizational form of the MNC[89].

Within the loosely connected body of research concentrating on the functioning of the MNC, the choice of structure (and, indeed, the structure itself) becomes a much more complicated matter[90]. Local conditions and capabilities predicate significantly different roles for subsidiaries (Bartlett and Ghoshal, 1986); and even the role of any headquarters becomes more diffuse, or diluted, as subsidiaries take on some of its responsibilities (Hedlund, 1986). Worse still, the structure can be seen as unstable over time (Hedlund, 1986). In the extreme, any notions of hierarchical relationships in a formal structure are irrelevant for all intents and purposes in the modern MNC (Hedlund, 1991a). The organizational capabilities, per se[91], of the MNC can be said to become the key structural characteristic.

Without "fit" or 'form', the question of choosing a structure must be interpreted as more one of how to manage interdependencies over time. Since these interdependencies are internal as well as external, we will concentrate on the two issues of possible limits to organizational capabilities and on conceptions of the firm[92]. An important caveat here

---

[88] Forerunners stressing the importance of informal means in MNCs are Bartlett (1979 and 1982), Hedlund (1980), Doz and Prahalad (1981), and Leksell (1981).

[89] With the introduction of several alignments (i.e. "fits") and including those between the macro-structure (i.e. corporate) and micro-structure (i.e. subsidiary), some limited variety in headquarters-subsidiary relationships is, however, now allowed for in the more traditional studies (e.g. as in Egelhoff, 1988a; and in Ghoshal and Nohria, 1989; both give much weight to local subsidiary conditions in rather traditional contingency models, which in the latter case perhaps is somewhat surprising, given the different focus evident in, for instance, Bartlett and Ghoshal, 1986 and 1989).

[90] Barlett (1979 and 1983) strongly emphasized that adaptation of MNCs to changing circumstances is more a question of managing processes than of formal reorganization, suggesting that changing the formal structure often was unnecessary.

[91] By emphasizing roles in the way done above, organizational capabilities are used here in a wider sense than the "strategic control capabilities" of Doz and Prahalad (1984).

[92] For a related discussion, but more specifically in the context of the importance of lateral relations internal to the MNC, see Hagström (1991).

is that the managerially-oriented theories of the 'emerging' MNC - be it the "heterarchical MNC" (Hedlund, 1986), the "transnational" (Bartlett, 1986), the "horizontal" (White and Poynter, 1990) MNC, or the new "diversified MNC" (Prahalad and Doz, 1987) - are evolutionary, have a strong normative bent, and can, so far, only claim fragmentary empirical support.

The academic interest in the usage of informal means[93] to hold the MNC together has decidedly come to dominate in more recent empirical studies, whereas its relative importance in MNCs can at present only be hypothesized to be of a commensurate magnitude (Martínez and Jarillo, 1989). As the empirical evidence accumulates, however, the respective roles of formal and informal means of control and coordination should become easier to ascertain. A wide spectrum of means is also required by the theoretical constructs, since coordination of the MNC along any single or dual dimension (e.g. product and/or area) is not sufficient (cf. Hedlund, 1986; and Bartlett and Ghoshal, 1990). Any restrictions on the use of informal mechanisms are less generously provided, however. One restriction that is commonly recognized (following Bartlett, 1986) is the MNC's administrative heritage. The legacy of a structure and of an idiosyncratic corporate culture puts a limit on what can be achieved[94]. Differently put, we can see time as an important ingredient in determining the scope of the structural opportunity set.

By inference, we can identify some additional restrictions. If organizational capabilities are of prime importance, then 'organizing' is a skill and such skills may be in more or less short supply. Moreover, many of the informal means, the use of which are exhorted, are more costly than formal ones. For instance, task forces, committees, corporate conferences etc., as well as extensive training and socialization are more expensive than

---

[93] We return to the question of various roles of organizational units in the following section.

[94] With reference to the administrative heritage, Bartlett and Ghoshal (1988) explicitly call for a "gradual approach" (1988:73, emphasis added) to building organizational capabilities in the MNC. The argument is somewhat at odds with related strategy-oriented views, where, for instance, Doz and Prahalad (1987) see strategic reorientation and implementation as a process, but as an intermittently recurring one with periods of stability in between.

using set rules and 'bottom-line reporting'[95]. In the same vein, geographical distance is a problem, since a very high internal communications intensity is a corollary of the MNC relying extensively on informal means of control and coordination.

The relative neglect of cost considerations in the 'functioning' main strand can be understood in terms of the development of MNC organizational capabilities being an investment, creating a valued potential for the future[96]. Learning, and building systems and procedures that foster continuous learning, are hallmarks of this view (particularly as developed by Nonaka, 1988 and 1990[97]). 'Structure' can then be interpreted to become the key competitive asset, enveloping 'strategy' or the strategic options (cf. Hedlund, 1986, although admittedly the terms really are inappropriate in this context[98]).

In consequence, longer term competitive potential is here seen as more important than strict economic efficiency criteria when designing 'structure'. Indeed, the <u>conceptions of the firm</u> itself are more organic and diffuse. In its most pronounced version, the modern MNC can be seen as a meta-institution (Hedlund, 1986 and 1991a). The MNC is becoming amorphous, constantly changing the interfaces with the environment and the internal relationships as new opportunities arise[99]. Less drastic conceptions stress the overriding need for internal and external flexibility in MNC structure in response to

---

[95] Arguably, the advocated use of normative mechanisms to achieve integration (e.g. Bartlett, 1986; and Hedlund, 1986; see also Baliga and Jaeger, 1984, on the alternative of "cultural control" vs. "bureaucratic control" by management in MNCs) can be relatively cheap. However, establishing and maintaining such shared values must be costly.

[96] A stricter formulation from economics (cf. Kogut, 1983 and 1989) takes duplication and maintaining slack in the organization as amounting to holding valuable options on future states.

[97] Note also that Nonaka (1988 and 1990) directly take issue with the information-processing perspective of organizations (e.g. Galbraith, 1977), by stressing that information is not only processed but, more importantly, <u>created</u> through learning in organizations.

[98] For an early, insightful argument of structure de facto determining strategy (since it is the organization that develops strategy), see Hall and Saias (1980).

[99] The idea (cf. Hedlund, 1991a) is that the management of an MNC continuously selects markets, hierarchies, <u>and</u> in-between forms of governance in its quest to survive and develop. Also creating advantages means that the MNC is not simply a select<u>ed</u> (cf. the transaction cost and internalization approaches), but a select<u>ing</u> governance form. Building new advantages, and structuring the MNC to have the capability to do so, imply that future transactions (or even the legal structure) cannot be specified today, although they influence the present MNC structure.

diverse and changing external demands (e.g. Bartlett and Ghoshal, 1987 and 1988; Doz and Prahalad, 1986; Kogut, 1983 and 1990; and also Vernon, 1979).

In our view, there is an unarticulated problem, particularly as regards the above managerially-oriented contributions, associated with the strong emphasis on the required flexibility of the modern MNC. Especially external flexibility, viz. changing scope of the MNC and types of interfaces with its environment, seems difficult to reconcile with the importance given to informal means of control and coordination. Informal means tend to demand some stability of organizational membership to be effective. A recognizable "administrative heritage" is also likely to be a prerequisite for a corporate culture to flourish[100]. For instance, it takes considerable time both to instill shared values or a corporate culture and to give people a chance to get to know one another for task forces, committees and the like to function. Socialization and maintaining something meaningful to socialize into put a limit to the flexibility that can be accommodated both internally and in interfaces with the environment. A flexibility/stability dichotomy is new but it follows a classic tendency in organizational research in general to elevate one trade-off to the pinnacle of organizational concerns[101].

Not wanting to inflate the trade-off between flexibility and stability to become an issue of preeminent importance to the MNC, it will nevertheless stay with us. So will the wide range of structural means at the disposal of management, both as regards the scope of the MNC and its internal cohesion. The jury is still out on the importance of the formal organizational structure, wherefore we cannot afford to disregard it. A question mark remains concerning the universality of structure for MNCs facing similar external conditions, which would severely limit managerial discretion in structural choices. However, we do find support (from the 'functioning' main strand) for firm idiosyncracies, and for the possibility of organizational innovation, to make the scope for choice greater

[100] Recall also our argument above of time being a restriction on choice of structure.

[101] Examples of such main balances to be struck are certainty within the organization vs. the uncertainty of the environment (Thompson, 1967), organizational differentiation vs. integration (Lawrence and Lorsch, 1969), and the information-processing capabilities vs. the same capacities of the organization (Galbraith, 1973 and 1977).

than traditionally assumed. Finally, control and coordination of activities stand out as prime motivations guiding managerial structural choice, and à fortiori so, since complexity (and not, for example, size) is the hallmark of the MNC.

3.2.2 Structural Configuration

Whereas we have hitherto focussed on the opportunity set of external and internal relationships of the MNC, we now shift our attention more to what the MNC does where. The location of MNC activities has a geographical as well as an internal organizational dimension[102]. The latter issue is closely related to classical arguments about centralization vs. decentralization and to the newer concerns about organizational roles. The particular complexity associated with MNC activity reflected in the discussion immediately above, naturally, also extends to the configuration of MNC activities. However, the subject overlap allows us to keep the present discourse considerably briefer.

We have already seen that conceptions of MNC structure are cast in an evolutionary mold (with the possible exception of some transactions cost/internalization approaches). Very broadly, the changing nature of competition, on the one hand, and the continuous development of means of control and coordination, on the other, determine how MNCs evolve over time. There is, however, less commensurate interest in how MNCs distribute activities across space other than in very general terms.

Within the main strand emphasizing the form of the MNC, proponents of the internalization approach are the most explicit about the missing element of physical space

[102] Recall that our third dimension of location (viz. 'institutional location' or externalization vs. internalization of activities) has been reviewed in conjunction with the scope, or extent, of the MNC being discussed above in Section 3.2.

as less than homogeneous and as relevant per se for the MNC[103]. Drawing on standard neo-classical economics, with factor price differentials reflecting varying resource endowments, and on Vernon's (1966) outline of the product life-cycle, where production of a product moves according to factor-price differentials as the product matures, a cost-minimizing theory of location results (cf. Buckley and Casson, 1976; and Casson, 1987). Here, the location theory fills the function of an adjunct theory, supporting claims of the internalization approach being a comprehensive theory for the MNC[104].

The richer tradition of inquiry into location issues in economic geography follows similar lines, at least as far as industrial location theory goes. Firm location questions find their clearest expression in research under the headings of "corporate geography" (also known as "geography of enterprise"); a branch of industrial location. Adding growth and strategic explanations for location decisions to least-cost considerations, corporate geography is firmly within the family we have labelled 'form' of the firm. The location decision is actually seen as an outcome of other business decisions (cf. McNee, 1974; and North, 1974), thus making the spatial implications of business decisions the focus of analysis. The main points for the present context[105] are that corporate geography has a tradition of concentrating on the role of external linkages for the location of firm activities[106], and, in practice, considers the location of very few activities or functions (production,

---

[103] One notable exception is Pennings et al. (1987), who argue that spatial structure could be the most important economic determinant of internal organizational structure on the basis of the domestic operations of a sample of large US firms. Their argument also concerns the geographical dispersion of production and (local) interorganizational linkages (making it very reminiscent of the "network" approach), and the strategy-structure combinations of the 'form' tradition (see Sections 3.2 and 3.2.1). However, their assessment (Pennings et al., 1987:44) that the significance of corporate spatial structure is largely ignored in organizational theory, and that future research should pay greater attention to the specifics of corporate spatial structure, is well in agreement with the thrust of the present argument.

[104] A parallel view and, indeed, function of location theory is found in Dunning's (1981) well-known "eclectic theory", where the MNC is in a position to exploit various location-specific advantages by virtue of its multi-locational presence.

[105] The argument is laid out in extenso, and is fully referenced, in Hagström (1990b).

[106] Although internal linkages are typically not considered, other internal locational factors can be. When firm growth is emphasized (e.g. Håkanson, 1979), firm internal factors are, of course, important. But penetration of foreign markets is perhaps best described as a 'ratchet process', where the firm's presence in a foreign market simply escalates. Which particular market is entered is, however, determined by external factors.

headquarters functions, research and development, and sales units in descending order of prominence in the relevant literature)[107].

Although considerably more varied firm activities are typically studied than in internalization approaches, corporate geography stops short of the set of activities entertained by business economists applying the micro-economic concept of a value(-added) chain. Perhaps the most complete and succinct such statement can be found in Robinson (1987). Subdividing links by time (from ideas to production of mature products), and highlighting key input activities at each stage, Robinson (1987) goes on to hypothesize a geographical location pattern for activities according to their (decreasing) capital/labor cost ratio. Geographical location of activities is, however, only divided in three categories (developed, newly industrialized and developing countries, respectively), but the scheme also suggests temporal variability, particularly within each category[108].

The related arguments on the MNC exploiting economies of scale and scope typically imply a concentration of relevant activities, coupled with a notion of least-cost location. More interestingly, there is also a link to 'organizational location' (and the subset of 'hierarchical location) through the question of centralization vs. decentralization in MNCs. Even if whole functions are more rarely seen to be centralized (as particularly finance, cf. Clague, 1977; but also purchasing, Corey, 1978), then parts of functions (e.g. basic research, Caves, 1982; and marketing training, service and sales support, and global advertising, Takeuchi and Porter, 1986) or coordination of functions (e.g. production,

---

[107] This assessment does not change if Porter's (1990) widely noted work is taken into account. His "clusters" are inherently local in character and essentially determined by external factors, viz. the local environment. Moreover, few activities are considered (notably the core activities production and R&D). - For a parallel, comprehensive statement within the industrial location tradition, see particularly McDermott and Taylor (1982). In both cases, the MNC, per se, is only incidental to the main thrust of the argument.

[108] Robinson's (1987) argument is comparative-static in that a particular activity is located according to comparative national advantage, but dynamic in that resources (and products) are transferred among MNC subsidiaries (and possibly to subcontractors) according to their locational advantage. However, with changing comparative advantage of nations and changing competitive advantage of internalising a transaction in the value-added chain, the MNC competes on flexibly adjusting both internal resource flows and the scope of the MNC itself (the argument is evident, but less clearly so, also in the earlier Robinson, 1978 and 1984).

Flaherty, 1986; purchasing, Davis et al., 1974) are commonly argued to become centralized in MNCs on theoretical, as well as on empirical, grounds[109].

Research more closely related to the over-all organizational form of the MNC provides another aspect of the issue by essentially discussing the degree of autonomy afforded local subsidiaries, given that MNC resources are geographically widely dispersed. Reformulating that question for our context, it becomes a debate over the scope of headquarter functions or activities. As such, the degree of centralization of coordination recurs from the functional perspective above but the extent of central control is added. Broadly, the more integrated the operations of the MNC are, the more centralized it will be in terms of exercising central control and coordination of overseas activities (Brooke, 1984)[110]. The development is particularly pronounced with the dominant global product divisions, where the tendency towards centralization is applauded (Hout, Porter and Rudden, 1982), or warned against (Davidson and Haspeslagh, 1982). But what about the influence of greater complexity (recall Thompson, 1967)? Increasing company-level complexity in MNCs indeed does seem to imply a pressure towards decentralization in order to cope, but the reverse appears to result when subsidiaries are faced with greater environmental complexity, viz. it fosters selective centralization of decision-making (Gates and Egelhoff, 1986)[111].

---

[109] Moreover, the centralization tendencies in MNCs are generally found to be stronger the need for "global" strategies (e.g. Gates and Egelhoff, 1986; and Hout, Porter and Rudden, 1982).

[110] In his very comprehensive work, Brooke (1984) sees global product and project organizations as being typically "highly" centralized, geographical divisions as having a "medium" degree of centralization, matrix organizations as spanning the two, and only the mother-daughter structure as possibly exhibiting a "low" degree of centralization by virtue of it being suited to all three categories (cf. 1984:262-263). On the functional level, the derived picture is more varied, but functions are argued to move in the same direction as the over-all structure.

[111] A critical review of the whole debate on the degree of centralization in MNCs would lead too far. Note, however, that the power-perspective, particularly as regards the external resource-dependence of organizations (cf. Pfeffer and Salancik, 1978), tends to yield additional decentralization pressures when applied to highly internationalized firms since subsidiaries command substantial resources. With reference to our discussion above, there is a link with internalization theory (cf. Buckley, 1990, see also n. 7 in Section 3.2). More specifically, Forsgren (1990, see also Section 3.2) employs a power-perspective as well, and finds strong evidence of on-going decentralization associated with high degrees of internationalization in a sample of Swedish MNCs. In our view, the contradiction with main line research is of a less dramatic nature than claimed (and that perspective thus is of less importance in our context). For instance, the seemingly relevant finding by Forsgren (1990) does not substantially contradict Brooke (1984), since Swedish MNCs have been particularly slow to replace a mother-daughter structure (cf. Hedlund, 1984) and

Still, we find that the traditional views on centralization in MNCs are of doubtful value for an understanding of the geographical location of activities. By implication, "centralization" simply means location at headquarters; in practice, location according to the nationality of the parent firm. Similarly, "decentralization" becomes dispersed location in an unspecified periphery.

Recall[112] that the newer tradition focussing on the functioning of the MNC appears much less keen to use the ingrained terms of centralization and decentralization and instead brings roles of different organizational units to the forefront. The relevant point here is that subsidiary roles are typically seen as determined both by local external and internal conditions (subsidiary capabilities, market structure, and locational advantage), and by the over-all strategic needs of the MNC (e.g. Bartlett and Ghoshal, 1986; Hedlund, 1986; and Håkanson, 1990[113]). The importance of the MNC in general terms to flexibly exploit also temporal locational advantages as a function of being geographically dispersed, is emphasized by Hedlund (1986) and Kogut (1983 and 1990).

There is less consensus on the role of MNC headquarters. Divisional or corporate, headquarters appears to be saddled with the role of directly controlling and coordinating the rather unwieldy set of organizational units with different and shifting roles (cf. Bartlett, 1986; Bartlett and Ghoshal, 1986 and 1989; and Prahalad and Doz, 1987; see also Kogut, 1983; and Doz and Prahalad, 1981). Hedlund (1986; see also Håkanson, 1990) strongly downplays the role of headquarters, stressing more that roles are assumed by (rather than assigned to) subsidiaries and comes out relatively stronger on the importance of normative control and diffusion of strategic knowledge in order to maintain MNC cohesiveness[114]. In still another version, roles in the modern MNC are assigned through mutual negotiation internally (Chakravarthy and Perlmutter, 1985) or

---

could thus well be relatively decentralized (see also the note immediately above).

[112] From Section 3.2.1, above.

[113] See also the discussion in Hagström (1990a).

[114] However, even with a more limited role for and, by inference, scope of activities performed by headquarters, time and geographical distance must remain as substantial restrictions on the 'emerging' MNC (cf. the arguments in Section 3.2.1, above).

are the outcome of de facto command of resources (Ghoshal and Bartlett, 1990). Thus, when broadening the centralization issue, we are richly rewarded in terms of complexity being acknowledged.

The conclusion from our, admittedly parochial, vantage point is quite dismal. The 'form' main strand of MNC research demonstrates that when the range of firm activities considered is increased, the location theory underpinning tends to be less developed, and vice versa. In the extreme, we have seen that geographical location remains altogether divorced from internal organizational location. The problem is that this state of affairs runs contrary to our established requirement of studying complexity and how it can be handled. The 'functioning' of the MNC perspective definitely adds complexity to the structural configuration issue, but is less than specific on geographical and internal organizational location.

Our initial and idiosyncratic question of "what is done where in the MNC" has got no easy answer from our selective search through the relevant literature. However, we argue that placing emphasis on the extent of and ability to exploit external locational advantages, as well as on the location of the locus of control and coordination, appears to find at least some broad support. We can also read in a need for awareness of differentiation by activity and over time.

3.3 Perspective and Limitations

Following the excursions into the nature of information systems and into the structural characteristics of MNCs, we are now in a better position to frame the problem of the former's possible role for the latter. In turn, better precision will allow a more direct route for choosing a perspective on organizational development than would a more random walk in the vast area of organization theory. We should also be in a better position to economically wade through, and to evaluate for our purposes, the considerable literature on organizational impacts of computer-based information systems.

3.3.1 New Information Systems and Activities

We have defined the data communications network as including basic communication services, although we are really interested in the combined use of corporate data communications and the attendant computer-based systems in MNCs. The reason for nevertheless treating the network separately is that the network itself is a basic means for communications, holding also the potential for communications. Our particular definition of network is guided by the wish to relate to MNC structure, viz. the network provides basic communication links between different organizational units and is thus interesting per se.

To clarify, the network can be seen as relating economies of scope, whereas the computer applications (commonly called "systems") belong to the realm of economies of scale. Economies of scope cannot be attributed to any particular product or function, while economies of scale relate to achieving an efficient scale for a specific product or function. The network can be used across activities, whereas the computer applications are intended for a more specific purpose. Types of, access to, and the actual use of computer-based systems by different organizational units then say more about the intended functionality of use. But just as economies of scale and scope are not neatly separable, we have seen that the network and systems categories exhibit significant overlap. The terms still have analytical merit, however.

A parallel argument is that the network allows the firm to exploit the economies of scale inherent in specific computer applications by virtue of providing access. Different organizational units thus have access to the services offered by these applications. In essence, services are transported across space and organizational boundaries. Also control and coordination can be seen as such services. The general point is that we have a transport system for information-based services, where the network provides the transport and the specific applications determine which services are transported[115]. In turn, that has implications for where geographically, and where in the organization, activities are carried out.

The not-too-distant idea of telecommunications-cum-computers constituting a new infrastructure of sorts is not new, though. Early, influential statements to this effect are McLuhan (1964), Porat (1977), Nora and Minc (1978), Masuda (1980/1984), Toffler (1980), Martin (1981b), Shelp (1981), Claisse (1983), Gershuny and Miles (1983), Feketekuty and Aronson (1984), Hawken (1984), Inose and Pierce (1984), and Miles et al. (1988). The main theme of the varied contributions are, however, the societal impact of new information technologies in the context of the rising service-based economy, which is said to characterize developed countries. Apart from more visionary and popular statements on the future that is to befall us, the concept of the societal infrastructure has survived in the academic literature primarily within the telecommunications policy tradition and in economic research into the sectoral composition of aggregate production.

Whereas, inter alia, McLuhan (1964) would lead us too far down the garden path to the "global village", our line of reasoning of a firm infrastructure as a transport system for information-based services gives us the first main rationale for studying the role of new information systems in MNCs: if the information systems are interesting at all then MNCs should be particularly interesting to study, since they provide great varietu in organizational and geographical dispersal[116].

Several implications follow from our more pragmatic interpretation (and have remained hidden in our discussion so far). First, we limit our inquiry to a subset of 'new information technology'. The reason is fairly straight-forward in that we would want a

[115] Here, we follow the route taken in Hagström (1990a). Recall also the underlying arguments of Section 3.1.

[116] Some indirect and limited support for our view can be had from the 'control-argument' as reviewed in Section 3.2 above, whereby communications technology represent a restriction on firm and, in particular, MNC growth. The general parallel is Chandler's (1965) unambiguous statement of the capabilities of the telegraph setting a limit to the expansion of the railroad companies in the US. The point is reiterated in Chandler (1990). For the converse statement, viz. the second rationale, see Section 3.2.2.

'new' technology, but one which is sufficiently 'old' and widely available to lend itself to ex post empirical investigation and one which constitutes a 'major' technology so as not to be of only marginal importance for complex organizations as the MNC. International data communications-cum-computer-based systems fit that bill. Arguably, they are the most pervasive to date for MNCs, comparing with alternatives such as Integrated Services Digital Network (ISDN) applications, mobile telephony/paging and teleconferencing, not to menti' the many futuristic services not yet available (cf. Pool and Solomon, 1980, Barras, 1986; Cleevely and Cawdell, 1986; and Ungerer, 1988 for succinct overviews). Old technologies (telegraph and voice telephony) will not be considered, nor will broadcast technologies (e.g. television). Telex and telefacsimile will only be considered specifically in passing, primarily since they allow only limited amounts of data to be transmitted (and, in any case, can safely be subsumed under our 'information systems' heading)[117].

Second, the technical development of information systems, as defined, has been remarkably fast in terms of improvements in quality and performance but has been fairly stable in terms of not having undergone any dramatic qualitative change, at least over the last two decades[118]. Whereas technical improvements are commonly detailed, price/performance indicators are rarely compared across technologies[119]. An obvious reason for the lack of detailed comparisons is the difficulty of meaningful measurement in cost terms (a difficulty which is much exacerbated in an international context). For our purposes, a robust rule-of-thumb is that processing, storage and transmission costs have fallen in real terms over the last two decades, and that the former two have fallen rather

---

[117] In this context, recall also the limitations implicit in focussing on international communications (cf. Section 3.1) and in paying attention to regulatory regimes only in so far as they affect access (cf. Section 2.1).

[118] For instance, see the concise overview in CSTD (1986), where the different contributions on developments in the respective technologies stress the radical improvements in performance, but without identifying any change relatively more important than the advent of powerful minicomputers in the early 1970s (CSTD, 1986:4).

[119] The general argument that information technology (generously defined) usage is predicated on its dramatic cost performance development rests on the evidence that whereas capital goods to labor price ratios have shown more modest gains over the last 30-40 years, information technology capital goods have recorded a many times greater fall in prices relative to other capital goods (for a succinct statement, see Benjamin and Scott Morton, 1986, who find the ratio of capital to labor costs to have improved 1.4 times in six industries over ten years; the equivalent ratio for information technology was as much as 25 times).

more rapidly than the latter[120]. It is sufficient (and non-controversial) here, to note that there is a reasonably stable economic trend favoring the use of information systems at all and that it favors processing and storage over communications (cet. par.).

Third, it should be spelled out that our view of networks and systems implies an element of standardization (directly or through interfaces) that goes beyond mere technical compatibility issues. Including the 'basic communications services', the network insures standardization in the sense that transmitted data are intelligible also at the receiving end[121]. Access, and remote usage of computer applications, thus presuppose such standardization.

The à priori potential for transporting information-based services is considerable. In a survey from 1986 of all Swedish manufacturing firms with more than 200 employees, only 20-25 percent of total internal labor costs (inclusive of international operations) could be attributed to direct production; the rest being different kinds of services, primarily found to be information-based services (Eliasson et al. 1990)[122]. In addition to the remaining 75-80 percent of labor costs, services were purchased externally to an amount equivalent to 22 percent of internal labor costs (Eliasson et al., 1990). Although measurement by labor costs gives an exaggerated view of the relative importance of services (with their high labor content), and although not even all information-based services are

120 This over-all argument recurs in different forms in, for instance, Gremillion and Pyburn (1988), Scott (1986), Eaton and Smithers (1982), and Martin (1981a and 1981b). Bergendorff (1982) quotes estimates of computer memory and logic as falling in the proportions of 4:1 and 2:1, respectively, in relation to the fall in communications costs during the 1970s. The cost of developing software is typically argued to increase, at least modestly in real terms (see the above references). However, it seems reasonable to us that the greater versatility of newer software would have the two broad implications of a) rendering comparisons even less meaningful than for hardware, and b) mitigating the pressure to develop user-specific applications (especially given the parallel growth of a market for standard applications).

121 On this point, see also Hagström (1988 and 1990a). Note, though, that standardization at this stage refers to use of information systems and not to the wider organizational processes; neither is the formalization of such processes implied here.

122 The approximate breakdown on the reported categories was "creation of new knowledge" (R&D, design etc.) - 10 percent; "coordination" (marketing, distribution, administration etc.) - 30 percent; "training costs" - 3 percent; "goods manufacturing" (of which less than half is direct production) - 57 percent. Interestingly, the findings coincide very closely to what a pilot study revealed regarding one Swedish manufacturing MNC (cf. Fries, 1984a and 1984b; see also Hagström, 1990a).

transportable by electronic means, the results constitute a strong - albeit indirect - indication of the possible significance of data communications networks. Recall their superior capacity to transport information-based services compared to other 'information technologies' available at present.

By offering transportation and automation of some information-based services, data communications-cum-computer applications can conceivably change the nature of activities performed in firms. Activities can be subdivided, or fragmented, differently by partial automation and recombined in new ways[123]. For instance, the keeping of sales records can be largely automated and then combined with other data for new kinds of analyses and forecasting. With transport, the activities can be performed in new locations, also outside the firm. The keeping of sales records can more readily be externalized, local records can be kept at a different location, dispersed sales records analyzed and used within the R&D function for planning purposes etc.[124] The argument is not that particular un- and rebundling of activities could not physically be achieved previously, but that the advent of new information systems can allow that to be done economically.

With a somewhat circular reasoning, the advent of new information systems then is a necessary condition for changing the scope of activities carried out at an organizational unit as indicated above. But is it also a sufficient condition? And which activities change, and how? These questions are within the realm of organizational repercussions of information systems.

[123] In an excellent assessment of the effects of the telephone, Pool (1983) provides an analogous argument on fragmentation by crediting the telephone with making the physical separation of headquarters and field operations possible.

[124] The point is also argued and illustrated further in Hagström (1990a and 1990b).

3.3.2 New Information Systems and Organization

Although the questions are not put as above, there is a recent, prolific tradition of research that addresses issues related to the impact of information systems (but typically with little or no specific reference to telecommunications[125]) on organizations[126]. The main roots of the tradition are in the fields of computer science, organization studies, and business strategy. Transaction cost economics has also found a related application with reference to information systems[127].

In the following, we will refer to two broad classes of studies dealing with information systems and organizations; one focussing broadly on strategic issues and one being more concerned with internal organization[128]. For reference, the strategy-grounded approach

---

[125] See Sections 2.2 and 3.1. However, Keen (1986) is a notable exception (his impressionistic managerially-oriented book being subtitled "Using Telecommunications for Competitive Advantage") as are Clemons and McFarlan (1986), Crowston and Malone (1987), and Davenport and Cronin (1988). Also, there are examples here of telecommunication systems being forecast to become much more important in terms of organizational impact when compared to the impact of computers and information systems to date (e.g. Straub and Wetherbe, 1989).

[126] Recall that economic geography has less of an impact in the present context, since the organization (notably the firm) more rarely is the unit of analysis (see the argument in Hagström, 1990b). Spatial effects of information systems are most commonly analysed from a regional perspective, and when firms are considered the conclusions tend to mirror the organizational debate (cf. Mandeville, 1983).

[127] Much more broadly, economists have tended to contribute primarily on issues of information systems from a macro-economic perspective or in the context of information economics, on the one hand, and in the micro-economics of telecommunications and in trade policy of telecommunications, on the other (for instance, see the contributions in Jussawalla and Ebenfield, 1984; and the review by Snow, 1988).

[128] Already at the outset, some significant branches of the literature on information systems in organizations can be excluded from consideration here. Systems analysis and design, including expert systems etc., fall outside our area of interest. Given our focus on organizational units' use of information systems, issues of cognition at the individual level (Winograd and Flores, 1986, provide a particularly comprehensive discussion) can also be put off the agenda. When it comes to evaluating information systems (IS) investment decisions (for a recent, succinct discussion see Clemons and Weber, 1990) and to more practical implementation issues (see Kwon and Zmud, 1987, for an authoritative review) the relevance for our purposes is less easily judged á priori. The same goes for the very voluminous treatments of "how to manage IS" from the point of view of general management and/or of IS functional management (prominent proponents, but with slightly different foci on these issues, are Earl, 1987 and 1989; Allen, 1987 and 1982; Scott, 1986; Sinclair, 1986; van Schaik, 1985; Millar, 1984; McFarlan and McKenney, 1983; McFarlan et al. 1983; Pava, 1983; Buss, 1982; and Nolan, 1982). It is particularly difficult to totally exclude these areas from further consideration since many contributions point to the strategic opportunities offered by electronic information systems and how to implant them in the organization. The organizational

to information systems clearly commands much more of a central position in the main-stream of strategy research[129] than is the corresponding case for research on organizations[130].

The two dominant strategic issues raised in connection with computer-based information systems are the possibilities to create new or modified products or services with a greater information content and the opportunities brought by inter-organizational information systems. Although improvements in the internal operations of the firm are acknowledged to be present in some contributions analyzing the strategic uses of information systems (e.g. Benjamin et al. 1984; Porter and Millar, 1985; and Earl, 1988), the impact of information systems on buyer-supplier relationships dwarfs those concerns in terms of the amount of research produced. The prime source of inspiration has been what is perceived as spectacular corporate success stories[131], and which now, arguably, have taken on folkloric characteristics.

Whereas information systems are generally seen as a new, powerful tool (i.a. Parsons, 1983) in the arsenal of strategic weapons, the relationship to strategy is less than unambiguous. The technology is seen to drive strategy (e.g. Rockart and Scott Morton, 1984), to enable strategies to be accomplished in response to external, environmental driving forces (e.g. Scott Morton, 1988), or the strategic use is seen to be the joint outcome of business needs and technology developments (e.g. Rockart and Short, 1989). Despite the varied perspectives, there is a fairly solid consensus on the paramount

---

perspective is, however, more narrow than ours, and we will only very selectively pick up on the investment and 'IS management' traditions in the following.

[129] For instance, see Porter (1985; and the related Porter and Millar, 1985) and Rumelt (1981 as quoted by Child, 1984b:245). For the view that the scholarly work has had too much of an impact, to the detriment of other ways of dealing with issues of competitive strategy, see, for instance, Warner (1987).

[130] To illustrate, in Scott's (1987) extensive, general review of organization research, computer-based information systems barely warrant a mention (cf. Scott, 1987:219 and :289), and Stinchcombe's (1990) book **Information and Organizations** has not been found by us to contain any (sic!) reference at all either to computer-based systems or to telecommunications.

[131] American Airlines, American Hospital Supply, Citibank, Merrill Lynch and McKesson, to name a few (see, for instance, Benjamin et al. 1984; Mason, 1984; Keen, 1986; Wiseman, 1985; Copeland and McKenney, 1988; and Clemons and Row, 1988 for case descriptions).

importance of the strategic role of information systems. It is therefore not surprising that the strategic bent, as a rule, yields strongly normative conclusions.

Although not termed as such, the main thrust of the argument is that information systems can create a monopoly position for the firm. That favored competitive position can typically be achieved by using information systems to add value to products (in the process changing the basis of competition in the industry), to create switching costs, to build barriers to entry, and to reduce the information available to the customer (particularly as regards alternative sources of supply). Most important for our purposes is the idea of using information systems to 'lock in' a customer[132] (e.g. as present in Parsons, 1983; McFarlan, 1984b; Cash and Konsynski, 1985; and Bakos and Treacy, 1986) and the usually corollary argument that there is a distinct first-mover advantage of doing so in an industry (e.g. Porter and Millar, 1985; Clemons and McFarlan, 1986; and Keen, 1986)[133].

Some controversy has, however, arisen recently regarding the sustainability over time of such strategic moves. They may provide only a very temporary advantage as they are readily copied by competitors (Vitale, 1986), or as they commonly have a strong tendency to evolve into electronic markets. Competitive dynamics force open exclusive electronic sales channels as the disadvantaged parties in exclusive relationships seek alternatives, and as provision of such alternatives is greatly stimulated by any strategic advantage accruing to any single player in an industry (Malone et al. 1989; and Hopper, 1990)[134]. An additional, supportive argument centers on standardization, notably through the arrival of many-to-many electronic data interchange (EDI) systems, something that is already beginning to speed up the process of eroding the viability of exclusive electronic buyer-seller links (Benjamin et al. 1990).

---

[132] Although the principle is the same, a supplier is more rarely considered.

[133] One of the notable exceptions to treating data, systems, and communications as one is Davenport and Cronin (1988). However, their conclusions simply mirror those already indicated in the paragraph.

[134] See also Hagström (1990a).

Similarly, the question of inter-organizational information systems has also attracted analyses much inspired by the transaction cost approach[135]. Antonelli (1988a and 1988b) provides a particularly comprehensive statement, in the process also outlining elements of a "new industrial organization approach" (Antonelli, 1988a). Governance mode is here the outcome of what is termed transaction (or market) costs vs. coordination (or firm) costs. The advent of new information systems, at least initially, is found to favor coordination within the firm over market transactions; one major reason being the difficulty with which market-specific communications networks are established. It is easier to accomplish with fewer parties involved[136]. Emerging "network firms"[137] (Antonelli, 1988b) centered around electronic information networks blur the market/hierarchies distinction by fostering intermediate types of relationships. Centered around electronic information networks, the "network firm" can achieve the best of both worlds: increased monopsonistic power vis-à-vis small contractors and increased monopolistic advantage by virtue of supplying more differentiated products or services (see also Cozzi, 1988).

Firms with high coordination costs (which should be large and complex firms) will benefit proportionately more from information systems usage than other firms (Ciborra, 1983; and Antonelli, 1988a[138]). The threshold optimum size for a firm would tend to increase, although information systems would simultaneously open up for small, highly specialized firms in intermediate markets (cf. Antonelli, 1988a). In relation to markets the conclusions are somewhat at odds: either markets lose out on the two counts of firm growth and replacement by intermediate relationships (Antonelli, 1988a and 1988b), or

---

[135] For a recent review and application, see Suomi (1990). See also Swanson (1987) for more of a traditional organizational perspective and overview, and Langlois (1984) for a general, theoretical discussion on internal organization. In addition to approaches within the broader industrial organization tradition, game-theory has been applied to inter-organizational information systems (cf. Venkatraman and Zaheer, 1990).

[136] However, for a contrary view from a similar vantage point, see Ciborra (1983 and 1987) and below.

[137] A term neither to be confused nor associated with the "network" approach discussed above (cf. Section 3.2).

[138] Earlier adoption by large firms carries the additional benefit that once acquired, the information channel will keep on being used (cf. Arrow, 1975).

markets are relatively strengthened by new markets emerging and old markets improving since standardized market transactions are particularly amenable to automation by computers (Ciborra, 1983 and 1987)[139].

The controversies surrounding buyer-seller relationships have counterparts regarding issues of the internal organization of firms. Much of the debate centers on centralization or decentralization following from the use of new information systems. Broadly, proponents of markets over hierarchies tend to favor decentralization over centralization, and vice versa. A case in point is Ciborra (1983 and 1987), who sees internal markets in the sense of profit centers as being stimulated[140], whereas Antonelli (1981, 1987 and 1988a) stresses the trend towards centralization[141].

Centralization vs. decentralization is, indeed, a very likely candidate for being the issue that has received the most attention in research on information systems from an organizational perspective. That is understandable, since the debate reflects a long-standing area of inquiry within general organization theory (cf. Scott, 1987; Brooke, 1984; and Pugh et al., 1963) and since it was the main issue raised by Leavitt and Whisler (1958) in their seminal article on the impact of computers on organizations.

Leavitt and Whisler (1958) argued for centralization resulting from extensive usage of computers in an organization. Whisler (1970) sustained the argument with empirical studies of insurance companies. Galbraith (1973 and 1977) provided more general, theoretical underpinnings for the reasoning with his "information-processing" model of organizations[142]. Investing in vertical information systems is here one organization

---

[139] That is, market transactions are more structured than the alternative semi-structured long-term contracts or unstructured internalized transactions (cf. Ciborra, 1987).

[140] Interestingly, the argument parallels the view emanating from the internalization approach to the study of MNCs (see Section 3.2).

[141] Recall also that increased centralization is the dominating view emanating from the other writings on the use of international data communications in MNCs (see Section 2.3).

[142] From a different information-processing vantage point (hinging on the bounded rationality of organizations and individuals), Simon (1977) also supported the centralization argument, but with the caveat of computerization not changing the fundamental hierarchical structure of organizations.

design strategy which improves the organization's capacity to process information. The strategy is associated with centralization of decision-making. However, Galbraith views global on-line-real-time systems as utopian, since they are deemed excessively costly and since creating the commensurate new organization structures is beyond foreseeable human ability (Galbraith, 1977:107)[143].

Looking back, very clear statements of computerized information systems prompting centralization (e.g. Wynne and Otway, 1982; and OECD, 1981) or decentralization (e.g. Gerstein, 1987; and Pfeffer and Leblebici, 1977) in organizations appear to have given way to different attempts at reconciling the contradictory and often confusing empirical evidence to date[144]. Various implicit or explicit efforts at dealing with the conundrum come across from the extensive literature reviews of the area (particularly by Markus and Robey, 1988; Crowston and Malone, 1987; Swanson, 1987; Robey, 1986 and 1977; and Kling, 1980). We find at least four such main approaches[145].

One avenue has been to argue that computers constitute an intervening or moderating variable instead of an independent variable (Robey, 1977 and 1981; and Crowston and Malone, 1987). More fundamental influences determine organizational structure, but the relationships are affected by computer usage in the organization. In what has become known as the "interactionist" view, the organizational change that is related to usage of information systems is a complex interaction between what the technology can do and what the organizational requirements are (Markus and Robey, 1983; and Robey, 1986).

---

[143] Galbraith's (1977) skepticism is in part predicated on his preferences for improving the information-processing capacity of organizations through creation of lateral roles (cf. discussions in Hagström, 1987 and 1988). Perhaps surprisingly, the apparent possibility to use information systems for such lateral relations is not investigated by Galbraith. A final twist to the story is that it was J. D. Thompson who influenced Galbraith to focus his research on organizations instead of on computers (sic!) (Galbraith, 1977:xi).

[144] It is also not uncommon to find no measurable effects even when such were expected (e.g. as by Robey, 1981), and to argue against any present or future impact, at least as far as top management goes (Dearden, 1983).

[145] Again, we will not attempt to provide a comprehensive review of organizational repercussions, but merely to structure the field so as to conform to our earlier discussions and to fill in some gaps in the same. For a particularly broad taxonomy of organization theories and their related treatment of information systems see Lyytinen (1987).

Another avenue has been to seize on the widely accepted conclusion that information systems allow for greater control of lower levels in the organization. Observed decentralization is then, in effect, delegation of decisions, but which are more closely monitored centrally (cf. Child, 1984a and 1984b; and Blau et al., 1976). The probable net effect could still be argued to be one of increased centralization (Child, 1984b) or decentralization (Blau et al., 1976).

A third avenue has been to stress the relatively strong malleability of the technology, making it more context dependent (Kling, 1980; Mohrman and Lawler, 1984; Björn-Andersen et al. 1986; and Boddy and Buchanan, 1986). The purpose of introducing the technology and/or the idiosyncracies of the particular situation (especially, existing power relations) then become commensurably more important for judging any effects.

A fourth avenue is to conclude plainly that the effects of information systems usage in organizations are "poorly understood...[and that] constructive theoretical progress has been minimal." (Swanson, 1987:196). A variation of this route is to acknowledge the theoretical uncertainty[146] and to hypothesize that information systems actually bring greater variety across organizations as to at what level decisions are taken (Huber, 1990:58).

A few related issues are hidden in the above arguments.

First, the centralization vs. decentralization conundrum (and proposed resolutions of the same) closely parallels that of the fate of middle managers in the face of computerization. To exemplify, early statements on the reduction in the number of managerial levels (e.g. Whisler, 1970; and Simon, 1977) can be juxtaposed with findings of an associated increase in the same (at least in government agencies, see Blau and Schoenherr, 1971; and Blau et al., 1976), and with the argument of an emerging

[146] And adding another level of complexity by arguing that information systems bring centralization to decentralized organizations and vice versa, but that it may also be the other way around (cf. Huber, 1990:57).

"diamond-shaped" organization by virtue of increased professionalization of work roles (Zuboff, 1982).

Second, causality is treated highly differently. Especially the early and strong statements assigned supremacy to the technology itself; viz. information systems 'cause' organizational change (e.g. Whisler, 1970; and Simon, 1977). There is a clear link here to (the already discussed[147]) views of technology driving, or determining, corporate strategy, in turn prompting structural change[148]. But the more plastic or the more embedded in a context the information technology is interpreted to be, the less of an 'impact' its use must have on organization structure. Some malleability, and the "interactionist" view, represent a middle ground, but implying weak or no predictive power on effects of using information systems[149].

A third, and recurring[150], issue regards requirements of "fit". There is a pervasive notion of information systems
having to be aligned with the firm's activities that goes beyond mere relevance or general applicability. In a comprehensive version, the information system should "fit" with the organization structure, the organization-environment interface, the users, and the power distribution in the organization in order to achieve the greatest effectiveness (Markus and Robey, 1983)[151]. It seems (from the previous paragraph) that the weaker the causality, the more "fit" becomes a question of design, and the stronger the causality, the more it becomes an issue of choice of technology. The "interactionist" views represent a mixture

---

[147] See Section 3.2.1 on MNC structure, and above for the strategic role of information systems.

[148] A clear illustration of this affinity is Benjamin and Scott Morton (1986) who succinctly argue for a causal chain from information technology to organization structure (here yielding integration).

[149] Rockart and Short (1989) represent a similar view emanating from the field of strategy in that they see information technology usage enabling firms to respond to business needs, in turn driving information technology usage.

[150] See Section 3.2.1 on 'fit(s)' in relation to MNC structure.

[151] Other explicit discussions on the need for "fit" are McKenney and McFarlan (1982) and Camillus and Lederer (1985) on "fit" with strategy; Tavakolian (1989) and Leifer (1988) on "fit" with organization structure; and Olson and Chervany (1980) on the "fit" between the information services function and the organization.

here, typically advocating iterative adaptation of information systems to ensure "fit" (e.g. Markus and Robey, 1983) and coordinated evolution of all business activities and information systems with integration as the catch-word (cf. Rockart and Short, 1989).

At this stage, we can conclude that many of the issues raised in previous research on organization and information systems parallel those we have reviewed in conjunction with our discussions on MNC structure, but only as far as the broad tradition of 'form' is concerned. Interestingly, there is, to our knowledge, no main strand of research corresponding to the 'functioning' perspective on MNC structure.

Admittedly, the "interactionist" perspective is closely associated with a processual view, stemming from the identified complexity of causal relationships (cf. Markus and Robey, 1988:592-593) but the approach is marred by the baggage of "fit". Also, authors emphasizing the importance of context (e.g. Kling, 1980) bring out the relevance organizational idiosyncracies but subsequent analysis all too easily can degenerate into an overriding concern with power relationships[152].

In short, any kinship of the organization-information systems research with the 'functioning' perspective (on MNCs) is tenuous, if one exists at all. The closest we have come so far in finding candidates who qualify for exhibiting a prime concern with the functioning of an organization coupled with the use of information systems are the inductive study by Antonelli (1981 and 1987) and the more speculative reasoning of Nanus (1969)[153].

However, there is one clear link to what we have termed the 'functioning' perspective, and a link that ties in both MNCs and information systems: Hedlund (1986), writing on the evolving "heterarchical" organization of MNCs[154], and Morgan (1986), writing on

---

[152] "Overall, automated information systems seem to be organized so that they enhance the power of already powerful groups in computer-using organizations" (Kling, 1980:101).

[153] See Sections 2.1 and 2.2, respectively.

[154] See the discussion in Section 3.2 (including Sections 3.2.1 and 3.2.2), and also Hedlund (1991a).

organizations in general[155]. Both place great emphasis on the metaphor of the firm/organization as a brain, and on the concomitant "holographic" principles of organizing[156]. Morgan (1986:105) argues that the insights gained into organizational learning and into the capabilities of self-organization are the key aspects of the brain metaphor.

Morgan (1986) is unusual in main-stream organizational research in that he specifically considers the implications of new information systems for how to organize[157]. The new technology is hypothesized to bring new ways of organizing beyond the often found simple reinforcement of bureaucratic principles (cf. Morgan, 1986:108). In the more distant future, organizations may cease to exist in physical terms, its members instead being linked through an advanced communications network, possibly with the physical work relegated to remote-controlled robots (cf. Morgan, 1986:84)[158].

Although we have been purposefully selective when highlighting issues raised in research connected to information systems and organizations, our discursive review of the field has not managed to transcend (or obscure) the fact that very few theoretical arguments or hypotheses have gained currency. That empirical evidence abounds to support a number of often contradictory arguments on the same issue exacerbates the difficulties of finding

---

[155] Morgan (1986) does devote considerable space to MNCs (cf. Morgan, 1986:299-315 and :380-381), but he consistently employs, for our purposes, an exceedingly limited and barren perspective on MNCs as instruments of economic exploitation only.

[156] These principles are identified by Morgan (1986:84-103 and :357-359) as requisite variety, minimum critical specification, redundancy of functions, and learning to learn, and their antecedents are traced to their origins (mainly in cybernetics and systems theory). Hedlund (1986) also explicitly draws on cybernetics.

[157] Morgan's (1986) over-all view of organizations exhibits a strong eclectic bent in that he presents eight overarching metaphors of organizations and argues that each contributes to our understanding of organizations, since "Organizations are many things at once!" (Morgan, 1986:339). But the impact of "micro-processing technology" on organization refers only to the brain metaphor (cf. Morgan, 1986:417; however, see also the following footnote on usage in practice).

[158] In this version, Morgan (1986) sees decentralization as the likely outcome. In a discussion of power relations, the argument very closely follows that of Child (1984a and 1984b, but not referenced in Morgan, 1986), viz. the emphasis on the control aspects of new information systems and the strong tendency to date of centralization to result (cf. Morgan, 1986:168).

a stable launching pad for further empirical inquiry. But, by way of summary, what can be salvaged for future reference?

Regarding the firm vis-à-vis the market, there seems to exist some consensus on a very general level: the boundary of the firm is most likely affected through information systems usage, and new points of interaction between firms arise. In relation to firm strategy, there is a pronounced preoccupation with the end-points of the firm's - sequential - "value-chain" of activities resounding already identified perceptions of the MNC[159]. The jury is still out on the issue of the sustainability of strategic use of information systems, as it is on the largely parallel question of information systems favoring market or firm-internal coordination of transactions.

Internal organization offers a varied menu of unresolved problems. An argued impetus toward centralization is, as a rule, associated with strong causality afforded the use of information systems, and the view echoes conclusions from earlier research on information systems in MNCs[160] and statements on the 'form' of the MNC[161]. The arguments for the opposite (viz. decentralization) and the objections we have raised to the terms themselves suggest, however, that the issue remains unclear. As with MNC structure[162], "fit" remains a problem here, and, similarly, invites great caution.

We do, however, find support in the field of information systems and organization for the recurring themes of increased control and importance of standardization. From our earlier discussions on networks, systems, and activities[163], we can recall the much

---

[159] See Section 3.2.1.

[160] See, particularly, Section 2.3.

[161] See Section 3.2.2. Moreover, Gates and Egelhoff (1986:90) briefly note that global communications systems clearly facilitate centralization of decision-making in MNCs.

[162] See Section 3.2.1.

[163] See Sections 3.1 and 3.3.1.

neglected[164] point of systems not being uniform (i.e. there are many different ones) and the point that the technology is versatile. In the name of consistency, we must then accept both a significant degree of malleability of the technology and the importance of intentions when information systems are brought in. In other words, information systems must, at this stage, remain a necessary, but not sufficient condition for certain kinds of organizational change.

Consequently, our view does not afford strong determinism to observed effects of using information systems in organizations. Rather, we expect to find common organizational changes taking place but changes that would differ depending on the information systems in use and changes that may differ across various organizations. Intentions, type of information systems, and the particulars of the organization will influence any probability of a given effect occurring.

At this, very general level our view can claim some kinship with, i.a., Kling (1980), Child (1984a and 1984b), and Crowston and Malone (1987). However, Crowston and Malone (1987) let 'commonness' of impacts largely be determined by the desirability of particular effects. In anticipation of our empirical inquiry and in keeping with the present serious lack of sound theory (cf. Swanson, 1987), we need to be more open about possible effects. Kling (1980), Argyris (1971) and Rogers (1984) emphasize the importance of resistance by users to information systems, or to dysfunctional effects. From a sociological viewpoint, Rogers (1984) also reminds us that there are unanticipated consequences, viz. consequences that are neither intended nor recognized[165].

In addition, Morgan (1986) alerts us to the possibility of totally new ways of organizing evolving from the use of information systems[166]. The relative closeness of the brain

---

[164] Notable exceptions to the tendency of neglect are Kling (1980), Markus and Robey (1988), and Huber (1990).

[165] The third dimension of Roger's classification scheme for consequences of (information) technological innovation is direct vs. indirect. That dimension is not an issue here (cf. the 'sufficiency' condition).

[166] See also Antonelli (1981 and 1987; cf. Section 2.3).

metaphor to the 'functioning' main strand in MNC research prompts recollection of other key aspects of MNC structural complexity: flexibility, scope for organizational innovation, capabilities for control and coordination, temporal variability, and the wide range of roles for organizational units[167].

In turn, we are led to the second main rationale for studying the role of new information systems in MNCs: if MNCs are interesting at all, then information systems should be particularly interesting since they make for a logical vehicle for studying the complex MNC[168]. Information systems touch on central processes in organization theory and they simultaneously offer one way of pursuing MNC structural complexity with a reduced risk of inundation (since all aspects of complexity need not be investigated). Although it not related to MNCs, we can take heart from one of Huber's (1990) very carefully considered recommendations that from an organizational perspective, advanced information technology should be studied "...as an intervention or jolt in the life of an organization that may have unanticipated consequences with respect to evolved organizational design..." (Huber, 1990:67). However, the methodological implications and issues are left for the following Chapter.

---

[167] For the first three aspects, see particularly Section 3.2.1, and for the latter (overlapping) three Section 3.2.2. Regarding flexibility and roles, see also Section 2.3. Moreover, control and temporal variability recur as key aspects of information systems in Sections 3.1.1 and 3.1.2, respectively.

[168] For the converse statement, viz. the first main rationale, see Section 3.3.1.

4. PURPOSE AND METHOD

Our ulterior motive for the whole exercise is the desire to gain additional insight into how complex organizations function and evolve. The operationalization of that purpose for the present inquiry has been to study the structure of MNCs and how it possibly changes, in particular with the advent, and usage, of computer-based information systems.

More specifically, the purpose of the empirical investigation has been to

- identify,
- better understand, and
- possibly explain

structural change in MNCs associated with information systems usage. We are particularly interested in the change of location of MNC activities and how the activities are controlled and coordinated. However, our analytical review of relevant empirical and theoretical antecedents in the preceding chapters has brought out three, particularly august problems intimately connected with any such inquiry; viz. the interdependent problems of

- complexity,
- chronology, and
- causality.

The phenomena under study are complicated structures and systems per se, and the associated change is clearly a diffuse process over time with no unequivocal basis for deducing any definite chain of effects.

These problems are addressed below, first, in connection with choice of empirical research strategy, and, second, with its execution.

The very cautiously stated ambition regarding attempts at explanation is, however, directly influenced by the stance ultimately taken on the issue of causality and related problems. At this stage, suffice it to recast the explanatory purpose as one of '<u>trying out theory</u>'. The somewhat irregular concept, and its application, require elaboration.

First, the term itself draws inspiration from the notion of "approximate knowledge"; a view that holds scientific theories to only be approximate descriptions of reality (cf. the version in Capra, 1985[169]). Given complexity and inter-connectedness, the criterion of "approximate knowledge" allows for explanations of phenomena without having to take everything into account. In terms of 'trying out theory', a similarly weak criterion is to confront theory with a real-life setting and 'test' for plausibility. Consequently, the goal is not a rigorous testing of hypotheses.

Second, recall that the established lack of theoretical maturity regarding MNCs, information systems, and information systems in organizations[170] does not imply that theory is absent but it does imply that there are ample theoretical opportunities. 'Trying out theory', then, would be to check existing theory for plausibility and to attempt to arrive at plausible propositions emanating from analysis of the empirical material. Any such propositions would consequently not strictly amount to theory-building as they would not be predictive other than in terms of likelihood.

Third, recall also that the arrived at view of information systems is one of information systems constituting a necessary, but not sufficient, condition for certain kinds of organizational change. That weak proposition itself invites being 'tried out' for possible refinement. The issues recur below.

4.1 Research Strategy

To a large extent, the research question determines the subsequent choice of method[171]. Given that the research question concerns recent phenomena inextricably

---

[169] The epistemological issue is the one if any certain knowledge exists at all. The tentativeness of all scientific statements are hallmark arguments of Popper (1968/34) and Kuhn (1962).

[170] See Sections 3.2, 3.1, and 3.3.2, respectively.

[171] A similar, but slightly more guarded, view is taken by Benbasat (1984).

set within a real-life context so that the researcher can exercise little control over events and that the purpose involves an attempt at understanding what is observed, then a situation is described which amounts to almost a blue-print of when case studies are recommended as a very suitable research strategy (cf. Yin, 1984:13ff, and also Duncan, 1979, and, particularly for information systems research, Benbasat et al., 1987)[172].

Alternative strategies were considered but were found not to fit the bill as well as a case study approach. For instance, a survey had to be rejected on the grounds that concise and unambiguous, but relevant questions could not be devised[173]. Given the complexity associated with any cause-and-effect, a survey is exceedingly likely to omit possibly significant variables and relationships (Crowston and Malone, 1987). Moreover, surveys typically yield correlations, not causes, when employed for explanatory purposes (Smith, 1990).

Experiments are more akin to case studies, differing from them primarily as to the degree of control over events allowed the researcher (Yin, 1984:16-20). Bonoma (1985) talks of the high data integrity achieved in experimental research as opposed to the "noisy settings" which characterize field, or case studies. The need for control rules out meaningful experiments for the present inquiry. However, careful case selection could, arguably, mitigate the difference between case and experimental research. Not that clear selection criteria should be confused with control, but the more specified even a relevant "noisy setting" can be the less damning is the risk of causal confusion and corruption.

Apart from the most important criterion of being well suited to the research issues at hand, some more mundane support for the initial choice of research strategy concerning opportunity can be noted. First, quantitative, hypothetico-inductive approaches still

---

172 The more general argument of the merits and demerits of case study research per se will not be pursued here. For an attack denouncing case studies as not transcending story-telling, see Miles (1979), and for the concomitant defense, see Yin (1981). That case studies are particularly underrated as a way to generate knowledge is argued by Hägg and Hedlund (1978).

173 Two survey designs were tried; one failed on the grounds of generating only trivial questions, and one of the survey questions becoming too lengthy and complicated (in practice, it meant a dismal response rate).

dominate, even in management-related (incl. information management) research (Smith, 1990; and cf. Bonoma, 1985). And, second, embarking on a case study journey holds a relatively greater promise of scientific "surprise" (Daft and Lewin, 1990) or "discovery" (Franz and Robey, 1987).

Following Yin (1981), a case study can more specifically be described as an empirical investigation of contemporary phenomena which are not clearly separable from the context and when multiple sources are used. The three main types of case studies, viz. exploratory, descriptive, and explanatory, all relate to the stated research purpose. Although there are no distinct boundaries between the types (Yin, 1984:16), designing a case study that embraces all types would face the near certainty of succumbing to internal logical contradiction. Two courses of action can mitigate that threat. First, a phased approach can be taken to the case study, viz. empirical studies are undertaken at different points in the research process. Second, in order to limit the empirical phases, studies can be directed at the the most pertinent (given the research purpose) intersections of the standard types of case studies, viz. exploratory/descriptive and descriptive/explanatory. An additional advantage with that characterization, notably of the second term, is that ambitions of explanation are down-played without rendering a critical use of theory irrelevant to the empirical research. Since we have rejected statistical inference, explanations in the proposed case study strategy would hinge on the quality of the logic of the analysis (cf. Smith, 1990). The acknowledged role even the single case study can fill by offering disconfirmation of theoretical propositions (e.g. Bonoma, 1985), or the stronger claim to contribute to confirmation by "testing" rival predictions in the same situation (e.g. Lee, 1989), also means that a more humble goal of possibly finding counter-factuals and arriving at propositions couched in likelihoods at least can be upheld à priori.

But more choices need to be made.

Whether to conduct a longitudinal or cross-sectional study does not represent much of a dilemma. In general, investigating organizational processes and structure, a longitudinal approach is all but a foregone conclusion (cf. Pettigrew, 1985). It is furthermore commonly recognized also in information systems-related research that without allowing for time to pass, possible effects will not be detected (e.g. Venkatraman and Zaheer, 1990; Rockart and Short, 1989; and Earl, 1987; see also Avison and Fitzgerald, 1991). Weick (1984) views sustained inquiry as perhaps the most essential dimension of research method for much the same reason. The relative failure to conduct longitudinal case studies can actually be seen to be prime testimony of the immaturity of the whole field (Franz and Robey, 1987). The number of longitudinal studies covering information systems is clearly very small (cf. Swanson, 1987), and the most notable exceptions appearing in the discussions in the previous chapters are Bakis (1980 and 1987) and Whisler (1970)[174]. However, there is reason to be aware of the fact that even longitudinal studies may not be sufficient in order to capture effects of adaptation over time, since learning is a continuous process. In effect, the arguments for longitudinal studies are also arguments for perpetual studies, something clearly beyond the scope of the present effort. Conveniently for us, the advent of information systems provides a natural starting point.

The next issue concerns the unit of analysis and the concomitant number of situations to study. The 'organizational correspondence' requirement[175] has already fixed both the distinct organizational unit in the MNC and the firm-level as focal points. The frequently mentioned complexity serves well to motivate limiting the present inquiry to a single case study. In Yin's (1984) terminology, the selected design is that of an "embedded (viz. multiple levels) single case". However, looking at the design from a different angle, one can say that the study of a single MNC holds one, admittedly very important, variable, the firm, constant[176]. Instead, time, countries, functions, communications, and systems

---

[174] The situation is not without its parallels with empirical research on MNC structure (as discussed in Section 3.2). With the renowned exceptions of Stopford and Wells (1972) and Franko (1976), studies are overwhelmingly cross-sectional up to, and including, Egelhoff (1988a and 1988b). It is especially intriguing since structural adaptation for long has been seen as fraught with a considerable time-lag (cf. the survey in Caves, 1980).

[175] The objective emanates from the previous discussion on the characteristics of information systems (cf. Section 3.1).

[176] Unfortunatley, the follow-on restrictions on variables such as administrative heritage, home-country and industry(ies) must be kept in mind.

are left to vary, and, consequently, in a rather more manageable complex context. An alternative where, say, the system is held constant and the firms are left to vary, the other enumerated variables would need to be significantly reduced or simplified. The point is that by 'controlling for' a crucial variable, a larger number of other variables can be left to be accounted for without ending up with a behemoth research task. The potentially hazardous implications hereof for validity will be considered in the following section.

Case selection issues, on the other hand, assume more of (research) strategic importance. Wärneryd (1985) strongly militates against studying a single case chosen on practioners' criteria of "success"; a procedure argued to be far too common in management studies. One way of reducing the vulnerability to that type of criticism is selection at random. That course is rejected on the grounds of information systems being such a recent phenomenon that a relatively quite experienced organization is needed as an object of inquiry to for any interesting results to obtain. Another way is to heed Weick's (1983 and 1984) pleas for joining in the quest for "prototype" cases in organization research in general and in information systems-related research in particular.

However, one problem with "prototype" cases must be that the epithet is earned ex post facto. Findings and interpretation cannot be specified in advance. Barring random choice, selection here implies some specified criterion, which makes the chosen object of inquiry a 'better' case than any alternative ones, given the research purpose. Two overriding criteria for the sought after MNC emerge:

1. The MNC should be highly internationalized, since the relevance of complexity has been stressed and since the focus on geographical and organizational location of activities requires variety.
2. The MNC should be an accomplished and experienced user of international information systems, since a wide range of applications in the organization is needed to be able to identify changes across activities and since organizational change takes time.

The consequences of the strategic choices made for research practice, and consequently for validity and reliability, are discussed in the following.

4.2 Research Practice

Reasons of practicality and manageability limited the search for the 'ideal MNC' to Sweden and, by implication, to manufacturing MNCs. However, neither of these limitations is particularly restrictive and could, in fact, to some extent be construed as advantages in disguise.

The degree of internationalization poses no real problem, since Swedish manufacturing MNCs, on average, are both extremely internationalized by any standard measure (shares of sales, employment, and production abroad) and have long international experience[177]. Any disturbing idiosyncracies due to home country nationality of the MNC is a trickier issue. Recall, for instance, that considerable national variation has been found regarding structural choices and subsidiary roles in MNCs[178]. Swedish MNCs have a history of greater reliance on informal means of control and coordination than, particularly, US MNCs[179]. On the other hand, those characteristics seem well in tune with a current trend indicating relatively greater use of informal means of control and coordination in MNCs in general (cf. Martínez and Jarillo, 1989; and Martínez, 1987). A Swedish case, then, could conceivably increase the topicality of the present study.

A largely parallel argument can be made concerning the use of information systems, especially as they pertain to international data communications. Sweden, and à fortiori

[177] See, for instance, Hörnell and Vahlne (1986) for a documentation.

[178] See, particularly, Section 3.2.1.

[179] See Hedlund (1981 and 1984), Hedlund and Åman (1983), and Otterbeck (1981); the contributions contain several nuances, which are glossed over here (see also the argument in Hagström, 1991). However, there is broad support for a general picture of more formalized, quantitative control in US MNCs than in European MNCs (see the reported accumulated evidence in Egelhoff, 1984 and 1988), and à fortiori than in Swedish MNCs (cf. Hedlund, 1984). Japanese MNCs add complications with patterns which defy easy classification (cf. Yoshino, 1976; Kagono, 1981; and Nonaka, 1988 and 1990), but that is less of a concern in the present context, since the internationalization of Japanese MNCs is both relatively quite limited and recent. (Japanese MNCs are, moreover, relative late-comers in the use of international information systems).

Swedish MNCs, exhibit relatively very intensive use of international data communications (cf. Thorngren, 1990; OECD, 1983a and 1983c; Bergendorff, 1982; and UNCTC, 1982), but no evidence of any general propensity for early adoption has been found[180]. However, there is an indirect argument lending some support to a view that Swedish MNCs at least are not late adopters: intensive usage of international telecommunications is coupled with a high quality of service in Sweden; a supply that has been forthcoming by virtue of Swedish MNCs having easy access to alternative suppliers of such services[181].

Swedish non-manufacturing MNCs are few in number and are not as internationalized as the typical manufacturing MNC[182]. The de facto limitation by industry constitute no real disadvantage, since the use of information systems by service industries typically make the 'product' indistinguishable from the firm's 'own' usage of information systems (cf. OECD, 1983c; and Hagström, 1991). In consequence, the probability of proper identification of structural changes should improve, and the effects on, particularly, construct validity should be positive (see further below).

---

[180] On the contrary, Antonelli (1985) found evidence from a sample of 40 US and European MNCs of earlier adoption of international data networks by large US firms. However, smaller, typically European MNCs tended to be quicker in the internal diffusion of network usage. Digressing slightly, the findings provide something of a parallel to the observed adoption pattern of "global" structures (cf. Stopford and Wells, 1972, and Franko, 1976): US MNCs were earlier, but European MNCs were faster (see Section 3.2.1).

[181] The fuller argument is two-fold: first, Swedish telecommunications have been less regulated and, on the whole, have recorded better service performance and availability than other countries (with the possible exception of the US) and, second, Swedish Telecom has been prodded into this position by very demanding customers, viz. Swedish MNCs (cf. Thorngren, 1990).

[182] That the sectoral composition of Swedish MNCs is heavily skewed against service industries (and computer manufacturers) gives additional support to the view of Swedish MNCs being rather avid users of international information systems. The logic behind the argument is that service industries (and computer manufacturers) have been found to be the relatively most intensive users of international information systems (e.g. OECD-BRIE, 1989; OECD, 1983c; and UNCTC, 1982), yet Sweden and Swedish MNCs score very high on usage (cf. above).

The resultant single, phased, longitudinal case is SKF, the world-leading roller-bearing producer, headquartered in Gothenburg, Sweden[183].

The choice was made simple by SKF coming out on top on both selection criteria: degree of internationalization regarding business operations and sophistication regarding information systems usage.

SKF is the most internationalized of Swedish MNCs and, indeed, is among the most internationalized manufacturing MNCs in the world[184]. SKF is also sufficiently large and experienced to satisfy any reasonable requirements for 'MNC-respectability'[185]. Two 'windfall' business characteristics greatly improved researchability by reducing unwanted complexity: SKF being little diversified[186] and active in a relatively 'simple' industrial setting[187]. An additional advantage is that the industry is far removed from

---

[183] Any information given regarding SKF in the following is taken from the conducted case studies (and is referenced therein where relevant), unless otherwise specified. Likewise, any qualitative judgments regarding SKF and its capabilities are argued more fully, and substantiated, in the same case studies. The combined study of SKF is contained in Hagström (1987b; as "Linking New Information Systems to Corporate Strategy and Structure: The SKF Experience"), and in Appendix 1 of this volume (as "The Role of Information Systems in the MNC: A(nother) Case Study of SKF"), respectively. Extensive flow-on references to Hagström (1987b) can be found in Appendix 1.

[184] SKF chalks up some 95 percent of sales, 90 percent of employees, 90 percent of assets, and 90 percent of R&D expenditure outside Sweden. However, Europe looms large in its activities, accounting for close to two-thirds of sales and employees.

[185] SKF was founded in 1907. As early as by the outbreak of World War I, it had manufacturing subsidiaries in Great Britain and Germany, an assembly plant in France, sales subsidiaries in all the major markets in Europe as well as in the US, and sales agents in far away places like Australia. Today, SKF has about 130 active subsidiaries in 47 countries. Close to 100 factories are operated in 17 countries and SKF is represented by sales subsidiaries and affiliates in more than 130 countries. Total net sales stood at approximately USD bn 4.8 (SEK bn 28), and the total number of employees at more than 50 000 at year-end 1990 (SKF Annual Report, 1990).

[186] Bearing products account for some three-fourths of sales, with the remainder being split between cutting tools and various components, the latter being more than twice the former as measured by sales. The dominance of bearings makes it relatively easier to understand SKF's business and to be attentive to industry influences. However, the related businesses also do serve to provide variation in industry setting, thus not insulating our study from such influences. We believe that, for our purposes, SKF represents a good trade-off between simplicity and variety on this score.

[187] 'Simplicity' refers both to technology and industry structure, and is seen from the point of view of not 'disturbing' the present inquiry. The products are quite mature and represent relatively uncomplicated product technologies with no recent dramatic technological break-throughs recorded. Consolidation and shifts in industry structures have been moving along steadily. SKF has also largely upheld its competitive

different computing and telecommunications industries, since the problem of possible confusion with production activities is reduced and since firms in those industries are likely to 'overinvest' in information systems for marketing and product development reasons.

SKF is, arguably, the most experienced and accomplished user of international information systems over-all within the considered population of Swedish MNCs. In fact, both in the recent past and at present, SKF's capabilities in the field rival that of the most accomplished users globally. Two qualifications are in order, though: first, recall that manufacturing MNCs outside the information systems-related industries are considered, and, second, the comparison is meant on an aggregate level[188]. SKF is not outstanding in each country where it operates; nor is it so for particular applications[189]; the gist of the argument being that SKF is a leading-edge 'run-of-the-mill' firm. SKF is, and has been, such a leader in its international capabilities; its corporate-wide communications

positions. Moreover, the characteristics apply a fortiori to bearings. - The main point is that neither the industrial setting nor SKF have experienced any significant jolts that compound research complexity.

188 SKF appears to have been the first (non-information technology) manufacturing firm to have installed a proprietary network of any significant size in Europe. No information contradicting that claim has been found. A further indication is given by UNCTC (1988b:48), where SKF is called "one of the leading industrial users of information technologies". Similarly, Antonelli (1981) identified a very advanced user firm that a careful reading reveals as the anonymized SKF standard bearings subsidiary in Turin. SKF also fares well when comparing with the numerous case studies in OECD-BRIE (1989), particularly as regards being early off the mark. However, it should be acknowledged that, especially US automotive MNCs can be argued to possess capabilities superior to those of SKF at present. A similar, but stronger, case can be made regarding firms diversifying early into the information systems service business, notably General Electric (viz. General Electric Information Services, GEIS) and McDonnell Douglas (viz. Tymnet; since acquired by British Telecom). On the other hand, private discussions with representatives of the telecommunications services industry (incl. GEIS and British Telecom) suggest that actual usage by the respective mother companies is less impressive than one can be led to assume. SKF actually also compares very favorably with GM regarding international usage of information systems (cf. OECD-Brie, 1989 and Appendix 1), notwithstanding the fact that GM has one of the main contenders in the information services industry in-house (EDS, Electronic Data Systems).

189 One possible exception is SKF's "CADalog" from 1986, which, by all accounts available, is the first of its kind. The "CADalog" contains a bearing selection program and a graphics program, both encompassing the standard product catalogue. The key feature making it special, however, is that the "CADalog" can interface with six different CAD-systems. (The "CADalog" is made available to SKF customers on tape, on diskette or by direct link-up to SKF mainframes. An advanced technical design software package completes the offering to SKF customers. However, access to this facility is only available by link-up for competitive reasons.)

network and the use thereof[190]. This state of affairs is fortuitous, when considering that the research focus being on more general organizational repercussions (as opposed to, for example, systems development capabilities per se, or diversification into information systems-related industries).

Whether SKF is a successful company in terms of profitability is less clear. It has not been more profitable than other Swedish firms over the las decade, rather the contrary. However, SKF has been considerably more profitable than its main competitors also seen over a longer time period. A contention of relative success is supported by the two major academic studies on SKF that we have encountered (Collis, 1991; and Wolf, 1985).

In short, it is possible to make a well-founded claim that a better case MNC than SKF, given the research purpose, would be difficult to find, even globally. An assumption so far only implied is that SKF is something of a trail-blazer, and a manageable one at that.

If selection was straight-forward, carrying out the study was not. In fact, SKF was selected twice.

Our first, formal request to gain access to SKF was declined by corporate management in October, 1986. Rather than the proposal, the suggested subject was cited by SKF as being a bit too sensitive to be approved at that juncture. However, some insistence yielded a hesitant offer of a 'consolation prize' in the form of a couple of informal discussions at a lower level in the organization. The result of the first round of contact was that the correctness of the original case selection was confirmed. In turn, it was then only natural to go ahead with the study but with the intention of almost exclusively relying on publicly available data[191].

---

[190] Several reasons why this is the case are given in Appendix 1, Hagström (1987), and in Hagström (1990a).

[191] A full account of the procedures followed is given in Hagström (1987). To avoid possible confusion, it should be noted that this first case study does not constitute a pilot study since the research problem had been both identified and formulated prior to starting the empirical work.

The resultant, draft case study not only further strengthened our conviction of having chosen the 'best' case, it provided a basis for a mutually beneficial exchange of information between researcher and 'researched'. The reported findings of the arm's-length study were only slightly adjusted, with some deletions and additions following a bargaining-type process.

At times, persistence pays off. In October, 1988, a series of interviews by the author on information systems usage were conceded by SKF, as well as access to some pertinent internal company material. The amount of secondary material available increased considerably as well, obviously as a result of writing later, but also in response to the previous study[192]. Still, the second case study differs from the first primarily as regards the degree of cooperation by SKF, albeit that no formal release of the empirical material has been required - and thus no responsibility for the contents assumed - by SKF[193].

The two research phases should not be confused with the stated ambitions to conduct a longitudinal study. In both instances, the relevant time period considered starts from the early conception of an international information systems at the beginning of the 1970s, bringing it, in the latter case, up to mid-1990. The period prior to the mid-1980s was then not observed concurrently, but reconstructed ex post facto. The data gathering (and observation) stretched over some five years.

Our chosen, somewhat unorthodox, design of the empirical inquiry raises the issues of whether validity and reliability can be said to have been upheld to an acceptable degree[194]. Reasonably good reliability is a precondition for satisfying any requirements

---

[192] One particular limitation was accepted at the behest of SKF; viz. that none of SKF's competitors or customers should be approached directly. This restriction has, however, been of little consequence for two reasons: first, the focus is on SKF's usage of information systems and as seen from SKF's perspective, and, second, relevant remaining information gaps could be filled to an acceptable extent by reliance on secondary sources.

[193] Similarly to the previous case, a full account of the procedures followed is given in Appendix 1.

[194] Practical aspects of reliability and validity are discussed in conjunction with the two case studies (see Hagström, 1987, and Appendix 1, respectively). In the following, the discussion mostly concerns general points and those specifics that to some extent set the whole study apart from more 'standard' case studies.

of validity. Data collection procedures have been specified in each case, and all primary and secondary empirical data, including interview protocols, have been kept. The prime claim to having achieved a measure of reliability is, however, that the phased approach meant that the same study was largely replicated, and without arriving at different findings[195].

Largely following Yin (1984), the problem of demonstrating construct validity of a case study can be dealt with tactically in three main ways; by having multiple sources, a chain of evidence, and drafts reviewed. All three routes were followed, but significantly adapted to the case in hand.

First, a considerable variety of sources, both primary and secondary, were used. One particular challenge to the construct validity of the empirical study has to do with the newness of phenomena. Regarding personal interviews it translates into many respondents being unfamiliar with considering information systems in the way proposed and being unable to give succinct answers to questions posed (often also because the information simply was not available). To minimize the potential damage, a brief outline with main questions was sent to the respondents in advance, the structured interviews were conducted in a discursive manner with ample time for clarification, and most respondents were sent a copy of the interview protocol for comments.

Further, one key aspect of data collection was precisely to maximize variation in sources of evidence. Initially faced with the prospects of having the inquiry limited to an arm's-length study, the use of less common secondary sources assumed greater importance. This 'insistent' approach vis-à-vis the object of inquiry has not been found to warrant mention in the standard literature on case study research.

The basic rationale of this kind of arm's-length study is one of the value of compilation. Large organizations tend to disseminate information in a variety of contexts for a variety of purposes. The point is that this fragmentation of information is decidedly an advantage

[195] However, the claim cannot be said to hold for the wider scope of the second case study.

from the research point of view, since the researcher can purposefully compile data from different observations along dimensions not foreseen by the organization. As such a study progresses, something of an 'automatic' learning process is also at work, extending the boundary of relevant source material. For instance, accumulated knowledge can give identity to 'anonymous' cases in academic reports and articles in the business press. A released, first case study also improves on the ability to 'vacuum' secondary sources for tidbits of information, if the researcher gains reputation effects. The described type of 'information leakage' is near-nigh impossible to prevent, and SKF is no exception. For example, company advertising was very useful, especially job vacancies[196] and advertising directed at customers[197]. Also, both 'anonymous'[198] and minor[199] references to SKF in reliable secondary sources were helpful in this respect.

Second, attempting to establish a chain of evidence and of trying pieces of information for fit in the case study jigsaw have been an integral part of the research process. Working with a somewhat recalcitrant object of inquiry makes cross-checking of data from multiple sources a must; the researcher becoming akin to a sleuth. One drawback, stemming from the informal nature of SKF's later collaboration, is that some of the information given in the study is not directly referenced. Consequently, any appeal to a chain of evidence has to rely on the internal logic of our account, a situation not too dissimilar from the way circumstantial evidence is judged in court.

Third, both draft case studies were carefully reviewed at the corporate level. Comments from corporate information systems management and from members of SKF Group Management were transmitted through the former. Subsequently, some marginal changes

---

[196] Where the immediate work environment for the position is specified, e.g. for information systems personnel.

[197] Which extols the virtues of SKF's products and services, e.g. the "CADalog".

[198] Three major such cases were identified beyond doubt but should not be named here, since they were meant to be "anonymous".

[199] Examples are SKF's old computer-based reporting system described in Pousette (1983), the configuration of SKF Group Telenet in RDF (1984), and SKF's direct ordering via wholesaler in Fredriksson et al. (1987).

were also made in the presented empirical material. One indication of at least some descriptive accuracy is that in conjunction with receiving the first draft case study, SKF decided to have a sweeping review of what information was released publicly in different contexts. It should be stressed, however, that our 'insistent' case study has not been perceived as being hostile in any way by SKF[200].

Possible subjectivity, though, is also an issue in terms of mode of inquiry. Hägg and Hedlund (1979), and Smith (1990) advocate that distance from the case situation is important in order to improve scientific control in case studies. Given the research purpose with modest explanatory ambitions (not to mention the later turn of events), it is also logical to have slavishly heeded that advice here[201].

Moving to the study's <u>internal validity</u>, the problem of making inferences in the presence of possible confounding variables arises (cf. Kish, 1959). Establishing causality is a demanding task when most events cannot be observed directly (cf. Bonoma's, 1985, "noisy setting").

A somewhat lame defense is to refer back to the cautious ambition of 'trying out theory'. However, since the design of the single case study of SKF encompasses several units of analysis, the element of having embedded matching cases would improve the score on internal validity[202]. Likewise, having evaluated rival theoretical explanations and having identified chronological sequences (without observed reversals of sequence) should have the same positive effect (cf. Yin, 1984). The empirical iteration inherent in the chosen phased approach, and the iteration between inductive and deductive research throughout

---

[200] On the contrary, our results have been much appreciated and deemed to be very useful by SKF.

[201] By implication, both clinical and explicitly contextual modes are ruled out. Clinical case studies requires strong identification with the research object (cf. Normann, 1975), and contextualist research demands close involvement with and commonly intervention in the case situation (as described by Pettigrew, 1985).

[202] Case evidence from companies other than SKF is also given in Hagström (1990b and 1991).

the present inquiry[203], should also contribute to better internal validity (cf. Glaser and Strauss, 1967; and Strauss and Corbin, 1990). Any remaining weakness regarding causality must be measured against the internal logic of the argument in the presented analyses of SKF. The tighter that logic, the stronger the resultant theory-building can be (Smith, 1990). On the basis of how internal validity has been dealt with in the present study, it appears as if the goal of theory-building couched in terms of likelihood is within reach.

But the tricky issue of external validity remains. Arguably, the extent to which findings can be generalized is the traditional Achilles heel of case studies in general, and of single cases in particular. Perhaps the easiest way to disarm criticism would be to take the position that SKF's experience is interesting in its own right (cf. Hägg and Hedlund, 1979). However, the discussion so far belies such a standpoint. The argument that a study of SKF actually is a series of case studies can provide only very weak support to claims on a wider domain for generalization.

Alternatively, it is possible to stress understanding at the expense of generalizability, as advocated by Crowston and Malone (1987; see also Benbasat, 1984). That avenue is in line with the stated purpose of the empirical investigation but the subsequent careful case selection has been put forth as extending the reach of the study's conclusions. More specifically, the strength of any generalization[204] hinges critically on the assumption of SKF as something of a 'trail-blazer'. Recall that the purpose of the rather stringent selection procedures was to identify the most relevant case MNC[205] but it was also to produce a 'fore-runner case'. Whether SKF is such a case, or, indeed whether such cases can be said to exist at all, is probably impossible to establish beyond doubt. At best, SKF can be seen as a reasonable approximation of an ideal. Therefore, any general statements emanating from the empirical evidence presented are expressed in rough likelihoods.

---

[203] As described, and as evidenced by the sequence of publication of the papers accompanying the present text.

[204] Other than those based on counter-factuals found.

[205] See Section 4.1.

Still, the bottom line on external validity for case studies is the quality of analytical generalization (cf. Yin, 1984; and Smith, 1990), although careful case selection can be argued to mitigate the quality requirements.

In conclusion, the decided advantage of a case study is that it permits taking account of complexity, particularly in relation to contextual variables. The cost can first and foremost be counted in terms of reduced external validity. Here, the attempt has been to try to minimize that cost, while retaining the gain in non-triviality. What sets our approach somewhat apart from common practice is primarily:

- the heavy emphasis placed on case selection,
- the two-phased design,
- the persistent exploitation of information-leakage from the, initially recalcitrant, object of inquiry, viz. the 'insistent' case study; and
- the notion of 'trying out theory'.

The subsequent fate of existing theory and the possible value of propositions generated through the interplay between theory and empirical findings in the course of the outlined research process take the center stage in the following chapter.

The case study in Appendix 1

- provides a discussion of SKF and its organization along more traditional lines without reference to information systems [Chapter 3],
- surveys the function and configuration of the data communications network in SKF from the corporate level to identifiable units in subsidiaries (e.g. a distant sales office) [Chapter 4],
- runs through SKF's information systems in some detail at the organizational levels corresponding to those of the communications network and comprehensively gauges the use that the systems have been put to [Chapter 5], and
- brings it all together in one story, giving a wide perspective on information systems usage in SKF [Chapter 6].

5. RESULTS AND IMPLICATIONS

Returning to the point of departure, the concept of 'changing location of activities' provides the logic for discussing the main results of the reported research. The specific conclusions in each of the accompanying papers will not be summarized here[206], since those papers are self-contained statements. Some overlap cannot be avoided, however, and the discourse below does draw on the accompanying papers both for general points and particular illustrations.

This chapter is structured along the original dimensions of location of MNC activities, viz. geographical and 'organizational' location of activities. Recall that the latter category is divided into two parts; 'hierarchical location' and 'institutional location'. From the previous discussions on the structure of MNCs (cf. Chapter 3), the two 'organizational location' concepts can conveniently be thought of in conjunction with the familiar dichotomies of externalization vs. internalization, and centralization vs. decentralization, respectively.

The reason for resurrecting the introductory terminology is to put our main findings in relief against previous research and to get a deeper understanding of the role of information systems in complex organizations. That is the purpose of the first main section, which constitutes the bulk of the present chapter. The most extensive treatment is given the least conventional concept of 'hierarchical location'.

In the second main section, some general characteristics of a 'wired' MNC are painted with broad strokes and put in perspective. The aggregated picture is based on the whole study's principal results. But the sketch is also slightly 'improved upon', invoking a license of informed extrapolation. Much of this 'improvement' reflects some disregard of detail, stemming from the desire to capture the whole MNC in one shot.

---

[206] A very brief summary of Appendices 1 and 2, and of Hagström (1987a, 1990a, and 1991) is given in Section 1.2.

Possible implications for further research are addressed at different points in the account. Specific conclusions indirectly beckoning further inquiry are found interspersed throughout the first main section. Some broader implications are left to the final section.

5.1 Main Findings

The role of information systems in complex organizations has turned out to be a rather varied one, however not really possible to promote beyond the 'necessary, but not sufficient' condition status. The underlying view of the communications network as essentially creating potential for economies of scope, and of computer applications as being more related to economies of scale, for the firm has been fruitful. It captures the firm infrastructural quality of information systems and specific uses of the same, respectively. Over-all, information systems represent an enabling condition and any causality inferred from usage needs to be guardedly qualified accordingly. Consequently, there should be little concern with any 'fits' between any dimension of organization structure and information systems but rather with the opportunities for organizational change that are offered[207]. In turn, any identified outcome is only a likely one, i.e. representing a trend, bias, direction of change. However, competitive dynamics drive the process and organizations ignore these opportunities at their peril.

Theoretical inference and induction from our empirical studies form the basis of the propositions on organizational change associated with information systems usage given below. The propositions exhibit a high level of abstraction and are given in condensed, at times telegraphic, form. The sparse illustrative evidence is elaborated on within the scope of the full story in Appendix 1. Much supportive evidence is suppressed since the

[207] We return to some additional aspects of the role of information systems in complex organizations in Section 5.1.4 below.

richness of a case study cannot be reproduced here[208]. Moreover, as indicated by the empirical caveats discussed in Appendix 1, the strength of the support for the presented general propositions varies.

In the interest of brevity preference is given to aspects of organizational change, which are contentious or neglected in previous research. In some cases, our evidence sheds some new light on unresolved theoretical issues and provides ammunition against some entrenched positions.

Although logically interdependent, the types of locational change are kept separate for the sake of clarity. The presented picture is cumulative, looking first at the geographical opportunity set, then at internal organizational repercussions before dealing with the boundary of the organization. The restriction of maintaining a sufficient degree of control over, and of being able to efficiently coordinate, activities is, of course, relevant for all the perspectives. However, control and coordination are given most attention in connection with internal organizational matters, and that for two reasons; first, the twin concepts occupy a prominent position in organization theory, and, second, they naturally recur when subsequently turning to the interface with the environment.

Finally, some general points on the role of information systems are given.

---

[208] Chapter 6 in Appendix 1 gives a summary review of, and conclusions pertaining to information systems in SKF, their role and their relationship to observed organizational change. The main difference between that account and the present chapter is one of vantage point and scope; in Appendix 1 the focus is solely on SKF, whereas here the arguments are 'cloaked' in the more general terms emanating from the discussion in the previous chapters. The end result are two related stories; one analytical narrative and one structured analysis.

5.1.1 Geographical Location[209]

Haig (1926) noted that firms are "packets of functions" and that the extent to which these functions with profit can be separated and located at different places varies. Physical separation of firm activities is limited by how closely they are tied to each other and by the need to maintain control and coordination. Haig's (1926) contention still holds. However, the greatly enhanced possibilities to transport information-based services by way of corporate information systems have lessened those restrictions. Both control and coordination can, in themselves, be seen as such 'services'. In addition, even manufacturing firms perform many non-tangible activities, the output of which can be similarly transported.

Information systems usage has been found to allow the firm and à fortiori the MNC to:

- separate and recombine activities across space in new ways.

  The increased potential for disaggregation of activities permits closer tailoring of activities according to very specific locational advantages or disadvantages, be they external or internal to the firm, and thus gives greater scope for exploiting scale economies through specialization. The proposition departs from standard views by emphasizing inclusion of locating away from something, of the importance of internal locational factors, and that concentration (and recombination) of activities is very much an issue of level of aggregation[210].

- continuously adjust geographical location.

---

[209] A more general, theoretical argument is developed in Hagström (1990b; reprinted here as Appendix 2). This section deals with the application of that argument to information systems usage.

[210] The last two points imply rejection of the traditional, implicit assumption in industrial location theory of 'automatic' agglomeration advantages accruing to activities within the same firm (cf. Hagström, 1990b). In SKF, basic research is concentrated and located away from other, potentially dominating SKF organizational units (thus also illustrating an internal locational factor). Production is seemingly geographically dispersed, but that dispersion obscures a concentration at a lower level, since manufacturing is specialized by product. In these cases, information systems have expanded the locational opportunity set.

Some activities become extremely foot-loose (e.g. can be 'unplugged', shifted, and 'replugged' into the network), and some 'disappear', i.e. are automated in the network (which then also can incorporate decision-rules). As a corollary of the previous proposition, there is also an implicit notion here of continuous relocation of activities among the existing sites of the MNC, viz. temporal locational advantages can more easily be exploited. In a related vein, the scope of operations at a particular location can be adjusted. For instance, remote access to specialized knowledge residing in computer applications or in specific organizational units can upgrade local capabilities or overcome temporary local bottlenecks.

- optimize the geographical distribution of sites (and activities at each) considering also future states of nature[211].

An upshot of this proposition is the option not to geographically relocate and concentrate activities, where one previously would have done it. For instance, particular expertise can be allowed to remain in a location although it 'should not' have, when considering the optimal range of activities at that location. One could say that electronic integration takes the place of physical integration, permitting more 'locational anomalies'.

5.1.2 'Hierarchical Location'

The organizational issues raised in Chapters 2 and 3, both in relation to MNC operations and to information systems "impact" recur here. The centralization/decentralization debate, aspects of control and coordination of activities, degree and type of (inter)dependence among organizational units, and the possible function of the formal

[211] Here, empirical support is scant but a certain 'redundancy' of activities and of operated sites can be seen. One such indication is the on-going regionalization of bearing operations, which is supported by information systems-mediated back-up of expertise. Another is the rather large number of sites that are still operated in Europe (with information systems attenuating the physical distance), in a sense constituting options on future states (cf. also the general argument in Kogut, 1983).

organization are discussed in turn. However, there is considerably more overlap in this section than what the headings below may suggest.

5.1.2.1 Centralization/decentralization

First, there is a need to disentangle some of the conundrum surrounding centralization vs. decentralization in organizations. The conceptualization of information systems employed here, and the experience of SKF as found, seem to afford a technical, or analytical, way to account for some of the difference of views. The proposition is that "centralization" is very much a question of time, function, and level of aggregation. The argument is quite straight-forward and can readily be illustrated with reference to SKF. Depending on when one were to look at SKF, at what function, and at what level in the organization (incl. which country of operation) one could find evidence of centralization or decentralization associated with information systems usage so as to support either position on the likely "impact" of information systems.

Recall first that many of the conflicting findings regarding the effects of information systems have largely been based on cross-sectional studies and often of whole organizations. Such a study of SKF would in the mid-1970s have shown clear tendencies of information systems-induced centralization, with the balance clearly shifting in favor of decentralization in a hypothetical study a decade or so later. A study of the financial function only at the two same points in time would have shown steady progress toward centralization and specialization. However, charting the course of the information systems function over the whole time period would largely indicate a sequence of change analogous to that of SKF as a whole, viz. first centralization and then decentralization but converse to that of the finance function. The examples could be multiplied, but the point is that the experience of SKF could easily be made up to provide ammunition for either camp in the classical battle of information systems-related centralization or decentralization depending of what was studied when. Moreover, the identified complex process of change clearly casts serious doubt over the efficacy of cross-sectional studies in this context.

Second, the very concept of centralization and its twin can be called into question. Given the analytical explanation offered above to the contradictory results of previous research, the usefulness of the term "centralization" becomes less than obvious. As commonly used, the term brings conjectures of concentrating an activity or decision-making, moving it up the organizational hierarchy, and physically locating it centrally, ultimately at the head-office. Limiting the meaning of "centralization" to the locus of authority (Pugh, 1973:69; and Pugh et al., 1968:76-78) and measuring that do not appear to ensure relevance. For instance, how "centralized" are decisions, the rules of which are embodied in mutually adjusting information systems?

More generally, 'concentration' and 'dispersion' (and 'automation' as the case may be) of activities or decision-making could be more useful terms as a first step. The importance of simultaneously treating degree of geographical concentration and level of aggregation has already been noted. Physical concentration often coincides, but need not always coincide, with concentration to an organizational unit. Recall first that specialization in production in SKF largely has meant geographical concentration by product but organizational dispersal to individual subsidiaries. However, it can get more complex as evidenced by SKF's recent organizational concentration of responsibility for standard bearing production to particular, new units for groups of products. The related manufacturing takes place in designated individual production lines which are physically located in different subsidiaries in different countries.

Leaving degree of concentration, the other step is to look at what, for lack of a better term, can be called de facto organizational proximity to headquarters, divisional or corporate. That a less "central" organizational unit or activity can be geographically located at headquarters is commonplace, but the converse is not. To see how a "central" hierarchical location can be at odds with a similar geographical location, consider SKF's Engineering and Research Centre in the Netherlands. Formally directly under corporate management in Gothenburg, Sweden, it is the key location for SKF Group research and quality control and houses the office of one of the seven members of the corporate management team. The differences in proximity can extend also to position in the formal organization. SKF's Forecasting and Supply Office (FSO) has the overall responsibility for coordinating standard bearing production with supply to the sales organization, and the logistics thereof; thus being something of a hub of the product flow within SKF. In terms of proximity, FSO undoubtedly represents a 'logistics overview' which is pivotal for SKF's dominant business[212]. Its de facto organizational closeness to headquarters is not matched by its geographical location or its peripheral position in the formal organization: FSO is located in Brussels and is simply listed as one of many subsidiaries in one division.

The examples given are all predicated on the usage of information systems, demonstrating how such usage can undermine the relevance of a familiar organizational concept, viz. degree of "centralization". It is fraught with imprecision, both on analytical and conceptual grounds. In consequence, "centralization" fails to capture the multidimensionality of information systems-supported, de facto, structural configuration of the MNC in terms of degree of 'concentration' of activities and proximity to headquarters.

By rejecting "centralization", most of the reviewed arguments and findings can be written off as insufficiently specified conclusions and/or misconceived answers to wrongly posed questions; information systems usage does not result in "centralization" or "decentralization" of organizations. However, control and coordination arguments relating to the traditional "centralization" debate cannot be dismissed as readily.

5.1.2.2 'Supply' of control and coordination

Control and coordination of activities has been a recurring theme, both when discussing organizations in general, and MNCs in particular. The limits of control and coordination

---

212 In fact, FSO's activities span two of SKF's five divisions; both are headquartered in Gothenburg. Some formal reporting from subsidiaries to divisional headquarters also goes through FSO.

are also the limits of organization structure, and information systems have been found to potentially enhance both.

The properties and functionality of information systems have made them very amenable for control purposes, also very early in their technological development. Information systems provide standardized channels for control information, information also often automatically generated as a by-product in systems filling some other function. In this light, improved coordination of firm activities is primarily a function of quicker, and of quantitatively and qualitatively better, central availability of control-related information[213]. In SKF the internal and external reporting systems, and the financial management system were the first to be put 'on-line' reducing administrative and financial 'floats'. In the process, better strategic overview and financial coordination were also achieved. However, it was the more ambitious coordination of product-flows and the reduction of product 'floats' that motivated SKF to build a proprietary corporate data communications network[214].

Of particular interest here is the greater scope for higher level control of performed activities afforded by information systems in a given organization[215]. The previously reviewed literature on information systems in organizations in general, and in MNCs, provides what in practice amounts to unanimous support for such a view. But whether the subsequent net result is one of "centralization" or "decentralization" is more contentious (but with the former commanding a clear majority support[216]).

---

213 The general argument is pursued most extensively in Hagström (1991), which also contains evidence from nine other Swedish MNCs.

214 The sequence of the use to which information systems tend to be put, both in general and in SKF, is most explicitly elaborated in Hagström (1990a). Recall also from Appendix 1 that the extreme rationalization was seen as prerequisite for corporate survival.

215 In control terms, geographically and organizationally distant units are brought 'closer' to headquarters.

216 One reason why this may be so is a classical argument in organization theory, which holds that lower costs of communication bring (re-)centralization of decision-making in organizations as geographic constraints become less pressing (Thompson, 1967:68).

The question cannot be unambiguously resolved here but a few observations are in order. The analytical explanation for differing conclusions still stands. Especially relevant is the change over time. That initially trimming a given organization tends to move decision-making up the line is borne out by SKF experience[217]. However, information systems facilitating greater specialization is also commonly recognized and that complicates the issue[218]. True, capturing scale economies typically implies higher level coordination of activities. But specialization has been seen to also take place in a geographically and organizationally 'dispersed' manner[219]. In SKF, specialized organizational units have proliferated (e.g. as for financial management) and some units have shouldered greater responsibilities but for more limited activities (e.g. development of a particular product).

It becomes more relevant to talk of roles, as in the 'functioning'-view of the MNC[220]. By being able to cope with more complexity both in terms of control and coordination, a greater variety of roles can be assigned to existing organizational units. Specialization implies a gain in importance concerning the specialized activity[221] and a relative loss for other activities and organizational units. One important implication is that a particular unit can have multiple roles, a contention supported by SKF experience[222]. Again, it is fruitless to talk of "centralization" or "decentralization" but rather of new, more specific

---

217 This, hypothetically generic, phase is labelled 'defensive' (and is more amply described) in Hagström (1990a). The 'defensive phase' is the first of three in an identified sequential action pattern, the subsequent two being named 'offensive' and 'integrative', respectively.

218 Specialization (as opposed to merely unbundling of activities) is a distinctive feature in the 'offensive phase' (following the 'defensive' one) in Hagström (1990a).

219 Also, it is worth noticing that systems theory here can offer a generally supportive argument: Miller (1972:133 and :171-172) draws a clear distinction between organizational and geographical decentralization, noting that increased (functional) specialization and spatial dispersion favor organizational decentralization.

220 The point echoes most closely the general arguments of Barlett (1986), Bartlett and Ghoshal (1986) and Hedlund (1986) on MNC subsidiary roles.

221 In corporate parlance, the terms are typically giving a "corporate" or "global" responsibility for the activity to an organizational unit.

222 Here, Bartlett and Ghoshal (1986) look at a higher level of aggregation. They discuss more in terms of archetypal main roles and the assignment of such a role per subsidiary. They specifically militate against what they term the "United Nations model assumption", whereby managers all-too often treat subsidiaries in a uniform manner although subsidiaries operate in very different circumstances around the world.

roles of organizational units, the complex network of which is contingent on maintaining control.

Another aspect is that better control can increase the readiness to devolve responsibility. The accelerated devolution of SKF corporate headquarter functions to divisions and to specialized organizational units during the first half of the 1980s does not contradict such a contention. In turn, the development apparently lends some credence to the general argument (cf., i.a., Blau et al. 1976; Kling, 1980; and Child, 1984a and 1984b) that information systems mask what amounts to a delegation of decisions with a simultaneous greater central overview. But, as noted above, SKF's experience hints at a more complex process, where new units also are created as a result of headquarters relinquishing responsibilities[223]. In this sense, headquarters is being geographically and organizationally 'dispersed'[224]. - For clarity, it should be stressed, though, that the increased propensity for devolution is a function of the perceived greater opportunity brought by information systems for quick intervention, should it be necessary.

The other, often forgotten, side of specialization is coordination of more interdependent activities. Typically, coordination requires more complex information system applications than does control. Many of the illustrations above of controlling subunits in SKF with the help of information systems also indicate how the more complicated coordination of their activities is supported by information systems. Moreover, from the discussion on geographical location we can recall that purposeful coordination of activities also has a

[223] A somewhat similar point is put forth by Perrow (1977), who (with a construed example involving only three people) argues that centralization and decentralization are just two aspects of the same bureaucracy; the illustration being how an added, intermediate level effectively takes on responsibilities when the higher level controls the premises of lower level activity. Perrow's (1977) message is that management already has more control than it generally perceives, and should therefore more readily decentralize decision-making (an assessment made without any reference to information systems).

[224] To avoid possible confusion, the point here is not one of using rules to allow for "decentralization", viz. local discretion within those rules (for instance, as held by Pugh, 1973). Rather, even rules can be relaxed, since information systems permit, de facto, moving closer to process control, typically seen as more costly than traditional output control.

temporal dimension, shifting activities in order to exploit transient locational advantages[225].

A general point, however, is that what initially tends to be conceived as active coordination changes towards quicker adjustment with less higher-level intervention as usage matures. In SKF, this trend manifests itself clearly in the shift from planning to clearing as mediating processes in the financial management and product flow systems. With sales orders feeding directly into production schedules, production capacity is allocated to actual demand rather than producing for a forecast demand. Differently put, traditional sequential dependence (as between production and sales[226]) graduates into more of reciprocal dependence, something that is largely contingent on information systems usage.

Improved control and coordination of MNC activities as discussed so far have been a matter of design. Information systems have been employed with the clear intention of reaching efficiency goals. However, empirically, that has been found not to be the whole story, wherefore we need to turn to the 'demand-side' of control and coordination.

5.1.2.3 'Demand' for control and coordination

Control and coordination are traditionally seen as a concern reserved for higher levels in the organization vis-à-vis lower levels. That perspective was also inherent in the 'supply' discussion above. However, information systems-mediated control and coordination reveal, perhaps surprisingly, a converse 'demand', which has less to do with intentional design, either of systems or of organization.

---

[225] Again drawing on the 'functioning'-tradition, information systems here improves the possibilities to benefit from what Kogut (1983 and 1990; see Section 3.2) calls the "sequential", or "network", advantages potentially accruing to the MNC.

[226] In fact, interdependence between subsidiaries is a much neglected phenomenon in the traditional body of research focussing on the 'form' of the MNC (cf. Chapter 3). Even the patent dependence of producing subsidiary-to-sales subsidiary is, as a rule, not recognized (see also Hagström, 1991).

It is worth stressing that what here is termed 'demand' lures us out into what is very much uncharted territory. In particular, a traditional issue of designing organizational structure is how the structure affects the information flows in the organization (e.g. Duncan 1979:426). Here the issue is how information flows seek out new routes in a given structure, possibly changing it. Whereas the 'supply' argument emphasized control aspects of information systems, the balance shifts towards coordination when considering the 'demand' side[227]. As found in SKF, information systems have stimulated what could be termed spontaneous coordination among organizational units. Some expressions hereof can be seen to have more general implications.

For instance, there is a tendency for internal markets to arise as usage matures. One fully-fledged electronic market for surplus products grew from a regional warehouse with low turnover, the internal participants using electronic mail and the corporate financial management system. Here, it is clearly not the superior capability of information systems to transport large volumes of data that is important but that 'buyers' and 'sellers' can be linked at all, organizing a 'market'. There are instances of internal services being marketed via information systems, which may also serve as the mode of delivery.

Related to the transport of information-based services is demand-driven remote usage of particular computer applications and databases[228]. The effect is not only one of upgrading local capabilities or of standardizing products and calculation techniques (as embedded in the systems), but also one of disseminating approaches to problem-solving and practical 'how-to-do' knowledge. Importantly, such seeking out of relevant knowledge has been seen to take routes not designated in the organization but rather to represent liaising with the 'best' counterpart.

'Demand' for control was found to manifest itself both in terms of differential perception, and in outright 'rebellious' use of information systems. Perhaps contrary to commonly

[227] Again, Duncan (1979) provides a good back-drop by identifying coordination between interdependent organizational units as a critical, but unexplored issue. Duncan specifically points to the logic of decentralization coming in conflict with such common interdependence.

[228] In SKF these are dominated by technical applications and databases.

held, there is apparently a clear wish by subsidiaries to be more tightly controlled by way of inclusion in the corporate reporting system. The motive for that is one of thus indirectly gaining quicker and better information on what goes on elsewhere in the organization and particularly at the head-office (sic!). Going further still, some subsidiaries were found to exchange reporting information among themselves, in effect circumventing corporate access rules.

The above examples suggest that the existence of a sophisticated information systems infrastructure fosters coordination at lower levels in the organization. From the sub-unit point of view, needs not catered for in the organizational structure as designed find outlets through information systems. In turn, roles can more easily be assumed and defined[229] by systems usage, in effect 'diffusing' coordination of activities further. A daunting ambiguity of the various multiple roles follows. The observed de facto dissemination of information (even of control-type information) and of procedures reinforce this development. The information monopoly typically accruing to higher levels in the organization is undermined. From the perspective of headquarters, much coordination takes on characteristics of being automatic or at least removed from higher-level intervention.

The points made show strong kinship with the notion of holographic design with self-organization (Hedlund, 1986; and Morgan, 1986) but the picture here is partial as it is tied to information systems usage. That is an advantage as we can be more specific[230]. A departure from Morgan (1986) is that more traditional, 'supplied' control is seen here, in practice, to be a something of a prerequisite for any "self-design" to become viable. Some such stability seems to make "self-design" more likely[231]. Furthermore, it seems clear that the MNC is in a favored position to take advantage of the identified

---

[229] As opposed to merely assigned.

[230] Morgan (1986) discusses practice only in very small groups of individuals, and Hedlund (1986) explicitly idealizes when referring to possible and disparate elements of the "heterarchy" in some MNCs.

[231] With reference to a wider concept, "administrative heritage" (Bartlett, 1986) can be an asset in creating the conditions for "self-adjustment". Naturally, the possibility of "self-adjustment" arising 'out of nowhere' cannot be dismissed, but it appears unlikely to be realized in the near future.

tendencies, since variety is internal and the requisite information infrastructure for reaping the benefits of variety is more likely to materialize[232].

Related to the above is the principle of double-loop learning (cf. Argyris and Schön, 1978). The principle is typically considered on the individual level only and consequently of less import here. However, the identified seeking out of relevant knowledge contains a non-trivial element of learning to learn. Recombination of existing information is also stimulated by the existence of an information systems infrastructure, although that may stop short of the requirements for "knowledge-creation" (cf. Nonaka, 1988 and 1990). Still, the conclusion is that information systems can foster at least some rudimentary learning processes also at the level of the organizational unit (or part of a unit)[233].

A few lesser issues raised in earlier chapters may also warrant some additional comment in the present context.

First, the information systems-induced appearance of internal markets is a much neglected phenomenon. The arguments for an evolution of exclusive interorganizational information systems linkages into electronic marketplaces for reasons of competition (Malone et al., 1989; and Hopper, 1990) or of standardization (Benjamin et al., 1990) naturally do not take account of internal markets, but here (internal) demand already exists and finding standardized information links already in place is much more likely. Moreover, internal market-type arrangements for products and services add to the labor market and shadow pricing mechanisms typically allowed for in internalization theory (e.g. Hennart, 1986; and Buckley, 1988). Note also that these new internal markets are not designed, but are rather more akin to classical, spontaneous markets, and that the improved transportability of information-based services also holds the possibility of internal markets for knowledge.

---

[232] A not mutually exclusive interpretation is that the inherent advantages in being an MNC parallel the potential benefits from the abstract notion of holographic design, wherefore it is only 'natural' to find such elements most explicitly in an MNC (for a variation on this theme, see Hedlund, 1991b).

[233] Whether it amounts to any "knowledge" in an epistemological sense is well beyond the scope of the present discussion.

Second, spontaneous coordination to some extent tends to restrict the scope for managerial choice of structure. But rather than paradoxically lending support to the traditional 'form'-view of the MNC, the observation falls more in line with the 'functioning' view[234]. Also, we have seen 'rebellious' use of formal systems and tendencies toward 'automatic' coordination of lower-level interdependencies. Apart from adding alternatives, those expressions are more 'tolerated' than managed, at least in SKF.

Finally, some clarification may be in order. The 'unanticipated' uses of information systems discussed clearly is removed from the "resistance by users" argument (e.g. Kling, 1980; Argyris, 1971; and Rogers, 1984), which emphasizes dysfunctional effects. More specifically, we also go beyond Rogers's (1984) "unanticipated consequences" since they are supposed to be unrecognized as well as unintended. Rather, we may see early indications of new modes of organizing following from the very nature of information systems; modes dismissed by Galbraith (1977) as humanly impossible[235], but foreshadowed in principle by Morgan (1986) who in a very abstract sense invokes McLuhan's (1964) dictum of the medium being the message. In principle having sided with the latter view, it is nevertheless worth stressing (in relation to Galbraith-type arguments) that it is the very human aspect of information systems usage which underpins our argument, viz. human ingenuity. Not only do people find ways to use information systems in unanticipated ways, the information systems can support and facilitate human interaction. An upshot of that is a significant twist to the established argument on the malleability of the technology[236]: here we downplay the importance of purpose (since that is largely divorced from the uses considered at present) and of power in favor of 'revealed demand'.

---

[234] However, recall that information systems have not really been given much weight in the 'functioning' tradition as surveyed (cf. Section 3.2.) and there is little of the 'funtioning' perspective in main-stream research on information systems in organizations (cf. Section 3.3.2).

[235] Galbraith's (1977) contention finds unrecognized but eloquent support in Boland's (1987) forceful argument against information systems "fantasies"; they fall on the grounds that organizations basically are face-to-face interaction, something information systems cannot provide.

[236] See Kling (1980), Mohrman and Lawler (1984), Björn-Andersen et al. (1986), and Boddy and Buchanan (1986); and Section 3.3.2.

5.1.2.4 Formal organization

The formal organization has received little attention by us when exploring organizational structure except in connection with the traditional 'form' treatment of MNC structure[237]. Recall that the possible role of the formal organization was found to remain unresolved. The issue cannot be totally neglected and a few words are in order although they are very far from including any final word on the matter. Instead, the contribution of information systems in this respect can be stated as whatever the traditional role of the formal organization, information systems usage tends to diminish it. That proposition rests on two main premises recurring from points made above:

- information systems significantly improves on the capability to have subunits formally organized according to several organizational principles, and, in parallel,
- information systems can provide for control and coordination along dimensions not present in the formal organization.

The notion of firms struggling to obtain a uniform, orthodox formal organization mirroring implementation of a chosen, coherent strategy is undermined. Most formal organizational principles can be traced in SKF[238] and that aspect of organizational complexity has tended to increase over time. The resultant mixed organization reflects adaptation to various external conditions and a wish for simultaneous coordination across several dimensions. The surmise is that information systems have made this mixed organization possible at all; a realized complexity going substantially beyond what any two-dimensional matrix arrangement could accommodate.

---

[237] See, especially, Section 3.2, where also our reluctance to use the terms "informal organization" or "informal structure" is explicated.

[238] Recall first that SKF is a rather 'uncomplicated' MNC in terms of operating in a quite stable industry environment, being relatively small, and having a very low degree of product diversification and low variety in product technologies. Nevertheless, even at the highest levels in the organization product, function, area, and customer-category have formal manifestations. Mother-daughter relationships and holding company organization can be found in divisions.

Note, however, that even a mixed formal organization is an understatement of the degree of 'mixture' in the de facto organization structure (cf. variety and variability of organizational roles). On the other hand, that does not obviate the need for formal organization, it merely suggests that its role can be less dramatic and can be allowed to take on other functions[239]. Apart from possible conjecture about functions, two tendencies receive some support from the SKF case; first, formal organizational change seems to have become more frequent but less of costly upheavals and, second, any formal status can more easily be assigned ex post, in effect legitimizing a de facto change in structure[240].

A final twist to the discussion is provided by the likely fate of the archetypal subsidiary. Broken up, stripped of many traditional activities, and having gained some new responsibilities (but which reside in parts of the subsidiary), the formally legal subsidiary becomes a platform or a shell for a changing set of activities subject to different coordinating mechanisms; mechanisms which extend outside the legal subsidiary. Although coordination can be complex, monitoring tends to remain simple[241].

---

[239] The formal organization can still reflect the legal structure of the firm, conceivably be more easily designed to correspond to different taxation requirements, be used for marketing purposes, providing a frame for formal management seniority etc. (cf. also Aoki's, 1990, general argument that the main role of the formal organization can be one of a reward structure for members of the organization as can be seen from Japanese firms).

[240] Greater central availability of detailed reporting information (since information systems tend to supply all data with aggregations, whereas manual systems only supplied aggregated figures) in itself makes changing formal boundaries less complicated (cf. Hagström, 1991). Rather than contradicting Bartlett's (1983) general point of managing processes being more relevant than the common but often misdirected formal reorganization in MNCs, our argument gives it additional support. With information systems in place, any need to dramatically alter the formal organization is reduced further. It becomes easier to live with any given formal organization and the greater tolerance for mixed formal arrangements makes it easier to effectuate smaller, idiosyncratic adjustments in the formal organization.

[241] The 'messy' illustration is in fact an understatement of the complexity involved in many standard bearing-producing subsidiaries in SKF. A fuller description of this remarkable complexity is given in Section 3.3 in Appendix 1. The juxtaposition of the parallel complicated information systems for coordination and the simple systems for control in the same type of subsidiary is brought out in Section 6.2.2 in Appendix 1.

5.1.3 'Institutional Location'

Most of the propositions made concerning geographical and 'hierarchical' location ostensibly relate to what happens inside the firm. There is, however, little need to impose that restriction as the propositions can be seen to be valid in a greater context, viz. also outside the firm as defined by its legal structure. Two general, main points stand out:

- a blurring of the organizational boundary, and
- a larger number of activities can be considered for possible externalization or internalization.

Although we have taken a view of the firm as a de facto organization, some of the terminology pertaining to a contractual/legal view is employed in order to highlight some of the conclusions reached.

As a point of departure, the observed effect of information systems to allow for 'unbundling', or fragmentation, of activities can be couched in terms of transaction costs. Unfortunately, the concept is less than ambiguous (cf. Dahlman, 1979) but in its most widely quoted version, a transaction is defined as occurring "...when a good or service is transferred across a technologically separable interface." (Williamson, 1985:1; see also Williamson, 1981). As given by the definition, with technological change, "technologically separable interfaces" must also change. In these terms, information systems would then add to the number of "interfaces" for information-based activities. The corollary argument suggesting itself, then, is that the contentious macro-question of information systems fostering more "market" or "hierarchy" governance of transactions can, simplistically, be answered with yes; both can be seen to increase in number[242].

However, from our chosen vantage point of the individual firm and with our focus on usage, we will concentrate on the situations where information systems make a difference, using the analytically idealized dichotomy based on the legal boundary of the firm. In organizational parlance, information systems can constitute something of a bridging

---

[242] Any change in proportions is a more difficult question and is beyond the scope of the present study.

strategy vis-à-vis the environment[243]. - An important observation in this context is that externalization or internalization need not be confined only to the end-points in a vertical chain of activities[244].

In order to bring out the point of the information systems alternative, we will focus on the properties of unbundling, control and differentiation of activities. The 'unbundling' property is only a restatement of the increased number of "interfaces" above, meaning that information systems can make it possible to externalize an activity at all, similarly to making it possible to get particular internal markets at all. By opening for possible specialization, as in the analogous case of internal specialization, 'unbundling' can, of course, also lead to the converse, viz. internalization. However, the scope for specialization is normally greater on the market. Information systems enabling new choices therefore tend to favor selective externalization of some 'old' internal activities rather than internalizing totally new activities; a conclusion broadly supported by SKF's experience.

However, there is an additional quality to many information systems-mediated external relationships, a quality that has to do with control (and, indirectly, with inter-firm coordination). First, 'marginal' cases of externalization (i.e. where the benefit thereof is very small) can change with the advent of information systems. A common argument has it that assuring quality control of critical upstream activities is an important motive for backward integration (e.g. Casson, 1987); a more general motive being reducing uncertainty (Arrow, 1975). The contention here is that those needs can be satisfied

---

243 Recognizing that there is great variety between the idealized institutional forms of markets and hierarchies is not unusual, also among organization researchers (e.g. as by Child, 1987a; Miles and Snow, Snow, 1986; and Powell, 1987). Information systems are typically cast in the role of being supportive in this portfolio of contracting alternatives (particularly Child, 1987a). Without rejecting that function of information systems (e.g. a common information system can support a joint venture), the argument here concerns the more fundamental role of information systems in shifting the balance as to whether activities are located inside or outside the organization.

244 Recall (cf. Sections 3.2 and 3.3.2) that the restriction to end-points is a common explicit or, more often, implicit assumption in strategic management (cf. particularly concerning inter-organizational information systems), but also in economics (cf. the treatment of vertical integration). For examples of non-end-point externalization or internalization, see Appendix 1.

through information systems[245]. The more general argument is that if control of a relationship improves with information systems, legal incorporation of that particular activity becomes less of a necessity[246]. We are also reminded by Ashby (1965) that it is always cheaper to control, or monitor, a system than to manage it outright. - Second, the combination of 'unbundling' and control means that many ostensibly 'unbundled' activities are externalized, not likely to an arm's-length market but to a 'controlled' external relationship[247].

Adding differentiation of external relationships to 'unbundling' and control, we broadly move downstream when running through new firm options brought about by information systems. Forward integration is a more complicated issue, however, since it implies entry into a new market, whereas backward integration simply means becoming one's own supplier (Thorelli, 1986:43). To some extent, information systems lower that higher threshold, stimulating internalization of some downstream activities. The key here concerns information systems as a distinct mode of delivery. Just as activities can be more closely tailored internally, so can customer relationships in terms of delivery of information-based services. That general point is relevant independently of whether or

---

[245] A significant instance is the decision by SKF to end seventy years of traditional backward integration into steel-making (see Section 3.3 in Appendix 1). However, the specialty steel business has been kept within the SKF communications infrastructure. Continued quality control (in a wide sense) is in this way maintained through fast feed-back on quality testing, quick dissemination of new requirements generated by SKF R&D, shared technical computer applications etc.

[246] 'Control' is thus here used in a very direct sense (cf. the notion of information technology being a "control technology" as in Ackoff, 1967; and Boddy and Buchanan, 1986). In consequence, 'control' is not used as a cloak for, or an expression of, power, e.g. as in Perrow's (1986) criticism of transaction cost economics (and by whom the two terms are, in practice, seen as equal). Recall also that we have found that control can be 'demanded' and that it may not be exercised although it could be (cf. above).

[247] From the 'middle' of the vertical chain of activities, physical transportation of bearings is a critical, mediating activity. Stripped of its planning aspects, it has become a simple activity that easily could be externalized. In particular, logistics and control of bearing shipments are handled through data interchange between the systems of the SKF production and sales organizations, while the actual transport has been externalized to specialists (trucking companies) running only a given transport capacity on a given schedule. Admittedly, shipping (on water) has, however, traditionally been externalized, but the reasons of high fixed costs and major indivisibilities (cf. Casson, 1987) have no parallel for trucking. In addition, they would become even less constraining with increased transport volume, which is exactly when SKF chose to externalize the activity (cf. the implementation of GFSS and the resultant greater demands on transshipment).

not the supplier has superior information systems capabilities to those of the customer[248] (or even concerning differential bargaining power).

Starting with the more obvious case, a supplier can 'lock-in' a customer through an information systems connection, as in the standard argument. That seems to represent a temporary phenomenon, not so much as a function of subsequent buyer pressure forcing neutral links (as argued by Malone et al., 1989) but more as a function of cost. Keeping exclusive, proprietary solutions up to date becomes increasingly costly with more sophisticated external markets for communications and systems. Moreover, it is cumbersome, since many parts of the 'host' organization have external links and there is a value in keeping down interface variation[249]. The argument holds à fortiori for the complex MNC. Cost to the supplier is a neglected driver of more open interfaces in customer-supplier relationships.

The more recent, largely parallel standard argument of add-on services to the product appears to have greater relevance and finds some support from SKF's experience. Information systems-mediated differentiation here goes hand-in-hand with selective internalization. For instance, many order-, payments- and inventory-related services essentially entail taking over activities from the buyer or intermediaries and this can be done on a case-by-case basis. 'Floats' can be reduced by interorganizational computer-mediated coordination[250]. In principle, these services can be copied by competitors (cf. Vitale, 1986)[251].

---

[248] Recall that the literature on interorganizational information systems is totally dominated by the issue of the supplier with superior information systems capabilities (cf. Section 3.3.2).

[249] SKF has a comparatively very standardized family of core systems and now promotes, as far as possible, the use of public standards also internally. SKF has also begun to introduce standard interfaces where not 'forced' to do so by competitors or buyers, thus ostensibly needlessly 'foregoing' [sic!] a competitive advantage.

[250] Who appropriates the gains in efficiency is more an issue of bargaining power.

[251] So far, the argument reasonably well follows wide-spread statements on what in effect are monopoly advantages vis-à-vis a customer (e.g. Parsons, 1983; Porter and Millar, 1985; Clemons and McFarlan, 1986 etc.; see Section 3.3.2; see also Antonelli, 1988a and 1988b). However, there are indications that the monopoly advantages can be less important than coordination advantages. For instance, when SKF introduced computers at, trained the people of, and established links to its network of more than fifty distributors in Italy, the greatest payoff seems to have come from SKF subsequently

A less than obvious demonstration of the value of information systems-mediated differentiation is how it holds a possibility to resolve more easily the higher-order conflict between strategies of rationalized production and product differentiation, viz. minimized diversity in production can be combined with customization through add-on services[252].

The threat of imitation by competitors is less acute concerning the internalization of knowledge than of "transactions". Accumulated knowledge about the customer improves the possibility to differentiate between customers. A database does not forget and it readily supplies a customer's historical buying pattern. In that sense, there is a significant first-mover advantage in linking a customer[253]. With an illustrative renegade use of transaction cost terms, it represents a quasi-internalization of <u>future</u> "transactions".

The less obvious case is when the customer possesses superior capabilities in information systems usage[254]. For the supplier, the issue becomes one of being able to accommodate dominant customer relationships. What we wish to highlight is that information systems can mean taking over activities, viz. selective internalization, also when the focal firm is in an inferior position in terms of information systems capabilities and/or bargaining power[255]; the point running contrary to what is normally assumed[256]. Information systems can make intensive customer-supplier relationships a viable proposition over great distances. In addition to the advantages of add-on services and inter-firm coordination, a more <u>fluid division of labor</u> concerning product customization and product development can be identified. Joint development and product

---

being able to rationalize its national aftermarket distribution.

[252] The description is directly applicable to SKF's standard bearing business.

[253] Thus, the advantage resides less in the customer connection per se or even the system (which otherwise is the standard argument; the first-mover advantage stemming first from the connection and, at times, second, from the system being the barrier that blocks out competitors).

[254] The situation is akin to that where SKF is the buyer (cf. above).

[255] For SKF particularly in relation to automotive manufacturers.

[256] Recall the arguments of monopoly through differentiation towards customers (e.g. Antonelli, 1988b; and Cozzi, 1988), or of 'locking in' the customer (cf. above). Our argument, of course, holds in these, more obvious cases as well.

modifications, but also transfer of 'how to' knowledge and additions to the knowledge base can be effectuated through cross-organizational information systems access[257]. The classical, very important boundary spanning roles of individuals for these purposes (e.g. Tushman, 1977) can to some extent be performed by information systems. The over-all task for the focal firm is to manage the differentiated relationships and to draw on the relevant pools of knowledge inside or outside the firm.

In the above cases, information systems support a new alternative between arm's length contracting and outright ownership. Concerning unambiguous externalization of activities, loss of control from loss of ownership can, in part, be compensated for by maintained control through information systems. Down-stream internalization of activities is clear in the case of add-on services, but more ambiguous in the case of more 'sub-contracting-type' relationships. The possibilities for 'unbundling' and control (cf. externalization) are necessary conditions when considering the contribution of information systems in this context but the final facet is one of information systems offering new opportunities for differentiation among customer relationships, not least by their offering a distinct mode of delivery. Competitive advantage has come to rest much more in information accumulated and in the experience gained on how to accumulate information and how to use it (rather than in the typically considered simple add-on services or even connections per se).

Finally, and reviving the idealized dichotomy, in the case of SKF information systems have meant more "transactions", and a shift toward more market in the internal "hierarchy", and more hierarchy in the external "market" relationships. The de facto boundary of the organization becomes blurred and the set of activities to be performed by the focal organization tends to be reconsidered with the advent of information systems.

---

[257] The general advantage to both parties compared to vertical integration is profiting from complementary innovation while retaining the competitive spirit (cf. von Hippel, 1976 and 1982; and Piore and Sabel, 1984). - Note also that stable external relationships often are cooperative in nature, rather than narrowly adversary (e.g. Perrow, 1986).

5.1.4 The Role of Information Systems in Complex Organizations

In what ways information systems constitute an enabling condition have been a recurring theme throughout this study. What has been less articulated, however, is how the notion of a firm infrastructure also implies some permanence. Information systems acquiring the status of an firm infrastructure to be maintained, as opposed to be built, is clearly found in SKF[258]. As it stands, the information systems setup has been seen to be more stable over time than organization structure itself. In fact, internal organizational change, or even turmoil, can more readily be reconciled with stability in external relationships (e.g. towards customers) with systems interfaces remaining in place. Reorganization can be facilitated, for instance, by temporarily running parallel internal reporting lines. We have also seen how new organizational units can more easily be added, old ones removed, and 'organizational abberations' maintained. In SKF, reorganization has become more frequent but also less dramatic.

However, the varying quality of data communications linkages (and through that systems access) suggests that the scope of induced stability needs to be qualified. In fact, quality and type of linkages have been shown to be a very good proxy for closeness to the core of firm operations, also in a strategic sense. Granted, the MNC will have to be very flexible concerning communications solutions depending on local conditions. But the need to bring closer parts of the organization deemed critical for efficient functioning of the MNC make readily observed linkages[259] a more than trivial measure for an inherently qualitative issue; how does the firm rank organizational units and dispersed activities in terms of strategic importance. At the far end, the measure also indicates which businesses or units are the most likely to be up for sale. The apparent keenness with which 'outlying'

[258] In very practical terms, it can be seen in the later reductions in dedicated information systems staff, less importance of idiosyncratic computer systems, and more monitoring than managing in the corporate and divisional information systems organization.

[259] Existence or non-existence and quality of connections.

organizational units want to be connected to the network testifies to the value attached to this proxy from 'below' in the organization. The observed differential treatment of acquisitions in this respect fits with the notion of closeness, and, moreover, it highlights the other side of the coin, viz. the role of information systems as a significant instrument of integration. Consequently, the degree of information systems-induced integration varies.

The less readily observed differential systems access is closely related to linkage quality but adds qualification to the role of information systems. It is particulary pertinent as regards external parties since closeness to core can be seen also to extend outside the focal organization. As a matter of fact, many important large customers are better served by SKF information system services than are some of its own subsidiaries. The offerings include remote usage of ostensibly 'internal' SKF technical applications. In this respect, access becomes something of a buffering issue, as information and 'how to' algorithms can be sensitive for competitive reasons. The point is relevant also when information systems are used as a forceful instrument of integration, in SKF illustrated by the use of information systems vis-à-vis many distributors.

Another aspect of the new infrastructure is that it lowers the communications threshold in a very general sense. Intentionally so in principle, the practice holds some surprises. As such, information systems complement other types of communication, also for more informal purposes[260]. Some systems are actively 'pushed' (e.g. reporting systems), whereas other only 'invite' usage (e.g. particular technical applications). However, as we have seen, there is not necessarily any implied conflict in the terms, 'pushed' systems can also be 'demanded' from below. As usage matures, the 'pull' aspect becomes relatively more important. Since the information systems infrastructure is less rigid than, for instance, defined reporting lines, ease of communication can stimulate organizational by-pass. Organizational units and, indeed, middle managers can rely less for their raison-

[260] Micro-level studies of electronic mail systems have demonstrated some similar effects. For instance, Foster and Flynn (1984) have described how ease of communication has led to more interaction through electronic 'dropping in' by subordinates at the manager's office in one General Motors subunit. In a similar situation, Kiesler (1986) found individuals forming new groups and engaging in new types of interaction (particularly around projects) within an organization.

d'être on formal status and traditional information-processing function than on expertise and other resources they can offer.

With stimulation of communication, an issue neglected so far warrants some comment: the threat of "information-overload". The conspicuous overconsumption of information by firms and managers that has been observed is, however, not limited to information systems usage (cf. Feldman and March, 1981; and also Culnan, 1983). The very readily suggested greater risk of inundation by information (or, more correctly, data) brought by new information systems does seem to have some inspiration from more solid, classical communication theory, where there is a conflict between information and meaning, and where communication should influence conduct (Shannon and Weaver, 1963/1949; see also Miller, 1972; and Jellis, 1988).

The simple point we wish to make is that information systems as treated here do not imply inundation although communication can be seen to increase. Either information or data need not necessarily be used for meaning; need not be 'received' (and influence conduct). A database or a system can be seen to represent both a buffer for transmitted data and an option on future states. Automatic adjustment between systems need not involve human agents and storage of data does not imply that the whole stock needs to be 'used'[261].

In addition, information systems themselves can be carriers of meaning. Reduction of variety through standardization and dissemination of 'best practice' or procedures alleviate the conflict but are not the whole story. As argued by Weick (1985), corporate culture is a carrier of meaning that makes computers more intelligible to individuals[262]. Changing the perspective to that of the organization, information systems constitute a structure in itself, de facto with embedded values of 'how to do things'. In SKF, the

261 For instance, recall the inter-locking information systems for the product flow and the storage of reporting information in SKF.

262 Weick (1985) discusses the micro-level issue of human-machine interface. Terminal work is seen to remain viable and relevant if the work situation is varied (people should leave the terminal and walk around etc.). Overload is decreased by making sure that different information inputs are present.

information systems are very much part of the firm culture, forging a certain cohesiveness. By way of illustration, SKF information systems were welcomed as bringing a soft 'Europeanness' by US subsidiaries and 'order' by the Spanish one.

In a more mundane way, information systems can support the forging of corporate culture, particularly by way of being an adjunct to informal means of control and coordination, mitigating some of the identified restrictions on their use[263]. Information systems can support the work of task forces, committees and the like, and even be the means by which they are convened and maintained, making the use of them less costly. Over-all, information systems are helpful as a channel for the required higher communications intensity, lessening the geographical constraints on informal means. At this stage, it should be re-emphasized that information systems have not been cast in the role of a panacea for complex organizations in terms of delivering efficient control and coordination and effective adaptation to changing conditions. Information systems enable improvements on those scores but, arguably, to a significant extent in many cases.

5.2 The 'Wired' MNC

Based on our main findings and with the associated caveats in mind, the plunge is taken and the contours of a 'wired' MNC are seen to emerge[264]. We choose to focus on the most likely scenario. In a speculative, idealized sequence, two, largely overlapping, generic states can be described; two states, which when fused epitomize the 'wired' MNC. After painting the portrait of the 'wired' MNC with broad strokes, the conceptualization is put in perspective.

---

[263] Recall the importance afforded such means in the 'functioning' view of MNCs (cf. Section 3.2.1).

[264] See also Hagström (1991) for a more restrained discussion on the internal characteristics of the 'wired' MNC with practical illustrations.

5.2.1 Conceptualizing the 'Wired' MNC

The information systems 'jolt' to the organization (cf. Huber, 1990) initially means presenting the organization with a new opportunity set for structural choice, although biased by the technological characteristics of the information systems. The choices made as to how information systems are to be employed are biased in turn by the needs and perceptions of the existing organization but the intentions broadly lead to the unorthodox organization. More than just automating a given organization, information systems tend to be established with the primary purpose of better central control and more hands-on coordination of dispersed activities (not least through better planning and better overview). Visions of an organization run by remote control would fit this picture. However, in practice, the main contribution of information systems is to be able to monitor activities across several dimensions and to redeploy resources closer in line with corporate objectives and particular local advantages. A leaner organization will simultaneously become more complex with specialized organizational units, often assigned multiple roles, and with the maintaining of idiosyncratic units which demonstrate that they function well. Better control does not necessarily mean enforcement of that control. A more integrated structure can be more flexible in adapting to external conditions and in its external relationships, particularly as regards differentiation towards customers.

However, the function of information systems as permitting better central control and coordination of an increasingly fragmented organization that motivated the very establishment of an elaborate information systems infrastructure, somewhat surprisingly, also unleashes the more interesting self-adjusting organization. The unorthodox organization being different from the initial organization means that subsequent choices regarding information systems and their use are different, particularly as the unorthodox organization has a wider scope of players, which 'demand' new organizational solutions. Better control gives quicker response as a function of getting the 'whole picture' but when the whole picture becomes available locally, response may be 'automatic'. The very notion of a 'center' in the MNC becomes ephemeral or even irrelevant, as organizational units initiate independent action. Coordination of activities becomes clearing and mutual adjustment rather than being achieved by rules or hands-on higher level optimization. Mutual adjustment thus takes place between non-contiguous agents, if not the information systems infrastructure is seen to make all parts of the dispersed MNC de facto contiguous.

The unorthodox, self-adjusting MNC thrives on the information systems infrastructure with relationships developing similarly to how unforeseen, irregular foot-paths soon get established in any planned housing development. Actively seeking out the best source of information or knowledge wherever in the network it resides places a premium on learning and retention. Variety and scope for dispersed experimentation stimulate innovation. The 'wired' MNC is populated by a mix of very idiosyncratic 'subsidiaries', where the locus of decision-making becomes diffused also on strategic issues. Roles are more likely to be assumed rather than imposed; roles which tend to be ambiguous, multiple, and highly prone to change. The traditional subsidiary may well survive, but only in a legal sense. In practice it tends to become a platform, or a 'home', for a changing set of activities, subject to different coordination mechanisms. It becomes more relevant to talk of the MNC as a population of 'auxiliaries'[265], with different competencies and only operating within the broad framework of corporate objectives.

Corporate management may initially have opted for 'remote control' through information systems, but in the 'wired' MNC it is likely instead ultimately to get remote monitoring with virtual management, i.e. mutual adjustment among 'auxiliaries' on-line (directly through systems) or as a consequence of spontaneous laterality springing from information systems-supported exchange. A confederation of 'auxiliaries' is likely to be exceptionally flexible in adapting to changing conditions but higher level influence over the process will be commensurably weakened. In addition, the centrifugal forces have an external dimension with the blurring of organizational boundaries through information systems-mediated external relationships. What can happen between parties legally internal to the firm can also take place across the legal boundary of the firm. More

[265] One meaning given to the word 'auxiliary' in the Oxford English Dictionary (1971:577) is "[o]ne who renders help or gives assistance; a helper, assistant, confederate, ally; also, that which gives help, a source or means of assistance".

internal market-like relationships and more external hierarchy-like relationships make the traditional difference between 'internal' and 'external' less clear. The threat of disintegration to the MNC is real.

Of course, the bottom line for a firm is literally the bottom line. Spontaneous laterality will be accepted by corporate management simply because it is seen to be strikingly effective. Stimulated by information systems, mutual adjustment in the 'wired' MNC also generates a record. Corporate management has an 'early-warning' mechanism in place through the same information systems. With good monitoring of activities performed, diffusion of traditional management functions becomes a more palatable proposition to corporate management. The prerogative to intervene remains real but the need to do so should, ideally, not materialize. In addition, informal means of achieving control and coordination, particularly as regards staffing and the forging of a corporate culture, will assume greater importance in the 'wired' MNC in order to maintain cohesiveness. Loyalty is best ensured through identification with corporate goals.

By implication, organizational design evolves more into an issue of infrastructure, far removed from supplying any detailed organizational blue-prints. The 'wired' MNC is both multinational and 'wired'. It is profitable to maintain and develop the inherent advantages of both. The information systems infrastructure is best served by safeguarding and extending the corporate communications network and by ensuring standardization of interfaces in a wide sense. The advantages of 'multinationality' are best exploited by nurturing the international network of dispersed resources and by preserving cohesiveness through incentives and informal means. As such, the 'wired' MNC also constitutes a platform which encompasses a set of options on future states of nature. Detailed 'design' at any given time lies within the purview of dispersed information systems users or of dispersed organizational subunits.

To create and maintain the conditions most conducive to achieve readaptation of the organization, reconfiguration of activities in response to changing external conditions are decisive factors for long-term corporate survival. For this to happen continuously, rather than in costly discrete leaps is probably destined to become the competitive advantage.

In turn, this capability is inexorably linked to mature usage of information systems. These broad organizational capabilities do, however, need to extend outside the organization. In a wider sense, competitive advantage would then reside in the governance structure and largely in information systems-mediated governance. In this respect, the 'wired' MNC represents a set of options on the future.

Complexity in the complex 'wired' MNC is a characteristic very much in the eyes of the beholder. From the point of view of the 'auxiliary', relationships and interaction appear 'natural', i.e. derived from local needs, rather than being particularly complex. For corporate management, complexity de facto is reduced to a remote keeping tabs on the over-all functioning of the MNC and to nurture the corporate infrastructure. For the detached observer, the 'wired' MNC remains exceedingly complex, defying any meaningful simple or reductionist description.

5.2.2 Perspective on the 'Wired' MNC

As to more visionary conceptions of future or emerging organizations, the 'wired' MNC broadly falls in line with "holographic" principles of organizing (Hedlund, 1986; and Morgan, 1986), the 'wiring' itself very much contributing to the principles being given some operational content at the organizational level[266]. In a similar vein, Huber's (1984) hypothesis that "postindustrial" organizations will use increased control to ensure compliance with corporate standards, in some cases possibly with the purpose of experimenting with self-designing organizations, finds a much stronger expression in the 'wired' MNC with its spontaneous mutual adjustment[267]. The later proposition (Huber,

[266] Given that the antecedents to the idea come from cybernetics, it is perhaps not surprising that a study highlighting the role of information systems should bear resemblance to this conception.

[267] Pava's (1983) micro-level "reticular organization" for non-routine office work warrants a mention in this context in that it represents an insightful statement linking cybernetic principles with traditional concepts in organization theory in a socio-technical framework. Apart from dealing with organization at the level of the individual, the "reticular organization" can be consciously designed with self-design as a discrete step in the process. In the 'wired' MNC continuous and spontaneous "self-design" is more important.

1990) of greater variety across organizations as an effect of information systems does not contradict the conceptualized 'wired' MNC but our findings suggest that internal diversity constitutes the relatively greater change.

Likewise, the 'wired' MNC shows close affinity with the 'functioning' main strand of research on the organizational structure of the MNC[268], although some difference in emphasis may be noted. The 'wired' MNC is less normative than either of the more managerially-oriented "transnational" (Bartlett, 1986; and Bartlett and Ghoshal, 1989) and "heterarchical" (Hedlund, 1986) MNCs. The stress on corporate monitoring of activities (and thus the 'threat' of intervention[269]) and on the spontaneous laterality appearing contrary to corporate intentions also take the 'wired' MNC down a somewhat different route. Moreover, the information systems infrastructure (not featured in the more general, managerially-oriented conceptions of the MNC) can alleviate some of the identified trade-off between flexibility and stability in the MNC. The relatively stable information systems infrastructure can support the required higher-order stable characteristics of corporate culture, norms etc. But information systems can also be a mechanism defining 'degree of belonging' in themselves through differential access and be a means for smoothening flexible interfaces with the environment.

Continuous structural change being the norm in the 'wired' MNC is somewhat at odds with the suggested periodic redirection of the organization (Doz and Prahalad, 1987). Vernon's (1979) "global scanner" implies more purposeful scanning and more central direction in the subsequent exploitation of opportunities than does the 'wired' MNC. The relationship with the "global scanner" can rather be seen as one of extension, where the 'wired' MNC through information systems moves close to a 'zero' information float, which is tantamount to sensing in the true sense of the word. With wide availability of 'sensing' information, the greater potential for exploitation of opportunities is then also present

---

[268] The 'wired' MNC is incompatible with with conceptions emanating from the organzationally-inclined 'form' tradition as regards 'fits' between the organization and its environment or technology (particularly information systems) and the subsequent selection of a formal organizational structure.

[269] The control aspect of information systems usage, in fact, constitutes the strongest link from the 'wired' MNC to the 'form' perspective on MNCs and organizations as it has developed from Chandler (1962; see also Chandler, 1986).

throughout the organization. The difference as to implied purposefulness is, however, more stark when contrasting the 'wired' MNC with the "information-based orchestra" (Drucker, 1986; see also Drucker, 1988). In the 'wired' MNC corporate management has no notes on the uncertain future and is hard put to orchestrate the activities of the organization.

Finally, our narrowly defined antecedents also offer visions of future organization. In OECD-BRIE (1989; synthesized by Bar and Borrus, 1989) organizational structure not being an issue, the key to future success is "telecommunications network flexibility", viz. success is determined by differential technical capabilities and national service availability. Although the information systems network obviously is critical also to the 'wired' MNC, it is neither a sufficient condition nor merely a technical or home country service-availability issue. Flexibility is wider than telecommunications network configuration or network resources. In fact, if anything is stable in the 'wired' MNC, it is the more widely defined information systems infrastructure.

The deep appreciation shown by Nanus (1969) and Antonelli (1981)[270] of both the enabling characteristics of information systems and of the intrinsic relation of those opportunities to MNC activities recurs with a vengeance in the 'wired' MNC. The very early conceptions of flexible utilization of a given MNC structure and set of resources apply to the 'wired' MNC, although the strengthening of inherent MNC advantages was not explicit. Predicted centralization and formal matrix arrangements clash with the characteristics of the 'wired' MNC, as does the implied efficient design of the MNC. However, Nanus's (1969) view of "the multinational computer" upgrading local capabilities and Antonelli's (1981) identified internal variety of subunits tally well with the 'wired' MNC[271].

---

[270] Restated in Antonelli (1987; see also Parry, 1983).

[271] Bakis's (1987) perceptive, but implicit mention of "telecommunications and teleprocessing" as being associated with coordination and control along multiple dimensions also deserves recognition in this context.

The later "network firm" (Antonelli, 1988b) has more adversarial relationships with suppliers and customers than the 'wired' MNC, although the blurred interfaces are similar. Still, the bias for growth is unequivocal in the "network firm" but less than definite for the 'wired' MNC, which is more likely to expand de facto than in terms of formal ownership[272]. The main dividing line, again, concerns the element of hands-on direction, particularly strategic decision-making, in a firm centered around an information network; strong in the "network firm" and ideally none in the 'wired' MNC.

5.3 Broad Implications for Further Research

Since the above discussion has been lengthy as it stands, we have made somewhat limited explicit allowance for the MNC aspect when rendering an account of the main findings of the present study. Another reason has been to put the exposé in the more general framework of change in complex organizations. The point to keep in mind, however, is that the conclusions apply à fortiori to MNCs, which have a more varied pool of resources to draw on (for instance as a result of exploiting particular locational advantages) and for which overcoming barriers of distance is a key managerial challenge. Naturally, the MNC stands to gain most from more internal cooperation across the board and across borders.

Even though the conclusions have specifically revolved around information systems, much of what has thus been 'revealed' should also apply to studies of MNC organization and structure. In fact, our main findings give a series of testable propositions, which would carry implications for the study of complex organizations or firms in general, for instance, the broad set of conclusions regarding:

- the usefulness of interpreting 'location' along more than one dimension,
- the analytical value of a disaggregated view of firm activities,

[272] Antonelli (1988b) considers only the firm as defined by law. But with information systems-mediated interfaces supporting alternatives to ownership, the legally defined firm could well shrink.

- the identified inadequacy of a term like "centralization" and the proposed alternatives for dealing with the implicit phenomena,
- the recognition of a 'demand' side embedded in the organizational structure, which expresses itself in spontaneous coordination as in the possible rise of internal markets,
- the variety in governance structure made possible and the organizational interpretation of de facto functionality of external relationships; and
- the outlined significant role of information systems in the evolution of complex organizations.

Apart from the purely theoretical inferences, much of the credibility of the generalized statements hinge on the assumption of SKF as something of a trailblazer. The case for such an assumption and the methodological rationale thereof have already been argued at some length. Suffice it to recall here that SKF represents, for our purposes, a maximization of the most relevant characteristics; degree of 'multinationality' and maturity of information systems usage. Still, the contention is that SKF is not an outlier, but a run-of-the-mill MNC, which for reasons of survival in a changing external environment was prompted to become an early adopter of information systems. In turn, SKF's usage has been free from 'folkloric' or outlandish particular applications, instead earning its laurels from more humdrum general capabilities in the area of international information systems.

In fact, the empirical study found a very complex and flexible SKF not readily reducible to any simple category, where we would have had reason to expect a very common MNC. This is surprising since a 'simple' MNC like SKF 'should not' need to be so messy according to the received wisdom. Our contention is also that SKF would not be quite so messy either, were it not for its well-developed information systems infrastructure. However, that leaves one important question outstanding, namely whether or not the 'Swedishness' of SKF amounts to a disqualification. Perhaps the combination of information systems and the heritage of relatively strong reliance on informal means of coordination and control is particularly fortunate and idiosyncratic? The question cannot be resolved without further research but our supposition is that SKF's 'Swedishness' is no serious liability for our results. Although present, effects of home-country nationality would at least be diluted by SKF's extensive and long-standing 'multinationality'. In addition, one may recall the likelihood of an on-going international trend towards relatively increased use of informal means of control and coordination in MNCs[273].

Fact remains that most propositions put forward here need further empirical verification (or falsification, as the case may be)[274]. The empirical base presented here clearly leaves a lot to be desired in terms of providing any test of theory or unequivocal prediction[275]. We can readily subscribe to the well-founded calls for further coherent theoretical development especially concerning MNC structure (Hedlund, 1991b) and information systems in organizations (Swanson, 1987; and Huber, 1990). The relative importance of information systems for coordination and control warrants much additional scholarly attention not least concerning inter-organizational information systems. Both theory and empirical study are needed on the possible implications of information systems usage for the theory of the firm and for firm location behavior. The likely role of the information systems infrastructure as a significant element of relative stability in an organization also needs to be critically explored in greater depth.

We surmise that the broad interdisciplinary approach taken here, the suggested analytical taxonomy of location of activities, the methodological extension (the 'insistent' case study and 'trying out theory'), and the usage perspective of information systems as developed are all modest contributions that could provide beneficial input to future research endeavors in the intersecting set of information systems and complex organizations.

The conception of the 'wired' MNC may have less practical usefulness but it may be noted that information systems are here provocatively elevated to and more clearly defined as being a key aspect of organization structure. By capturing the de facto

---

[273] On the score of liability or possibly asset, see also the more specific argument in Hagström (1991).

[274] Studies of other organizations in different environments and clever research designs using large samples readily spring to mind as being worth-while.

[275] Recall, however, that such aims were beyond the purpose of this study already at the outset (cf. Chapter 4).

functioning of the MNC, the information infrastructure and flows are a better determinant of the de facto scope of the MNC than either the formal organization structure or the de jure ownership structure.

REFERENCES

Ackoff, R. L. (1967), "Management Misinformation Systems", **Management Science**, Vol. 14, No. 4, pp. (B)147-(B)156.

Ågren, L. (1990), **Swedish Direct Investment in the U.S.** Stockholm: Institute of International Business, Stockholm School of Economics.

Allen, B. (1982), "An Unmanaged Computer System Can Stop You Dead", **Harvard Business Review**, Vol. 60, No. 6, pp. 77-87.

Allen, B. (1987), "Make Information Services Pay Its Way", **Harvard Business Review**, Vol. 65, No. 1, pp. 57-63.

Allen, T. J. and Hauptman, O. (1987), "The Influence of Communication Technologies on Organizational Structure: A Conceptual Model for Future Research", **Communications Research**, Vol. 14, No. 5, pp. 575-587.

Andersson, P. (1989), "Informationsteknologi i organisationer: Bestämningsfaktorer och mönster" ["Information Technology in Organizations: Determinants and Patterns"], **Linköping Studies in Arts and Science**, No. 46, Linköping (doctoral thesis, with a summary in English).

Anthony, R. N. (1965), **Planning and Control Systems: A Framework for Analysis**. Boston: Harvard University Press.

Antonelli, C. (1981), "Transborder Data Flows and International Business - A Pilot Study", **Directorate for Science, Technology and Industry**, Working Party on Information, Computer and Communications Policy, Expert Group on Transborder Data Flows, DSTI/ICCP/81.16. Paris: OECD.

Antonelli, C. (1984), "Multinational Firms, International Trade and International Telecommunications", **Information Economics and Policy**, Vol. 1, No. 4, pp. 333-343.

Antonelli, C. (1985), "The Diffusion of an Organizational Innovation: International Data Telecommunications and Multinational Industrial Firms", **International Journal of Industrial Organization**, Vol. 3, No. 1, pp. 109-118.

Antonelli, C. (1987), "TDF and the Structure and Strategies of TNCs", **The CTC Reporter**, No. 23, pp. 43-44.

Antonelli, C. (1988a), "A New Industrial Organization Approach" in Antonelli, C., ed., **New Information Technology and Industrial Change: The Italian Case**. Dordrecht: Kluwer Academic Publishers for the Commission of the European Communities, pp. 1-12.

Antonelli, C. (1988b), "The Emergence of the Network Firm" in Antonelli, C., ed., **New Information Technology and Industrial Change: The Italian Case**. Dordrecht: Kluwer Academic Publishers for the Commission of the European Communities, pp. 13-32.

Aoki, M. (1990), "Toward an Economic Model of the Japanese Firm", **Journal of Economic Literature**, Vol. XXVIII, No.1, pp. 1-27.

Argyris, C. (1971), "Management Information Systems: The Challenge to Rationality and Emotionality", **Management Science**, Vol. 17, No. 6, February, pp. 275-292.

Argyris, C. and Schön, D. A. (1978), **Organization Learning**. Reading, Mass.: Addison-Wesley.

Aronson, J. D. and Cowhey, P. F. (1988), **When Countries Talk: International Trade in Telecommunications Services**. Cambridge, Mass.: Ballinger Publishing Company.

Arrow, K. J. (1975), "Vertical Integration and Communication", **Bell Journal of Economics**, Vol. 6, No. 1, pp. 173-183.

Ashby, W. R. (1965), **An Introduction to Cybernetics**. London: Methuen & Co.

Astley, W. G. and Van de Ven, A. H. (1983), "Central Perspectives and Debates in Organization Theory", **Administrative Science Quarterly**, Vol. 28, No. 2, pp. 245-273.

Avison, D. E. and Fitzgerald, G. (1991), "Information Systems Practice, Education and Research", **Journal of Information Systems**, Vol. 1, No. 1, pp. 5-17.

Bakis, H. (1980), "The Communications of Larger Firms and Their Implications on the Emergence of a New World Industrial Order: A Case Study: I.B.M.'s Global Data Network", Contributin[g] Report to the **24th International Geographical Congress** (pre-Congress Meeting), August 26-30, Commission on Industrial Systems, International Geographical Union, Chuo University, Tokyo (mimeo).

Bakis, H. (1987), "Telecommunications and the Global Firm" in Hamilton, F. E. I., ed., **Industrial Change in Advanced Economies**. London: Croom Helm, pp. 130-160.

Bakos, J. Y. and Treacy, M. E. (1986), "Information Technology and Corporate Strategy: A Research Perspective", **MIS Quarterly**, Vol. 10, No. 2, pp. 107-119.

Baliga, B. R. and Jaeger, A. M. (1984), "Multinational Corporations: Control Systems and Delegation Issues", **Journal of International Business Studies**, Vol. 15, No. 2, pp. 25-40.

Bar, F. and Borrus, M. with Coriat, B. (1989), "Information Networks and Competitive Advantages: The Issues for Government Policy and Corporate Strategy: Final Report" in OECD-BRIE, "Information Networks and Business Strategies: An OECD-BRIE Project on Competitiveness and Telecommunications Policy", BRIE Working Paper 38, **Berkeley Roundtable on the International Economy**, University of California, Berkeley, pp. 1-47.

Barras, R. (1986), "New Technology and the New Services: Towards an Innovation Strategy for Europe", **Futures**, Vol. 18, No. 6, pp. 748-772.

Bartlett, C. A. (1979), "Multinational Structural Evolution: The Changing Decision Environment in International Divisions", **Harvard Graduate School of Business Administration**, Harvard University, Boston, Mass. (unpublished doctoral dissertation).

Bartlett, C. A. (1982), "How Multinational Organizations Evolve", **Journal of Business Strategy**, Vol. 3, No. 1, pp. 20-32.

Bartlett, C. A. (1983), "MNCs: Get Off the Reorganization Merry-Go-Round", **Harvard Business Review**, Vol. 61, No. 2, pp. 138-146.

Bartlett, C. A. (1986), "Building and Managing the Transnational: The New Organizational Challenge" in Porter, M. E., ed., **Competition in Global Industries**. Boston, Mass.: Harvard Business School Press, pp. 367-401.

Bartlett, C. A., Doz, Y. and Hedlund, G. (1990), "Introduction: The Changing Agenda for Researchers and Practitioners" in Bartlett, C. A., Doz, Y. and Hedlund, G., eds., **Managing the Global Firm**. London: Routledge, pp. 1-12.

Bartlett, C. A. and Ghoshal, S. (1986), "Tap Your Subsidiaries for Global Reach", **Harvard Business Review**, Vol. 64, No. 6, pp. 87-94.

Bartlett, C. A. and Ghoshal, S. (1987), "Managing Across Borders: New Organizational Responses", **Sloan Management Review**, Vol. 29, No. 1, pp. 43-53.

Bartlett, C. A. and Ghoshal, S. (1988), "Organizing for Worldwide Effectiveness: The Transnational Solution", **California Management Review**, Vol. 31, No. 1, pp. 54-74.

Bartlett, C. A. and Ghoshal, S. (1989), **Managing Across Borders: The Transnational Solution**. Boston, Mass.: Harvard Business School Press.

Bartlett, C. A. and Ghoshal, S. (1990), "Matrix Management: Not a Structure, a Frame of Mind", **Harvard Business Review**, Vol. 68, No. 4, pp. 138-145.

Benbasat, I. (1984), "An Analysis of Research Methodologies" in McFarlan, F. W., ed., **The Information Systems Research Challenge**. Boston, Mass.: Harvard Business School Press, pp. 47-85.

Benbasat, I., Goldstein, D. K. and Mead, M. (1987), "The Case Research Strategy in Studies of Information Systems", **MIS Quarterly**, Vol. 11, No. 3, pp. 369-386.

Beniger, J. R. (1986), **The Control Revolution: Technological and Economic Origins of the Information Society**. Cambridge, Mass.: Harvard University Press.

Benjamin, R. I., de Long, D. W. and Scott Morton, M. S. (1990), "Electronic Data Interchange: How Much Competitive Advantage?", **Long Range Planning**, Vol. 23, No. 1, pp. 29-40.

Benjamin, R. I., Rockart, J. F., Scott Morton, M. S. and Wyman, J. (1984), "Information Technology: A Strategic Opportunity", **Sloan Management Review**, Vol. 25, No. 3, pp. 3-10.

Benjamin, R. I. and Scott Morton, M. S. (1986), "Information Technology, Integration, and Organizational Change", 90s Working Paper 86-017 and Sloan WP # 1769-86, **Management in the 1990s, Sloan School of Management**, Massachusetts Institute of Technology, Cambridge, Mass.

Bergendorff, H. (1982), "International Data Communications in the OECD Area: 1976 and 1981", **Directorate for Science, Technology and Industry**, Committee for Information, Computer and Communications Policy, Expert Group on Transborder Data Flows, DSTI/ICCP/82.27, OECD, Paris.

Björn-Andersen, N., Eason, K. and Robey, D. (1986), **Managing Computer Impact: An International Study of Management and Organizations**. Norwood, N.J.: Ablex Publishing Corporation.

Blau, P. M., McHugh Falbe, C., McKinley, W. and Tracy, P. K. (1976), "Technology and Organization in Manufacturing", **Administrative Science Quarterly**, Vol. 21, No. 1, pp. 20-40.

Blau, P. M. and Schoenherr, R. A. (1971), **The Structure of Organizations**. New York, N. Y.: Basic Books, Publishers.

Boaden, R. and Lockett, G. (1991), "Information Technology, Information Systems and Information Management: Definition and Development"; **European Journal of Information Systems**, Vol. 1, No. 1, pp. 23-32.

Boddy, D. and Buchanan, D. A. (1986), **Managing New Technology**. Oxford: Basil Blackwell.

Boeckhout, I. J. and Molle, W. T. M. (1982), "Technological Change, Location Patterns and Regional Development", **FAST Occasional Papers**, No. 16, June, Commission of the European Communities, Brussels.

Boland, R. J. Jr. (1987), "The In-Formation of Information Systems" in Boland, R. J. Jr. and Hirschheim R. A., eds., **Critical Issues in Information Systems Research**. CHichester: John Wiley & Sons, pp. 363-379.

Bonoma, T. V. (1985), "Case Research in Marketing: Opportunities, Problems, and a Process", **Journal of Marketing Research**, Vol. 22, No. 2, pp. 199-208.

Brooke, M. Z. (1979), "Multinational Corporate Structures: The Next Stage", **Futures**, Vol. 11, No. 2, April, pp. 111-121.

Brooke, M. Z. (1984), **Centralization and Autonomy: A Study in Organization Behaviour**. London: Holt, Reinhart and Winston.

Brooke, M. Z. (1986), **International Management: A Review of Strategies and Operations**. London: Hutchinson.

Brooke, M. Z. and Remmers, H. L. (1970/1978), **The Strategy of Multinational Enterprise**. Harlow: Longman (1st edn.) and London: Pitman (2nd edn.).

Buckley, P. J. (1988), "Organizational Forms and Multinational Companies" in Thompson, S. and Wright, M., eds., **Internal Organization, Efficiency and Profit**. Oxford: Philip Allan, pp. 127-144.

Buckley, P. J. (1989), **Multinational Enterprise: Theory and Applications**. London: Macmillan.

Buckley, P. J. (1990), "Problems and Developments in the Core Theory of International Business", **Journal of International Business Studies**, Vol. 21, No. 4, pp. 657-665.

Buckley, P. J. and Casson, M. (1976), **The Future of the Multinational Enterprise**. London: Macmillan.

Buckley, P. J. and Casson, M. (1985), **The Economic Theory of the Multinational Enterprise: Selected Papers**. London: Macmillan.

Burns, T. and Stalker, G. M. (1961), **The Management of Innovation**. London: Tavistock.

Business International (1983), "Transborder Data Flow: Issues, Barriers and Corporate Responses", New York, N.Y.

Buss, M. D. J. (1982), "Managing International Information Systems", **Harvard Business Review**, Vol. 60, No. 5, pp. 153-162.

Buss, M. D. J. (1984), "Legislative Threat to Transborder Data Flow", **Harvard Business Review**, Vol. 62, No. 3, pp. 111-118.

Camillus, J. C. and Lederer, A. L. (1985), "Corporate Strategy and the Design of Computerized Information Systems", **Sloan Management Review**, Vol. 26, No. 3, pp. 35-42.

Capra, F. (1985), "Criteria of Systems Thinking", **Futures**, Vol. 17, No. 5, pp. 475-478.

Cash, J. I. Jr. and Konsynski, B. R. (1985), "IS Redraws Competitive Boundaries", **Harvard Business Review**, Vol. 63, No. 2, pp. 134-142.

Casson, M. (1987), **The Firm and the Market: Studies on Multinational Enterprise and the Scope of the Firm**. Oxford: Basil Blackwell.

Caves, R. E. (1980), "Industrial Organization, Corporate Strategy and Structure", **Journal of Economic Literature**, Vol. XVIII, No.1, pp. 64-92.

Caves, R. E. (1982), **Multinational Enterprise and Economic Analysis**. Cambridge: Cambridge University Press.

Chakravarthy, B. S. and Perlmutter, H. V. (1985), "Strategic Planning for a Global Business", **Columbia Journal of World Business**, Vol. XX, No. 2, pp. 3-10.

Chandler, A. D. Jr. (1962), **Strategy and Structure: Chapters in the History of the American Industrial Enterprise**. Cambridge, Mass.: The M.I.T. Press.

Chandler, A. D. Jr., ed. (1965), **The Railroads: The Nation's First Big Business**. New York, N.Y.: Harcourt, Brace & World.

Chandler, A. D. Jr. (1977), **The Visible Hand**. Cambridge, Mass.: The Belknap Press of Harvard University Press.

Chandler, A. D. Jr. (1986), "The Evolution of Modern Global Competition" in Porter, M. E., ed., **Competition in Global Industries**. Boston, Mass.: Harvard Business School Press, pp. 405-448.

Chandler, A. D. Jr. (1990), "The Enduring Logic of Industrial Success", **Harvard Business Review**, Vol. 68, No. 2, pp. 130-140.

Child, J. (1972), "Organizational Structure, Environment and Performance: The Role of Strategic Choice", **Sociology**, Vol. 6, No. 1, pp. 1-22.

Child, J. (1984a), "New Technology and Developments in Management Organization", **Omega International Journal of Management Science**, Vol. 12, No. 3, pp. 211-223.

Child, J. (1984b), **Organization: A Guide to Problems and Practice** (2nd edn.). London: Harper & Row.

Child, J. (1987a), "Information Technology, Organization, and the Response to Strategic Challenges", **California Management Review**, Vol. 30, No. 1, pp. 33-50.

Child, J. (1987b), "Managerial Strategies, New Technology, and the Labor Process" in Pennings, J. M. and Buitendam, A., eds. **New Technology as Organizational Innovation: The Development and Diffusion of Microelectronics**. Cambridge, Mass.: Ballinger Publishing Company, pp. 141-178.

Ciborra, C. U. (1983), "Markets, Bureaucracies and Groups in the Information Society: An Institutional Appraisal of the Impacts of Information Technology", **Information Economics and Policy**, Vol. 1, No. 2, pp. 145-160.

Ciborra, C. U. (1987), "Research Agenda for a Transaction Costs Approach to Information Systems" in Boland, R. J. Jr. and Hirschheim, R. A., eds., **Critical Issues in Information Systems Research**. Chichester: John Wiley & Sons, pp. 253-274.

Civildepartementet (1984), **Sveriges datakommunikationer med utlandet: En inventering** [Sweden's data communications with other countries: A survey]. Stockholm: Liber, Ds C 1984:4A.

Clague, L. with Haizman, K. and Kochevar, J. (1977), "Organizing for International Finance: Structuring, Managing and Implementing the Function", **Business International Corporation**, New York, N.Y.

Claisse, G. (1983), "Transport and Telecommunications" in European Conference of Ministers of Transport, **Report of the Fifty-Ninth Round Table on Transport Economics**. Paris: OECD.

Cleevely, D. and Cawdell, R. (1986), "A Telecommunications Taxonomy", **Telecommunications Policy**, Vol. 10, No. 2, pp. 107-119.

Clemons, E. K. and McFarlan, F. W. (1986), "Telecom: Hook Up or Lose Out", **Harvard Business Review**, Vol. 64, No. 4, pp. 91-97.

Clemons, E. K. and Row, M. (1988), "McKesson Drug Company: A Case Study of Economost - A Strategic Information System", **Journal of Management Information Systems**, Vol. 5, No. 1, pp. 36-50.

Clemons, E. K. and Weber, B. W. (1990), "Strategic Information Technology Investments: Guidelines for Decision Making", **Journal of Management Information Systems**, Vol. 7, No. 2, pp. 9-28.

Coase, R. H. (1937), "The Nature of the Firm", **Economica**, Vol. 4 (new series), pp. 405-448.

Collis, D. J. (1991), "A Resource-Based Analysis of Global Competition: The Case of the Bearings Industry", **Strategic Management Journal**, Vol. 12, Special Issue, pp. 49-68.

The Conference Board (1972), "Information Technology: Some Critical Implications for Decision Makers", New York, N.Y.

Copeland, D. G. and McKenney, J. L. (1988), "Airline Reservation Systems: Lessons from History", **MIS Quarterly**, Vol. 12, No. 3, pp. 353-370.

Corey, E. R. (1978), "Should Companies Centralize Procurement?", **Harvard Business Review**, Vol. 56, No. 6, pp. 102-110.

Cozzi, G. (1988), "Supply Conditions of Telematic Network Services and Public Policy Implications" in Antonelli, C., ed., **New Information Technology and Industrial Change: The Italian Case**. Dordrecht: Kluwer Academic Publishers for the Commission of the European Communities, pp. 133-149.

Crowston, K. and Malone, T. W (1987), "Information Technology and Work Organization", 90s Working Paper 87-040 and Sloan WP # 1960-87, **Management in the 1990s, Sloan School of Management**, Massachusetts Institute of Technology, Cambridge, Mass.

CSTD (1986), "New Information Technologies and Development", **Advance Technology Alert System (ATAS)**, Centre for Science and Technology for Development, United Nations Secretariat, New York, N.Y., Issue 3, June.

The CTC Reporter (1984), "TNCs and TDF", **United Nations Centre on Transnational Corporations**, United Nations, New York, N.Y., No. 17, pp. 11-12 and 48-50.

Daft, R. L. and Lewin, A. Y. (1990), "Can Organization Studies Begin to Break Out of the Normal Science Straitjacket? An Editorial Essay", **Organization Science**, Vol. 1, No. 1, pp. 1-9.

Dahlman, C. J. (1979), "The Problem of Externality", **Journal of Law and Economics**, Vol. XXII, No. 1, pp. 141-162.

Daniels, J. D., Pitts, R. A. and Tretter, M. J. (1984), "Strategy and Structure of U.S. Multinationals: An Exploratory Study", **Academy of Management Journal**, Vol. 27, No. 2, pp. 292-307.

Daniels, J. D., Pitts, R. A. and Tretter, M. J. (1985), "Organizing for Dual Strategies of Product Diversity and International Expansion", **Strategic Management Journal**, Vol. 6, No. 3, pp. 223-237.

Davenport, L. and Cronin, B. (1988), "Strategic Information Management: Forging the Value Chain", **International Journal of Information Management**, Vol. 8, No. 1, pp. 25-34.

Davidson, W. H. and Haspeslagh, P. (1982), "Shaping a Global Product Organization", **Harvard Business Review**, Vol. 60, No. 4, pp. 125-132.

Davis, H. L., Eppen, G. D. and Mattson, L. -G. (1974), "Critical Factors in Worldwide Purchasing", **Harvard Business Review**, Vol. 52, No. 6, pp. 81-90.

Davis, S. M. and Lawrence, P. R. (1977), **Matrix**. Reading, Mass.: Addison-Wesley.

Dearden, J. (1983), "Will the Computer Change the Job of Top Management?", **Sloan Management Review**, Vol. 25, No. 1, pp. 57-60.

Diebold, J. (1986), "Information Technology as a Competitive Weapon", **Advance Technology Alert System (ATAS) Bulletin**, Centre for Science and Technology for Development, United Nations Secretariat, New York, Issue 3, June, pp. 104-106.

Doll, D. R. (1978), **Data Communications: Facilities, Networks, and Systems Design**. New York, N.Y.: John Wiley & Sons.

Dordick, H. S., Bradley, H. G., Nanus, B. and Martin, T. H. (1979), "Network Information Services: The Emergence of an Industry", **Telecommunications Policy**, Vol. 3, No. 3, pp. 217-234.

Doz, Y. L. (1986), **Strategic Management in Multinational Companies**. Oxford: Pergamon Press.

Doz, Y. L. and Prahalad, C. K. (1981), "Headquarters Influence and Strategic Control in MNCs", **Sloan Management Review**, Vol. 23, No. 1, pp. 15-29.

Doz, Y. L. and Prahalad, C. K. (1984), "Patterns of Strategic Control within Multinational Corporations", **Journal of International Business Studies**, Vol. 15, No. 2, pp. 55-72.

Doz, Y. L. and Prahalad, C. K. (1986), "Controlled Variety: A Challenge for Human Resource Management in the MNC", **Human Resource Management**, Vol. 25, No. 1, pp. 55-71.

Doz, Y. L. and Prahalad, C. K. (1987), "A Process Model of Strategic Redirection in Large Complex Firms: The Case of Multinational Corporations" in Pettigrew, A., ed., **The Management of Strategic Change**. Oxford: Basil Blackwell, pp. 63-83.

Drucker, P. F. (1986), "Playing the Information-Based 'Orchestra'", **Advance Technology Alert System (ATAS) Bulletin**, Centre for Science and Technology for Development, United Nations Secretariat, New York, Issue 3, June, pp. 102-103.

Drucker, P. F. (1988), "The Coming of the New Organization", **Harvard Business Review**, Vol. 66, No. 1, pp. 45-53.

Duncan, R. B. (1979), "Qualitative Research Methods in Strategic Management" in Schendel, D. E. and Hofer, C. W., eds., **Strategic Management**. Boston, Mass.: Little, Brown and Company, pp. 424-447.

Dunning, J. H. (1981), **International Production and the Multinational Enterprise**. London: Allen & Unwin.

Dyas, G. P. and Tanheiser, H. T. (1976), **The Emerging European Enterprise: Strategy and Structure in French and German Industry**. London: Macmillan.

Dykert, L. (1984), "Datakommunikationer med utlandet: Stora företag och koncerner" ["Data communications with foreign countries: Large firms and corporations"], **Bohlins Revisionsbyrå AB**, March 14, Stockholm (mimeo).

Earl, M. J. (1987), "Information Systems Strategy Formulation" in Boland, R. J. Jr. and Hirschheim, R. A., eds., **Critical Issues in Information Systems Research**. Chichester: John Wiley & Sons, pp. 157-178.

Earl, M. J. (1988), "IT and Strategic Advantage: A Framework of Frameworks" in Earl, M. J., ed., **Information Management: The Strategic Dimension**. Oxford: Clarendon Press, pp. 33-53.

Earl, M. J. (1989), **Management Strategies for Information Technology**. Englewood Cliffs, N.J.: Prentice-Hall.

Eaton, J. and Smithers, J. (1982), **This Is It**. Oxford: Philip Allan Publishers.

Ebenfield, H. and Jussawalla, M., eds. (1984), **Communication and Information Economics**. Amsterdam: North-Holland/Elsevier Science Publishers.

Eckelmann, R. (1983), "A Study of the International Competitive Position of the U.S. Telecommunications Equipment Industry" in **U.S. Department of Commerce**, "The Telecommunications Industry", International Trade Administration, Washington, D.C.

Egelhoff, W. G. (1982), "Strategy and Structure in Multinational Corporations: An Information Processing Approach", **Administrative Science Quarterly**, Vol. 27, No. 3, pp. 435-458.

Egelhoff, W. G. (1984), "Patterns of Control in U.S., U.K., and European Multinational Corporations", **Journal of International Business Studies**, Vol. 15, No. 2, pp. 73-83.

Egelhoff, W. G. (1988a), **Organizing the Multinational Enterprise: An Information Processing Perspective**. Cambridge, Mass.: Ballinger Publishing Company.

Egelhoff, W. G. (1988b), "Strategy and Structure in Multinational Corporations: A Revision of the Stopford and Wells Model", **Strategic Management Journal**, Vol. 9, No. 1, pp. 1-14.

Eliasson, G., Fölster, S., Lindberg, T., Pousette, T. and Taymaz, E. (1990), **The Knowledge Based Information Economy**. Stockholm: Almqvist & Wicksell International.

Ergas, H. (1984), "Corporate Strategies in Transition" in Jacquemin, A., ed., **European Industry: Public Policy and Corporate Strategy**. Oxford: Clarendon Press, pp. 327-342.

Feketekuty, G. and Aronson, J. D. (1984), "Meeting the Challenges of the World Information Economy", **World Economy**, Vol. 7, No. 1, pp. 63-86.

Feldman, M. S. and March, J. G. (1981), "Information in Organizations as Signal and Symbol", **Administrative Science Quarterly**, Vol. 26, No. 2, pp. 171-186.

Flaherty, M. T. (1986), "Coordinating International Manufacturing and Technology" in Porter, M. E., ed., **Competition in Global Industries**. Boston, Mass.: Harvard Business School Press, pp. 83-109.

Forsgren, M. (1990), "Managing the International Multi-Centre Firm: Case Studies from Sweden", **European Management Journal**, Vol. 8, No. 2, pp. 261-267.

Foster, L. W. and Flynn, D. M. (1984), "Management Information Technology: Its Effects on Organizational Form and Function", **MIS Quarterly**, Vol. 8, No. 4, pp. 229-235.

Francis, A. (1985), "Work Organisation, Industrial Organisation and New Technology: Some Research Questions", **Economic and Social Research Council**, October, London (mimeo).

Francis, A. (1986), **New Technology at Work**. Oxford: Clarendon Press.

Franko, L. G. (1976), **The European Multinationals: A Renewed Challenge to American and British Big Business**. Stamford, Conn.: Greylock Publishing.

Franz, C. R. and Robey, D. (1987) "Strategies for Research on Information Systems in Organizations: A Critical Analysis of Research Purpose and Time Frame" in Boland, R. J. Jr. and Hirschheim, R. A., eds., **Critical Issues in Information Systems Research**. Chichester: John Wiley & Sons, pp. 205-225.

Fredriksson, O., Holmlöv, P. G. and Julander, C.-R. (1987), "Distribution av varor och tjänster i informationssamhället" ["Distribution of goods and services in the information society"], MA Rapport, **Economic Research Institute at the Stockholm School of Economics**, Stockholm.

Freese, J. (1979), **Data över gränserna** [Data across borders]. Lund: Studentlitteratur.

Fries, H. (1984a), "Datateknik och koncernstyrning - fyra fallstudier" ["Computer technology and corporate management - four case studies"] in Industridepartementet (1984), **Det moderna företaget - studier av organisation och styrsystem**. Stockholm: Liber, Ds I 1984:3, pp. 137-228.

Fries, H. (1984b), "Datateknik och koncernstyrning - fyra fallstudier" ["Computer technology and corporate management - four case studies"] in Eliasson et al., **Hur styrs storföretag?** Stockholm: Industriens Utredningsinstitut & LiberFörlag, pp. 129-190.

Galbraith, J. R. (1973), **Designing Complex Organizations**. Reading, Mass.: Addison-Wesley.

Galbraith, J. R. (1977), **Organization Design**. Reading, Mass.: Addison-Wesley.

Galbraith, J. R. and Kazanjian, R. K. (1986), **Strategy Implementation: Structure, Systems, and Process** (2nd edn.). St. Paul, Minn.: West Publishing Company.

Galbraith, J. R. and Nathanson, D. A. (1978), **Strategy Implementation: The Role of Structure and Process**. St Paul, Minn.: West Publishing Company.

Gassman, H. P. (1980), "Introduction by the Secretariat" in OECD, **Policy Implications of Data Network Developments in the OECD Area** (No. 3 in the "Information, Computer and Communications Policy" Series). Paris: OECD, pp. 11-19.

Gates, S. R. and Egelhoff, W. G. (1986), "Centralization in Headquarters-Subsidiary Relationships", **Journal of International Business Studies**, Vol. 17, No. 2, pp. 71-92.

Gershuny, J. I. and Miles, I. D. (1983), **The New Service Economy: The Transformation of Employment in Industrial Societies**. London: Frances Pinter (Publishers).

Gerstein, M. S. (1987), **The Technology Connection: Strategy and Change in the Information Age**. Reading, Mass.: Addison-Wesley.

Ghoshal, S. and Bartlett, C. A. (1990), "The Multinational Corporation as an Interorganizational Network", **Academy of Management Review**, Vol. 15, No. 4, pp. 603-625.

Ghoshal, S. and Nohria, N. (1989), "Internal Differentiation within Multinational Corporations", **Strategic Management Journal**, Vol. 10, No. 4, pp. 323-337.

Glaser, B. G. and Strauss, A. L. (1967), **The Discovery of Grounded Theory: Strategies for Qualitative Research**. Chicago, Ill.: Aldine Publishing Company.

Graham, E. M. (1978), "Transatlantic Investment by Multinational Firms: A Rivalistic Phenomenon?", **Journal of Post Keynesian Economics**, Vol. 1, No. 1, pp. 82-99.

Gremillion, L. L. and Pyburn, P. (1988), **Computers and Information Systems in Business: An Introduction**. New York, N.Y.: McGraw-Hill.

Hägg, I. and Hedlund, G. (1978), "'Case Studies' in Accounting Research", **Accounting, Organizations and Society**, Vol. 4, No. 1/2, pp. 135-143.

Hagström, P. (1987), "Linking New Information Systems to Corporate Strategy and Structure: The SKF Experience", Research Paper 87/11, **Institute of International Business**, Stockholm School of Economics, Stockholm.

Hagström, P. (1988), "New Information Systems in MNCs: Outline of a Research Project", Research Paper 88/3, **Institute of International Business**, Stockholm School of Economics, Stockholm.

Hagström, P. (1990a), "New Information Systems and the Changing Structure of MNCs" in Bartlett, C. A., Doz, Y. L. and Hedlund, G., eds., **Managing the Global Firm**. London: Routledge, pp. 164-185.

Hagström, P. (1990b), "Unshackling Corporate Geography", **Geografiska Annaler**, Series B, Human Geography, Vol. 72 B, No. 1, pp. 3-12 [Reprinted here as Appendix 2].

Hagström, P. (1991), "Inside the 'Wired' MNC" forthcoming in Antonelli, C., ed., **The Economics of Information Networks**. Amsterdam: North Holland/Elsevier Science Publishers, (provisionally) pp. 305-325.

Haig, R. M. (1926), "Toward an Understanding of the Metropolis: II. The Assignment of Activities to Areas in Urban Regions", **Quarterly Journal of Economics**, Vol. XL, pp. 402-434.

Håkanson, L. (1979), "Towards a Theory of Location and Corporate Growth" in Hamilton, F. E. I. and Linge, G. J. R., eds., **Spatial Analysis, Industry and the Industrial Environment; Volume I: Industrial Systems**. Chichester: John Wiley & Sons, pp. 115-138.

Håkanson, L. (1990), "International Decentralization of R&D: The Organizational Challenge" in Bartlett, C. A., Doz, Y. L. and Hedlund, G., eds., **Managing the Global Firm**. London: Routledge, pp. 256-278.

Hall, D. J. and Saias, M. A. (1980), "Strategy Follows Structure!", **Strategic Management Journal**, Vol. 1, No. 2, pp. 149-163.

Hauptman, O. and Allen, T. J. (1987), "The Influence of Communication Technologies on Organizational Structure: A Conceptual Model for Future Research", 90s Working Paper 87-038 and Sloan WP # 1892-87, **Management in the 1990s, Sloan School of Management**, Massachusetts Institute of Technology, Cambridge, Mass.

Hawken, P. (1984), **The Next Economy**. London: Angus and Robertson.

Hayes, R. H. and Abernathy, W. J. (1980), "Managing Our Way to Economic Decline", **Harvard Business Review**, Vol. 58, No. 4, pp. 71-79.

Hedlund, G. (1980), "The Role of Foreign Subsidiaries in Strategic Decision-Making in Swedish Multinational Corporations", **Strategic Management Journal**, Vol. 1, No. 1, pp. 23-36.

Hedlund, G. (1981), "Autonomy of Subsidiaries and Formalization of Headquarters-Subsidiary Relationships in Swedish MNCs" in Otterbeck, L., ed., **The Management of Headquarters-Subsidiary Relationships in Multinational Corporations**. Aldershot: Gower, pp. 25-78.

Hedlund, G. (1984), Organization In-Between: The Evolution of the Mother-Daughter Structure of Managing Foreign Subsidiaries in Swedish MNCs", **Journal of International Business Studies**, Vol. 15, No. 2, pp. 109-123.

Hedlund, G. (1986), "The Hypermodern MNC - A Heterarchy?", **Human Resource Management**, Vol. 25, No. 1, pp. 9-35.

Hedlund, G. (1991a), "Assumptions of Hierarchy and Heterarchy: An Application to Multinational Corporations" forthcoming in Ghoshal, S. and Westney, E., eds., **Organization Theory and the Multinational Corporation.**

Hedlund, G., ed. (1991b), **Organization and Management of the TNC**. New York, N.Y.: United Nations Centre on Transnational Corporations (forthcoming).

Hedlund, G. and Åman, P. (1983), **Managing Relationships with Foreign Subsidiaries**. Stockholm: Sveriges Mekanförbund.

Hedlund, G. and Hagström, P. (1986), "Styrning av Multinationella Företag: Utvecklingstendenser och Framtidsperspektiv" ["Management of Multinational Corporations: Development and Perspectives"], Research Paper 86/7, **Institute of International Business**, Stockholm School of Economics, Stockholm.

Hedlund, G. and Rolander, D. (1990), "Action in Heterarchies: New Approaches to Managing the MNC" in Bartlett, C. A., Doz, Y. L. and Hedlund, G., eds., **Managing the Global Firm**. London: Routledge, pp. 15-46.

Hennart, J. F. (1982), **A Theory of Multinational Enterprise**. Ann Arbor, Mich.: University of Michigan Press.

Hennart, J. F. (1986), "What Is Internalization", **Weltwirtschaftliches Archiv**, Vol. 122, No. 4, pp. 791-804.

von Hippel, E. (1976), "The Dominant Role of Users in the Scientific Instrument Innovation Process", **Research Policy**, Vol. 5, No. 3, pp. 212-239.

von Hippel, E. (1982), "Get New Products from Customers", **Harvard Business Review**, Vol. 60, No. 2, pp. 117-122.

Hopper, M. D. (1990), "Rattling SABRE - New Ways to Compete on Information", **Harvard Business Review**, Vol. 68, No. 3, pp. 118-125.

Hörnell, E. and Vahlne, J.-E. (1986), **Multinationals: The Swedish Case**. London: Croom Helm.

Hout, T., Porter, M. E. and Rudden, E. (1982), "How Global Companies Win Out", **Harvard Business Review**, Vol. 60, No. 5, pp. 98-108.

Huber, G. P. (1984), "The Nature and Design of Post-Industrial Organizations", **Management Science**, Vol. 30, No. 8, pp. 928-951.

Huber, G. P. (1990), "A Theory of the Effects of Advanced Information Technologies on Organizational Design, Intelligence, and Decision Making", **Academy of Management Review**, Vol. 15, No. 1, pp. 47-71.

Hughes, P. and Sasson, R. (1980), "The Usage of International Data Networks in Europe" in OECD, **Policy Implications of Data Network Developments in the OECD Area** (No. 3 in the "Information, Computer and Communications Policy" Series). Paris: OECD, pp. 25-34.

Hymer, S. H. (1976/1960), **The International Operations of National Firms: A Study of Direct Investment**. Cambridge, Mass.: The MIT Press (previously unpublished doctoral dissertation, MIT, 1960).

Inose, H. and Pierce, J. R. (1984), **Information Technology and Civilization**. New York, N.Y.: W. H. Freeman and Company.

International Organization for Standardization (1986), "Open Systems Interconnection", **Advance Technology Alert System (ATAS) Bulletin**, Centre for Science and Technology for Development, United Nations Secretariat, New York, Issue 3, June, pp. 33-34.

Jarillo, J. C. and Martínez, J. I. (1990), "Different Roles for Subsidiaries", **Strategic Management Journal**, Vol. 11, No. 7, pp. 501-512.

Jellis, J. (1988), "Information Management: Meaning and Learning", **International Journal of Information Management**, Vol. 8, No. 1, pp. 35-42.

Johanson, J. and Mattson, L.-G. (1988), "Internationalization in Industrial Systems - A Network Approach" in Hood, N. and Vahlne, J.-E., eds., **Strategies in Global Competiotion**. London: Croom Helm, pp. 287-314.

Johanson, J. and Vahlne, J. -E. (1977), "The Internationalization Process of the Firm - A Model of Knowledge Development and Increasing Market Commitments", **Journal of International Business Studies**, Vol. 8, No. 2, pp. 23-32.

Johanson, J. and Vahlne, J. -E. (1990), "The Mechanism of Internationalization", **International Marketing Review**, Vol. 7, No. 4, pp. 11-24.

Jussawalla, M. and Cheah, C.-W. (1983), "Emerging Economic Constraints on Transborder Data Flows", **Telecommunications Policy**, Vol. 7, No. 4, pp. 285-296.

Jussawallah, M. and Ebenfield, eds. (1984), **Communication and Information Economics: New Perspectives**. Amsterdam: North Holland/Elsevier Science Publishers.

Kagono, T. (1981), "Structural Design of Headquarters-Division Relationships and Economic Performance: An Analysis of Japanese Firms" in Otterbeck, L., ed., **The Management of Headquarters-Subsidiary Relationships in Multinational Corporations**. Aldershot: Gower, pp. 147-185.

Kane, M. J. and Ricks, D. A. (1989), "The Impact of Transborder Data Flow Regulation on Large United States-Based Corporations", **Columbia Journal of World Business**, Vol. 24, No. 2, pp. 23-29.

Kantrow, A. M. (1980), "The Strategy-Technology Connection", **Harvard Business Review**, Vol. 58, No. 4, pp. 6-16.

Keen, P. G. W. (1986), **Competing in Time: Using Telecommunications for Competitive Advantage**. Cambridge, Mass.: Ballinger Publishing Company.

Kiesler, S. (1986), "The Hidden Messages in Computer Networks", **Harvard Business Review**, Vol. 64, No. 1, pp. 46-48 and 52-60.

Kirsch, W. (1983), "Transborder Data Flows: A Current Review", **International Institute of Communications**, Tavistock House East, London.

Kish, L. (1959), "Some Statistical Problems in Research Design", **American Sociological Review**, Vol. 24, No. 1, pp. 328-338.

Kling, R. (1980), "Social Analyses of Computing: Theoretical Perspectives in Recent Empirical Research", (ACM) **Computing Surveys**, Vol. 12, No. 1, pp. 61-110.

Knickerbocker, F. T. (1973), **Oligopolistic Reaction and Multinational Enterprise**. Boston, Mass.: Graduate School of Business Administration, Harvard University.

Kogut, B. (1983), "Foreign Direct Investment as a Sequential Process" in Kindleberger, C. P. and Audretsch, D., eds., **The Multinational Corporation in the 1980s**. Cambridge, Mass.: The M.I.T. Press, pp. 38-56.

Kogut, B. (1989), "Research Notes and Communications: A Note on Global Strategies", **Strategic Management Journal**, Vol. 10, No. 4, pp. 383-389.

Kogut, B. (1990), "International Sequential Advantages and Network Flexibility" in Bartlett, C. A., Doz, Y. and Hedlund, G., eds., **Managing the Global Firm**. London: Routledge, pp. 47-68.

Kozmetsky, G. and Ruefli, T. W. (1972), "Newer Concepts of Management, Profits, Profitability" in **The Conference Board**, "Information Technology: Some Critical Implications for Decision Makers", New York, N.Y., pp. 61-95.

Kwon, T. H. and Zmud, R. W. (1987), "Unifying the Fragmented Models of Information Systems Implementation" in Boland, R. J. and Hirschheim R. A., eds., **Critical Issues in Information Systems Research**. Chichester: John Wiley & Sons, pp. 227-251.

Kuhn, T. S. (1962), **The Structure of Scientific Revolutions**. Chicago, Ill.: University of Chicago Press.

Langlois, R. N. (1984), "Internal Organization in a Dynamic Context: Some Theoretical Considerations" in Jussawalla, M. and Ebenfield, H., eds., **Communication and Information Economics: New Perspectives**. Amsterdam: North-Holland, pp. 23-49.

Lawrence, P. R. and Lorsch, J. W. (1969), **Organization and Environment**. Homewood, Ill.: Richard D. Irwin.

Leavitt, H. J. and Whisler, T. L. (1958), "Management in the 1980's", **Harvard Business Review**, Vol. 36, No. 6, pp. 41-48.

Lee, A. S. (1989), "A Scientific Methodology for MIS Case Studies", **MIS Quarterly**, Vol. 13, No. 1, pp. 33-50.

Leifer, R. (1988), "Matching Computer-Based Information Systems with Organizational Structures", **MIS Quarterly**, Vol. 12, No. 1, pp. 63-73.

Leksell, L. (1981), **Headquarter-Subsidiary Relationships in Multinational Corporations**. Stockholm: Institute of International Business and the Economic Research Institute, Stockholm School of Economics.

Lemak, D. J. and Bracker, J. S. (1988), "Research Notes and Communications: A Strategic Contingency Model of Multinational Corporate Structure", **Strategic Management Journal**, Vol. 9, No. 5, pp. 521-526.

Lessard, D. R. (1986), "Finance and Global Competition: Exploiting Financial Scope and Coping with Volatile Exchange Rates" in Porter, M. E., ed., **Competition in Global Industries**. Boston, Mass.: Harvard Business School Press, pp. 145-184.

Lessard, D. R. and Nohria, N. (1990), "Rediscovering Functions in the MNC: The Role of Expertise in Firms' Responses to Shifting Exchange Rates", in Bartlett, C. A., Doz, Y. and Hedlund, G., eds., **Managing the Global Firm**. London: Routledge, pp. 186-212.

Locke, R. M. and Antonelli, C. (1990), "International Competitiveness, Technological Change and Organizational Innovation: Strategy and Structure of the Italian Apparel Industry in the 1980's" in Lessard, D. and Antonelli, C., eds., **Managing the Globalization of Business**. Naples: Editoriale Scientifica, pp. 151-173.

Lyytinen, K. (1987), "A Taxonomic Perspective of Information Systems Development: Theoretical Constructs and Recommendations" in Boland, R. J. Jr. and Hirschheim, R. A., eds., **Critical Issues in Information Systems Research**. Chichester: John Wiley & Sons, pp. 3-41.

McDermott P. and Taylor, M. J. (1982), **Industrial Organization and Location**. Cambridge: Cambridge University Press.

McFarlan, F. W. (1984a), "Current Research Issues: An Alternative Perspective Discussion" in McFarlan, F. W., ed., **The Information Systems Research Challenge**. Boston, Mass.: Harvard Business School Press, pp. 309-322.

McFarlan, F. W. (1984b), "Information Technology Changes the Way You Compete", **Harvard Business Review**, Vol. 62, No. 3, pp. 98-103.

McFarlan, F. W., ed. (1984c), **The Information Systems Research Challenge**. Boston, Mass.: Harvard Business School Press.

McFarlan, F. W. and McKenney, J. L. (1983), **Corporate Information Systems Management: The Issues Facing Senior Executives**. Homewood, Ill.: Richard D. Irwin.

McFarlan, F. W., McKenney, J. L. and Pyburn, P. (1983), "The Information Archipelago - Plotting a Course", **Harvard Business Review**, Vol. 61, No. 1, pp. 145-156.

McGee, J. and Thomas, H. (1988), "Technology and Strategic Management: A Research Review" in Earl, M. J., ed., **Information Management: The Strategic Dimension**. Oxford: Clarendon Press, pp. 7-32.

McKenney, J. L. and McFarlan, F. W. (1982), "The Information Archipelago - Maps and Bridges", **Harvard Bussiness Review**, Vol. 60, No. 5, pp. 109-119.

McLuhan, M. (1964), **Understanding Media**. London: Routledge and Kegan Paul.

McNee, R. (1974), "A Systems Approach of Understanding the Geographic Behaviour of Organizations, Especially Large Corporations" in Hamilton, F. E. I., ed., **Spatial Perspectives on Industrial Organization and Decision-making**. London: John Wiley & Sons, pp. 47-75.

Malone, T. W., Yates, J. and Benjamin, R. I. (1989), "The Logic of Electronic Markets", **Harvard Business Review**, Vol. 67, No. 3, pp. 166-170.

Mandeville, T. D. (1983), "Spatial Effects of IT", **Futures**, Vol. 15, No. 1, pp. 65-72.

Mansell, R., Holmes, P. and Morgan, K. (1990), "European Integration and Telecommunications: Restructuring Markets and Institutions", **Prometheus**, Vol. 8, No. 1, pp. 50-66.

Markus, M. L. and Robey, D. (1983), "The Organizational Validity of Management Information Systems", **Human Relations**, Vol. 36, No. 3, pp. 203-226.

Markus, M. L. and Robey, D. (1988), "Information Technology and Organizational Change: Causal Structure in Theory and Research", **Management Science**, Vol. 34, No. 5, pp. 583-598.

Martin, J. (1981a), **Computer Networks and Distributed Processing**. Englewood Cliffs, N.J.: Prentice-Hall.

Martin, J. (1981b), **Telematic Society**. Englewood Cliffs, N.J.: Prentice-Hall.

Martínez, J. I. (1987), "The Evolving Nature of Coordination Mechanisms in MNCs: A Framework and a Survey", Research Paper No. 125, **Instituto de Estudios Superiores de la Empresa**, Universidad de Navarra, Barcelona.

Martínez, J. I. and Jarillo, J. C. (1989), "The Evolution of Research on Coordination Mechanisms in Multinational Corporations", **Journal of International Business Studies**, Vol. 20, No. 3, pp. 489-514.

Mason, R. O. (1984), "Current Research Issues" in McFarlan, F. W., ed., **The Information Systems Research Challenge**. Boston, Mass.: Harvard Business School Press, pp. 279-304.

Masuda, Y. (1984), **Informationssamhället** (translation from: The Information Society. Tokyo: Institute for the Information Society, 1980). Stockholm: LiberFörlag.

Miles, I., Rush, H., Turner, K. and Bessant, J. (1988), **Information Horizons: The Long-Term Social Implications of New Information Technologies**. Aldershot: Edward Elgar Publishing.

Miles, M. B. (1979), "Qualitative Data as an Attractive Nuisance: The Problem of Analysis", **Administrative Science Quarterly**, Vol. 24, No. 4, pp. 590-601.

Miles, R. E. and Snow, C. C. (1986), "Organizations: New Concepts for New Forms", **California Management Review**, Vol. XXVIII, No. 3, pp. 62-73.

Millar, V. E. (1984), "Decision-Oriented Information", **Datamation**, Vol. 30, No. 1, pp. 159-162.

Miller, J. G. (1972), "Living Systems: The Organization", **Behavioral Science**, Vol. 17, No. 1, pp. 1-182.

Mintzberg, H. (1979), **The Structuring of Organizations**. Englewood Cliffs, N.J.: Prentice-Hall.

Mohrman, A. M. Jr. and Lawler, E. E. III (1984), "A Review of Theory and Research" in McFarlan, F. W., ed., **The Information Systems Research Challenge**. Boston, Mass.: Harvard Business School Press, pp. 135-164.

Morgan, G. (1986), **Images of Organization**. Beverly Hills, Calif.: Sage Publications.

Nanus, B. (1969), "The Multinational Computer", **Columbia Journal of World Business**, Vol. IV, No. 6, pp. 7-14.

Nanus, B. (1978), "Business, Government and the Multinational Computer", **Columbia Journal of World Business**, Vol. XIII, No. 1, pp. 19-26.

Nolan, R. L. (1982), "Managing Information Systems by Committee", **Harvard Business Review**, Vol. 60, No. 4, pp. 72-80.

Nonaka, I. (1988), "Toward Middle-Up-Down Management: Accelerating Information Creation", **Sloan Management Review**, Vol. 29, No. 3, pp. 9-18.

Nonaka, I. (1990), "Managing Globalization as a Self-Renewing Process: Experiences of Japanese MNCs" in Bartlett, C. A., Doz, Y. and Hedlund, G., eds., **Managing the Global Firm**. London: Routledge, pp. 69-94.

Nora, S. and Minc, A. (1978), **L'informatisation de la société**. Paris: La Documentation Française and Editions du Seuil.

Normann, R. (1975), **Skapande företagsledning** [Creative management]. Stockholm: Aldus.

North, D. J. (1974), "The Process of Locational Change in Different Manufacturing Organizations" in Hamilton, F. E. I., ed., **Spatial Perspectives on Industrial Organization and Decision-making**. London: John Wiley & Sons, pp. 213-244.

OECD (1980), **Policy Implications of Data Network Developments in the OECD Area** (No. 3 in the "Information, Computer and Communications Policy" Series). Paris: OECD.

OECD, (1981), **Information Activities, Electronics and Telecommunications Technologies** (No. 6 in the "Information, Computer and Communications Policy" Series). Paris: OECD.

OECD (1983a), "Preliminary Interpretations of a OECD/BIAC Survey", **Directorate for Science, Technology and Industry**, Committee for Information, Computer and Communications Policy, DSTI/ICCP/83.19, Paris.

OECD (1983b), "Trade in Information, Computer and Communications Services", **Committee for Information, Computer and Communications Policy**, ICCP (83)12, Paris.

OECD (1983c), "Transborder Data Flows in International Enterprises: Based on Results of a Joint BIAC/OECD Survey and Interviews with Firms" (Note by the Secretariat), **Directorate for Science, Technology and Industry**, Committee for Information, Computer and Communications Policy, DSTI/ICCP/83.23, Paris.

OECD (1987), **Trends of Change in Telecommunications Policy** (No. 13 in the "Information, Computer and Communications Policy" Series). Paris: OECD.

OECD-BRIE (1989), "Information Networks and Business Strategies: An OECD-BRIE Project on Competitiveness and Telecommunications Policy", BRIE Working Paper 38, **Berkeley Roundtable on the International Economy**, University of California, Berkeley.

Olson, M. H. and Chervany, N. L. (1980), "The Relationship Beween Organizational Characteristics and the Structure of the Information Services Function", **MIS Quarterly**, Vol. 4, No. 2, pp. 57-68.

Otterbeck, L. (1981), "Introduction and Overview" and "Concluding Remarks - And a Review of Subsidiary Autonomy" in Otterbeck, L., ed., **The Management of Headquarters-Subsidiary Relationships in Multinational Corporations**. Aldershot: Gower, pp. 1-9 and 337-343.

The Oxford English Dictionary (1971). Oxford: Oxford University Press.

Palmer, D., Friedland, R., Jennings, P. D. and Powers, M. E. (1987), "The Economics and Politics of Structure: The Multidivisional Form and the Large U.S. Corporation", **Administrative Science Quarterly**, Vol. 32, No. 1, pp. 25-48.

Parry, T. G. (1983), "Multinational Enterprises' Structure and Transborder Data Flows: Main Trends in the Evolution of Multinational Enterprise Structure", **Directorate for Science, Technology and Industry**, Committee for Information, Computer and Communications Policy, DSTI/ICCP/83.24, Paris.

Parsons, G. L. (1983), "Information Technology: A New Competitive Weapon", **Sloan Management Review**, Vol. 25, No. 1, pp. 3-14.

Pava, C. H. P. (1983), **Managing New Office Technology: An Organizational Strategy**. New York, N.Y.: The Free Press.

Pennings, J. M. (1975), "The Relevance of the Structural-Contingency Model for Organizational Effectiveness", **Administrative Science Quarterly**, Vol. 20, No. 3, September, pp. 393-410.

Perlmutter, H. V. (1969), "The Tortous Evolution of the Multinational Corporation", **Columbia Journal of World Business**, Vol. IV, No. 1, pp. 9-18.

Perlmutter, H. V. (1984), "Building the Symbiotic Societal Enterprise: A Social Architecture for the Future", **World Futures**, Vol. 19, No. 3/4, pp. 271-284.

Perrow, C. (1977), "The Bureaucratic Paradox: The Efficient Organization Centralizes in Order to Decentralize", **Organizational Dynamics**, Vol. 5, No. 1, pp. 2-14.

Perrow, C. (1986/1972), **Complex Organizations: A Critical Essay**. New York, N.Y.: Random House (3rd edn., 1st edn. 1972).

Pettigrew, A. M. (1985), "Contextualist Research: A Natural Way to link Theory and Practice" in Lawler, E. E. III, ed., **Doing Research That Is Useful in Theory and Practice**. San Francisco, Calif.: Jossey-Bass, pp. 222-274.

Pfeffer, J. and Leblebici, H. (1977), "Information Technology and Organizational Structure", **Pacific Sociological Review**, Vol. 20, No. 2, pp. 241-261.

Pfeffer, J. and Salancik, G. R. (1978), **The External Control of Organizations: A Resource Dependence Perspective**. New York, N.Y.: Harper and Row.

Piore, M. J. and Sabel, C. F. (1984), **The Second Industrial Divide: Possibilities for Prosperity**. New York, N.Y.: Basic Books, Publishers.

Pitts, R. A. and Daniels, D. D. (1984), "Aftermath of the Matrix Mania", **Columbia Journal of World Business**, Vol. XIX, No. 2, pp. 48-54.

Pool, I. de Sola (1983), **Forecasting the Telephone: A Retrospective Technology Assessment**. Norwood, N.J.: Ablex Publishing Corporation.

Pool, I. de Sola and Solomon, R. J. (1980), "Transborder Data Flows: Requirements for International Co-operation" in OECD, **Policy Implications of Data Network Developments in the OECD Area** (No. 3 in the "Information, Computer and Communications Policy" Series). Paris: OECD, pp. 79-139.

Poppel, H. L. (1982), "Who Needs the Office of the Future?", **Harvard Business Review**, Vol. 60, No. 6, pp. 146-155.

Popper, K. L. (1968/1934), **The Logic of Scientific Discovery**. New York, N.Y.: Harper and Row, Publishers (originally published as **Logik der Forschung** in 1934).

Porat, M. U. (1977), "The Information Economy: Definition and Measurement", **U.S. Department of Commerce**, U.S. Government Printing Office, Washington, D.C.

Porter, M. E. (1985), **Competitive Advantage**. New York, N.Y.: The Free Press.

Porter, M. E. (1986a), "Changing Patterns of International Competition", **California Management Review**, Vol. XXVIII, No. 2, pp. 9-40.

Porter, M. E. (1986b), "Competition in Global Industries: A Conceptual Framework" in Porter, M. E., ed., **Competition in Global Industries**. Boston, Mass.: Harvard Business School Press, pp. 15-60.

Porter, M. E. (1990), **The Competitive Advantage of Nations**. New York, N.Y.: The Free Press.

Porter, M. E. and Millar, V. E. (1985), "How Information Gives You Competitive Advantage", **Harvard Business Review**, Vol. 63, No. 4, pp. 149-160.

Pousette, T. (1983), "Datakommunikation i företag" ["Data communications in firms"], Rapport nr. 9, **Teldok**, Stockholm and Forskningsrapport nr. 24, **Industriens Utredningsinstitut**, Stockholm.

Powell, W. W. (1987), "Hybrid Organizational Arrangements: New Form or Transitional Development?", **California Management Review**, Vol. 30, No. 1, pp. 67-87.

Prahalad, C. K. (1975), "The Strategic Process in a Multinational Corporation", **Harvard Graduate School of Business Administration**, Harvard University, Boston, Mass. (unpublished doctoral dissertation).

Prahalad, C. K. (1976), "Strategic Choices in Diversified MNCs", **Harvard Business Review**, Vol. 54, No. 4, pp. 67-78.

Prahalad, C. K. and Doz, Y. L. (1981), "Strategic Control - The Dilemma in Headquarters-Subsidiary Relationship[s]" in Otterbeck, L., ed., **The Management of Headquarters-Subsidiary Relationships in Multinational Corporations**. Aldershot: Gower, pp. 187-203.

Prahalad, C. K. and Doz, Y. L. (1987), **The Multinational Mission: Balancing Local Demands and Global Vision**. New York, N.Y.: The Free Press.

Pugh, D. S. (1973), "The Measurement of Organization Structures: Does Context Determine Form", **Organization Dynamics**, Vol. X, No. 1, pp. 19-34.

Pugh, D. S., Hickson, D. J., Hinings, C. R., Macdonald, K. M., Turner, C. and Lupton, T. (1963), "A Conceptual Scheme for Organizational Analysis", **Administrative Science Quarterly**, Vol. 8, No. 3, pp. 289-315.

Pugh, D. S., Hickson, D. J., Hinings, C. R. and Turner, C. (1968), "Dimensions of Organization Structure", **Administrative Science Quarterly**, Vol. 13, No. 1, pp. 65-105.

RDF (1984), "Datakommunikation i 80-talets centrum" ["Data communications in the center of the 80s"], Rapport nr. 19, **Riksdataförbundet**, Stockholm.

Robey, D. (1977), "Computers and Management Structure: Some Empirical Findings Re-examined", **Human Relations**, Vol. 30, No. 11, pp. 963-976.

Robey, D. (1981), "Computer Information Systems and Organization Structure", **Communications of the ACM** (Association for Computing Machinery), Vol. 24, No. 10, pp. 679-687.

Robey, D. (1986), **Designing Organizations** (2nd edn.). Homewood, Ill.: Richard D. Irwin.

Robinson, R. D. (1978), **International Business Management: A Guide to Decision Making** (2nd edn.). Hinsdale, Ill.: The Dryden Press.

Robinson, R. D. (1984), **Internationalization of Business: An Introduction**. Chicago, Ill.: The Dryden Press.

Robinson, R. D. (1987), "Preface" in Robinson, R. D., ed., **Direct Foreign Investment: Costs and Benefits**. New York, N.Y.: Praeger Publishers.

Rockart, J. F. (1988), "The Line Takes the Leadership - IS Management in a Wired Society", **Sloan Management Review**, Vol. 29, No. 4, pp. 57-64.

Rockart, J. F. and Scott Morton, M. F. (1984), "Implications of Changes in Information Technology for Corporate Strategy", **Interfaces**, Vol. 14, No. 1, pp. 84-95.

Rockart, J. F. and Short, J. E. (1989), "IT in the 1990s: Managing Organizational Interdependence", **Sloan Management Review**, Vol. 30, No. 2, pp. 7-17.

Rogers, E. M. (1984), "A Sociological Research Perspective" in McFarlan, F. W., ed., **The Information Systems Research Challenge**. Boston, Mass.: Harvard Business School Press, pp. 167-179.

Rugman, A. M. (1982), "Internalization and Non-Equity Forms of International Involvement" in Rugman, A. M., ed., **New Theories of the Multinational Enterprise**. London: Croom Helm, pp. 9-23.

Rumelt, R. P. (1981), "The Electronic Reorganization of Industry", Paper presented at the **Conference of the Strategic Management Society**, London, October.

Sambharya, R. B. and Phatak, A. (1990), "The Effects of Transborder Data Flow Restrictions on American Multinational Corporations", **Management International Review**, Vol. 30, No. 3, pp. 267-289.

Samiee, S. (1984), "Transnational Data Flow Constraints: A New Challenge for Multinational Corporations", **Journal of International Business Studies**, Vol. 15, No. 1, pp. 141-150.

Sauvant, K. P. (1983), "Transborder Data Flows and the Developing Countries", **International Organization**, Vol. 37, No. 2, pp. 359-371.

Sauvant, K. P. (1986), "The International Politics of Trade in Data Services", **Advance Technology Alert System (ATAS) Bulletin**, Centre for Science and Technology for Development, United Nations Secretariat, New York, Issue 3, June, pp. 153-156.

Schaik, E. A. van (1985), **A Management System for the Information Business: Organizational Analysis**. Englewood Cliffs, N.J.: Prentice-Hall, Inc.

Schoonhoven, C. B. (1981), "Problems with Contingency Theory: Testing Assumptions Hidden within the Language of Contingency 'Theory'", **Administrative Science Quarterly**, Vol. 26, No. 3, pp. 349-377.

Schumann, G. (1984), "The Macro- and Microeconomic Social Impact of Advanced Computer Technology", **Futures**, Vol. 16, No. 3, pp. 260-285.

Scott, B. R. (1973), "The Industrial State: Old Myths and New Realities", **Harvard Business Review**, Vol. 51, No. 2, pp. 133-148.

Scott, G. M. (1986), **Principles of Management Information Systems**. New York, N.Y.: McGraw-Hill Book Company.

Scott, W. R. (1987), **Organizations: Rational, Natural, and Open Systems** (2nd edn.). Englewood Cliffs, N.J.: Prentice-Hall.

Scott Morton, M. S. (1988), "Strategy Formulation Methodologies and IT" in Earl, M. J., ed., **Information Management: The Strategic Dimension**. Oxford: Clarendon Press, pp. 54-67.

Scott Morton, M. S. (1984), "The State of the Art of Research" in McFarlan, F. W., ed., **The Information Systems Research Challenge**. Boston, Mass.: Harvard Business School Press, pp. 13-41.

Seitz, N. B. (1980), "Data Communication and Data Processing: A Basis for Definition", **Telecommunications Policy**, Vol. 4, No. 1, pp. 49-62.

Shannon, C. E. and Weaver, W. (1963/1949), **The Mathematical Theory of Communication**. Urbana, Ill.: University of Illinois Press (originally published 1949).

Shelp, R. K. (1981), **Beyond Industrialization: Ascendancy of the Global Service Economy**. New York, N.Y.: Praeger Publishers.

Simon, H. A. (1977), **The New Science of Management Decision**. Englewood Cliffs, N.J.: Prentice-Hall.

Sinclair, S. W. (1986), "Information Technology and Strategy Revisited", **Multinational Business Quarterly**, No. 4, pp. 8-15.

SKF (1990), **Annual Report 1990**. Gothenburg.

Smith, N. C. (1990), "The Case Study: A Useful Research Method for Information Management", **Journal of Information Technology**, Vol. 5, No. 3, pp. 123-133.

Snow, M. S. (1988), "Telecommunications Literature: A Critical Review of the Economic, Technological and Public Policy Issues", **Telecommunications Policy**, Vol. 12, No. 2, pp. 153-183.

Söderström, R. (1984), "Datakommunikationer med utlandet: Konkurrensmedel och marknad för svenska dataföretag" ["Data communications with other countries: Competitive tool and market for Swedish computer firms"], **Informotor Kommunikation AB**, April 10, Stockholm (mimeo).

Sölvell, Ö. (1987), **Entry Barriers and Foreign Penetration - Emerging Patterns of International Competition in Two Electrical Engineering Industries**. Stockholm: Institute of International Business, Stockholm School of Economics.

Stinchcombe, A. L. (1990), **Information and Organizations**. Berkeley, Calif.: University of California Press.

Stopford, J. M. and Wells, L. T. Jr. (1972), **Managing the Multinational Enterprise: Organization of the Firm and Ownership of the Subsidiaries**. New York, N.Y.: Basic Books.

Straub, D. W. and Wetherbe, J. C. (1989), "Information Technologies for the 1990s: An Organizational Impact Perspective", **Communications of the ACM** (Association for Computing Machinery), Vol. 32, No. 11, pp. 1328-1339.

Strauss, A. L. and Corbin, J. M. (1990), **Basics of Qualitative Research: Grounded Theory Procedures and Techniques**. Newbury Park, Calif.: Sage Publications.

Suomi, R. (1990), "Assessing the Feasibility of Inter-Organizational Information Systems on the Basis of the Transaction Cost Approach", **Publications of the Turku School of Economics and Business Administration**, Series A-3:1990, Turku.

Swanson, E. B. (1987), "Information Systems in Organization Theory: A Review" in Boland, R. J. Jr. and Hirschheim, R. A., eds., **Critical Issues in Information Systems Research**. Chichester: John Wiley & Sons Ltd., pp. 181-204.

Takeuchi, H. and Porter, M. E. (1986), "Three Roles of International Marketing in Global Strategy" in Porter, M. E., ed., **Competition in Global Industries**. Boston, Mass.: Harvard Business School Press, pp. 111-146.

Tanenbaum, A. S. (1989), **Computer Networks**. Englewood Cliffs, N.J.: Prentice-Hall International.

Tavakolian, H. (1989), "Linking the Information Technology Structure with Organizational Competitive Strategy: A Survey", **MIS Quarterly**, Vol. 13, No. 3, pp. 309-317.

Teece, D. (1985), "Multinational Enterprise, Internal Governance, and Industrial Organization", **American Economic Review**, Vol. 75, No. 1, pp. 233-238.

Teece, D. (1986), "Transaction Cost Economics and the Multinational Enterprise: An Assessment", **Journal of Economic Behavior and Organization**, Vol. 7, No. 1, pp. 21-45.

Thompson, J. D. (1967), **Organizations in Action**. New York: McGraw Hill Book Company.

Thorelli, H. B. (1986), "Networks: Between Markets and Hierarchies", **Strategic Management Journal**, Vol. 7, No. 1, pp. 37-51.

Thorngren, B. (1990), "The Swedish Road to Liberalization", **Telecommunications Policy**, Vol. 14, No. 2, pp. 94-98.

Toffler, A. (1980), **The Third Wave**. London: Collins.

Toyne, B. (1989), "International Exchange: A Foundation for Theory Building in International Business", **Journal of Internationall Business Studies**, Vol. 20, No. 1, pp. 1-17.

Trauth, E. M. (1986), "An Integrative Approach to Information Policy Research", **Telecommunications Policy**, Vol. 10, No. 1, pp. 41-50.

Tushman, M. L. (1977), "Special Boundary Roles in the Innovation Process", **Administrative Science Quarterly**, Vol. 22, No. 4, pp. 587-605.

Tushman, M. L. (1979), "Work Characteristics and Subunit Communication Structure: A Contingency Analysis", **Administrative Science Quarterly**, Vol. 24, No 1, pp. 82-98.

Tushman, M. L. and Nadler, D. A. (1978), "Information Processing as an Integrating Concept in Organizational Design", **Academy of Management Review**, Vol. 3, No. 3, pp. 613-624.

UNCTAD (1984), "Services and the Development Process", **United Nations Conference on Trade and Development**, The Secretariat, TD/B/1008, United Nations, Geneva.

UNCTC (1982), "Transnational Corporations and Transborder Data Flows: A Technical Paper", **United Nations Centre on Transnational Corporations**, ST/CTC/23, United Nations, New York.

UNCTC (1983), "Transborder Data Flows and Brazil: Brazilian Case Study", **United Nations Centre on Transnational Corporations**, ST/CTC, United Nations, New York.

UNCTC (1984), "Transborder Data Flows: Transnational Corporations and Remote-Sensing Data", **United Nations Centre on Transnational Corporations**, ST/CTC/51, United Nations, New York.

UNCTC (1988a), "Data Goods and Data Services in the Socialist Countries of Eastern Europe", **United Nations Centre on Transnational Corporations**, ST/CTC/80, United Nations, New York.

UNCTC (1988b), "Transnational Corporations in World Development: Trends and Prospects", **United Nations Centre on Transnational Corporations**, ST/CTC/89, United Nations, New York.

Ungerer, H. with Costello, N. P. (1988), "Telecommunications in Europe", **European Perspectives Series**, Commission of the European Communities, Brussels/Luxemburg.

Varis, T. (1976), "Aspects of the Impact of Transnational Corporations on Communications", **International Social Science Journal**, Vol. 28, No. 4, pp. 808-830.

Venkatraman, N. and Zaheer, A. (1990), "Electronic Integration and Strategic Advantage: A Quasi-Experimental Study in the Insurance Industry", **Information Systems Research**, Vol. 1, No. 4, pp. 377-393.

Vernon, R. (1966), "International Investment and International Trade in the Product Cycle", **Quarterly Journal of Economics**, Vol. 80, No. 2, pp. 190-207.

Vernon, R. (1979), "The Product Cycle Hypothesis in a New International Environment", **Oxford Bulletin of Economics and Statistics**, Vol. 41, No. 4, pp. 255-267.

Vitale, M. (1986), "The Growing Risks of Information Systems Success", **MIS Quarterly**, Vol. 10, No. 4, pp. 327-334.

Warner, T. N. (1987), "Information Technology as a Competitive Burden", **Sloan Management Review**, Vol. 29, No. 1, pp. 55-61.

Wärneryd, K. -E. (1985), "Management Research and Methodology", **Scandinavian Journal of Management Studies**, Vol. 2, No. 1, pp. 3-18.

Weick, K. E. (1983), "Organizational Communication: Toward a Research Agenda" in Putnam, L. L. and Pacanowsky, M. E., eds., **Coomunication and Organizations: An Interactive Approach**. Beverly Hills, Calif.: Sage Publications, pp. 13-29.

Weick, K. E. (1984), "Theoretical Assumptions and Research Methodology Selection" in McFarlan, F. W., ed., **The Information Systems Research Challenge**. Boston, Mass.: Harvard Business School Press, pp. 111-132.

Weick, K. E. (1985), "Cosmos vs. Chaos: Sense and Nonsense in Electronic Contexts", **Organizational Dynamics**, Vol. 13, No. 3, pp. 50-64.

Welge, M. K. (1981), "The Effective Design of Headquarter(s)-Subsidiary Relationships in German MNCs" in Otterbeck, L., ed., **The Management of Headquarters-Subsidiary Relationships in Multinational Corporations**. Aldershot: Gower, pp. 79-106.

Wells, L. T., ed. (1972), **The Product Life Cycle and International Trade**. Cambridge, Mass.: Harvard University Press.

Whisler, T. L. (1970), **The Impact of Computers on Organizations**. New York, N.Y.: Praeger Publishers.

Whitaker, M. and Miles, I. with Bessant, J. and Rush, H. (1989), **Bibliography of Information Technology: An Annotated Critical Bibliography of English Language Sources Since 1980**. Aldershot: Edward Elgar.

White, R. E. and Poynter, T. A. (1990), "Organizing for World-Wide Advantage" in Bartlett, C. A., Doz, Y. and Hedlund, G., eds., **Managing the Global Firm**. London: Routledge, pp. 95-113.

Williamson, O. E. (1975), **Markets and Hierarchies: Analysis and Antitrust Implications**. New York, N.Y.: The Free Press.

Williamson, O. E. (1981), "The Modern Corporation: Origins, Evolution, Attributes", **Journal of Economic Literature**, Vol. XIX, No. 4, pp. 1537-1568.

Williamson, O. E. (1985), **The Economic Institutions of Capitalism: Firms, Markets, Relational Contracting**. New York, N.Y.: The Free Press.

Williamson, O. E. (1989), "Transaction Cost Economics" in Schmalensee, R. and Willig, R., eds., **Handbook of Industrial Organization**, Vol. I. Amsterdam: North Holland, pp. 135-182.

Winograd, T. and Flores, F. (1986), **Understanding Computers and Cognition: A New Foundation for Design**. Norwood, N.J.: Ablex Publishing Corporation.

Wiseman, C. (1985), **Strategy and Computers: Information Systems as Competitive Weapons**. Homewood, Ill.: Dow Jones-Irwin.

Wolf, B. M. (1985), "The Bearing Industry: Rationalization in Europe" in Casson, M., ed., **Multinationals and World Trade**. London: Allen & Unwin, pp. 175-195.

Woodward, J. (1965), **Industrial Organization: Theory and Practice**. London: Oxford University Press.

Wynne, B. and Otway, H. J. (1982), "Information Technology, Power and Managers" in Björn-Andersen, N., Earl, M. J., Holst, O. and Mumford, E., eds., **Information Society: For Richer, for Poorer**. Amsterdam: North-Holland Publishing Company, pp. 207-217.

Yin, R. K. (1981), "The Case Study Crisis: Some Answers", **Administrative Science Quarterly**, Vol. 28, No. 1, pp. 58-65.

Yin, R. K. (1984), **Case Study Research: Design and Methods**. Beverly Hills, Calif.: Sage Publications.

Yoshino, M. Y. (1976), **Japan's Multinational Enterprises**. Cambridge, Mass.: Harvard University Press.

Zuboff, S. (1982), "New Worlds of Computer-Mediated Work", **Harvard Business Review**, Vol. 60, No. 5, pp. 142-153.

APPENDIX 1

THE ROLE OF

NEW INFORMATION SYSTEMS

IN THE MNC

A(nother) Case Study of SKF

Contents

1. INTRODUCTION

What is the role of international data communications and the related use of information systems in the way multinational corporations (MNCs) carry out and structure their activities? How can, and do, MNCs exploit the new means of communication? What are the longer-run implications thereof for the MNC as we now know it? - This study represents one approach in the quest to find answers to these over-arching questions.

In particular, we set out here to somewhat redress what we surmise to be the painful near-absence of empirical investigations in the area. To this end, an extensive case study of SKF has been carried out, trying to explore the various uses, and effects, of SKF's information systems infrastructure. SKF has been - and still is - very much of an international pace-setter in information systems usage, and is one of the singularly most internationalized MNCs to boot. Our hope - indeed, belief - is that SKF's experiences provide fertile ground for uncovering salient features of complex application of new information systems internationally, and for practitioners to learn from.

To our knowledge, no similar studies have been undertaken (not within SKF either, in the specific case), which does cast some doubt over the efficacy of the chosen approach, but that can arguably be seen instead as the main contribution of the investigation; viz. the attempt to provide a <u>comprehensive</u> view of the role of international data communications and attendant systems in an MNC[1]. In the process, a novel conceptual separation of the communications network from the systems available on the same network is proposed.

Immediately following, in Chapter 2, the background to, and practicalities of, conducting the present study are briefly discussed.

---

[1] The more theoretical aspects of this argument are explored in the main text.

The logic implicit in the initial questions is reflected in the structure of how our findings are reported. The body of the study is broken down into three main parts: the context in which the pursued phenomena are embedded (i.e. company operations), the data communications network, and the related computer-based systems. This sequence yields a cumulative account, successively expanding in complexity, but with continuous reference back to the preceding discussions. In particular, the network is later (re-)merged with systems to form the wider concept of information systems (IS). That exercise provides us both with a clearer understanding of the phenomena under study and with a somewhat non-conventional conceptualization of information systems.

Relating IS to the strategic and organizational capabilities of an MNC requires something of a 'report-card' on the MNC in question. Chapter 3 reviews SKF from the corporate perspective as well as SKF's different businesses. The present organizational conundrum is given special attention and the complicated position of a standard bearing manufacturing subsidiary is examined in some detail.

A working definition of a data communications network is developed initially in Chapter 4. The functions and differential reach (viz. the hierarchical configuration) of SKF's proprietary international 'Group Telenet' are identified and classified. The vantage point then shifts to the local one; a perspective which is illustrated in five selected countries of SKF operations. Chapter 4 concludes with a first, indicative gauging of the importance attached to international data communications in SKF.

Chapter 5 starts with a conceptual discussion about the basic rationale for data communications networks and the resultant meaning of the term information systems. SKF's systems are then surveyed according to a suggested taxonomy based on functionality with corporate, divisional and local systems, respectively. The systems are described in a non-technical manner[2] and usage patterns are identified where possible. Most effort has been expended on divisional systems, both by SKF and, consequently, by the author. Almost half of Chapter 5 is, however, devoted to a more thorough review of

---

[2] Note, however, that a list of abbreviations recurring in the text (particularly system acronyms) appears in Appendix 3.

the effects of information systems usage in SKF related to SKF company objectives and IS strategy priorities. Internal efficiency and effectiveness, as well as effects for external relationships, are assessed to the extent our available data permit. Finally, a quick look at the main competitors' IS capabilities provides an additional point of reference.

The conclusions in Chapter 6 are structured differently from the body of the study. First, the differential use of IS in SKF is explored. It varies over time, type of activity, geographical location, and type of business. The substantive change over time (from the mid-1970s to the present) is in stark contrast to the remarkable stability of SKF's competitive environment and scope of operations. Coupled with other aspects (e.g. different product technology, process technology, and internal conditions), a notion of degree of 'centrality' of activities in SKF emerges. Also, the simple quality of data communications links comes out as a good and ready alternative to more traditional and complicated company analyses for judging closenes to the 'core' of operations.

Moreover, Chapter 6 addresses directly the role of IS in SKF in the over-all context. IS is shown to be a means for strategy implementation and organizational design. Strategic capabilities are clearly enhanced and the organizational 'degrees of freedom' increase significantly with the help of IS. More interestingly, IS creates conditions for more 'organic' coordination of activities. Dispersed units often spontaneously take on coordination tasks, exploiting the potential for lateral communication brought by IS. Central management can tolerate this development due to the greatly improved possibilities for monitoring complex and dispersed activities, and is rewarded by more flexible and efficient company operations.

The final part of Chapter 6 calls some of our conclusions into question, identifies some uses of IS found lacking in SKF, and speculates on the infrastructural quality of IS giving the MNC the capability to readapt the organization and to reconfigure activities in a more flexible manner and in novel ways.

2. A NOTE ON METHOD AND SOURCES

The relevance of studying the use of international data communications-cum-systems, the research strategy, and the choice of case, viz. SKF, are all discussed at some length elsewhere[3]. We will not reiterate all the arguments here, only some main points. In this relatively short section, space is also given to the specific circumstances pertaining to the present inquiry.

The observation that exploratory research is needed still holds, since information systems use in organizations is fraught with a high degree of uncertainty due to the relative newness of the phenomenon (ample support for that view can be found in McFarlan, 1984a; see also Earl, 1988). Likewise, it holds à fortiori regarding information systems use by MNCs, where there is a continued dearth of relevant empirical studies (notable exceptions are Antonelli, 1981; OECD 1983a and 1983b; and OECD-BRIE, 1989; see also Hagström, 1988 and 1990b). Relevance, in our context, is paying attention to the possible role of international data communications and attendant systems for how MNCs perform and structure their operations. Moreover, there is as yet no need to go beyond data communications when considering new means of communications, since, for instance, ISDN applications remain in the pilot stage (cf. Ungerer, 1988; and OECD-BRIE, 1989). In any case, there are arguably no major qualitative differences regarding strategic and structural impact between data communications and still emerging, blue-print types of more integrated communications. Building on the same core technology, differences are marginal.

The most plausible explanation for the scant attention paid to MNCs, and their over-all activities, in information systems research is the complexity represented by the MNC itself. It is only to be expected that in a new field of research, there is a strong, and prudent, tendency to shy away from the most complex of cases, at least initially. Our main reason for nevertheless braving this quagmire is that new means of communications

[3] In a prior study (Hagström 1987b) and even more so in the main text.

should be particularly relevant for MNCs where geographic and hierarchical distances are great[4]. In fact, MNCs are also the dominant users of international data communications (UN, 1982; and OECD, 1983a and 1983b).

However, we do simplify our task by excluding service MNCs and MNCs active in the computer and telecommunications equipment businesses. Since we concentrate on user aspects, it is helpful to avoid cases where information systems are an integral, core element of the firm's business already by definition. Such company usage is furthermore likely to be constrained by its own range of product offerings, and/or to be difficult to disentangle from product development for external sales. In particular, in these industries there is a propensity to 'over-invest' in information systems (not least for marketing reasons), wherefore conclusions on the role of information systems run the risk of being both exaggerated and highly idiosyncratic.

Still, the problems of complexity and newness obviously remain significant. Intensive case studies have their strongest merits in situations characterized by unclear causal relationships, uncertainty, importance of processual development, and relevance of contextual variables (cf. Duncan, 1979; Hägg and Hedlund, 1979; and Yin, 1981 and 1984), wherefore we stick with the single case, viz. MNC. Applications, functions, time and countries vary, though.

SKF combines an extremely high degree of internationalization of its operations ('multinationality') with leading use of international data communications-cum-systems. Not least important is the fact that SKF also was a pioneer in establishing a proprietary international data communications network, giving us a comparatively very long period to study. These attributes of SKF are appropriate even in an international context[5]. In fact, SKF being such an eminently suitable case is a prime reason for complementing our

[4] A more comprehensive argument can be found in Hagström (1989) and in the main text.

[5] See also UN (1988:48) and Thorngren (1990), where SKF is mentioned by name. For specific qualifications, see the following chapters and Hagström (1989); for additional advantages of studying SKF, see Hagström (1987b); and for an argument why Swedish MNCs are particularly interesting, given this area of research, see Hagström (1991). - All aspects are also covered in the main text.

previous study with the present one (rather than, for instance, investigating another company).

The main difference between the way the two studies have been conducted is that some access to primary data (particularly personal interviews and internal company material) was ultimately conceded for the present study. Of course, the amount of secondary material available to us also increased considerably, obviously as a result of writing three years later, but also in response to our earlier study. A qualitative difference is that the insights already gained permitted a much better use of existing and new secondary material. We were also able to ask more pertinent and focussed questions in the interviews. Learning, on the part of the researcher, has, I hope, significantly added to our possibilities to handle the complexity involved.

The two studies are related in two main ways. First, this study clearly supercedes the previous one, but does not re-search all the issues covered in the earlier inquiry. In particular, the historical evolution of the company, its strategy, and its structure are not reiterated here. Second, the prior study was a prerequisite for carrying out the present one. The results of the initial arm's-length case study 'provoked' (in a positive sense for both parties) subsequent access to SKF. In effect, the two studies add up to a phased case study design, labelled an 'insistent' case study in the main text.

SKF's cooperation has been of paramount importance for the completion of this study, and thanks are due in rich measure. However, the generously offered replies to interview questions and subsequent commentaries on our written material are best characterized as informal in nature. This generosity does not imply that the present account is guaranteed to be free from errors. All judgments are solely those of the author and they do not purport to reflect SKF policy or views. To emphasize, **the description and analysis presented in this study have in no way been either authorized or officially sanctioned by SKF.**

One particular limitation of our investigation is that we agreed not to approach any of SKF's competitors or customers directly. This restriction has, however, been of little consequence for two reasons; first, our focus is on SKF's usage of IS and as seen from SKF's perspective, second, relevant remaining information gaps could be filled to an acceptable extent by reliance on secondary and indirect sources[6]. Market conditions were a recurrent theme during the data collection, regarding both product and geographical markets.

All the sources directly providing data for our study are listed in Chapter 7 below, except some miscellaneous internal company material (and advertisements). If we were to rank the sources used by broad category in terms of accuracy and content (both qualitative and quantitative), the different SKF publications (cf. Section 7.3) clearly come out on top. The two measures coincide in this ranking, the explanation being that the underlying rationale for these publications is to disseminate information internally or externally, and that published material is carefully 'vetted' for legal reasons. Internal company material was similarly helpful in a few, very particular instances (for Figures 4.1-4.5, and in understanding the interlocking systems of Section 5.2.2.1)[7].

Interviews (cf. Section 7.4) scored high on content, but lower on accuracy. The converse can be said of other researchers' publications and additional bibliographic sources (cf. Section 7.1).

The main reason for the interviewees giving less than totally reliable answers was that our questions were 'unusual' (cf. Appendix 1). Respondents were unused to considering information systems in the way proposed, and were in many cases unable to give succinct answers (often because the information simply was not available). Other standard caveats, of course, also apply (personalized perspective, respondents' possible ulterior motives, cultural differences, possible misunderstandings etc.).

---

[6] Section 5.3.3 below is devoted to a discussion on competitors' use of information systems.

[7] SKF advertising provided some isolated, but valuable, tidbits of information, notably regarding the CADalog (Section 5.2.2.2 below) and services offered to customers by SKF (cf. Hagström, 1987b).

The bibliographic material rarely addresses issues of direct relevance for our study, but information contained therein could be 'recycled' by interpreting it in the light of our research questions (e.g. Beckholmen; 1982, Håkanson and Zander, 1986; and Wolf, 1985). In other cases, the issues are relevant, but only covering a more limited aspect of information systems and, typically, with SKF figuring as one of several examples or only incidentally (e.g. Fredriksson et al., 1987; Hammarkvist, 1986; Pousette, 1983; RDF, 1984; and Televerket, 1989). When providing significant input to the text below, sources are indicated in each instance.

Articles in the trade and general press (cf. Section 7.2) proved to be less accurate and to contribute less than the other sources consulted. However, they have been very useful as background material and in some particular cases giving important data on SKF for our inquiry (notably The Financial Times, Affärsvärlden, and Datavärlden).

All in all, the comparatively rather rich source material has furnished ample information for description and analysis, and sufficient variety for satisfying reasonable demands on reliability. The latter is not least important, since variety has given a certain broadness of perspective and good opportunities for cross-checking on the accuracy of the information presented in the following sections. On the whole, the research process has followed standard intelligence-gathering procedures in the sense of relying mostly on secondary sources to piece together as consistent a picture as possible. The strength of the approach derives much more from compilation and structuring of information than from any access to superior sources.

The structural logic (cf. Chapter 1 above), and the exploratory nature in general, of this case study have meant that the main body (Chapters 3 - 5) is far from free from deductive interpretation. Ideally, evidence should be presented without much running commentary, but the importance of the over-all context of company operations prompts more of an inter-woven analysis. An additional reason is that the study otherwise would have become considerably longer (sic!), since subsequent interpretation would have required more repetition. Sections 4.3 and 5.3 are particularly biased in this respect, but their placement is motivated by the need to maintain the logic of our perspective.

However, great care has been taken to indicate when our reasoning is more than mere description, and we trust that is clear when reading the text.

Moreover, the present study draws on other research by the author, bringing - perhaps somewhat tedious - recurrent references to own publications. The reason for this apparent lack of humility is twofold: first, the writings are very closely related, and, second, we did not wish to extend an already lengthy work by repeating arguments readily available to the reader in other publications.

The remaining complexity and the extent of the task set before us will unfold in the following chapters.

3. SKF REVIEW

Prior to delving into the main issue of the use of information systems in SKF, the context of overall company activities needs to be reestablished. Most of the historical description will be omitted here, as will the details on the evolution of the particular businesses. Instead, a purpose of the present overview is to complement our previous study (Hagström, 1987b) by, among other things, bringing it up to date. Moreover, this chapter represents more of an analysis than a straight description of SKF, since we are setting the scene specifically with information systems use in mind.

We start by briefly looking at SKF from the corporate perspective, before turning to each of SKF's three major business areas. A recent reorganization of the standard bearing business merits some special attention. The new organization and its position relative to the over-all organization of SKF is the subject of the following section. Lastly, the discussion is complemented by touching upon a few SKF units, logically falling less well within the divisional organization.

3.1 SKF - The Company

The current structure of the SKF Group dates back to September, 1987. The organizational chart, presented in Figure 3.1 below, is a manifestation of the 'new' SKF as a specialized manufacturer of certain industrial goods; the structure emerging, as it did, a year after SKF divested itself of its main upstream activity, its large specialty steel business. The other major change involved the bearing business shifting from an area-based organization to a purported customer-oriented setup. The Bearing Industries division became responsible for sales of standard bearings to original equipment manufacturers (OEMs), while Bearing Services was to handle the aftermarket. Specialty Bearings got the role of catering for customers with needs not satisfied by standard bearings. The Tools and Component Systems businesses survived these last upheavals as virtually unchanged global product divisions, dating back to 1977 and 1983, respectively[8].

All units shown in the chart are headquartered in Gothenburg, Sweden, with the exception of Specialty Bearings, where the divisional headquarters is located in Wayne, Pennsylvania. However, the headquarters of the Tools division is scheduled to be moved to Frankfurt, Germany (in late 1990 or early 1991) following a planned merger with a West German tool company (see Section 3.2.1 below).

Figure 3.1

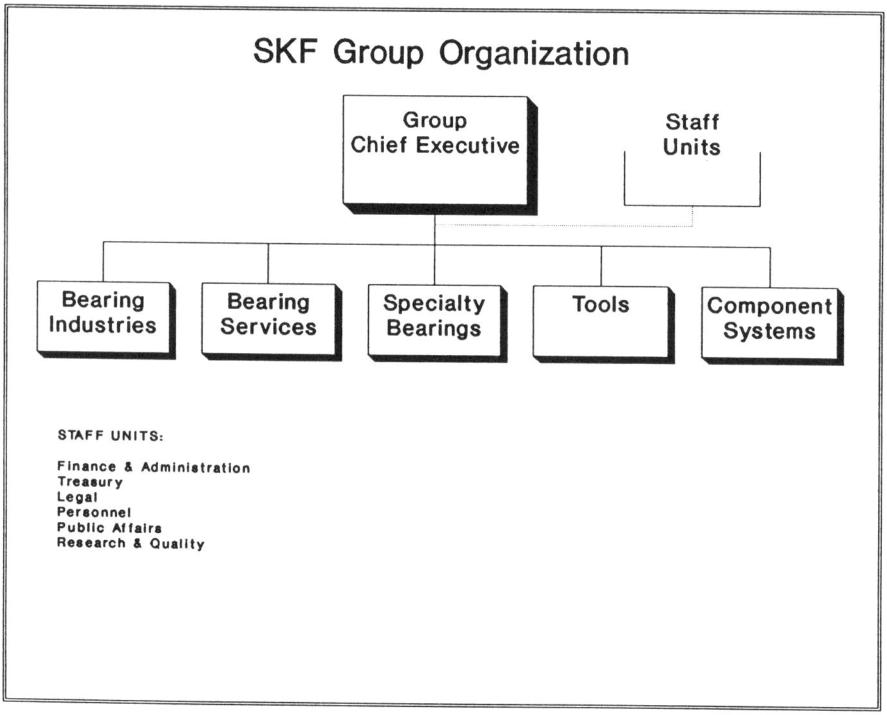

[8] In SKF parlance, all these entities are referred to as 'business areas', but the standard generic term 'division' is used throughout the present study.

This Group structure sits on top of a large, geographically very dispersed organization generating sales of SEK 25 billion, or USD 4 billion[9], in 1989. SKF has about 130 active subsidiaries in 47 countries. The number of factories operated is close to 100 in 17 countries, and SKF is represented by sales subsidiaries and affiliates in more than 130 countries[10]. With very few exceptions, subsidiaries are wholly-owned by SKF, but are operated as separate profit centers with its own boards of directors. SKF explicitly[11] pursues a policy of employing host country nationals in senior management positions.

At the beginning of 1990, SKF employed almost 50 000 people world-wide, with a large majority found in Western Europe (see Figure 3.2 below[12]). The most important countries of operation are the largest market economies, with Japan - where SKF only had 77 employees - as a notable exception. Of course, Sweden hardly qualifies for the epithet of large economy; its prominence instead due to being SKF's home country. On the other hand, it is the home country's modest relative position that is more remarkable. Extremely few, if any, major MNCs would show a foreign country (here West Germany) boasting about twice as many company employees as the home country[13].

[9] SKF net sales reached SEK 25 066 million in 1989. Converted at the exchange rate of 1 USD = SEK 6.21 at December 31, 1989, the figure translates into USD 4 036 million. At the average yearly rate of 1 USD = SEK 6.44, as used by SKF, the net sales stood at USD 3 892 million.

[10] The figures on the number of SKF sites are marginally inflated by inclusion of a recent acquisition, CR Industries, see further Section 3.2.2, below. Other data given in this study excludes acquisitions after 1989, unless otherwise specified.

[11] See Annual Report on Form 20-F, 1990.

[12] SKF registered 49 413 employees on December 31, 1989. Due to data availability, Figure 3.2 shows the distribution of the average number of employees at work the same year, which amounted to 46 667.

[13] The acquisitions during the first half of 1990 bring increases in the number of employees in particular for West Germany and the US. In the latter case, it means that both Sweden and Italy are overtaken in the ranking in Figure 3.2.

Figure 3.2

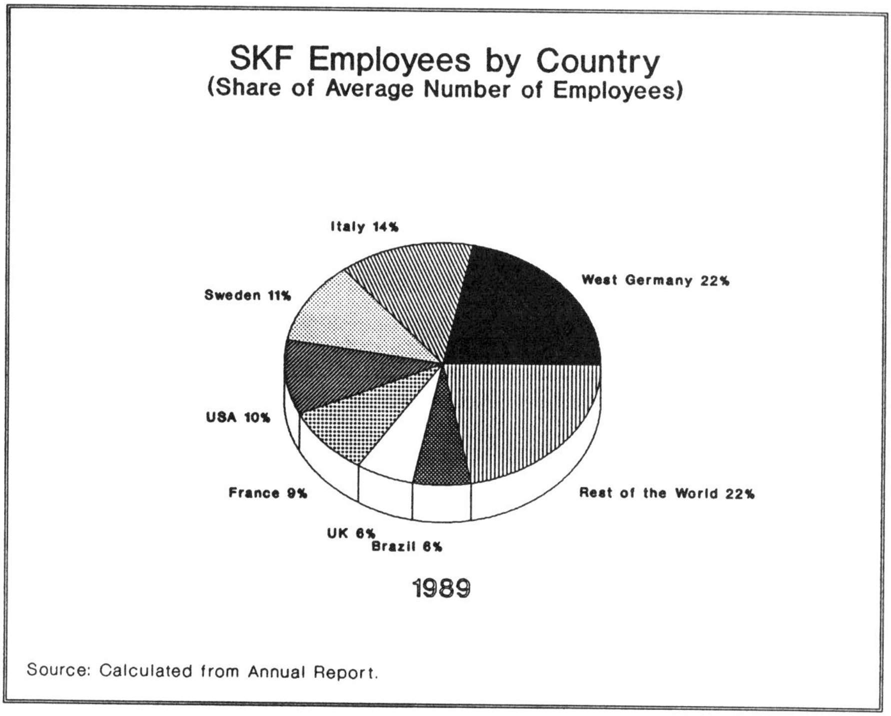

With 89 percent of its employees abroad, SKF is the most internationally based of all major Swedish MNCs. In spite of its purported manning policy for managers of foreign subsidiaries, SKF is somewhat less international in outlook, at least judging from the proportion of Swedes as heads of major subsidiaries abroad, where SKF clocks just slightly below average for major Swedish MNCs[14]. However, there are indications that SKF has the smallest proportion of Swedes as heads of foreign sales subsidiaries, notably small distant ones[15]. According to SKF, it is the only Swedish MNC with an institutionalized international trade union for its employees (meeting every third year).

---

[14] As reported in the background data to Danielsson and Synnerstad (1990).

[15] About 90-95 percent of sales subsidiary managing directors were identified as non-Swedish in the late 1980s. (Affärsvärlden, December 7, 1988).

With more than 95 percent of its sales abroad, SKF is again the most internationalized among major Swedish MNCs. In fact, SKF is by this measure possibly one of the very most internationalized large industrial MNCs in the world[16]. Looking at the regional distribution of Group sales (see Figure 3.3, below), SKF emerges as a heavily West European-biased MNC, with that region accounting for almost two-thirds (63 percent) of sales[17]. The same characteristic shows up regarding the distribution of activities[18]. Further, there is little variation in the regional distribution of sales for the three major businesses, underlining the relative uniformity of SKF's geographical emphasis. There are no indications that there have been any significant changes in the relative importance of the different regions during the last few decades, at least not at this aggregate level[19].

[16] In an attempt by Business Week (May 14, 1990) to identify the most international manufacturing companies in the world, SKF ties for second place, after Nestlé, with Sandoz and Hoffman-La Roche (three Swiss companies), regarding share of foreign sales; and is placed third, after Nestlé and Sandoz, when measured on the share of assets outside the home country (SKF here reaches 90 percent).

[17] Sales to Eastern European markets have so far been minimal.

[18] Using number of employees as a proxy, a full 62 percent of the total are located only in the five most important West European countries (cf. Figure 3.2, above).

[19] Comparable figures back to 1985 (cf. Annual Report on Form 20-F, 1988) show only minor changes, with the exception of the Tools division, where Europe has increased its share a dozen percentage points, mainly due to acquisitions. The longer-term relative stability of the regional distribution of SKF sales was echoed during the interviews. No information to the contrary has been encountered. The aggregates hide some shifts in emphasis, however. The one worth mentioning is the increased relative importance of the Far East for bearing sales (see Section 3.2.3 below).

Figure 3.3

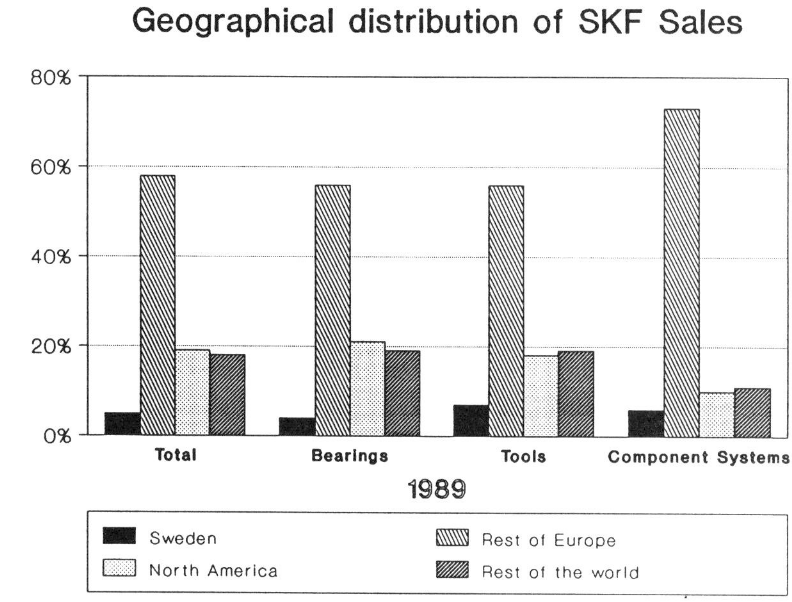

Source: Annual Report 1989.

Since the mid-1980s, SKF pursues a corollary strategy of largely manufacturing in each region what it sells there[20]. Dubbed the 'Currency Zone' concept, it divides the world into three regions: the D-mark zone (Europe, Africa and the Near East), the dollar zone (the Americas), and the yen zone (the Far East and Oceania). The main reasons behind the policy is to be less vulnerable to currency fluctuations and protectionist measures, to economize on transports, and to benefit from the psychological value of local presence.

The three-zone division has most bearing on the main business, with the Tools and Component Systems divisions being rather too small to match the regional distribution

[20] For instance, as expounded in 1989 and 1990 by Mauritz Sahlin, Chief Executive Officer, SKF AB (see Section 7.4).

of sales with manufacturing capacity. In fact, of the two only Component Systems has any manufacturing in Asia (in Singapore).

The dominant position of the bearing business in SKF shows up clearly when Group sales are broken down by division (see Figure 3.4, below). The two largest divisions, which only cover standard bearings, together account for more than three-fourths of SKF's external sales[21]. By this measure, the Components Systems division is bigger than Specialty Bearings, with the Tools division trailing rather far behind.

SKF's concentration on bearings has been a constant theme since the inception of the company in 1907[22]. Growth was mainly achieved through geographical expansion and, to a lesser extent, through vertical integration. The major moves were SKF getting into steel manufacturing in 1916, foundry products in 1917, and proprietary engineering in 1929 (starting on a small scale in 1912). SKF has on the whole desisted the lure of integrating forward (as particularly manifest in SKF's divestment of its growing automotive subsidiary, Volvo, in 1935).

[21] The share for Bearing Industries and Bearing Services combined was 77-78 percent in 1989. The distribution between the different bearings divisions in Figure 3.4 is not exact, due to lack of precision in the underlying data as reported by SKF.

[22] A fuller account of the historical developments is given in the accompanying study (Hagström, 1987b).

Figure 3.4

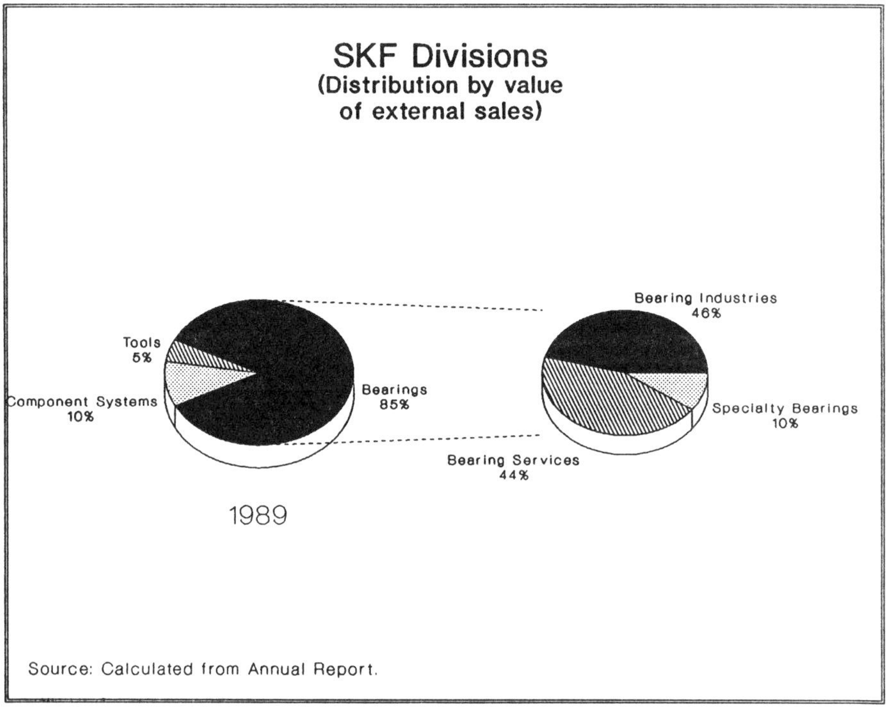

SKF was Sweden's largest company (both by sales and number of employees) a quarter of a century ago, but now barely squeezes in among the top ten. In the intervening period SKF has been busy maintaining its leading position in the bearings industry, fighting off new, primarily Japanese, challengers. Over-capacity and depressed profit-margins marred the industry until the latter half of the 1980s.

SKF was not, however, totally immune to the trend to diversify, which was a common corporate strategy for large industrial enterprises one to two decades ago. In the late 1970s the thrust to diversify outside bearings was limited to developing external sales for its upstream activities, to cutting tools, and to miscellaneous niche components.

Now, SKF is more focussed in its business strategies. Of the upstream activities, only very specialized machinery and castings remain. The components portfolio is leaner, and the tools business is expanding slowly along the traditional pattern followed earlier for bearings. The center of gravity in the bearings business is, to some extent, moving downstream with more differentiated products and a greater service component. More resources have also successively come to be devoted to research and development[23].

The repercussions of the strategic shifts at corporate headquarters have meant a continuous slimming down of activities. In 1965, when SKF had a traditional mother-daughter organizational structure, SKF headquarters had 375 employees and 140 managers reported directly to the chief executive officer. In 1971, corporate staff units were introduced, and the head-office made do with 220 people. The area organization for the bearings business came into effect in 1978, and headquarters could be reduced to 120 employees. Now, the Group head-office has a total staff of only 48 people, and no more than 15 managers report directly to the chief executive officer.

The main responsibilities of headquarters in today's SKF are commensurably rather fewer than they used to be. Overall strategic plans and competitor analyses (since they are very much the same ones) are still a corporate task. Financial coordination and human resources (notably training and job rotation across divisions) are key corporate concerns, and they appear to have gained in importance. Having a strong, competent department for handling legal issues world-wide, nurturing the corporate image, and shouldering the responsibility for basic research and product quality complete the list[24]. The enumerated items conform well to the present staff units (cf. Figure 3.1, above).

Other traditional head-office functions in SKF, such as production, product development, marketing and sales, have been moved to the divisional level. Following suit, the respective businesses will now be given more attention.

---

[23] R&D expenditure stood at, for instance, 1.2 percent of turnover in 1980 and are now, a decade later, 2.0 percent. They are targeted to grow up towards 3 percent of turnover in the coming few years.

[24] The identification of the present role of SKF Group headquarters draws largely on a presentation in 1989 by Mauritz Sahlin, Chief Executive Officer, SKF AB (see Section 7.4).

3.2 SKF - The Businesses

The following survey of the SKF businesses will be exactly that, viz. an overview, since something of a bird's-eye - or corporate - view is maintained. The purpose is to give some insight into the peculiarities of the different businesses; characteristics which form a backdrop to, and which will recur in, this study. Naturally, the overwhelming bearing business occupies the center stage, but we shall begin with the tools and component systems businesses. In the concluding section, only the companies with a bearing on the ensuing discussion are given space as background information.

3.2.1 Tools

Diversification into cutting tools on any significant scale was less than a calculated strategic move. This, the smallest division, traces its origins to 1969 when SKF acquired Malcus AB in Halmstad, Sweden. The Head and owner had just died in an airplane accident, and SKF was approached to take over. Further major acquisitions in Brazil, 1970, and in the UK, 1975, formed the nucleus of a separate division, which came into existence in 1977.

Tools are manufactured in five countries and dedicated sales subsidiaries are maintained in another seven countries[25]. In addition, other SKF sales subsidiaries are used as outlets. Since its inception, the Tools division has largely maintained its relative position in SKF, generating between 4 percent and 6 percent of SKF's sales[26]. It has consistently

[25] There are manufacturing units in the UK, Brazil, West Germany, Sweden and Italy by descending order of size (number of employees). If the acquisition in January, 1990, of Cofler & C. S.p.A., with 200 employees (and yearly sales of around SEK 100 million) is included, Italy edges past Sweden. Complementing sales companies are found in Austria, Belgium, Canada, France, the Netherlands, Spain and the US.

[26] The range is given exclusive of steel sales (see also Figure A.1 in Appendix 2 for details). Including steel up to October, 1986, the range of Tools sales would be 3 percent to 6 percent of total SKF sales during the period 1978-1989.

been more profitable than bearings. The division is headed by a small staff of less than a dozen people in Gothenburg. Much of the operational coordination emanates from the largest producing unit, located in the UK (Sheffield).

However, significant changes are in the offing for the Tools division. In July, 1990, it was decided to merge the division with Günther & Co. (Titex) of West Germany, thus forming a new company, Cutting Tools Technology. CTT is to be 70-percent owned by SKF, with the remaining 30 percent, at least initially, to be held by Günther & Co. CTT will operate as a division within the SKF Group. The SKF Tools headquarters will be transferred to Frankfurt, Germany as a new head-office for CTT will be established.

Titex adds some 1 400 employees and SEK 700 million in sales to the Tools division. Adding the recent merger and acquisitions[27] to SKF's 1989 figures, tools (viz. CTT) would have increased their share of Group sales to some 7-8 percent, but still remaining the smallest of SKF divisions.

The 'old' Tools division produces a wide range of twist drills, taps and dies, milling tools and other cutting tools, like reamers and shank cutters. Both standard products and special designs are offered, primarily made of high-speed steel. There is some expansion into cutting tools of hard materials (cemented carbide), which are now supplied in a few markets. This diversification move is boosted by the inclusion of Titex, which basically sports the same product program as SKF Tools, but is relatively stronger in hard material tools (and tools with diamond coatings).

By itself, SKF Tools is the world leader in cutting operations using high-speed steel tools (drilling, milling and thread cutting). It is the world's largest full-range producer in this industry. Specialists are bigger in some segments, but SKF is the only manufacturer with sales and service being available basically world-wide. Still, SKF only commands a market

[27] Titex, Cofler S.p.A., CR Industries and Gallino Gomma (the latter two by the Component Systems division, see Section 3.2.2 below). Especially the formation of CTT and the purchase of CR Industries are too significant to be ignored in this overview of SKF. But by virtue of being so recent, the merger and acquisitions have negligible bearing on the topic of the present study - use of information systems in SKF - wherefore they will not figure in the following unless explicitly stated.

share of around 7 percent, due to the very fragmented nature of the industry. That characteristic extends to customers as well. Typically, they make small purchases and primarily through distributors, which take more than three-fourths of the Tools division's external sales. End-users make up the remainder (22 percent in 1989).

Somewhat surprisingly, SKF sees little, if any, synergy between the tools and bearings businesses[28]. Still, the main input (steel) is the same, and some of the manufacturing steps are similar to those of bearings (heat treatment, turning and grinding, but also quality controls). The customers are largely different (see further below), but the Tools division apparently can make at least some minor use of SKF's sales network for bearings.

3.2.2 Component Systems

Synergy is even less of a concern regarding the Component Systems division. From the vantage point of SKF as a whole, the division contains the non-bearings-, non-tools-related end-products. Component Systems is actually a portfolio of seven, fairly distinct, businesses, as shown in Figure 3.5, below. They are operated separately, with only a skeleton divisional staff of half a dozen people in Gothenburg, essentially filling the limited function of a holding company management (viz. primarily financial and portfolio-strategic coordination). All in all, the division fields 32 companies in 13 countries, and there are 23 manufacturing facilities[29].

---

[28] See Footnote 20, above.

[29] In Western Europe, Brazil, the US, and Singapore.

Figure 3.5

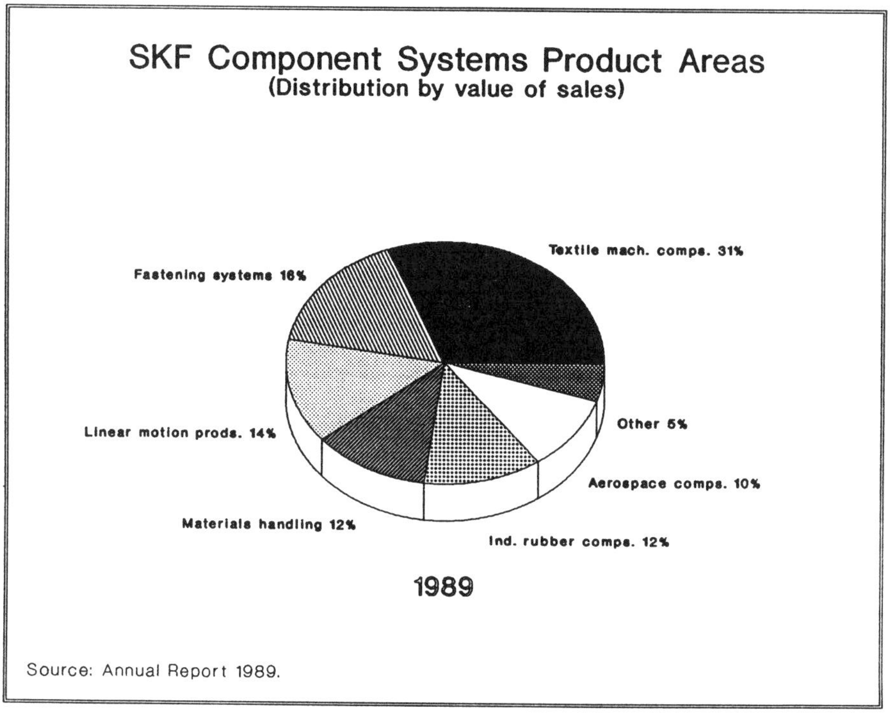

Briefly,

- Textile machinery components refer to the manufacture of spinning spindles, open end rotors, drafting systems, and bearing units for the textile industry. SKF has a very strong position in the industry, especially with more than a 50 percent world market share in ring spinning spindles.

- The Fastening systems product area is centered around the production of retaining rings, snap rings, and other miscellaneous fasteners. SKF is broadly the world market leader, reaching an approximate 40 percent world market share for the main, retaining ring, product.

- Ball and roller screws, linear bearings, way guides, drive units and positioning tables, and electromechanical actuators and controls are the major Linear motion products. SKF is the world's largest manufacturer of roller screws.

- Materials handling consists of conveyor systems, conveyor hollies, wheels, rollers, castors, and some bearing housings. Much is made of plastic.

- Different seals and vibration dampening products are manufactured within the Industrial rubber components area.

- Aerospace components entails production of a variety of control rods and cables, other different electromechanical flight control devices, and air-frame bearings.

- The 'Other' segment is mainly measuring tools for bearing manufacture and for other industries.

Each of the above product areas is built around one or a few producing companies, which are highly specialized in their respective niches. Typically, they command a high, or a very high, market share. The Component Systems division's few sales subsidiaries concentrate on linear motion and materials handling products. Otherwise, sales are organized very much separately by the different companies. All in all, the division's own sales organization accounts for approximately a quarter of turnover. However, other SKF sales subsidiaries are also used as outlets[30].

[30] Around one-fifth of the division's sales takes this route (Hagström, 1987b).

The Component Systems division has grown considerably in relative importance, increasing its share of SKF's sales from less than 8 percent to more than 12 percent since the various businesses were collected under one hat in the early 1980s[31]. It is something of a cash cow for SKF, having been its most profitable division after it came into being.

Expansion has chiefly come through acquisitions since the end of the 1960s, thus also before the various businesses migrated out of the bearings organization. A recent, exceptionally big acquisition actually alters some of the data already given, even at the company level.

In March, 1990, SKF purchased Chicago Rawhide Industries, which would add sales of nearly SEK 1.7 billion[32], or almost 7 percent, on the total 1989 figures for SKF. CR Industries manufactures fluid sealing devices for the automotive and machinery OEM and replacement markets. Being strongly centered on the North American market, SKF plans to exploit the Bearing Services sales organization in order to expand sales of CR Industries' products[33]. Bearing Services will also take over CR Industries' aftermarket sales organization.

Including all of CR Industries (and another minor acquisition[34], the Component Systems share would rise from 10 percent to 15-16 percent of SKF Group sales (cf. Figure 3.4). By the same token, the industrial rubber components business would grow from 12

---

[31] Component Systems has operated as a separate division from 1984 onwards. However, figures can be traced back to 1982, when the division's businesses were still lodged within bearings. Again, the range is given exclusive of steel sales, which, if included, would put the earliest figure at slightly more than 6 percent (see Figure A.2 in Appendix 2 for details).

[32] CR Industries had a turnover of USD 270 million in 1989 (SKF Annual Report on Form 20-F, 1990). At the year-end rate this figure converts to SEK 1 677 million.

[33] CR Industries employs some 3 000 people, and has 10 manufacturing units in the US and one in Canada. The addition of CR Industries only marginally influences the statistics on the degree of internationalization of SKF as a whole. The regional distribution of employees and of sales will, of course, be more affected.

[34] In July, 1990, SKF bought the fluid sealing devices business of the Italian Gallino Gomma company. The business had sales of about SEK 100 million and 250 employees in 1989. - The developments in the Tools division (see Section 3.2.1 above) are also taken into account.

percent to well over 40 percent of the Component Systems division's turnover (cf. Figure 3.5).

There have been no notable divestments in the Component Systems portfolio since its elevation to the status of separate division. However, the logically related SKF Automotive Group was kept within the bearings business organization and sold off in 1987. The Automotive Group was centered around the company McQuay-Norris, supplying a full line of automotive parts to OEMs and the aftermarket almost entirely for the North American market. Mainly engine parts were manufactured and other components traded. At the time of its acquisition by SKF, in 1976, McQuay-Norris had 1 400 employees. It was heralded as one of the main new roads for expansion and diversification of SKF. The subsequent sale of the automotive components business is the second largest divestment (after steel) by SKF in the last quarter of a century. That decision having been anticipated could explain its exclusion from the Components System division in 1984.

Although its portfolio-character has been emphasized, the Component Systems product areas are not totally unrelated to the bearing business. Among the connections worth mentioning are the (rubber) seals and the measuring tools, which both are used for bearings. Retaining rings are used in connection with the mounting of bearings. Linear motion products have some overlapping technology and components with the dominant circular motion products. Materials handling products are widely used in the bearing plants, notably the so called Flex-Link conveyor systems, which are an integral part of the automatic production lines for bearings. Fastening systems and Industrial rubber components also have the important automotive manufacturing and replacement customer segments in common with bearings. A similar concurrence exists between Specialty Bearings and Aerospace components, which also includes some bearings among its products. Lastly, the especially profitable Textile machinery components have a long history of association with bearings, going back to the founding of SKF[35]. The

[35] The invention of the double-row, self-aligning ball bearing was made by SKF's founder, Sven Wingquist, while employed at a textile mill. The need for such a bearing was prompted by the experienced frequent stoppages due to unaligned shafts in the mill.

components have traditionally been manufactured in SKF's bearing plants, and various types of bearing units are part of its offering to the textile industry.

Seen from the outside, the Component Systems division clearly represents fairly closely related diversification vis-à-vis the basic bearing business. The McQuay-Norris case, and the rather loose management of the Component Systems portfolio, indicate, however, that these remain side businesses for SKF.

3.2.3 Bearings

SKF manufactures and sells both standard and specialty bearings. The main standard types are various ball bearings, taper, cylindrical and spherical roller bearings, and thrust bearings. Specialty bearings are often custom-designed for a specific application and include aerospace bearings, miniature and thin section bearings, slewing bearings, machine tool bearings (and spindles), spherical plain, gas and ceramic bearings, and bearings made of polymer materials.

The bearings make SKF fundamentally a global specialist, almost a single-business company. Sales of bearings, including some miscellaneous, closely related products (notably for the mounting, dismounting, and maintenance of bearings), accounted for 81 percent of SKF's sales in 1970, and were only a few percentage points higher twenty years later[36]. The share reached a low of 68 percent in 1980; a figure that rises to 81

[36] See Figure A.3 in Appendix 2 for the period 1978-1989 (for which comparable figures are available).

percent if specialty steel is excluded[37]. The dominance of bearings in SKF's operations has not only been maintained, its position has been remarkably stable over the years[38].

SKF's leading position in the bearings industry has also remained relatively unchanged during the last few decades. Its share of world market economy demand peaked at almost 25 percent in the mid-1960s, but settled at 20 percent a decade later with only very minor subsequent divergences[39]. SKF has held on to its existing markets, and during the last decade even been able to compensate for the faster growth of the Far Eastern markets (where SKF traditionally has had a small market share).

The world market economy demand for bearings is rather evenly distributed between Europe, North America and the rest of the world[40]. The regional distribution of SKF's bearing sales is heavily skewed in favor of Europe, with three-fifths of sales and with one fifth each for the other two regions. These shares have changed little during the 1980s, for which comparable figures are available[41].

The regional approach to manufacturing - as made explicit in the 'currency-zone' concept - has begun to make its impact, though. SKF is moving from about 80 percent local production a few years ago towards 90-95 percent in the US, where SKF holds an approximate 12 percent market share. Whole production lines are in the process of being

---

[37] The 'low' figures constitute a slight exaggeration of the drop, since bearings sales are calculated on the basis of SKF's gross sales (without elimination for internal deliveries). By comparison, the 1989 share of net sales in Figure 3.4 above would be reduced to 83 percent (from 85 percent) if calculated the same way (see also Appendix 2 for more details).

[38] Even the acquisition of CR Industries and the formation of CTT only dent the bearings share. Hypothetically included for 1989, the bearings share would drop to 77 percent. However, recall that parts of CR Industries are to be transferred to Bearing Services, wherefore even this small reduction is slightly overestimated.

[39] The development during the 1970s and the first half of the 1980s is discussed more extensively in Hagström (1987b).

[40] More precisely, bearing demand is divided between North America 34 percent, Western Europe 30 percent, Japan 23 percent, and the rest of the world 13 percent. (The figures exclude Eastern Europe and the centrally planned economies.)

[41] See Figure A.4 in Appendix 2.

transferred from Europe to a new plant in Georgia. Another wholly new factory, in Kentucky for complete hub units, is planned to start production in 1992. A recent almost doubling of the capacity in Brazil and a take-over in Mexico are aimed at expanding operations in the rest of the region.

In the Far East, SKF only manufactures some 20 percent of local sales at present. However, a major new plant in Malaysia is planned to come on stream in 1992. Increasing its presence in the Far East is an important long-term objective for SKF. So far, the expansion has mainly concerned the sales organization, with half a dozen new sales companies having been opened in the last few years[42].

Apart from wanting to exploit faster market growth and to improve the balance of local sales and production, SKF has a need for a stronger presence on the 'home ground' of some of the major competitors in the industry. Japanese bearing producers dominate in the Far Eastern markets and have emerged in the last decade or so as SKF's most significant global competitors in terms of market presence and size (growth), including overseas production[43]. That is also SKF's perception[44]. - Market shares are one indication of the competitive line-up, albeit rough and aggregated.

---

[42] New sales companies opened 1987-1988 in Hong Kong, Indonesia, the Philippines, South Korea, Taiwan, and Thailand. In these markets, the new sales companies meant a doubling of the sales volume, an average 30 percent price increase due to better customer service, and a resultant doubling of profits already in 1989 (according to Mauritz Sahlin, in October, 1990).

[43] The 'threat' of growing Japanese exports of bearings to particular markets in some product segments was, however, acutely felt as early as in the late 1960s (see further below).

[44] Collis (1991) comes to similar conclusions (see also Section 5.3.3). However, in comparison with Table 3.1, Collis (1991) approximates the bearings world market with the combined sales of an unspecified number of companies (they are likely to be some 20+ companies). The top end of his market share ranking for 1987 was SKF, FAG, NSK, NTN, Timken, and Koyo Seiko. For 1970 it was SKF, Timken, New Departure Hyatt (of the US), FAG, NTN, and Koyo Seiko.

Table 3.1

Leading Bearing Manufacturers

(1988)

Company	Home country	Market share (%) World*	Market share (%) Europe*
SKF	Sweden	20	34
NSK**	Japan	12	5
NTN	Japan	10	3
FAG	West Germany	8 ½	17
Timken	US	8 ½	6
Koyo Seiko	Japan	6	2
Torrington	US	5 ½	2
Ina	West Germany	5	13

*) Excluding Eastern Europe and centrally planned economies.
**) Here including UPI of the UK, a company acquired in January, 1990.

Source: SKF/Financial Times, January 18, 1990.

Of the eight largest bearing companies, only SKF does not have a large domestic market to fall back on. All the other seven companies are domiciled in one of the three biggest market economies of the world. SKF is, however, the top foreign contender in each of those three national markets[45]. In terms of production, SKF is clearly the geographically most broadly-based company in the industry, even if all of Western Europe is designated as SKF's 'home market'.

The large volumes in world bearing sales emanate from OEM customers, and SKF has its most significant such relationships in Europe. The challenge from Japanese producers has, so far, been concentrated to this market segment. The major Japanese manufacturers are first and foremost volume producers of standard bearings, competing

[45] For more details, see Section 5.3.3 below.

primarily on price. Japan itself is self-sufficient in bearings, and SKF is only able to sell small quantities of specialty products[46] on that market.

SKF sports the most complete range of bearings in the industry and offers that range most internationally. Further, SKF is relatively stronger than its competitors in the aftermarket. Roughly, the industry distribution between direct OEM sales on the one hand, and sales to distributors and for replacement on the other, is 70/30. For SKF's bearings the corresponding proportions are about 55/45 (cf. Figure 3.6 below).

The margins are generally higher in the aftermarket, as they often also are for specialty bearings. SKF has consistently been more profitable than almost all of its major competitors. The exception is Torrington, which concentrates on pursuing high-margin market niches. Torrington focusses on specific customer segments and, consequently, has a product range biased towards special applications. In general, the bearing industry has, however, chalked up considerably smaller profits than other manufacturing industries.

One important reason already mentioned for the low profitability is the over-capacity, which has plagued the industry from the late 1960s and onwards. Another reason is that the commonly much larger OEM customers have been successful in squeezing prices for what is a rather mature, standard product. That holds for SKF as well, in spite of its size.

[46] Primarily high precision bearings and machine tool spindles (see also below), the latter of which also are assembled in Japan.

Figure 3.6

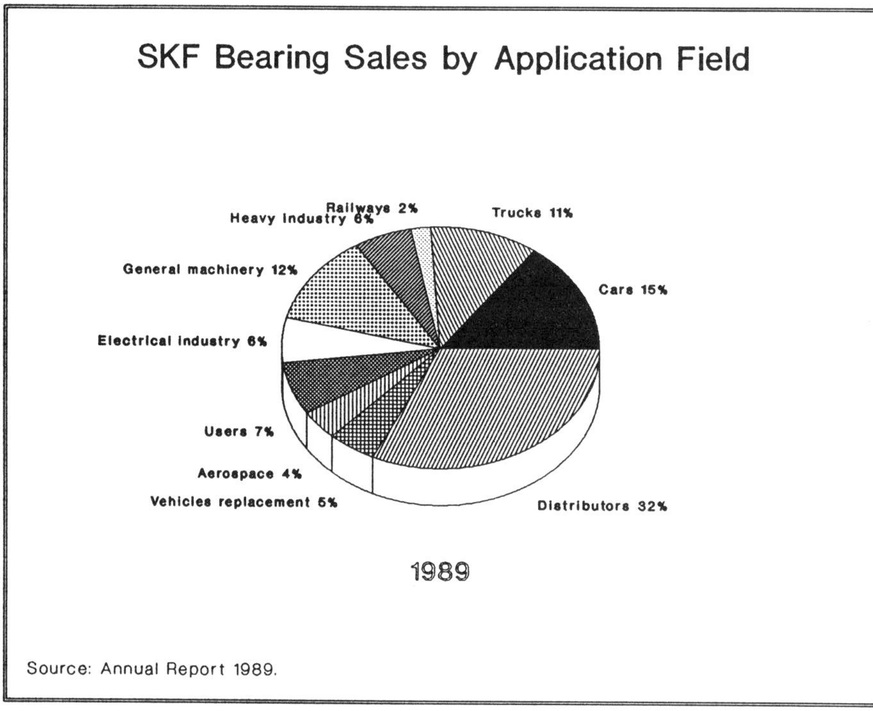

OEM-customers still dominate in SKF bearing sales, and most of them are large and very professional buyers. SKF's main customers are also found in some of the most concentrated industries.

The distribution of SKF's customer categories shown above has been remarkably stable over time[47]. Among OEM-customers, the railways and heavy industry segments have lost somewhat in importance for SKF over the last decade. There has also been a weak downward trend for the shares of the machinery and electrical industries. Customers in

[47] See Figures A.5 and A.6 in Appendix 2 for details. Data availability does, however, only permit bearing sales by application field to be traced back to 1985. On the other hand, the same series for total company sales goes back to 1977. The dominance of bearings in SKF's product portfolio means that the distribution of customer categories only deviates marginally between bearings and total company sales (cf. Figure 3.6 above, and Figure A.7 in Appendix 2).

the automotive sector, at present taking a quarter of bearing sales, have only marginally gained in relative importance. The aerospace industry has grown considerably, but remains a fairly small customer category.

Selling to OEM-customers, as a rule, means that the customer captures the replacement market. SKF has sought steadfastly to increase its share of this more lucrative market. The efforts have been most successful regarding the automotive sector, where the final consumer is more prone to take care of any required bearing replacements himself, rather than to turn to the car or truck manufacturer.

Like the vehicles replacement market, most aftermarket customers are reached through distributors. SKF now has more than 7 000 industrial distributor outlets for bearings, located in over 130 countries. In addition to increasing in number, distributor relationships have been considerably strengthened as SKF has continued to give the aftermarket special attention. Distributor sales of SKF bearings have also increased slightly faster than total bearing sales over the last decade (cf. Figures A.5 and A.6 in Appendix 2).

SKF's raised ambitions regarding the aftermarket were manifested in the 1987 reorganization of the bearing business. All sales of standard bearings to distributors and the after-sales market were collected in the Bearing Services division. The 'user' category in Figure 3.6 is also included here. 'Users' are customers for whom bearings are a critical component in their production equipment. Good examples are steel and paper mills.

Bearing Services employed approximately 3 500 people and recorded sales of SEK 9.6 billion in 1989. The division operates 48 sales companies around the world. Bearing Services produces no bearings.

The largest division, Bearing Industries, registered a total of 29 000 employees in 16 manufacturing companies the same year. Bearing Industries' external sales of some SEK 10 billion covered deliveries of standard bearings to OEM customers. Bearing housings and accessories are also included here. Deliveries of standard bearings to Bearing Services are, however, not included.

The Specialty Bearings division is responsible for all manufacture of specialty bearings and handles almost all sales of such bearings itself. Specialty bearings are often custom-designed and, consequently, are typically sold directly to OEM customers. Relationships with customers will tend to be very intimate, and where the technological sophistication of the resultant product is the most important feature. Moreover, the products fall in very distinct categories, which gives the division a strong portfolio-character beside the main, standard bearing business. In total, the division had some 4 000 employees in 14 companies in 1989 with gross sales amounting to SEK 2.3 billion.

Although the three bearing divisions seemingly combine well to give SKF a complete product offering of bearings for all types of customers wherever they are located, the possible complementarities are more complex and elusive in practice. Recall that the three bearing divisions display some quite different business characteristics. In short:

- Bearing Industries is in a very competitive, high-volume, low cost business with rather few, large customers typically demanding just-in-time delivery. On the whole, particular types of bearings are earmarked for specific user industries, and the onus is on product development of standard bearings closely tied to the user industry requirements. Bearing Industries is also responsible for all manufacturing of standard bearings.

- Bearing Services broadly supplies a wide range of standard bearings to a large number of customers usually in small lots, or a very specific bearing to a very specific customer at a very specific time. The numerous distributors and dealers need a more varied package of continuous sales and application support. The specific users primarily need reliable around-the-clock stand-by service and very precise, often idiosyncratic, application support. The substantial service component in the product offerings is a prime source of competitive advantage and is recoverable in the price charged. The competition is more of the wholesaler or special service provider type, rather than strict bearing manufacturers.

- Specialty Bearings competes in a more technology-driven environment, where satisfying an exact customer need is the key. This involves more basic research, commonly in close contact with the customer. The resultant product will take a variety of non-standard forms. Competitive advantage primarily rests on technological competence, and competitors are often specialists, reflecting that Specialty Bearings, in effect, operates in several different businesses.

How the separate bearing divisions then fit in the formal organizational context is the subject we now turn to.

3.3 Business Organization

The differences identified in the previous section provide one logic for why SKF has chosen to split its bearing operations along the present dimensions. A similar logic can be said to most likely underlie the establishment of the much more distinct Tools and Component Systems divisions. But, conversely, what then about the needs for:

- a cohesive approach to a geographical market?;
- catering to a customer with various requirements?;
- adequately responding to competitor moves in more than one business or market?;
- exploiting economies of scale in functions, such as R&D and distribution?;
- exploiting economies of scope across products?;
- safeguarding the flow of knowledge from research and product development, through manufacturing, to customer application?;

- assimilating the feedback flow of experiences from field applications to research, product development and manufacturing?; etc.

These questions are relevant, even if we only consider the more closely related bearing divisions.

Answers to all the questions will not be provided in this section. The issues raised will instead recur at various points in the present study. Now, the discussion is limited to the formal organization, and it focusses especially on the elaborate organization of standard bearing operations. The discussion is important as a backdrop for the remainder of the present study, but is also of interest per se, as organization charts beyond the stylized aggregate depicted in Figure 3.1 above are extremely rare in SKF. Our suspicion is that standard organization diagrams simply cannot in any meaningful way represent the complex formal organization in SKF.

Officially, SKF is a decentralized organization, where a more monolithic company has been replaced by 27 separate business organizations[48]. For SKF, the sought business orientation translates into a mixture of product- and customer-based such organizations, as displayed in Table 3.2 below.

The different businesses vary greatly in size. For instance, "linear motion" accounted for 1.5 percent of SKF sales in 1989. Another business encompassing both production and sales, for example, "cars" contributed almost ten times as much, or 14 percent, to corporate sales. Still, each of the businesses has world-wide product and/or customer responsibility.

As has been mentioned above, divisional staff units are small and most product development, manufacturing, and sales and marketing functions are carried out by the different business areas. This is especially true of the 'stand-alone' product businesses of Specialty Bearings and Component Systems, and of the Tools division. Some of the

[48] See Footnote 20, above.

smaller product businesses are concentrated at a single location, such as slewing bearings in Avallon, France. More often, even small businesses have sizeable production outside the main location, such as aeroengine bearings with manufacturing in Jamestown, N.Y., and in Villar Perosa, Italy.

The customer-defined businesses in Table 3.2, viz. the areas under Bearing Industries and Bearing Services, are relatively few (9), but account for some three-quarters of SKF sales and almost as much of SKF employees. Here, the organization becomes more complicated as the product-customer gap is bridged.

Behind the Bearing Industries businesses there lurks a product organization, meaning that the six businesses in Table 3.2 actually primarily refer to the OEM sales organization. As of 1989, the corresponding product organization is defined according to "product lines"[49], each of which constitutes a particular part of the Bearing Industries product range. The new product organization at present comprises 15 such "product lines". Profitability is said to be measured globally for these product lines. The overall responsibility for a "product line" rests with a "product line board", which is appointed by the divisional management of Bearing Industries. Board members meet intermittently and are drawn from various SKF companies.

[49] Quotation marks are used in the following where SKF terminology may cause confusion due to it diverging from standard use of the words.

Table 3.2

SKF Business Organization

Division	'Business'	Total number
Bearing Industries	Cars Trucks Electrical industry General machinery industry Heavy industry Railways	6
Bearing Services	Auto distributors & dealers Industrial distributors & dealers Users	3
Specialty Bearings	Non-metallic bearings Magnetic bearings Thin section bearings Specials Aeroengine bearings Miniature bearings Machine-tool spindles Plain bearings Gas bearings Slewing bearings	10
Tools	Tools	1
Component Systems	Textile machinery components Fastening systems Linear motion products Materials handling Industrial rubber components Aerospace components Other	7
Total:		27

Sources: See text and Chapter 2.

The largely supervisory role assigned to the "product line" boards does not include continuous strategic product management. That key role is delegated to what has been designated "product centers" by SKF. In practice, they are institutionalized management teams collected around a "product line" or part of a "product line". The day-to-day operational responsibility is left to "product divisions"; SKF's term for what essentially is the various physical manufacturing locations for the respective types of bearings.

This three-tier setup is very similar to a corporate level organization with a board, a group management and product divisions. However, the 'divisions' in Bearing Industries' product organization primarily have a more limited manufacturing responsibility. Still, the product organization, in effect, creates a set of quasi-companies within Bearing Industries. They cut across existing subsidiaries, individual plants, and international borders along the predetermined product dimensions. The different units making up these quasi-companies also have their own, separate profitability targets, and are monitored individually while still legally and physically remaining apart (for instance one production line) of an existing national subsidiary.

This neat dividing up of the manufacturing organization is not complete, however, as most products have manufacturing locations outside the designated "product divisions". These locations play a more passive role. Most of them are found in markets where the subsidiary is a stand-alone operation, basically supplying the local market only. Another reason is small scale of production of the particular bearing at the location. An overriding point, though, is that the "product divisions" have a strong European bias, which goes over and above the region's relative importance in Bearing Industries' manufacturing. The explanation is most certainly that the new product organization springs from, and is an institutionalization of, the extreme specialization of SKF's bearing production in Western Europe during the 1970s. Previously full range local production was then restructured to become manufacturing at each plant of narrowly defined products for the whole European market (and overseas exports)[50].

Armed with the principles of the Bearing Industries' product organizations, and the qualifications given above, we can now look at the new organization in some more detail.

---

[50] SKF's drastic rationalization of the production and distribution of standard bearings, and its manifestation in the Global Forecasting and Supply System (GFSS), are discussed extensively in Hagström (1987b) The main points recur in Section 4.2 below.

Table 3.3 represents an attempt at structuring the new product organization, stressing the geographical location of the relevant entities.

In practice, there is some overlap between "product centers" and "product divisions" (cf. Table 3.3 below). Both are commonly centered on the same site, and the "product division" manager (or one of them, if there are many) is often also one of the "product center" managers. However, the "product center" is typically a function at a national subsidiary's head-office, while the "product division" is a factory-located operation. They may, but very often do not, coincide physically.

Table 3.3

SKF Bearing Industries' Product Organization

Product Line (main products)	Product Line Chairman	Product Center	Product Division (*)	Also manufactured in
Deep groove ball bearings	Italy	Italy	Sweden UK France (2) Spain Italy (2) US	Brazil India Germany Mexico Argentina South Africa US
Self-aligning ball bearings	Sweden	Sweden	Sweden	Austria
Angular contact ball bearings - single row	Germany	Germany	Germany	Austria US
Angular contact ball bearings - double row	US	US	US	Italy
Cylindrical & needle roller bearings	Germany	Germany	Germany (2) Austria	US
Spherical roller bearings	France	Sweden	Sweden UK France US (2)	Brazil
Taper roller bearings	Germany	Germany	Germany (2) Spain US	Mexico Brazil India Italy Argentina South Africa
Thrust ball bearings	(none)	Germany	Germany	
Spherical roller thrust bearings	Sweden	Sweden	Sweden	
Bearing accessories and housings	Sweden	Sweden	Sweden	
Y-bearings	Italy	Italy	Italy	Mexico
Hub bearing units	France	France Italy	France Italy	Spain (2) Brazil Argentina
Railway bearing units	Sweden	Italy France	Italy France	
Automotive specials	Sweden	France Germany Italy	France Germany (2) Italy	
Large size bearings	Sweden	Sweden Germany	Sweden Germany	US

(*) Indicates if more than one location is applicable.

Source: Based on Bearing Bulletin, October 1989.

The division of responsibilities between "product centers" and "product divisions" is nevertheless very important, also when the entities are 'co-located' and when there is personnel over-lap (recall the financial follow-up per entity). It is also important if we are to be able to put the new product organization in its context. In Table 3.4 below some major tasks of the "product centers" and "product divisions" are classified according to where the responsibility appears to rest.

Table 3.4

Loci of Some Task Responsibilities in the SKF Bearing Industries' Product Organization

Tasks	PCs	Mainly PCs	Jointly	Mainly PDs	PDs
Development of manu- factu- ring techniques	X				
Product design coordination	X				
"Product knowledge" and training materials			X		
Current product development plan	X				
Product development work					
			X		
Product plans (incl. range, capacity, pricing and investments)		X			
Final product line forecasts					
Manufacturing				X	
Product quality assurance					X
Special delivery or technical demands					X
					X
Non-local stocks and delivery times					
Internal product promotion			X		
	X				

Note: PC = product center
PD = product division

Sources: See text and Chapter 2.

Obviously, the tasks listed in Table 3.4 are neither of equal importance, nor do they constitute an exhaustive list of relevant responsibilities. Table 3.4 does, however, demonstrate the ambiguity of respective roles that comes with the new product organization, and, by implication, the need for intensive liaison between "product centers" and "product divisions". In turn, it should be noted that the required close coordination is not only a challenge strictly in terms of the formal organization. The additional challenge posed by the concomitant geographical distances is evident from Table 3.3 above. Organizational ambiguity spans continents.

Moreover, the combined picture emerging from Tables 3.3 and 3.4 actually represents an understatement of the complexities involved. Recall that the links to the sales organization for standard bearings have been suppressed so far. The sales organization (implicit in the customer-defined "businesses" in Table 3.2 above) covers both Bearing Industries and Bearing Services[51]. It is logically separate from the product organization, which refers only to Bearing Industries. The interface between production and sales of standard bearings thus takes place within Bearing Industries or between Bearing Industries and Bearing Services. We will attempt to clarify the intricacies of this combined organization.

First, some of the tasks enumerated in Table 3.4 pertaining to the product organization are shared also with the sales organization, and primarily with the sales organization for OEM-customers. The over-all product development programs, enveloping the product development plans and actual work in Table 3.4, are determined by the product line board in close cooperation with the OEM-sales organization. A similar close cooperation concerns the accumulated "product knowledge" and preparation of training material in Table 3.4. The identified shared responsibility within the product organization for this task is to be exercised in collaboration with the OEM-customer sales organization. Special delivery demands and connected support in technical matters (cf. Table 3.4) is ultimately the responsibility of the OEM-customer sales organization, but in effect shared with the "product divisions".

Second, and more importantly, the organizational hand-over between production and sales has not been specified. The standard bearings leaving the product organization have to be picked up by the sales organization for delivery to OEM-customers and the

---

[51] The other three divisions, Specialty Bearings, Tools and Component Systems, handle their 'own' sales. To a varying, but limited, degree they also draw on the extensive net of Bearing Services subsidiaries for sales.

aftermarket. Differently put, the sales organization constitutes the internal 'customers' for the product organization. That relationship explains the task of internal marketing in Table 3.4. A "product center" has to actively market its product line wares to the sales organization, indirectly in competition with other "product centers", since they are also laying claim to sales effort of the sales organization vis-à-vis external customers.

The nine customer segments, or 'businesses', of Bearing Industries and Bearing Services (cf. Table 3.2 above) are organizationally collected into three separate sales forces. The "automotive business unit" brings together the large volume car, truck, and electrical industry segments. The small to medium volume businesses associated with general machinery industry, heavy industry, and railways are collectively designated the "machinery business unit". The three aftermarket customer segments are, naturally, handled by the Bearing Services organization. It should be noted, though, that the Bearing Services' auto distributors and dealers segment has much in common with Bearing Industries' "automotive business unit", and similarly the users segment with the "machinery business unit".

External sales are essentially local, meaning that the sales forces are represented on the different national markets. The "automotive" and the "machinery business units" have their local personnel attached to the Bearing Industries' subsidiary, and the aftermarket sales personnel belong to the Bearing Services' subsidiary. Where Bearing Industries is less able to service 'its' local customers due to its more limited geographical market coverage, Bearing Services takes over.

One significant limitation to sales being local needs to be pointed out at this stage. Some large OEM-customers deal directly with the Bearing Industries subsidiary which manufactures the bearings it purchases. To exemplify, Ford UK has more business directly with the German Bearing Industries subsidiary than with the local UK "automotive business unit" organization.

By now, the contours of the over-all organization for standard bearings have, I hope, become more distinct. Nevertheless, to further that objective Figure 3.7 below summarizes some salient features as they have been identified so far. Figure 3.7 illustrates the organizational principles as they have been deduced, and thus suppresses much of the detail in the preceding discussion. Moreover, the figure represents only one cut through the organization in order to be able to accommodate the product, sales and subsidiary dimensions. It is noteworthy that there is a pronounced functional influence in the organization.

Obviously, Figure 3.7 is grossly oversimplified. Only one full product line with sales organization interface is shown (top one in Figure 3.7), and it is the simplest type with only one "product center" and one "product division". This hypothetical product line is, however, assumed to deliver to both OEM-customer sales organizations, which is not the case for a few lines (the aftermarket sales organization is always a recipient).

The second product line displayed in Figure 3.7 (bottom one) is assumed to have two "product divisions", but is still very uncomplicated (cf. the actual product lines in Table 3.3 above). Here, the physical product flow to the sales organization is omitted for the sake of presentational clarity (as are the reporting lines to divisional headquarters).

The scope of a typical manufacturing subsidiary (with sales to external customers), and of a corresponding sales subsidiary, is indicated in Figure 3.7. The latter is the simplest case. It depicts a national sales subsidiary serving the local aftermarket and reporting to its divisional head-office. Of course, the subsidiary takes deliveries from all other product lines as well wherever they may be located (and as a rule also from the three other divisions outside the standard bearing business; none of those flows are shown in Figure 3.7).

Although simplified in the figure, the hypothetical manufacturing subsidiary is rather more complicated. Some points of clarification relating to Figure 3.7 are in order.

Figure 3.7

Schematic View of the Organization for Standard Bearings

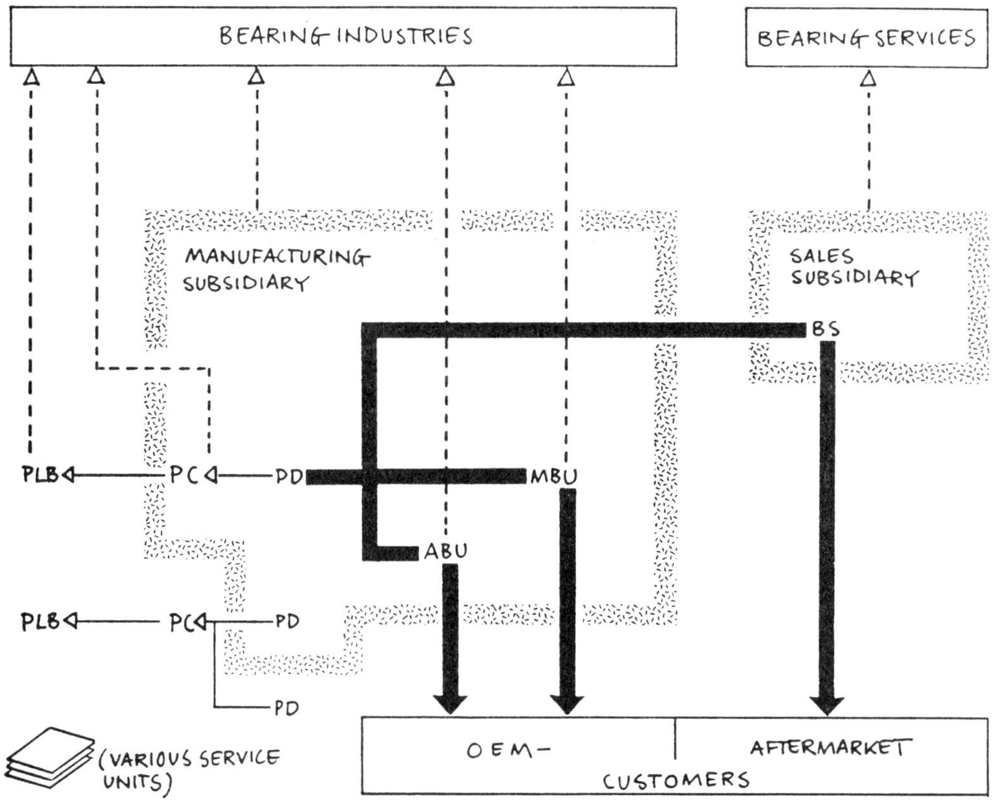

NOTE: PLB = PRODUCT LINE BOARD
PC = PRODUCT CENTER
PD = PRODUCT DIVISION
ABU = AUTOMOTIVE BUSINESS UNIT
MBU = MACHINERY BUSINESS UNIT
BS = BEARING SERVICES
——— PRODUCT LINE REPORTING
- - - - (GLOBAL) DIVISIONAL REPORTING
▬ PHYSICAL PRODUCT FLOW

Sources: See text.

First, the "automotive" and "machinery business units" are local sales units, supplied also from other product lines (not shown). They are parts of the manufacturing subsidiary, but their activities are quite distinct from those of the subsidiary, wherefore their (sales) reporting to the divisional headquarters are displayed.

Second, all reporting on the manufacturing subsidiary's activities de facto go from the subsidiary to divisional headquarters. However, since the "product center" of a "product division" present in the subsidiary often is located at another manufacturing subsidiary, the "product center's" reporting is indicated[52]. The "product division(s)" in the manufacturing subsidiary constitute the very 'heart' of subsidiary operations, wherefore that reporting is not singled out in the figure.

Third, and although perhaps self-evident, "product divisions" are located at factories, of which there typically are several in a manufacturing subsidiary. For instance, this means that a factory manager is evaluated both on company performance and on the performance of the "product division(s)" operating in the factory.

With production and sales now largely organized de facto independently from the legal and physical scope of the manufacturing subsidiary company, the latter's role has changed considerably. Its responsibilities have been much diffused. It retains a much diminished company staff primarily for finance, legal matters and public affairs. Company human resource and quality management are also attended to, but they are secondary priorities.

The main locus of staff activities is the "product division", which has sizeable staff for manufacturing, logistics, quality and personnel. Actually, the sum total of the "product divisions" makes up the bulk of Bearing Industries' resources in terms of capital and labor employed, and indeed also of SKF as a whole.

The "product center" is a skeleton operation, maintaining a small staff for product marketing, product development, and manufacturing development. Loosely put, its role

[52] The converse situation - viz. when a "product center" is located within a subsidiary, but also having "product divisions" in other subsidiaries - is naturally also relevant here.

is 'thin and wide'. The "product center" has coordinating responsibilities along key production functions (product development, manufacturing, and sales) and across legal - national and company - boundaries (global product responsibility).

At the Bearing Industries divisional level (i.e. the global divisional level) there is a strong management group for the finance, manufacturing, marketing and human resource functions. Purchasing, material flow, product development, information systems, and quality assurance are staff functions of lesser importance. These latter functions (as well as financial management) have additional significant coordinating units with divisional or corporate scope of activity. These units' considerably varying roles fall outside the present discussion. Instead, they will crop up in the following sections (some in Section 3.4 immediately below). One of the functions, purchasing, is particularly relevant in the present context, though.

Purchasing also brings us to the subject of "various service units" in Figure 3.7. A set of international purchasing centers falls in this category. Ten international purchasing centers covering the main material inputs[53] have so far been established. They are to coordinate globally the purchasing activities of the "product divisions" in order to exploit economies of scale leading to improvements in quality, delivery conditions and prices. The potential here should be sizeable, as indicated by a benchmark cost distribution in the bearing industry being 20 percent direct labor, 30 percent fixed costs, and 50 percent material content[54].

Other service units worth mentioning on the sales side are Autech in the automotive customer segment and the business support teams in the machinery segment (e.g. the pulp & paper, mining & construction, gearbox and metalworking teams). They primarily work toward OEM-customers but also assist the aftermarket sales organization. They give technical support, work with special customer requirements, and coordinate sales to

[53] For steel, tube, bar/wire, rings, brass cages, seals, grinding wheels, diamond tools, lubricants, and cartons.

[54] For reference, manufacturing costs ("costs of goods sold" in the income statement), but for the whole SKF Group, amounted to SEK 16.9 billion in 1989.

customers in what is seen as global industries. - The service units are normally geographically located in conjunction with the central manufacturing location for the most relevant product(s), e.g. Schweinfurt, Germany, for the gearbox support team.

To sum up, the organization for the standard bearing business means control and coordination of activities according to many dimensions. It thus goes further than any traditional (two-dimensional) matrix arrangements. The wish to achieve this multiple, simultaneous coordination carries with it a certain ambiguity as to the specific roles of the different organizational units. In parallel, specialization is driven further, be it in a function (like production), a customer segment, local market (sales), or particular product.

The traditional national subsidiary has little to do with the picture in Figure 3.7. It is instead something of a 'home' for a variety of smaller units, which coordinate their activities amongst themselves and with other units in other subsidiaries. We have also seen how these various smaller units have taken on responsibilities previously residing at the subsidiary level. Indeed, de facto 'reach' may actually go further in that a "product division" (being a part of a subsidiary) can be the key location globally for a "product line".

In addition, it appears as if the divisional head-office has stronger control over subsidiary activities than is traditionally the case. In the process some historical subsidiary responsibilities now have been put at the divisional level.

The bottom line for SKF's business organization is increased complexity. It is especially evident for the standard bearing business. The tortuous review of the organization has also indirectly demonstrated the inadequacy of the terms at hand to describe this labyrinth. However, the following section presents some additions to this organizational complexity.

3.4 Other Organizational Units

A few, rather disparate, organizational units warrant mention because of their importance, although they do not fit well with the business organization. In the case of Eurotrade, this situation may be temporary as it is due to a changing context of operations (responsibility for bearings in the Eastern European market), while backward integration into machine tools (LMT) and steel (Ovako Steel), as well as SKF's basic research unit (ERC), traditionally have filled roles separate from the more narrow bearing, tools and component businesses. We will briefly look at them in turn and, lastly, just note a few other organizational bodies.

Starting with Eurotrade in Gothenburg, it has recently changed from selling on commission to Eastern Europe to assuming full sales responsibility for the region. The sales companies in Hungary, Czechoslovakia, and Yugoslavia, as well as agents, are to be coordinated through Eurotrade. Import restrictions and other government regulations prevented such coordination previously.

SKF's East European sales are very limited at present (they are expected to grow as a result of the political changes in the region during the last couple of years). Our interest, however, stems from Eurotrade representing something of an organizational aberration. Eurotrade and the SKF subsidiaries in Eastern Europe belong to Bearing Industries. This is the case in spite of only two small joint ventures with the Yugoslav Government (and where SKF holds small minority shares) having anything to do with manufacturing. Faced with external uncertainty, SKF chooses to institute a regional sales 'headquarters' (called Area Europe East) centrally in Bearing Industries. It has been built on collecting what earlier were rather insignificant units left over in Bearing Industries from the time when the Bearings Europe division existed (prior to 1987, see Hagström, 1987b).

Another unit that has defied organizational orthodoxy, and consistently so, is Lidköping Machine Tools (LMT) in Lidköping, Sweden. Lidköping primarily manufactures grinding machinery. Grinding is commonly held to be the most critical operation in the manufacture of bearings, which is why LMT is of strategic importance for SKF. It is something of a competence center. LMT also makes process control equipment, most notably for continuous production.

Out of sales amounting to some SEK 300 million/year, about half goes to external customers and half to internal ones (i.e. the bearing, but also the tool, manufacturing subsidiaries). The state-of-the-art models are sold internally, while external customers typically can only buy the second-latest version. Around four-fifths of sales are exports and LMT has a sales subsidiary of its own in Erkrath, Germany. The relatively small LMT does not belong organizationally to any of SKF's five divisions. LMT's separateness, and importance, is manifest in it being the only manufacturing subsidiary reporting directly to the Chief Executive Officer of SKF.

Another company representing upstream vertical integration is Ovako Steel. It is half-owned by SKF, and ownership of the other half has recently been concentrated in the hands of the Finish Oy Wärtsilä AB. SKF's contribution to the joint venture was its specialty steel division (cf. Hagström, 1987b). Ovako Steel is now a much bigger operation with annual sales of about SEK 5.6 billion (1989). It is not formally part of SKF and its organization, but tied to SKF in other ways, notably through a five-year supply agreement due to expire in 1991.

According to SKF corporate management[55], the reasons for the divestment in 1986 were strategic in the context of the steel business itself. SKF Steel was not big enough to successfully compete in the long run on the global specialty steel market. Corporate management neither wanted to close it down, nor to undertake the investments necessary to remedy the situation. No suitable buyers (from SKF's point of view) could be found, wherefore a merger was seen as the only viable alternative in order to achieve a sufficiently strong market position in the specialty steel business.

[55] See Footnote 20, above.

A competing explanation is given by Lundgren (1990). From a corporate perspective, he argues for the steel business being hived off as a result of the need for know-how feed-back from customers. Tying the particular case to a careful theoretical argument, vertical integration is seen as denying the upstream activity external user information. The combination of high quality specialty steel becoming an industry commodity, and SKF Steel's shortcomings in developing its 'market' know-how then led to SKF's decision of vertical disintegration.

It is worth emphasizing, though, that Lundgren's (1990) point is one of principle, since ownership is the key issue, and is seen in an 'all-or-nothing' context. That perhaps also explains why no mention is made of the fact that the 'old' SKF Steel only sold about one quarter of its output to internal, SKF customers. A diluted SKF share of Ovako's sales and of ownership must then have been assumed by Lundgren (1990) to be enough for non-SKF customers to become more forth-coming with their knowledge.

Recall also that this in-between organizational solution for the steel business is consistent with SKF's over-all strategy of moving the center of gravity in its operations downstream, viz. closer to the activities of its (bearing) customers (cf. Hagström, 1987b).

In addition to the area- and production-based units mentioned, there is a whole host of functional entities outside the divisional organization. Apart from exploiting economies of scale, they provide a measure of functional coordination at the corporate level[56]. They are active in areas such as financial management, insurance, information systems, real estate management, consultancy, and research and product development[57]. Most date back to the mid-1970s (cf. Hagström, 1987b). More recent (1987-1988) additions are SKF Capital S. A., SKF Fastighetsförvaltning AB, and SKF Support AB. SKF Fastighetsförvaltning (real estate management) is primarily a function of SKF having concluded sale-lease-back arrangements for some Swedish properties (incl. the

[56] In addition, there are several committees, boards and the like supporting functional coordination within SKF (see Hagström, 1987b).

[57] Financial management and information services are discussed further in Section 5.2.1.3 and Section 5.2, respectively.

Gothenburg head-office). SKF Support is a fairly large (93 employees in 1989) internal consultancy operation for general technical and management services.

Apart from the small capital market subsidiary in Brussels and the SKF Engineering & Research Centre (ERC) in Holland, the functional entities are located in Sweden. ERC is a strategically important unit, accounting for about a quarter of SKF R&D expenditure[58]. It reports directly to the Chief Executive Officer of SKF, and the Research Director in the SKF Group Management team sits at ERC. In 1988 ERC received a boost to its status by the establishment of the SKF College of Engineering at ERC. The College is an internal training institution for SKF's sales personnel, and for sales and application engineers.

ERC carries out most of SKF's basic research (materials, bearing life, lubrication etc.). In addition, it is the corporate center for product testing, quality assurance, process control, measuring techniques, and development of heat treatment processes (an important stage in the production of bearings and tools, cf. LMT's corresponding role concerning grinding above). Moreover, ERC is an important marketing instrument, a large portion of its approximately 1 800 visitors per year being SKF customers.

ERC is owned[59] by the largest Bearing Industries subsidiaries which, together with the corporate headquarters, are represented on its board. ERC was located away from these major subsidiaries and headquarters in order to avoid it straying from its corporate role. Some more traditional location-specific advantages added to the attraction of the chosen site (see further Hagström, 1990b).

---

[58] SKF's strong reliance on R&D carried out abroad is also illustrated by the fact that Sweden actually only accounts for about 10 percent of SKF's R&D expenditure (according to the background data to Danielsson and Synnerstad, 1990).

[59] Ownership has recently been adjusted to include also the US and Spanish subsidiaries. The German subsidiary now holds a 30 percent stake, the Italian 21 percent, the Swedish 15 percent, the French 12 percent, the US 12 percent, the UK 7 percent, and the Spanish subsidiary 3 percent. This division is a very accurate ranking of the subsidiaries' relative importance in SKF.

In terms of ownership and location, ERC is very similar to the Forecasting & Supply Office (FSO) in Brussels (cf. Hagström, 1987b). But FSO has a coordinating role for the production and distribution of standard bearings (see Section 5.2.2.1 below) and belongs to the Bearing Industries division.

The conclusion from the previous section of daunting organizational complexity has thus been reinforced. However, we have primarily described a formal organizational framework, which is far from the whole story. The main points are the multi-dimensionality of, and the variety of loci of responsibility in the organization identified already at this stage of our inquiry. We now go further, turning to the role of computer-based information systems in the complex web of SKF activities.

4. NETWORK

SKF Group Telenet is designated as a corporate resource. Its main purpose is twofold: to provide communications links, and to offer access both to different computers and to computer applications. At this stage, the Telenet can conveniently be regarded as constituting one communications infrastructure of the firm, while the applications refer to one information systems infrastructure. This chapter deals with the communications links between selected sites and, consequently, with communications access for different organizational units. Access to, and use of, information systems is the subject of the next chapter.

Here, we first discuss some points of principle regarding how to delimit the communications infrastructure. The following two most extensive, main sections in this chapter are dedicated to the actual workings of the data communications network in SKF. Both the functions and configuration at different levels of the network structure are run through in some detail. The chapter is concluded with a somewhat cursory review of the specific role of the network in SKF.

4.1 What Is a 'Network'?[60]

The term 'network', and indeed also 'communications' and 'information systems', is much wider than the use implied here. Our more narrow focus is on corporate data communications networks; a specific, but by no means uncomplicated, category. Data communications networks are as a rule defined and discussed from a technical perspective (good overviews are Doll, 1978; Eaton and Smithers, 1982; Martin, 1981; Tanenbaum, 1989; and United Nations, 1982). That tradition is followed, but as a point of departure only.

[60] Section 4.1 is an adapted and abbreviated version of the conceptual discussion in the main text. The same is true of Section 5.1 below. These discussions are included here to provide a context for the benefit of those who do not wish to read the more extensive exposé in the main text.

A physical telecommunications network can be said to be comprised of different transmission media (twisted-pair cables, coaxial cables, fiber optic cables, microwave links, and satellites) and different repeater equipment along the links.

Logical networks operate on the physical telecommunications network, but are kept logically separate by idiosyncratic equipment. For instance, telephone switches, telex stations, (data) concentrators, (data) packet-assembler/disassemblers, (data) cluster controllers, and data switches are parts of the different logical telephone, telex, packet-switched data, and circuit-switched data networks.

Different telecommunications services use the physical network and one of the logical networks. Several services are available on the same logical network. For example, the common (voice) telephone service, telefacsimile, and data transmission via modem (leased line or dial-up) are all offered via the logical telephone network. Conversely, data transmission can be effectuated on different logical networks. A final distinction is that there are interfaces between logical networks allowing some services to interact, like telex and some types of data transmission.

A corporate data communications network is in essence a bundle of data communications services[61]. The main point for our purposes is that the firm has control over the network in the sense that it decides over access to the network. Thus we define the data communications network from the user end (elaborated in Hagström, 1988).

The firm purchases data communications services or provides them fully in-house. In practice, a firm rarely builds physical telecommunications links other than within a site or between adjacent sites. These Local Area Networks (LANs) are not considered further, except indirectly when local data interchange between terminals or computers

[61] The problems of definitions of communications networks and communications services suffer from both regulatory and technical complications. For different angles to these questions especially in relation to international data communications, see Aronson & Cowhey (1988), Cleevely & Cawdell (1986), ISO (1986), OECD (1980), Seitz (1980), Trauth (1986), and Ungerer (1988). By choosing the user firm's perspective, we can safely disregard these issues here.

is not possible, viz. when a site has separate, non-interfacing connections into a data communications network.

Corporate data communications networks are largely private networks. The firm 'builds' a proprietary network by leasing lines from telecommunications carriers. The alternative is to use public networks, leaving switching and transmission control to a service provider. The main reason for choosing the former is that firms often find that their communications needs outstrip what is offered publicly. Some value-added service providers can compensate for this lack of performance in common carrier networks. However, many services tailored to the needs of a large corporation have so far tended to be most cost-effectively supplied in-house.

In the end, what constitutes a typical corporate communications network are elements drawn from all the above categories. Private leased lines, dial-up connections, common public packet- and circuit-switched links, and value-added communications services more often than not coexist in a corporate data communications network. Exactly how the different individual users are tied is of little or no consequence when defining the extent of a corporate data communications network. What is important is that they <u>are</u> linked, viz. that the individual user perceives that he is connected to the corporate network.

By taking the vantage point of the individual user, our definition of a corporate data communications network then basically overrides all the distinctions so painstakingly made above. The reason for nevertheless establishing the taxonomy is twofold:

a) it makes it possible to relate our definition to mainstream literature on data communications;

and, more importantly,

b) there are qualitative differences concerning usage depending on what type of link is chosen in a particular case.

As a rule, using leased lines is more reliable, is faster, gives higher capacity, is more secure, and offers better availability than using a dial-up connection. It is also considerably more expensive and demands more network management by the using firm.

Consequently, the choice of communications link from a particular site into the network is an indication of the communications requirement. In a geographically dispersed firm, different organizational units will have qualitatively different types of links, and this configuration of the network is likely to change over time.

Naturally, the choice of links is not only a question of weighing price against performance but is also subject to availability. The relevant range of options for a specific site at a specific time varies and has to be taken into consideration. For a given communications requirement, availability has a bearing on if and when a site is connected to the network. For instance, the existence of a public circuit-switched data network in the Nordic countries makes local connections technically simple and very attractive on a price/performance basis. In South America, the range of options is not only much more limited, but the alternatives are also more expensive and more cumbersome to implement. The 'threshold value' of a communications requirement for being connected to the corporate network will then tend to be higher in South America than in the Nordic countries.

In sum, our view of corporate data communications networks will differ from standard, technically-oriented definitions (e.g. Martin, 1981; and Tanenbaum, 1989) in that we focus on the user-function of the network[62]. Our approach yields a wider concept since the whole range of electronic data transmission alternatives are seen to be part of the same network. Hence, the ability and need to communicate are here more important than exactly how it is done technically.

[62] We have also avoided the additional complication of different technical architectures in data communications networks. When a gateway exists between, say, an IBM SNA network and DEC's DECNET network, we regard them as parts of the same corporate network (see further below).

4.2 SKF Group Telenet

In SKF, the term 'Telenet' dates back to 1975-1976 when the linking of the company's main computer centers in Europe was evaluated and specified. Until then, SKF had experimented with dial-up connections, but with poor results. The first set of leased lines were established in 1976, providing only very rudimentary mainframe-to-mainframe links. During the latter half of the 1970s, SKF supplemented its own efforts by using a third-party value-added network, General Electric Information Services' Mark III.

However, the story of Telenet goes back further and we need to pause for a moment to briefly recall the context within which Telenet appeared[63].

At the end of the 1960s SKF found itself with an eroding competitive position, in particular in its 'home' region, Europe[64]. SKF chose to remain a full range producer of bearings, meeting the challenges with a production coordination and inventory system, the Global Forecasting and Supply System (GFSS), which was developed and decided upon 1970-1971. The key idea was to cut both production and capital costs by specializing production. First, the product range was more than halved to about 20.000 items. Second, production was concentrated by plant down to the point of allocating it according to dimension of standard roller bearing. These measures permitted a change from batch to continuous production in automated lines and reductions of inventories, both of work in progress and of finished goods.

---

[63] The early evolution of information systems in SKF and the broader context is discussed in Hagström (1987b). Here, only the relevant main points reappear. Any new information now available to us is, of course, also included.

[64] During the latter half of the 1960s, SKF's technological lead began to shrink. International competition intensified as demand growth slowed and new, in particular Japanese, competitors started to appear on the scene. Multilateral tariff reductions stimulated international trade, particularly for industrial goods. In Europe, the rules of the game changed with the elimination of tariffs on industrial goods both within the European Communities (EC) 1960-1968, and among the members of the European Free Trade Association (EFTA) 1960-1967. Subsequently, tariffs between the groupings were successively lowered.

Implementation of GFSS primarily concerned the European operations. It began in mid-1972 and was completed on schedule six years later. Production costs were brought down by one fifth. Out of 22 plants, six were closed. Five main national subsidiaries (with several plants) came to dominate SKF's European bearing production[65]. In the longer run, the old standard relationship of 80 percent of production for the local market and 20 percent for exports changed for the converse. The mother-daughter organization was replaced by a divisional organization in 1973 as the realization of GFSS required supranational decisions on coordination of production[66].

GFSS itself is not a computer but a logical system. However, GFSS was conceived as functioning on-line from the outset. During the early to mid-1970s the development of an SKF Totally Integrated Computer System (STICS) was attempted. It was supposed to be one mammoth company-wide system encompassing all relevant applications. Despite repeated efforts, the integrated system failed and had to be dropped in favor of less ambitious temporary solutions. The Forecasting and Supply Office (FSO), established in 1973 to handle the operational aspects of GFSS, had to operate on stand-alone-basis. Abandoning STICS opened the way for concentrating on communications without having to simultaneously accommodate, with hindsight, unrealistic requirements of systems development[67].

The final decision to go ahead and build a fully-fledged proprietary data communications network was taken during the autumn of 1977 by Mauritz Sahlin, then Head of the European Bearing Division, now Chief Executive Officer of SKF. The main driving forces leading up to the decision was still the on-going implementation of GFSS, but also the prospects of being able to better utilize expensive computer capacity in the company. The latter consideration is reflected in the original full name, where 'Telenet' stood for

[65] In France, Italy, Sweden, the UK, and West Germany.

[66] See further Section 5.2.2.1.

[67] Note that the conception of STICS was well in line with thinking on information systems at the time (see main text).

'Teleprocessing Network'. Furthermore, it was stressed that a data communications network had the potential of becoming a vital strategic asset for the whole company.

The SKF Group Telenet was successively installed and began to provide service in the beginning of 1979. Five computer centers in five countries (Sweden, West Germany, Italy, France and UK, viz. the main GFSS units) were included. SKF was a pioneer in the area, being the first industrial company outside the computer industry (at least in Europe) to implement an international data communications network.

4.2.1 Telenet Functions

Some basic communications services are required for a network to function as a data communications network. A physical connection is not sufficient for allowing a terminal user to transmit data throughout the network in a coherent format and to access application programs located in different computers connected to the network. In order to make communications practicable, a number of communications services are offered on the SKF Group Telenet. The main services are interactive traffic, remote job entry, file transfer, and message transmission. A host of other services (different gateways, connections to external systems and networks, and calculation and text applications) are also provided.

In consequence, our initial distinction between communications and information systems does not appear to hold up as neatly as one would hope. However, the problem is not serious as the set of services provided by SKF Group Telenet is largely a function of practical administrative concerns. Some corporate applications and systems are most conveniently supplied as an integral part of Telenet, while others ended up as Telenet functions for more haphazard reasons. An example of the former is the message transfer system, or electronic mail system, MEST (SKF Electronic Message Transmission). Some technical calculation applications can illustrate the latter category. They were some of the first common applications and were in some cases used for building Telenet[68]. Subsequently, they more or less just 'remained' as a part of Telenet.

For analytical purposes we can maintain the distinction, if we include the, in some sense, basic communications services in 'communications'. Interactive traffic, remote job entry, file transfer, gateways and some external connections will then merit some further consideration here[69]. MEST is left for the next section. Many of the other minor systems are supportive in character (like word processing, simulation packages and calculation programs) and will not be discussed further other than in very general terms.

Remote job entry is a way to access processing power. A user enters a job to be processed at any of the computer centers connected to the network.

Interactive traffic simply means that a user with the proper authorization can access a particular on-line application program located in a computer connected to the Telenet. This facility incorporates access to common applications, i.e. different standardized systems for special-purpose information exchange in the company.

Files can be transmitted between the computer centers and also to/from some smaller minicomputers. The requested file is copied and sent to the receiving computer. An important use of file transfers is for transmitting information between (and within) standardized common systems.

---

[68] The MEST of today also actually grew out of a technical message transfer system used when Telenet was being set up. It was a message-switching (logically similar to circuit-switching, but a route is established for a message rather than for a conversation) system. In this type of system, messages are filed, usually at a single location, for subsequent retrieval (cf. Martin, 1981). This centralized filing and the system's intimate connection to switching for the initial network were good reasons for MEST becoming a Telenet service.

[69] Our term 'basic' is not as indistinct as it may seem. It corresponds quite well to the International Standards Organization's (ISO) Open Systems Interconnection (OSI) model for data communication, although that model was developed for technical and regulatory purposes (cf. ISO, 1986; and Tanenbaum, 1989). The services we include below in Telenet relate to the three top layers of the model (i.e. session, presentation, and application). For instance, file transfer is specified in the top layer. The excluded services, to be discussed in the following section, go beyond the OSI-model in that they constitute more complex applications.

Some external connections go via Telenet. For instance, external databases are, in principle, utilized through one connection to Telenet instead of users spread around the world having their own, separate connections. There are also central interconnections through MEST with GEIS' message-handling network and with the similar Scandinavian network for MEMO-users. A special case is a leased line from Gothenburg to IBM for technical support world-wide and for access to IBM's own network.

Telenet also provides a gateway (via MEST) to the public telex network. Virtually all of SKF's international telex messages are sent from Gothenburg, irrespective of where in the organization they originated. In this way, SKF subsidiaries around the world can exploit the lower Swedish telex rates. Via connections to the public telephone network, telefacsimile messages can also be sent through Telenet.

Finally, there are internal gateways between DEC and IBM computers. The Telenet uses IBM's Systems Network Architecture (SNA). IBM compatibility is the rule for Telenet connections. However, SKF has several DEC computers for technical uses. Many of those are linked in an international DECNET[70], which has gateways into Telenet. Telenet 'overlaps' the SKF DECNET, wherefore we can regard it as one network.

4.2.2 Telenet Configuration

The extent of the SKF data communications network remains to be accounted for. The SKF Group Telenet covers only part of the story. In turn, the Group Telenet consists, first, of a 'backbone' network, linking the main computer centers or nodes in Europe and the US, and, second, of links to a large number of peripheral nodes around the world.

The different main and peripheral nodes are themselves more often than not centers of local networks, not uncommonly extending outside the borders of the country where the

[70] Schweinfurt, Clamart, Turin, Gothenburg, Lidköping, and ERC in Holland are linked on a DECNET (see also Section 5.2.2.2 below).

node is located. These 'national' networks are the responsibility of the respective node to which they are connected and thus technically not part of the SKF Group Telenet. However, some Telenet peripheral nodes are located in the same countries as (and are indeed connected to) a main node. The rule is that connections to the main subsidiary of each of the respective SKF business divisions in the same country are also called peripheral nodes. Their status is thus defined by the formal organization of the company. That becomes a source of confusion, since the organization structure is prone to change while the communications network configuration is more stable. Consequently, unclear node status has less to do with data communications structure than with the organization structure of the day.

The picture is further complicated by overlapping networks in the Nordic region. Main nodes and the extensive Nordic "national" network are not readily separable.

We will choose to disregard some of these technical, operational and administrative intricacies, and instead impose a clearer hierarchical structure based on de facto communications functionality.

The main nodes are linked by communications 'highways' in the backbone network. Peripheral nodes in distinct national markets are termed collectively the peripheral network. The backbone and peripheral networks make up the Group Telenet. National or domestic networks are then geographically determined. We introduce the term 'subsidiary node' for what is a peripheral node in Telenet parlance, but is within a national network as we have defined it. For instance, the Tools division subsidiary in Milan is seen as a subsidiary node in the Italian national network, and the Lisbon bearings sales subsidiary is seen as a peripheral node, since it is the only node in Portugal[71].

The distinction is useful since it improves correspondence with the organizational setup where the different subsidiaries are national companies. Without having an 'extra'

---

[71] The connection to Telenet in the latter case is routed through the Madrid main node.

national hierarchy the Milan subsidiary node would assume the same status in relation to Turin as, say, the peripheral node in Auckland, New Zealand[72].

We also term connected subsidiaries 'nodes', and most of them are just that (in a technical sense), in keeping with the organizational correspondence objective. Still, some minor such 'nodes' are technically 'end-points', as they have no lower level links. Perhaps a more accurate term would be 'potential nodes' since, should the need arise, these latter peripheral and subsidiary nodes can quickly attain (technical) node status. The minor gain in exactness has little practical relevance here, though, and does also add considerably to expository complexity, wherefore that fine distinction is ignored in the following.

A final caveat to keep in mind concerns the geographic routing (and choice of carrier) for data communications traffic. The identified relative stability of the communications network configuration refers to connections having been established between locations. The specific routing of these links between the locations may change considerably, however, as advanced users of data communications will continuously assess existing traffic-carrying arrangements. When a cheaper and/or better way of routing a particular link becomes available, traffic can be switched to the new route (and sometimes to another carrier). Therefore, when specific routing is indicated in the following, it only provides a snap-shot in time of the physical network configuration. The functional configuration, viz. that connections exist between units, remains stable, though.

4.2.2.1 Backbone network

The geographical location of the main nodes of SKF Group Telenet is shown in Figure 4.1. The leased lines linking the nodes portray the configuration as it stood at the beginning of 1990.

---

[72] However, some minor overlap between peripheral nodes and subsidiary nodes within national networks cannot be avoided, depending on the particular issues being discussed.

Figure 4.1

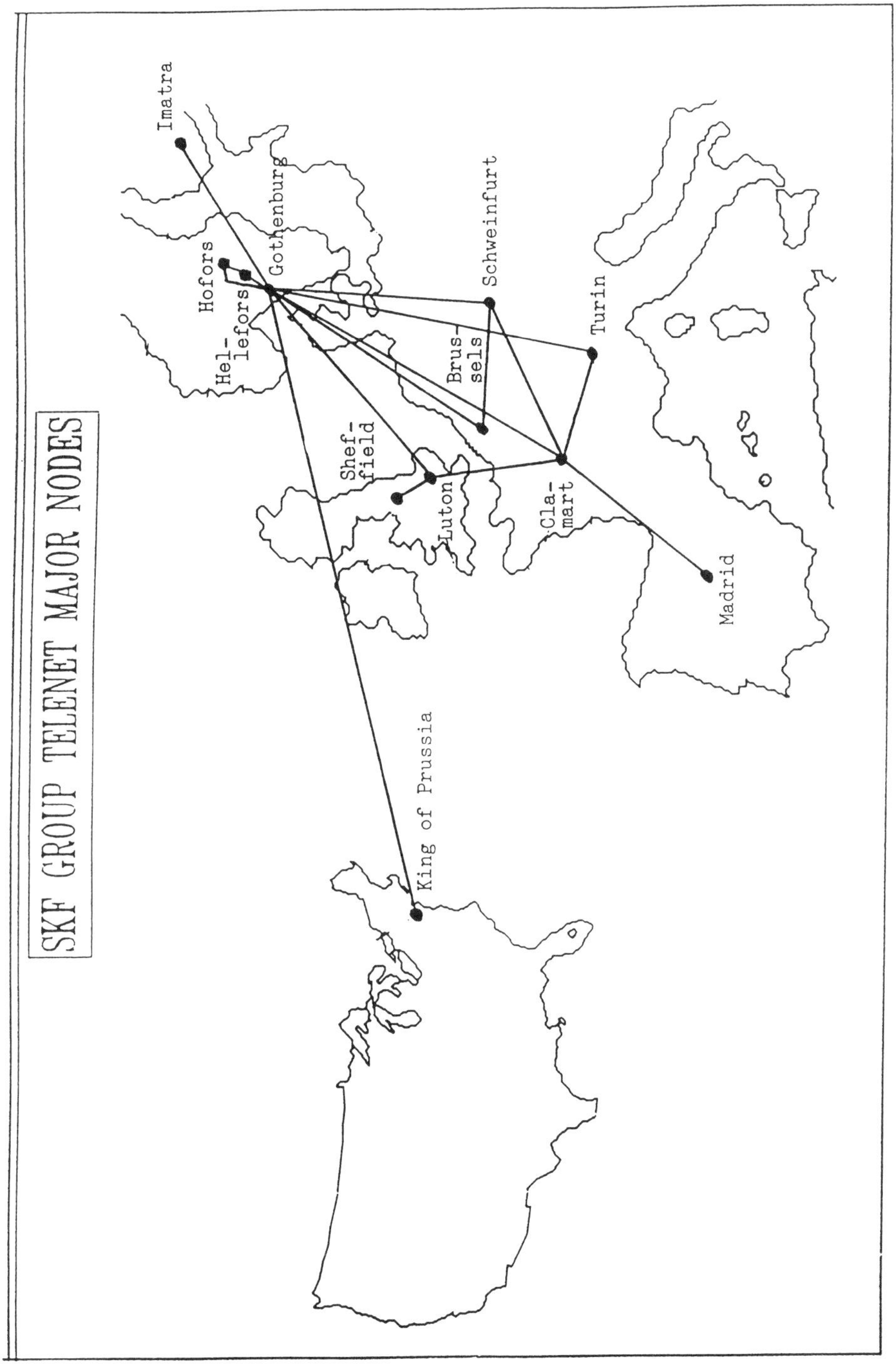
SKF GROUP TELENET MAJOR NODES
Imatra
Gothenburg
Hofors
Hel-
lefors
Schweinfurt
Turin
Brus-
sels
Shef-
field
Luton
Cla-
mart
Madrid
King of Prussia

A decade earlier, the first backbone network linked the five main European bearing manufacturing units. It consisted of a set of leased lines from Gothenburg to Schweinfurt, Turin, Clamart and Luton, respectively. Each of these locations housed a major computer center.

The computer centers of Hellefors and Hofors in Sweden, and Sheffield in the UK were added to the network in 1983. Hellefors and Hofors are steel mills and were part of the SKF Steel division at the time. Sheffield was, and still is, the largest manufacturing unit and computer installation in the Tools division.

During the following couple of years the network was consolidated, with complementing lines being established from Clamart to Schweinfurt, Turin and Luton.

Madrid was added to the network in connection with SKF's complete takeover of its Spanish bearing manufacturing subsidiary from the Spanish Government in 1985. That same year, SKF's large computer center at the bearings head-office in King of Prussia, Pennsylvania, was tied to the network through a leased satellite link.

SKF's divestment of the Steel division in 1986 subsequently brought changes to the configuration of the backbone network. Hellefors and Hofors have so far maintained main node status but the computer center in Hellefors is being dismantled. The steel mill in Imatra, Finland, has been added to the network, or, more correctly, the computer service bureau handling Imatra's data processing has been made a main Telenet node. When the new Ovako Steel (half-owned by SKF) was formed, it was agreed that the company would remain in SKF Group Telenet at least for another five years.

Lastly, the Forecasting and Supply Office (FSO) in Brussels - the hub of GFSS - has been included as a main node. This is contrary to SKF practice, since FSO has for almost a decade formally been a peripheral node, linked to the Gothenburg (or Nordic) 'national' network. With the establishment in 1988 of a second leased line (this time to Schweinfurt) FSO is functionally a main node. Indeed, FSO together with the five largest bearing plants in Europe form an 'inner circle' in SKF. Functioning data communications between these sites is deemed sufficiently important as to warrant back-up links, thereby radically reducing the risk of interruptions in data traffic. In addition, transmission of large volumes of data can be speeded up by using both routes simultaneously.

The SKF Group Telenet functions 99.5 percent of the time (average for 1990), a very high figure by international standards[73]. SKF is now on par with specialist suppliers of international data communications services (like GEIS and Tymnet) in terms of network availability offered[74]. The record for public packet-switched networks operated by telecommunications authorities, on the other hand, leaves a lot to be desired: by a slightly different measure, as much as about 25 percent of data transmitted across borders within the European Community on the public packet-switched networks never arrive (Financial Times, September 18, 1989).

The cost of leasing an international line within Europe is typically USD 30 000 - 50 000 per year. More or less double that amount is required for an intercontinental line. These highly imprecise figures only serve to indicate the approximate, and rather substantial, threshold value attached to maintaining a functioning data communications link by the leasor. The traffic-carrying capacity of a leased line is typically far in excess of even the most avid user's needs. SKF clocks a peak hour lineload of approximately 25 percent on the communications 'highways' in the backbone network. With very few exceptions (see OECD, 1980; and OECD, 1987), the leasor is prohibited to resell excess carrying capacity (so called third-party traffic).

The relatively high cost of fixed international communications links, coupled with increased competition in the provision of such links, puts a premium on flexibility in the choice of carrier. When the Telenet was built, competition was restricted to value-added service providers, which could demand high prices as a result of the difficulties involved in establishing communications links. SKF had to negotiate individually with the

---

[73] Typically, international corporate proprietary networks reach 89-90 percent availability.

[74] During the last few years of 1980s, the specialists reached about one percentage point higher than SKF.

telecommunications authorities through whose area a leased line passed. At present, SKF maintains a large measure of flexibility by only entering into quarterly agreements with carriers. However, the market for very basic transmission services is still strictly limited to a few, quite sophisticated users capable of managing an international proprietary communications network. Swedish MNCs are by international comparison very accomplished users (cf. OECD, 1983a and 1983b; and Thorngren, 1990). In November, 1987, SKF became the very first customer of (indeed, it is likely to have prompted the formation of) STS Telecom[75]. SKF had plans to route its link with King of Prussia via the UK, using British Telecom International for the last leg. The new STS Telecom was set up in order to provide non-regulated, competitive pricing by reselling transmission capacity leased from Swedish Telecom, which was not allowed to do so itself[76]. By mid-1990, SKF was renting capacity (in practice leased lines) on about ten main international routes in this way.

The responsibility for planning, managing and supervising SKF Group Telenet rests with a special unit within SKF Dataservice in Gothenburg. The SKF Group Telenet unit consists of five people. The basic communications services (cf. Section 4.2.1) are administered out of Gothenburg. The Telenet unit is further charged with implementing the stringent corporate standards regarding computer hardware and software connected to the network. Finally, they are the corporate level counterpart to the different node managers regarding corporate data communications[77].

The cost of data communications is distributed internally on a fixed basis. Hardware costs are borne by the respective nodes where the equipment is physically located. Communications costs are shared equally between nodes according to a hierarchical principle, assuming that a node sends about as much as it receives. The opposite number

[75] STS Telecom was owned jointly by the Nordic telecommunications authorities. However, in January, 1990, the Swedish part of STS was reconstituted as part of a new Swedish Telecom International to provide a wide variety of competitive international network services.

[76] For reference, the Swedish Government formally lifted the restrictions on third-party traffic on Swedish Telecom lines, January 24, 1991.

[77] For the wider, information systems, organization, see Section 5.3.2 below.

to main, peripheral and subsidiary nodes is Group Telenet in Gothenburg. For example, the Turin node pays half of the cost of the leased line to Gothenburg, which pays the other half. In fact, Turin transmits about twice as much data as it receives. The upshot of this debiting principle is that the variable cost of usage of fixed links is zero. For dial-up connections, the sender pays, but only to the node connecting the sender to the Telenet. Onward transmission is 'free'. Thus, corporate policy (cf. 'Telenet is a corporate resource') and excess transmission capacity combine to stimulate usage of the data communications network.

The issues discussed in this section become more diverse as we leave the backbone network and move to the peripheral network.

4.2.2.2 Peripheral network

The variability of connections is greater for peripheral nodes, not only because of changes in availability, performance and price for telecommunications services, but also because of changing communications requirements of SKF Telenet users. There are few peripheral nodes that merit international leased line connection to the Group Telenet. Leased lines are more common in the different national networks.

Connection to the Telenet is purported to generally be judged on the basis of the local company's turnover and the technical feasibility of establishing a link. In keeping with our geographically determined hierarchy of the data communications network, we can list the countries with SKF subsidiaries and whether or not a connection exists[78]. The extent of the peripheral network as of January, 1990 is given below, juxtaposed with data on the divisional affiliation of SKF subsidiaries in the respective countries. Note, however, that

[78] We omit sales offices and agents, both selling on a commission-basis, since such links are within the purview of the local node managers and thus a 'national' issue (cf. Section 4.3 below). However, such links can cross international borders, the full extent of which has not been possible to establish. We do know, though, that they are extremely few outside the countries in Table 4.1. But fact remains that Table 4.1 represents an understatement, albeit very slight, of the number of countries with a connection to Telenet.

the table is an incomplete guide to the number of subsidiary locations, as a division may have more than one subsidiary company in a country. For instance, the Component Systems division has five very different subsidiaries in (West) Germany.

The summary enumeration of countries with main and peripheral nodes in Telenet is a fair picture of the state-of-the-art concerning to which countries meaningful connections can be established. Most peripheral nodes employ common public dial-up, packet-switched connections (CCITT recommendation X.25), which is the preferred mode when the alternative is a value-added service provider. However, common public dial-up circuit-switched links (CCITT recommendation X.21) are often the superior alternative in terms of price/performance ratio, but this service is poorly diffused internationally. Where available, it is still rather 'national' in character. SKF uses this type of link in the Nordic countries and within some national networks (notably in Germany).

Western Europe and North America present few technical problems. South East Asia/Far East and beyond have had some problems with long response times. SKF's ongoing expansion of its bearing operations in South East Asia carries with it a commensurate expansion of Telenet. The new data traffic is linked via the Singapore node. In keeping with the strategy of regionalization of bearing operations, this intermediary role for Singapore is set to grow.

Table 4.1

SKF Group Telenet Connections by Country

(1990)

Country (with local subsidiary)		Division (represented by subsidiary)					
Connected	Unconnected	Bearing Industries	Bearing Services	Specialty Bearings	Tools	Component Systems	Other companies
Argentina		X	X				
Australia			X				
Austria		X	X		X	X	
Belgium		X	X		X	X	X
Brazil		X	X		X	(X)	
Canada			X		X		
Chile			X				
Colombia			X				
	Czechoslovakia	X					
Denmark			X				
Finland			X				
France		X	X	X	X	X	X
Greece			X				
	Hungary	X					
Hong Kong			X				
India		X					
	Iran		X				
Italy		X	X	X	X	X	X
Japan			X				
	Kenya		X				
Malaysia			X				
Mexico		X	X				
	Morocco		X				
Netherlands		X	X		X	X	X
New Zealand			X				
Norway			X			X	
Panama			X				
Peru			X				
	Philippines		X				
Portugal			X				
Singapore			X		X	X	
South Africa		X					
South Korea			X				
Spain		X	X		(X)		
Sweden		X	X	X	X	X	X
Switzerland			X			X	
Taiwan		X	X				
Thailand			X				
	Turkey		X				
UK		X	X		X	X	
USA		X	X	X	X	X	X
Venezuela			X				
West Germany		X	X	X	X	X	X
	Yugoslavia	X					
	Zambia		X				
	Zimbabwe		X				
Total: (36)	(10)	(19)	(41)	(5)	(12)	(12)	(7)

Note: ( ) = Unconnected, not included in total.

Sources: See text and Chapter 2.

Latin America is more complicated in terms of establishing communications. SKF has largely been forced to use the value-added carrier Infonet via the US. Argentina and the bearing operations in Brazil have been easier to connect directly to Sweden. However, recent improvements in inter-American communications made it possible to switch this Brazilian link, instead routing it through the US. The Tools subsidiary in Brazil still uses Sheffield in the UK as a communications intermediary. The Brazilian components subsidiary remains unconnected to the network. (See also Section 4.3.5 below). The medium-sized sales subsidiary in Venezuela is a very special case in that the only way to establish communications was by leasing a line to Panama. Similarly to Singapore, the US can be expected to gain in importance as a communications intermediary. Recall though, that actual routing of lines from the perspective of corporate communications is a price/performance issue. It is largely irrelevant exactly where traffic is piped into Telenet. However, for the node providing entry it means enhancement of its communications status and commensurate local capabilities.

Eastern Europe has so far not been a viable proposition. Also Africa and the near East are largely unconnected. South Africa and India are exceptions, both representing sizeable bearing manufacturing locations. However, they almost exclusively serve their national markets and their communications needs are commensurably limited, only warranting rudimentary links with Telenet.

The growth of SKF Group Telenet has in the main been cumulative, starting from the early backbone network. The dominating position in SKF commanded by Western Europe in terms of production and sales, and by bearings in terms of products, shows up in the order by which sites have been connected to Telenet. Recall also that SKF Europe (Bearings) was a separate division in SKF up until late 1986[79].

The simple rule of connection determined by size of turnover/technical feasibility does not tally well with the observed development of the network. Rather, it needs to be amended as: manufacturing sites were connected before the sales subsidiaries; bearing

[79] See Section 4.2 above and Hagström (1987b).

locations before steel, after which came Tools and Component Systems; and Europe before the rest of the world. These sequences hold for peripheral nodes as well as for other internal connections. The dimension that appears to hold up the strongest is that of business areas.

To illustrate, the medium-sized sales subsidiaries in Switzerland and Australia (countries where SKF had no other activities) were connected to Telenet well before the Tools manufacturing subsidiary (at the time fourth largest), located in Milan very close to the main Turin node. Also, the bearings sales subsidiaries in the Nordic countries were connected (without using the public Nordic data communications network) earlier than even the Tools main node in Sheffield.

Acquisitions provide another opportunity for tracing the degree of urgency as it relates to connections to the Telenet, although the population is limited. Cases in point are Seeger-Orbis (Component Systems) and Prototyp-Werke (Tools) in West Germany, acquired by SKF in 1970 and in June, 1986 respectively. Both manufacturing units have a turnover in excess of a medium-sized bearings sales subsidiary and both still only have very limited dial-up connections to the Schweinfurt main node. Prototyp-Werke is the third largest production location within the Tools division.

A very good comparison is Steyr, an Austrian bearing manufacturer bought by SKF in September, 1988. An expensive leased line connection to Schweinfurt was installed as early as in February, 1989. In spite of Steyr's turnover being some 2.5 times higher than that of Prototyp-Werke, the swiftness of action is very impressive for several reasons: first, an international connection was required; second, Steyr has DEC computers (rather than the SKF standard IBM); and, third, there was a serious security problem associated with Steyr being part of another large local data communications network[80].

Two acquisitions within Specialty Bearings point in the same direction. The instances concern establishing subsidiary nodes in national networks (see the following section) but

---

[80] Steyr belonged to the Austrian Group, Steyr-Daimler-Puch.

nevertheless serve to further illuminate SKF's implicit policy of connection to the Telenet. MRC in Jamestown, N.Y., is about one-third again larger than Steyr in terms of turnover. MRC was purchased by SKF in July, 1986. One year later, the MRC computer center had been shut down with operations taken over by the King of Prussia center and its network had been integrated with the SKF US national network (and Telenet). Similarly, it took less than a year to establish a leased-line connection for Gamfior in Italy. Again, the problem of Gamfior using DEC computers had to be overcome in the process. And, Gamfior can be estimated to be only one third the size of Prototyp-Werke.

Finally, the category 'other companies' in Table 4.1, contains a mix of corporate level service units, some specialized manufacturing, 'left-overs' from the steel business, and the US holding company (cf. Section 3.4 above). Most important for SKF operations are the Lidköping Machine Tools for proprietary engineering (in Sweden, plus a sales subsidiary in Germany) and the specialized corporate service units, notably for financial services (see Hagström, 1987b). The center of SKF Group Telenet, SKF Dataservice AB, also falls within this category. SKF Engineering & Research Centre (in the Netherlands) is an important peripheral node. It was among the very first to be connected to the Telenet, but originally as a part of the 'national' Swedish network. ERC is still linked to the Gothenburg main node with leased lines and has a status in communications terms bordering on that of a main node. - We will return to these issues when discussing the information systems in the next chapter. Now we continue down the line to the outer boundaries of the SKF data communications network.

4.3 National Networks

In addition to the node interface with SKF Group Telenet, the local node information systems manager is responsible for other connections to the local node and onto Telenet. The local possibilities, requirements and ambitions shape the national networks. Consequently, the national networks are very different from one another.

In theory, the national networks fall within the purview of the local node information systems manager. In practice, corporate recommendations severely limit this apparent freedom. The corporate concerns go beyond the rather obvious, straight-forward Telenet issues (such as equipment to be connected, transmission protocols and required capacity). Questions of access to and control of the data communications network become more relevant as connection points are located hierarchically further from the center of the Group Telenet.

As far as the linking of only SKF subsidiaries is concerned, the problem largely remains in the mould outlined in the previous subsection. Both at the corporate level and from the different divisions, there is an overriding wish to connect all the different subsidiaries. Below the peripheral and subsidiary node level, the subsidiaries themselves are left to decide whether or not to connect their own sites, and, if so, with what type of link. In this respect, communications between factories, warehouses and offices within one SKF company are a truly local concern. Local interchange between subsidiaries - notably between Bearing Industries and Bearing Services subsidiaries - is also a local issue, but it is encouraged from the corporate and divisional levels.

As the network diffuses into the environment, connections become trickier. External parties are connected on widely different premises. On the whole, the SKF companies function as a united front towards external parties, relaying communications internally if need be. In practice, this means that customer connections are 'local' in character. For instance, an order is placed with SKF locally but it may be processed and effectuated elsewhere in the network. This internal relay of information can, however, be more or less left to the discretion of the external party, depending on the degree of access he has been afforded once he has been linked to the network. Those filtering mechanisms reside in the different information systems and are left for consideration in the following section.

The first filter towards external parties is the type of connection, which also relates to the extent of the SKF data communications network. Most business is local and that type of connection is left for the local information systems manager to decide over. More sophisticated interfaces are subject to corporate level approval and recommendations.

Some suppliers belong to this latter category. Recall the Telenet gateways to the public telex network, external databases and IBM. Ovako Steel is, in essence, 'adopted' into the SKF family in communications terms and the transactions are thus similar to other internal deliveries. In bearing manufacture, some 70 percent of material inputs are steel, and the only international supplier is Ovako Steel. Otherwise, relations with banks, transport companies, public authorities, and suppliers of material inputs are still very much in the hands of the local subsidiary and, hence, so is also the commensurate communications interfaces. In general, the external suppliers to SKF companies are very few. Of those, very few are linked to the data communications network.

Internal purchases of tools and components (e.g. rubber seals for bearings) are very limited[81]. Some bearing houses and other castings are supplied by SKF Mekanprodukter in Katrineholm but these deliveries are primarily for the Gothenburg bearings plant. Machine tools, notably grinding machines from SKF's Lidköping Machine Tools, are strategically very important, as much of SKF's technological edge in manufacturing resides in that phase of the manufacturing process. However, the information needs associated with these investment goods are largely technical in nature (loads, process control, maintenance etc.), which explains Lidköping's DECNET links.

External customers form a larger and much more varied group. Connecting customers to the SKF network began in earnest in 1983. The total number of customers linked has increased by about 100 per year since 1986/1987, and in 1990 is standing approximately at the 500-mark[82]. Some four-fifths of those use dial-up, packet-switched connections for interactive terminal usage. One-fifth have file transfer capabilities, usually via similar dial-up links. A small number of customers, less than 10 percent, have access similar to that of SKF's own sales companies, i.e. application-to-application.

---

[81] The largest cross-product flow in SKF is Component Systems's use of primarily the Bearings sales organization for about one-fifth of its output (1986 figures). The Tools division similarly disposed of 3 percent of its production. (See also Hagström, 1987b, on synergies between products in SKF.)

[82] No exact figure, or break-down on customer categories, is given (known?) by SKF.

However, the network fans out further for two reasons. First, one customer connection may in fact be many, for instance, when one distributor has many locations. He may also, in turn, have interfacing links with his customers. Second, third-party value-added networks and public videotext-applications have begun to be used in some national networks. The first category clearly falls within the SKF data communications network as we have defined it. The second category is a border-line case, as some loss of control is associated with it.

Using value-added networks for connection to external parties essentially means leaving the SKF communications standard. The applications are those of the host network and in principle open to any subscriber. Simply put, a particular application coupled with data transport is bought from the external host. Closed user groups can be defined, i.e. access to an SKF initiated application on such a network can be controlled. However, the communications package the SKF customer gets in this way, and is trained to use, is not dedicated to communications with SKF (as has been the case above). It can easily be used for, say, communications with a competitor to SKF. Further, the public nature of the network makes applications relatively easy to copy. The advantage of this kind of limited communications link is that it is a lot cheaper than establishing its own links using only a common carrier.

SKF has so far shunned these more 'open' solutions for competitive reasons. SKF's leadership in communications is deemed a major competitive asset, and SKF has vowed to maintain its lead. However, the more sophisticated the local market for value-added services, the more difficult it is to offer superior communications services to customers. The customer, say a distributor, will also be more likely to resist a communications solution dedicated to only one supplier if comparable 'open' and standardized alternatives are available. On the bonus side, from SKF's perspective, marginal customers not warranting a fully SKF-controlled connection, can justify a link via a third party, which is better than no link at all.

So, contrary to SKF policy, customer connections via third-party networks are used in the US and the UK. Both have well developed markets for value-added communications services. A videotex application is used in West Germany, but because of the exceptional cost differential between that and any standard SKF alternatives. In neither of these three markets is SKF the undisputed industry leader in national communications.

This discussion of national networks characteristics can be made specific by looking closer at a few different national networks. We have chosen four fairly extensive but, we hope, representative networks and one more idiosyncratic situation. Italy represents the standard main node (the two other similar ones being France and West Germany). The UK is interesting, since it encompasses the only Tools node. Spain is included as the most recent major addition to the network[83]. The US was selected on the basis of its relatively lesser integration with SKF's European core operations. Finally, Brazil illustrates the problems of being an outlier in terms of communications.

4.3.1 The Italian Network

The Turin node is operated by the Bearing Industries subsidiary. It also serves the Bearing Services subsidiary in Turin, Specialty Bearings' three subsidiaries (two at the same site in Vilar Perosa and Gamfior in Turin), the Tools subsidiary in Milan, the Component Systems subsidiary in Turin[84], and Ovako Steel's sales subsidiary in Milan. However, that is not the whole story as can be seen from Figure 4.2 below which depicts the locations of SKF sites linked to the Italian national network.

The Bearing Industries subsidiary has its six factories[85] and its Milan branch office linked to Turin and the head-office via leased lines. The central Italian warehouse is located adjacent to the factory in Airasca but has its own connections to Turin. These

[83] Sweden was excluded from consideration since the Group Telenet itself overlaps the 'national' network. In addition, Sweden figures so prominently throughout the whole study that there is little additional information to present here. The latter also goes for West Germany. However, West Germany is discussed fairly extensively in Section 5.3, where the network-systems relationship is discussed.

[84] A Components Systems' subsidiary in Asti and a small one in Milan are not connected.

[85] In Airasca, Bari, Cassino, Massa, Pinerolo, and Vilar Perosa (see Figure 4.2).

locations generate more than half (54 percent in 1989) of the traffic (measured in Mb/day) on the Italian national network.

Bearing Services' head-office in Turin and ten branch offices[86] are the source of more than one-third of the national traffic. All lines are leased, although one line may link more than one branch office (so called multi-drop connections). The number of branch offices have been reduced by a third during the last few years, thereby also reducing the SKF Italian network (one factory has also been closed down). Fourteen dial-up connections are at the disposal of distributors, representing less than one percent of traffic volume. Bearing Services is in the process of establishing the separate site in Turin as a subsidiary node and taking over the distributor connections.

The sites belonging to Specialty Bearings, Tools, and Component Systems have leased line connections, generating five percent, less than one percent, and two percent of domestic traffic respectively. Ovako Steel is the only supplier and Fiat Auto in Turin the only end-customer who have access to the network. Both transmit less than one percent of data traffic on the network. Fiat's connection is switched over the public telephone network. Notably, Fiat's Iveco truck company is not hooked-up as yet. The rather rudimentary link(s) with Fiat is all the more surprising as Fiat is SKF's single largest customer over-all with yearly purchases of SEK 0.7 billion for its cars and SEK 0.3 billion for its trucks.

With multiple and back-up lines (a total of 45) mostly leased, domestic lines feed off the Turin main node. The hard to come by figures on traffic volume are representative of traffic flows in national networks. By comparison, the domestic traffic is more than four times as large as the international traffic to and from the Turin node. However, there is some double counting, since some domestic traffic goes on to locations outside Italy. The shares are, however, a good indication of the distribution of data communications flows on the SKF data communications network.

---

[86] In Ancona, Bologna, Catania, Florence, Genoa, Milan, Naples, Rome, Udine, and Vicenza (see Figure 4.2).

Figure 4.2

SKF Italian Data Communications Network

(Leased line configuration by geographical location, 1990)

Note: There may be more than one node/site at each location (see text).

It is noteworthy that the Italian node has the lowest performance, viz. network availability, among the SKF main nodes, and that, contrary to the norm, the national network performs worse than the international connections. On both counts, this is a reflection of the relatively poor standard of Italian telecommunications in general.

The first connection outside the Turin head-office was installed in 1975 to the central warehouse in Airasca. That coincided with the first, rudimentary dial-up connections to other main bearings subsidiaries in Europe being tried. The Italian bearing factories got their first links in the following year. The branch offices (fifteen at the time) were connected over a period of three years, starting in 1977.

The next phase in the development of the Italian network began in the mid-1980s. Distributor links were initiated in 1985, making SKF the very first company in Italy to do so. Today, some 85 distributors have the capacity for on-line communication with SKF. SKF has both trained and helped supply the necessary equipment, to its distributors.

At about the same time (1985-1986), Tools, Component Systems, Ovako Steel and Fiat Auto had their connections installed. Specialty Bearings had to wait another couple of years.

For the near future, the growth of the network can primarily be expected to come with more end-user connections. Another key area is to connect local transporters used by SKF in Italy. Finally, the present physical transport of computer tapes to local banks and social security authorities can also be expected to become replaced by direct computer links relatively soon.

4.3.2 The UK Network

Of the two main Telenet nodes in the UK, Luton is the primus inter pares. It is possible to talk of a national 'backbone' network, linking main computer centers. First, there is a triangle, connecting Luton, Sheffield and Birmingham with leased lines. Birmingham is a sales office and a local depot for bearings. It earns its status from its role as a node for connections in the Black Country. Second, there is a leased line link to the main computer of the National Coal Board (NCB) from Luton to Birmingham. In that way, the NCB's own network is accessed by SKF. The primary locations are shown in Figure 4.3 below.

Luton is the only bearing factory in the UK and is also the site of the head-office of UK Bearing Services. The central UK warehouse is located in the vicinity. The lack of internal local impetus meant that the national network got off to a relatively slow start comparing with other parts of the SKF data communications network. Around 1980, SKF began to use dial-up connections first for its own branch offices and then for a couple of distributors. The interest paid to distributors was, however, very early both by SKF and UK standards.

The fact that distribution of industrial goods in the UK market is highly concentrated helped pave the way for forging distributor links early. Distributors are few and commonly national in coverage. The first distributor was connected in 1981, through a simple dial-up connection. In turn, that triggered an internal rationalization of the Birmingham-based distributor. It set up a small network of its own, linking its customers and branch offices. The number of sites were quickly reduced from 21 to four, more than halving the number of employees. Sales volume dropped only marginally, and customer service was improved[87]. After this trial link, connecting distributors really got underway from 1983 and on.

[87] Sigvardsson (1985) more fully describes the internal changes at the (anonymous) distributor.

Figure 4.3

SKF UK Data Communications Network

(Leased line configuration by geographical location;
SKF sites only, 1990)

Note: There may be more than one node/site at each location (see text).

The first fixed connections in the SKF UK national network outside the Luton site coincided with Sheffield becoming a main node in the international backbone network. In 1983, two stocking points-cum-sales offices, three branch offices[88], and the Luton warehouse (all bearing locations) got leased line connections to the Luton main node.

SKF was still well ahead of competition in the UK market when it began to upgrade its distributor links in 1984. Eight distributors got leased lines to either of the three points in the UK 'backbone triangle'[89]. SKF's largest distributor has, in turn, eleven sites thus connected to the SKF network. Some fifteen distributors continue to use dial-up connections.

The NCB fixed link was established during the same phase. The coal mines around the UK remain the only end-users of bearings with such connections to SKF. Two large OEMs have dial-up links. Perhaps surprisingly, there are no substantial links with the big local car manufacturers, although a hook-up to FORDNET (similar to the NCB-link) is in the offing.

SKF's lead in the local market in terms of superior communications has successively eroded, making exclusive links with SKF less attractive. Standardized communications solutions are gaining ground. Other customers choose to communicate with SKF through ISTEL's EDIT, a private third-party videotex network and SKF has installed a link to that network.

Few suppliers have data communications links with SKF. No banks or transport companies are connected to the UK network. One consultancy firm in London has a temporary (three years) leased line to Luton for work on systems development. Of the steel suppliers, only Ovako Steel is linked[90].

---

[88] In Leeds and Swanley, and in Birmingham, Bristol, and Glasgow, respectively (see Figure 4.3).

[89] Distributor connections are not shown in Figure 4.3 and not identified for reasons of competition.

[90] A leased line from Birmingham to Wolverhampton (not shown in Figure 4.3).

Component Systems has one leased line from Milton Keynes to Luton. It is unclear if the other three Components Systems companies in the UK have any dial-up links to Milton Keynes.

The Tools subsidiary has its own history of data communications. Recall that the whole Tools division was created in 1977, following the acquisition of The Sheffield Twist Drill and Steel Company (mother company of the better known Dormer Tools) in 1975. Sheffield had already started to worry about data communications with its own three overseas sales subsidiaries.

Since the overall integration into SKF dragged on, and since data communications in SKF in practice was a prerogative of bearings, it was natural for Sheffield to go ahead on its own. Just like SKF (see Hagström, 1987b), it started by physically transporting tapes and diskettes between computers. The first dial-up connections were installed in 1978 to the sales subsidiaries in Canada and the US. A similar link to Tools in Sweden came in 1980. The Belgian sales company followed a year later. Then Dormer's other UK sites (four factories and a handful branch-offices) got dial-up connections. Tapping into the Tools sales organization, the sales subsidiaries in West Germany, France, Italy and Spain (the latter though not on-line) were connected consecutively 1982-1984. SKF Group Telenet took over 1984-1985.

At present, the UK national network links Tools' two factories and three sales offices[91], in addition to the main Sheffield site. The Tools node has, however, retained a large measure of independence, and SKF standards are less pervasive here. There are locally administered dial-up links with eleven end-users and eleven distributors. Another 30-40 UK distributors are in the process of being separately linked to the Sheffield mainframe, the first ones having started in 1989. The present forced pace is a reflection of attempting to stay ahead in the face of competitor moves. The pressure towards standardized, 'public' communications links is felt, but they are still probably a couple of years or so off.

[91] In Aldridge and Nuneaton, and in London, Bristol and Glasgow, respectively (the two latter locations also have Bearing Services sales offices; see Figure 4.3).

Supplier communications links are poorly developed also from the horizon of the Sheffield node. They exclusively consist of a stand-alone personal computer (but which can down-load from the Tools mainframe), offering an elementary link to the local bank.

4.3.3 The Spanish Network

The Madrid node is comparatively modest and the national network it supports is commensurably small. Indeed, data communications were not a concern until SKF could move from a small minority stake to full ownership of the Spanish bearings company in 1985[92]. Immediately following the acquisition, the antiquated Madrid computer center was connected to the SKF Group Telenet. Local capabilities are now reinforced by relying on other main nodes for backup, including processing.

Bearing Industries and Bearing Services are located at the same site. A leased line links the near-by Madrid factory and warehouse to the computer center. The other plant in Tudela and two branch offices each for Bearing Industries and Bearing services also have leased-line connections.

Connecting distributors began in 1986 but was a cumbersome process, mainly because of the insufficient local computer. By the beginning of 1990, and after a new computer had been installed, some fifteen distributors had dial-up links with Madrid. The number is planned to rise to approximately 50 in the course of the next couple of years, giving a good coverage of the distributor network. Distributors are generally small, one site operations and SKF has a total of approximately 70 distributors in Spain.

The first Bearing Industries link to its OEM-customers came in 1987, when Renault got a dial-up line via the public network. Ford followed in early 1989. GM, Peugeot, and

[92] The company has a chequered history with the Spanish Government being the other owner. The important point is that SKF could not operate the company on standard commercial terms until it was allowed to acquire the company outright.

SEAT/Volkswagen are soon to follow suit. In all these cases, the interface with the Madrid mainframe is mediated by a PC, which can up- and down-load from the mainframe but not provide on-line access to the rest of the national network.

No suppliers are linked to the network, as is also the case for the Tools sales subsidiary in Barcelona. SKF has no other operations in Spain.

In little more than four years, SKF has laid the solid foundations for a substantial network with extensive coverage, also of external parties. It is worth noticing that this has been done in the face of adverse local conditions as reflected in the poor state, almost by any standard, of Spanish public telecommunications.

4.3.4 The US Network

In the fall of 1980, a so-called 'consent decree' regarding SKF's US bearings subsidiary was finally lifted after 30 years. What amounts to direct competition between SKF in the US and the rest of SKF had been imposed for anti-trust reasons. Communication between the US subsidiary and the head-office in Gothenburg had to go through a US court. Consequently, the national data communications network evolved very independently up until a decade ago, just as in other aspects of SKF's US operations. However, integrating the US national network with SKF Group Telenet only really began when King of Prussia, immediately outside Philadelphia, Pennsylvania, became a main node in 1985. The acquisition of MRC in the following year gave added impetus to the process of integration.

In the second half of the 1970s, leased lines began to connect the bearings plants with the computer center in King of Prussia. As a rule, other locations would rely on dial-up connections over a third-party network (Tymnet). General Electric's Transnet was used for the first, elementary customer links, amounting to SKF 'lifting' customer orders entered into Transnet and printing them off. By then, in the early 1980s, SKF's US national network had largely reached its present extent, excluding MRC and some external links. With those exceptions, local network development was in a sense put on 'hold'. Over the last few years, SKF efforts in the area of data communications and systems have in the main been confined to consolidating the US network, to bringing it in line with the SKF corporate network, and to making King of Prussia a node for the Americas[93].

King of Prussia plays an outstanding role in a national network, since there are no outlying processors. All major data processing for all SKF units in the US is done in King of Prussia since July, 1987. The relatively low cost and high quality of local data communications stimulated this pronounced concentration of computer processing.

Both the national head-quarters for Bearing Industries and for Bearing Services are located at the same site in King of Prussia. Bearing Industries operates six main factories in Eastern US, all of which are linked to King of Prussia via leased lines (see Figure 4.4 below). One plant (in Hornell, New York) is closing and its connection discontinued. A plant in Bremen, Indiana (mainly foundry products and needle bearings) uses a simpler dial-up connection. A factory for miscellaneous industrial equipment in Canton, Ohio was sold a few years ago to American Switchgear Corporation (ASC) but it has retained its leased line to King of Prussia, using the node's services for a fee.

The main US warehouse is located together with one of the main factories in Allentown, Pennsylvania. Four other main factories also have sizeable warehouses. In addition, Bearing Industries runs one separate sales office in Detroit for customers in the automotive industry. It also uses a leased-line connection. Most Bearing Industries' sales go through Allentown, and basically all are administered out of there (see Section 5.3.1.3).

Bearing Services operates an additional twelve sales offices and three large warehouses. The former have dial-up public data network connections (Infonet having replaced

---

[93] Eventually, all the Latin American peripheral nodes are likely to be connected to King of Prussia.

Tymnet) and the latter employ leased lines. Through MRC in Jamestown, New York, Bearing Services is linked to another twelve warehouses around the country, formerly serving only MRC. The network linking these latter warehouses is operated by MRC's former parent, TRW. The setup goes back to the 1986 acquisition of MRC and it is temporary, pending a decision of how to organize bearing distribution in the US market. So far, only one customer has a fixed link with SKF. Bearings Inc. has a leased line connection from its head-office in Cleveland to King of Prussia since the end of 1986. All the thirteen stocking points of Bearings Inc. and two of its sales offices can be reached indirectly through this link. Down the line, the other 250 sales offices of Bearings Inc. may be included. Bearings Inc. is a key partner, roughly equal in size to SKF bearing operations by turnover and at present taking some ten percent of SKF's output.

Other Bearing Industries and Bearing Services customers can be reached via GE's Transnet (cf. above). Ford is the leading data communications user among OEM-customers and is in the process of requesting better communications links with its suppliers. SKF is unlikely to be an exception, though it is not the local leader, probably not even among the top three in the bearings industry, when it comes to external data communications links.

SKF Specialty Bearings has its world-wide divisional head-office in Glenhardie/Wayne, just down the road from King of Prussia. It also fills the role of head-office for the US market. The old MRC headquarters in Jamestown, New York, still functions as head-office for the revamped MRC Bearings within Specialty Bearings. Both sites are linked to King of Prussia through leased lines. At 2 Mbs, the latter has the highest capacity of all lines in the SKF data communications network.

MRC Bearings operates three plants in Northeastern US outside of Jamestown. In addition a Specialty Bearings plant and a sales company for imported specialty bearings are located together in Kulpsville, Pennsylvania[94]. All sites are linked with King of

[94] Somewhat curiously, the Kulpsville plant and Ford are installing a simple, PC-based dial-up link for the administration of direct sales of steering column bearings. This is a stand-alone connection without interface with the SKF US national network.

Prussia through leased lines. Lastly, a plant for foundry products in Washington, Missouri has recently had its leased-line connection down-graded to a dial-up link[95].

SKF Tools and Component Systems sales companies in Trumball, Connecticut, and Allentown/Bethlehem, Pennsylvania, respectively, have leased lines to King of Prussia. The three minor manufacturing locations of the Component Systems division[96] are not part of the SKF US national network[97].

The Ovako Steel sales subsidiary in Avon, Connecticut, similarly has a fixed link into the US network. Two suppliers of minor manufacturing equipment have dial-up connections. A similar link for a local bank completes the list of supplier links.

Finally, the SKF Tools and Bearing Services sales subsidiaries in Canada (Toronto and Scarborough, both in Ontario) are effectively part of the US national network. They share a leased line straight to the King of Prussia node. In addition, the Bearing Services central warehouse for all of Latin America has been shifted from Panama to Port Everglades, Florida. The move came in response to the mounting political uncertainty in Panama and was in part carried out successively from April to July, 1988, shipping from Panama and building up new stocks in Port Everglades. The final transfer of remaining stocks and other material took place during July. Customers noticed little or nothing of the move. Naturally, the new SKF Latintrade Inc. has a leased line to King of Prussia.

---

[95] It is the only remaining part of SKF automotive parts replacement business which was discontinued in 1986-1987.

[96] In South Hackensack and Somerset, New Jersey, and Long Island City, New York.

[97] With the recent acquisition of CR Industries (cf. Section 3.2.2 above), headquartered in Chicago, another ten manufacturing locations in the US and one in Canada are, so far, outside the network.

Figure 4.4

SKF US Data Communications Network

(Configuration by geographical location, 1990)

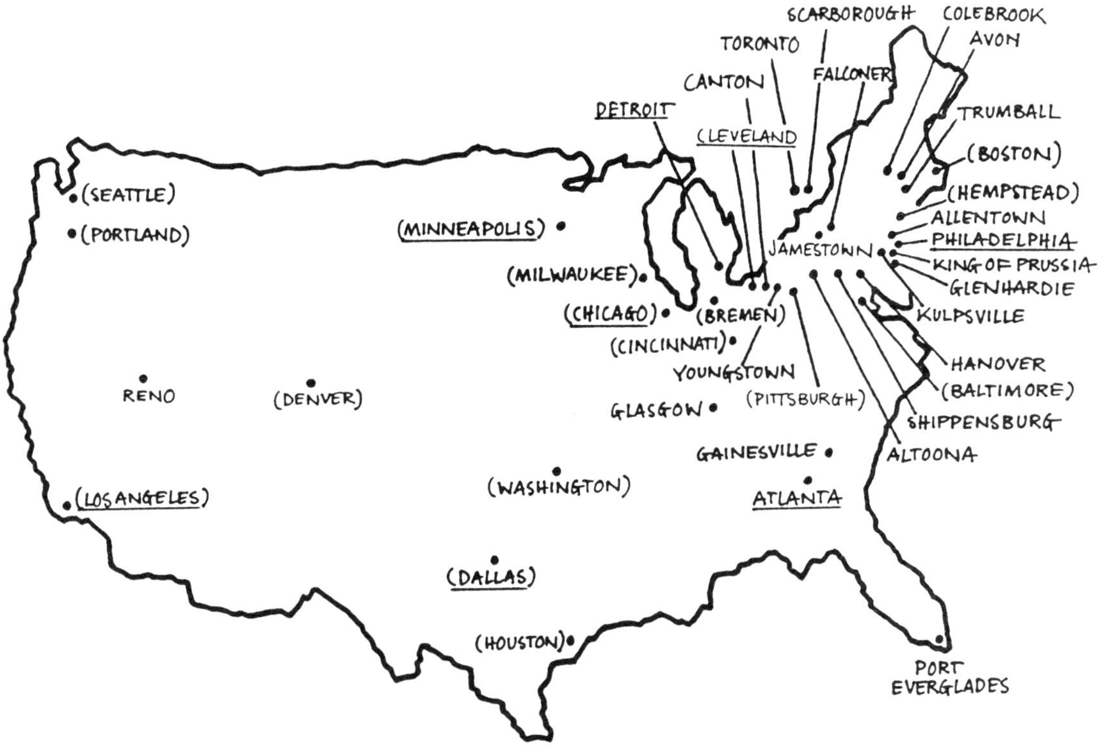

Note: Places indicated as	only name	leased line connection (but may also have additional links)
	parenthesis	public data network or TRW network link
	underlined	more than one site with a connection at a geographical place name (see below and text)

Nodes in the US Network

(may be more than one node/site at one location; see text)

Location	Bearing Industries	Bearing Services	Specialty Bearings	Other
Allentown	Plant Sales office			National warehouse SKF Component Systems
Altoona	Plant			
Atlanta		Warehouse Sales office MRC warehouse		
Avon				Ovako Steel
Baltimore				
Boston				
Bremen	Plant			
Canton	(ASC)			
Chicago		Sales office MRC warehouse		
Cincinnati		Sales office		
Cleveland		Sales office MRC warehouse Customer		
Colebrook			Plant	
Dallas		Sales office MRC warehouse		
Denver		Sales office		
Detroit	Sales office	MRC warehouse		
Falconer			Plant	
Gainesville	Plant			
Glasgow	Plant			
Glenhardie			Head-office	Divisional headquarters
Hanover	Plant			
Hempstead		MRC warehouse		
Houston		MRC warehouse		
King of Prussia	Head-office	Head-office		National data center
Kulpsville			Plant Sales office	
Jamestown		MRC sales	Plant	
Los Angeles		Sales office MRC warehouse		
Milwaukee		Sales office		
Minneapolis		Sales office MRC warehouse		
Philadelphia		Sales office	Plant	
Pittsburgh		Sales office		
Port Everglades				Regional warehouse
Portland		Sales office		
Reno		Warehouse		
Seattle		MRC warehouse		
Scarborough		Sales office		
Shippensburg	Plant			
Toronto				SKF Tools
Trumball				SKF Tools
Washington			Plant	
Youngstown		Warehouse		

In sum, the very extensive US national data communications network is highly centralized and has very good internal connections. The bearing manufacturing and warehousing sites are comparatively better served than other units. External links are rather poorly developed. In part, the situation reflects the US network being installed relatively early and quickly. There has also been a stronger emphasis on computer hardware and the technical aspects of internal data communications than in Europe to the detriment of especially customer relationships. With continued integration vis-à-vis the rest of SKF, this modus operandi is, however, likely to change more toward the European style, especially as regards the rationalization and upgrading of distribution in the US market.

4.3.5 The Brazilian Network

The perceived need to protect domestic, hopefully growing, 'infant' industries that has brought a restrictive trade regime has a counterpart in the telecommunications and computer sectors. A national "informatics law" basically prohibits the import of computer hard- and software, and severely regulates international data traffic (see UN, 1983; and Hobday, 1990). In the process, any international communications services are effectively barred from being offered to customers in Brazil. Company internal communications crossing the Brazilian border are subject to governmental scrutiny, also in terms of content. However, the biggest obstacle in the last instance is the exceptionally high cost, e.g. for a low-speed international leased line (approximately USD 6 000 per month).

In view of the above, it is not surprising that SKF's local operations in general, and in computer-related activities in particular, are largely isolated from those of the rest of the company.

In addition, and not unrelated to existing regulations, the price/performance ratio for communications is very high in Brazil. That has both hampered local network development and has made it difficult to substitute internationally for the local shortage of resources and capabilities. The SKF Brazilian network is therefore something of an aberration and is not commensurate with the economic importance of SKF's operations in the country. The local bearings business is larger than that of Spain, the Tools subsidiary is the second biggest in the division, and the Components Systems subsidiary is somewhere in the middle among the division's companies. Brazil can also claim historical importance as SKF's presence goes back to a sales subsidiary established in 1914.

The main Bearing Industries plant and head-office in Guarulhos, just outside São Paulo, is the hub of the domestic network. Almost all data processing for bearings-related operations is carried out in Guarulhos. Leased lines connect Guarulhos with the two Bearing Services sites in São Paulo, the head-office and the main sales branch. That connection dates back to 1985, when the four regional sales branches got their dial-up links through the public network[98]. No distributors are linked as yet.

A new bearings plant, which will almost double the manufacturing capacity, began production in late 1988. The factory was located in Cajamar, some 50 kms from Guarulhos, in spite of space being available at the original site. That land could be sold and a cheaper block of land purchased in Cajamar. A mammoth establishment could be avoided and the production units could be maintained at a more manageable size. The solution was explicitly contingent on functioning data communications being available. The Cajamar site got its leased line link in January, 1989. It only has very limited local computer-processing capabilities.

As of last year, Guarulhos has simple dial-up connections to a local bank and to Autolatina, Brazil's largest car manufacturer, a local joint venture between Volkswagen and Ford. In both cases, the link is between the external mainframe and a PC at Guarulhos. There is thus no direct interchange of data but the PCs can up- and down-load from the mainframe.

---

[98] They are located in the main industrial centers (outside the state of São Paulo) in the southern part of Brazil, viz. in Belo Horizonte, Minas Gerais, in Curitiba, Paraná, in Pôrto Alegre, Rio Grande do Sul, and in Rio de Janeiro, Rio de Janeiro.

There are no links either to the Tools or the Component Systems subsidiaries. They are both located in the greater São Paulo area. The Tools company is in the process of establishing distributor links and is doing so ahead of its competitors. The Component Systems subsidiary has what in practice is a one-way link with Autolatina, the latter releasing data to a stand-alone PC at the SKF site. There are no supplier links but the Component Systems subsidiary has a local bank branch on its site, an office which in turn has a simple link to its parent.

Overall, the SKF subsidiaries are well ahead of local competitors in the areas of data communications and computer use. In relation to the main customers (viz. the car industry), the situation is the reverse but the difference rather smaller. As to international communications, SKF is easily quite as well placed as any foreign MNC in Brazil.

Digressing slightly into international communications, there are actually three different links with SKF Group Telenet. First, Guarulhos got a direct dial-up link to Gothenburg in August, 1988. It replaced a very short-lived, simple connection from a stand-alone PC via modem. That indirect type of arrangement is at present actually used separately by Bearing Services since the Guarulhos link had limited capacity. In mid-1990, the Guarulhos-Gothenburg connection was transferred virtually unchanged to run via King of Prussia as a result of lower charges coming into effect on the latter route. The Tools subsidiary has a PC-based dial-up link as of February, 1988. In the latter case, the role of the PC is to 'translate' between the local mainframe and the international network, though only managing batch-transmission. Here, the Sheffield node functions as a communications intermediary. Component Systems subsidiary has no link to the Group Telenet.

To reemphasize, the bearings, tools and components businesses are separate in communications terms. Somewhat curiously, the restrictive local environment has led to three international connections for SKF from Brazil (although Component Systems has none).

The limited local availability of hardware, software and services stemming from the existing "informatics law" explains some of the described aberrations. The apparent penchant for totally, or almost totally, stand-alone PC-based links is not at all an exclusive SKF trait. It is simply a function of, literally, the relative ease of getting a PC around the local regulations as opposed to a minicomputer, or even a mainframe. Moreover, and in the specific case of SKF, both national and international communications capabilities are severely restricted by the existing local computer capacity and the difficulty associated with obtaining a new one. For instance, simple technical incompatibility becomes a problem, when a previously stand-alone computer with a particular communications architecture is to be connected to a network using a different standard (cf. the Tools subsidiary). These technical limitations effectively stop both some national and international data interchange even if that traffic in itself is approved by the authorities.

Another hampering effect of the informatics policy is the local shortage of skilled manpower. Relatively good international communications capabilities can help, though. First, SKF has found that some processing and communications skills abroad, and which are obtainable through the network, actually can help in alleviating some local skill bottlenecks. Second, and more importantly, it is easier to retain scarce talent. The international data communications network allow Brazilians to keep up better with developments in their field and to indirectly use applications not available locally. There is also the added advantage of qualified job opportunities abroad being available.

4.4 Network Revisited

The upshot of the discussion in this section is that the full extent of the SKF communications network is difficult to establish. It is basically impossible to identify a unequivocal cut-off point, given the range of connections in use. Recall, for instance, links to multiple location distributors and gateways into other networks, like the NCB in the UK and TRW in the US. It is also a moving target as new connections are continuously being added and as third-party connections are notoriously foot-loose. Indeed, as the data communications network peters out into the environment and constantly changes, its actual extent is most probably not even known internally, at the Group Telenet center.

Apart from being complex, we have, however, seen that the SKF data communications network is very extensive, not least in relation to the geographical dispersal of SKF operations. Few of its own sites are outside the network. An even larger number of non-SKF sites than SKF locations have some form of connection to the SKF network, albeit in many cases the links are rudimentary. Another way of stating essentially the same thing is that the national networks taken together have more links than the backbone and peripheral networks combined (viz. Group Telenet). The local influence on the configuration of SKF's data communications network is consequently also great.

Hard data on different aspects of the data communications network are not readily available, and when available, they are often imprecise. In Table 4.2 below, commonly used illustrations of the network size are given. The information has been collected from various sources, both public and informal[99]. Although frequently recurring, the table demonstrates how even these, fairly specific, measures leave a lot to be desired in terms of accuracy. Still, the continued growth of the network unequivocally comes across.

The few existing attempts at gauging the importance and impact of data communications in companies generally employ attitudinal measures (e.g. OECD, 1983a, and 1983b). Respondents are typically invited to judge their present and future use according to specified categories, like "plays an important role", "plays some role, but not a determining factor", and "is not important" (this is the case in OECD, 1983a:19). Given our more detailed approach, this type of information is of little value.

[99] Sources are publications, presentations for different fora, and personal interviews. They are not specified to avoid identification, but each source is, prima facie, reliable. Some discrepancies may possibly be attributed to varying definitions of the network.

Table 4.2

Commonly Used Indicators of Network Size
(SKF Data Communications Network)

Number of: SKF sources

Countries	Central processing units	Mid-size computers	Lines	Terminals*	Point in time
10	8	-	-	3 500	1984
20	9	62	300	5 000	Jul., 1986
26	-	-	3-400	5 000	Jun., 1987
-	11	40	-	4 000	Nov., 1987
26	11	60	> 300	> 6 000	Nov., 1988
30	13	80	> 300	> 8 000	Nov., 1988
32	13	80	665	> 11 000	Dec., 1988

*) Includes printers, approximately 10 per cent of the total.

Source: See text.

More relevant measures of the importance attached to the data communications network would be to look at the costs (and revenues) associated with the network. Such figures are, however, closely guarded secrets or simply not available. In part, that may be a function of data communications and information systems issues hitherto not having attracted either much systematic corporate attention or scholarly interest. The accounting systems in use are, as a rule, not geared to specifically take account of such categories. Moreover, the incentives for the first companies to reveal their costs would be weak. Perhaps it is fair to say that, in general, data communications and information systems are considered to be strategically important by companies but that there is considerable confusion as to exactly how important they are and as to in what ways, specifically, they are important. Under these circumstances, it may be wise to be tight-lipped.

Some circumstantial evidence can be obtained, however. First, and for comparison, the Financial Times (in collaboration with Price Waterhouse) regularly surveys a panel of more than 100 senior information technology directors in leading UK organizations, finding that information technology costs (incl. investments) run to some 5-7 percent of sales in "some major companies" (Financial Times, Jan. 26, 1990). The very ambitious

OECD-BRIE study of corporate use of information networks in seven major countries[100] laments that precise figures are very difficult to attain, but that telecommunications claimed up to five percent of the costs in the investigated companies (OECD-BRIE, 1989:21, n. 14). It should be noted that in the two comparisons, expenditure is related to total sales and costs respectively, wherefore the prima facie difference between them is slightly exaggerated.

Exactly what is meant by 'information technology' and 'telecommunications' above is unclear, to say the least. The former clearly includes investment in computer hardware but may not include communications costs. The latter category most probably includes some computer costs as they are inexorably linked with communications and should also include communications other than data, such as voice telephony, telex and telefacsimile over external networks. Internally, telex and telefacsimile can commonly use the corporate data communications network (e.g. SKF, see Section 4.2.1 above) and in some cases so can voice telephony.

Returning to SKF, the cost of data communications and information systems at the individual manufacturing subsidiary level can be 'guesstimated' to vary between two and four percent of turnover[101]. The figure excludes depreciation, voice telephony, and stand-alone factory automation installations. The corresponding figure for a sales subsidiary would be lower, say 1-2 percent of turnover, since turnover is high relative to the size of the company and since its greater number of customers pay for their hardware and part of the cost for connections.

If we inflate the costs to the company-wide level, it seems reasonable to arrive at a higher figure than at the subsidiary level, as some costs are borne by the divisions and the corporate head-office. An interval of 3-4 percent of turnover, leaning towards the

[100] US, UK, France, West Germany, Italy, Spain and Japan.

[101] Exactly how these figures were arrived at is not described for reasons of confidentiality.

higher end, seems likely[102]. For 1989, that would give an approximate magnitude approaching SEK 900 million for SKF as a whole, a sizeable amount.

By chance, the only more detailed account of a company's information systems costs (an example given in Allen, 1987) that we have found show some remarkable similarities between the unnamed company and SKF[103]. Like SKF, "A" is "...widely respected for its computer management expertise." (Allen, 1987:60). "A's" computer and data communications budget stood at 2 percent of company turnover, considerably less than our estimate of closer to 4 percent for SKF. Rather than revising our figure, the discrepancy can well be put down to SKF being highly internationalized and to SKF operating a larger, more dispersed IS network[104].

For another comparison, recall that the total research and development costs in SKF are in the process of being raised from 2 to 3 percent of turnover. That rise is heralded as a strategically very important move. The amount spent on IS would still be greater according to our findings.

We can conclude that SKF maintains a high level of ambition regarding data communications and is willing to pay for it. In terms of costs, much is self-inflicted and not automatic or uncontrollable, thus betraying the important role having been assigned to data communications in SKF.

---

[102] The estimate is not at odds with the fact that designated IS staff comprise 2 percent of total SKF employees (cf. Section 5.3.2 below). IS staff is more skilled than the average SKF employee, thus commanding a higher-than-average salary, and IS similarly claims a fair share of other, non-labor, costs.

[103] The company "A" had close to the same turnover, operated almost as many plants, and employed roughly the same number of IS staff at its IS department as SKF had company-wide. Also, "A" could only field about a quarter of the number of terminals and had less communications equipment compared to SKF at the time.

[104] Allen (1987) makes no reference to international operations, which is an important element explaining cost. Moreover, the centralized structure of IS operations implied for company "A" tallies well with US practice (see Section 4.3.4).

In the end, we were not able to distinguish between data communications and information systems, wherefore it is also high time to turn to what the SKF data communications network is used for in some detail.

5. SYSTEMS

With the network in place, the missing link is the more specific uses which the network can be put to. These uses are embodied in the systems operating on the network. The systems set the framework for the information flows routed through the communications network. Types of, access to, and the use of systems in the SKF data communications network are the topic of this chapter.

First, however, the subject matter itself needs to be clarified and the initial main section addresses the connection between systems and the network. SKF's systems are then surveyed in turn, moving from the corporate, through the divisional, to the local level. The final main section takes a more comprehensive view of SKF's systems, relating them to avowed own objectives and priorities, and to some competitiors' system use.

5.1 The Systems-Network Relationship[105]

Conceptually, the standard argument explaining why a data communications network is established is twofold:

a) utilization of distant computer processing power, and

b) the need to access data located elsewhere (cf. Martin, 1981:24).

The first reason springs from a need to overcome local insufficient processing power and the second from data being collected and stored in different locations, notably, different from the locations where they may be needed. The advent of relatively cheap and more powerful small computers means that the second reason has come to dominate, especially since commercial transactions are "the bread and butter of data processing", and since these transactions do not require much in the way of computer power (Ibid.).

---

[105] See Footnote 60 in Chapter 4 above.

We need to extend, and, alas, complicate, the traditional argument.

First, recall that computer processing is not just a matter of place, but also of time. Local power per se may well be sufficient for a transaction but the sheer number of simultaneous uses may cause temporary congestion. Other processing units can then handle the 'overflow' from time to time. Further, and if designed for this to occur regularly, a data communications network can be motivated for reasons of efficient capacity utilization (in addition to the straight access to superior capacity needed for a particular type of transaction).

Second, and more importantly, not only data but also applications are normally found at different locations. In order to highlight the point, we can construct an example: a user in one location may fetch data from another location to feed to an application in a third location. (The actual processing can, in turn, 'overflow' to a fourth location.) This illustration describes what actually can, and does, happen in the SKF data communications network. Indeed, access to applications, as opposed to data, was one of the main reasons for establishing the network in the first place.

Third, the important function of being a system for communication needs to be given its due weight. This function can be perceived as divorced from 'obtaining data for computer processing' (cf. Martin, 1981), unless the latter is given such a wide domain as to render it virtually meaningless. Consider, for instance, electronic mail. True, processing is involved, but it is minute and largely confined to enabling transmission. True, data are transmitted, but not really for local machine processing at the receiving end. Rather, we can typically conceive of electronic mail primarily as a delivery system; a message is sent to be received unchanged for subsequent human 'processing'[106]. Another example is remote systems maintenance. It has less to do with processing at either end, or with transmission of data, than with providing a means for 'hands-on' maintenance of a computer system in a distant location. So, the idea of enhanced communications, without

[106] The gist of the argument remains, although electronic mail messages frequently have attached files, or contain other information, which eventually is processed by a computer.

reference to the twins 'processing' and 'data', is an additional motivation for having a data communications network.

Our extended version of the rationale for data communications networks demonstrates the need to move beyond the now restrictive focus of Section 4, above. Especially access to dispersed data and to applications, and use of communications systems shift the question more toward what the network is used for.

We choose to use the term information systems as the wider concept. Databases are subsumed under the same heading. The network of the previous chapter essentially constitutes the infrastructure for making information systems (and therewith associated data) available at geographically dispersed locations. The information systems also determine the type of data that can be handled within the data communications network, subject to the restrictions set by the communications hard- and software (and, in exceptional cases, government regulations[107]. The set of systems, and pattern of availability or access, make up the information systems infrastructure of the organization.

The existence of a communications link is a necessary, but not sufficient, condition for access to information systems, in principle available through the communications network. Control over access is thus a relevant issue also at the system level[108]. The details of access to a system can be an extremely complicated affair. It can be linked to a person, a position, an organizational unit, a site or specific hardware, or combinations thereof. It is also a matter of degree, defining which transactions can be processed, which data are available for entry, and when the system can be used. None of these classifications is confined to internal use of a system. External parties may enter at any point.

---

[107] The regulations primarily refer to different national privacy laws (see, for instance, UN, 1982; and Aronson and Cowhey, 1988) but they are of very limited relevance for the case of SKF.

[108] Similarly to the case of communications links, ownership of a system is not really an issue. A system may be housed in an external computer and maintained by an external party, without that impinging on the control of access to that system by the user organization (see further Hagström, 1988).

Here, we are primarily concerned with the larger, organizational (as opposed to the individual or particular information system) perspective. Consequently, access tied to organizational unit and geographical site, as well as degree of access afforded these categories in terms of transactions permitted and data availability, will take the center stage. The overview of information systems in SKF is structured according to organizational level and access, similarly to the treatment of the corporate data communications network. But we need to pause a moment to review the particular SKF setting for its information systems.

5.2 The SKF Family of Systems

Historically, computerized information systems have been handled locally, simply as a function of economically feasible local computer processing arriving before economically feasible data transmission over large distances. In SKF, that time passed with the establishment of the Group Telenet.

The same way that processing and communications hardware and software need to be standardized to ensure compatibility, information systems are subject to standardization. When using a particular system, there is little flexibility in format, type of data and kind of processing. Parameters are set by the system. By analogy, if we think of communications compatibility as having the same rail gauge, systems 'compatibility' is packing information in containers. The former concerns delivery, the latter relates to a user being able to easily accommodate what is being delivered. Standardization of the former naturally takes precedence over efforts at standardizing the latter.

At SKF, standards for communications are more strictly enforced than for systems. The reasons for that are not only historical but also that some systems are very local in nature, for instance, a payroll system adapted to national legislation. Simply put, the degree of standardization needed for a system depends on how wide access is envisioned.

The data communications network is at one extreme, and the local payroll system at the other. Between them, there is a family of systems.

A few information systems are corporate in that they are used across divisions. The larger systems are tied to product areas, or rather, in practice to SKF's bearing operations. The largest number of systems are local.

Both the data communications network and the set of systems are the responsibility of the Director, Group Information Systems. He (in the person of Håkan Landahl since 1977) reports to the Director of Finance and Administration, one of six staff unit directors in the eight-member SKF Group Management[109].

It is noteworthy that information systems was a staff unit in its own right 1973-1976, reporting directly to the Chief Executive Officer. It was moved down one notch when the number of corporate staff units was halved as of 1977. Recall that this change coincided with the decision to start building the Group Telenet.

Albeit small, the information systems have, however, remained firmly at the corporate level. By comparison, SKF at present has no corporate staff units for product development, marketing, manufacturing and engineering. The skeleton information systems (IS) staff consists of five people. They are responsible for Group IS policies, standards, data communications, common applications and databases, and overall coordination and follow-up of IS plans.

The Group IS Plan for over-all coordination is developed and agreed upon at formal IS meetings 2-3 times per year. The IS staff is then complemented by a representative from each of the divisions and by the IS managers of some main nodes. Bearing Industries and Bearing Services have formal IS departments. Specialty Bearings has informal IS

---

[109] The recently (1989) appointed Director of Finance and Administration, Kaj Thorén, has a well documented interest in information systems. He was previously (since 1985) Head of the Tools division, and before that Corporate Controller. He came to SKF from a position as an information systems specialist [sic!] at Atlas Copco.

representation[110]. For Tools, the IS responsibility is ceded to Sheffield. Component Systems is represented by secondment from SKF Dataservice. In total, some 15 people make up the Group Information Systems Board, and about half of them, in practice, come from Bearing Industries. However, "Group IS Plan" is really something of a misnomer, since it is less of a plan and more of general guidelines for the systems infrastructure, for applications, and for support activities. The specific, more traditional, IS planning takes place at the divisional level.

In so far as one can talk of 'an inner circle' drawing up the agenda for SKF IS policy, it would consist of Håkan Landahl (since 1983 also Head of Dataservice), two members from his Group IS staff, and the four IS Heads of the divisions. They meet informally in different constellations when the need arises. They also make up the Group Telenet Board, betraying the very central role afforded the communications infrastructure in SKF.

Overall coordination of company IS activities thus follow two main tacks: enforcement of corporate standards and informal agreement (or cooption). Much of the corporate coordination thus comes at the planning stage, and is achieved by being present and influencing early in systems development. While still a project, a major new system gets a coordinating group with representation from interested parties, including the IS staff and/or SKF Dataservice. Actual systems development is in practice done locally by the operating companies and SKF Dataservice. It is commonly done jointly by the most interested subsidiaries at several locations (see further Hagström, 1987b, and Section 5.3 below).

The cost of systems development is primarily borne by the divisions and the operating companies themselves, although slightly more than half of the total cost is for common applications (incl. the many applications 'common' only for bearings).

Each common system is then given a board of directors, responsible for support and further development of the system on an internal profit and loss basis. Corporate

---

[110] There is a continuous dialogue with the division controller in the head-office in Glenhardie, Penn.

coordination is commonly supported by representation on these boards. Once implemented, the responsibility for systems support and maintenance is passed on to a local company, most often at a main node.

There is thus no corporate behemoth running the SKF information systems. That is otherwise still not uncommon, even in large companies. There were tendencies in that direction, however, in the early 1970s. Recall that GFSS prompted an attempt at building one single, company-wide integrated computer system (STICS)[111]. The attempt failed. The existence of a large corporate staff unit, and the establishment of SKF Dataservice in 1975, were probably also reflections of the strong technical bias in information systems so prevalent in general at the time.

The present set of SKF information systems is instead an unwieldy lot. As shown above, a convenient way of approaching them is by organizational level and access. We start from the highest, and widest, point.

5.2.1 Corporate Systems

Apart from the basic functions offered by the SKF Group Telenet, there are only three systems that are universal in the SKF world in that they cross all divisional lines. They are electronic mail, a system for reporting, and a system for internal financial flows. They will be discussed in turn.

[111] See Section 4.2.

5.2.1.1 Electronic mail

As a rule, access to Telenet implies that SKF's electronic mail system, MEST, is available. Since it began as a message switching system for technicians building the Telenet during 1978 (see also Section 4.2 above), it is a bit cumbersome to use and slightly old-fashioned in terms of features offered, but it shares the generic characteristics of electronic mail systems.

The decided advantages of SKF's system are its very wide geographical coverage through Telenet, and being 'oldish' means that it has had time to penetrate the organization. MEST has been in widespread use since 1980, when non-technical uses began to dominate. Since traditional message switching systems as a rule are single systems with centralized archiving of messages (cf. Martin, 1981), it was very unusual at the time when MEST almost immediately (months) was made a multi-site system, making it very reliable and versatile in communication terms. The original set of five inter-connected installations has since grown to ten.

The volume of pages transmitted over the system has increased from 120 000 pages/month in 1982, through 733 000 in 1986, to some 900 000[112] today. The average MEST message is two pages long. The average number of messages sent per day is up to 15 000. The number of registered users has roughly doubled since 1986 to 12 300 at the end of 1990.

The figures reflect that usage has largely followed the S-shaped logistics curve with rapid growth in the first half of the 1980s and subsequent saturation towards the end of the decade. The early users are also the most avid, with latecomers tending to bring down average usage. Later, more modest growth in total usage primarily come from local, as opposed to international, message transmission. For the bigger national networks the

112 Estimated figure, exact figure not avilable.

distribution is about 50/50 between local and international MEST traffic. By main (SKF) country, Sweden is at the top in terms of overall usage and the US at the other end.

Electronic mail is not dedicated to transmitting a specific type of information, and MEST is no exception. It is a simple system with few frills, but also with few restrictions other than those set by the data communications network. These characteristics make it similar to other, non-data-based, means of communication. By qualitative judgement, MEST usage is both a complement to and a substitute for such other means.

Briefly, MEST is always preferred over telex when both are available (except when telex is needed for legal reasons). Telefacsimile has less limitations in terms of format, but suffers from lack of confidentiality, since reception is tied to a machine rather than to a person. Voice telephone is easier, more readily interactive, but depends on finding the interlocateur at a specific time and at a specific telephone[113]. Both voice telephone and telefacsimile are less reliable than MEST, since they exclusively use the public telephone networks instead of the SKF Group Telenet. Moreover, reliability and speed are MEST's strongest advantages over ordinary mail. In terms of degree of formality, however, a MEST message has a different status, sandwiched between a written letter and a telephone conversation. Finally, few trips have probably been replaced by better information exchange through MEST according to what we have gathered from the interviews. But further probing indicated that many trips were made more efficient and/or shorter by the traveller having prepared the meeting etc. much better through MEST use. The bottom line is, that with a given increased need for communications, there are strong indications[114] that other costs of communication would have increased much more, were it not for MEST.

Electronic mail comes closest to being a substitute in relation to telex and telefacsimile. Here, electronic mail has a clear cost advantage as well. An average MEST message costs

[113] An illustrative quote from SKF is: "Call twice, then MEST!".

[114] By qualitative judgement, but an inference allegedly supported by internal SKF cost data.

only SEK 1. Corresponding figures in SKF for telex is SEK 28 and telefacsimile SEK 10-11.

Still, more important benefits of MEST to SKF stem from its complementary function in relation to other computer-based information systems. Other systems rarely allow the more 'free format' and universal information exchange that is associated with electronic mail. MEST can supplement other systems, e.g. adding general comments to a transmitted drawing in a CAD/CAM application or asking for clarifications to items in the reporting system. The case is most clear-cut for cases when a particular system for a special activity do not exist. For instance, joint systems development, mentioned above, is largely supported by MEST exchanges in lieu of having people work at the same geographical location.

MEST is also to a limited extent made available to external parties. Naturally, Ovako Steel uses MEST, both internally and often vis-à-vis SKF. When direct order systems do not exist, an SKF subsidiary can order steel via MEST. Ovako Steel, on its own, also uses MEST as a gateway to an 'external' service for booking land and sea transports from Sweden[115]. - Also distributors and OEM customers can get access to MEST. With a good-quality link to Telenet, MEST often follows. They will, however, have very little use for MEST, although some distributors (notably in the UK) use MEST between its different sites.

Internally, MEST is most extensively used within Bearing Industries. To illustrate, the main internal news publication (Bearing Bulletin) as a rule gives the relevant MEST address for requesting further information in connection with an article. That is definitely not the case for other divisions, including Bearing Services. Some Tools and Component Systems companies actually do not use MEST at all, casting some doubt over its universality.

---

[115] MARKIS, an information system offered by Swedish Transocean Lines, responsible for line shipping within the Transatlantic Group, which in turn is part of Bilspedition (originally a road-haulage firm).

Still, MEST has found some use for disemination of more general company information. Press releases and the like are sometimes distributed via MEST, albeit to a remarkably limited extent. One practical reason is that MEST does not have a 'cc' function, and all messages have to be addressed individually.

In the end, we return to the lead integrative role played by MEST. Usage is strongly encouraged, especially from the corporate level and not least because of its cost advantage. From the local users' vanatage point, it is more likely perceived as 'free', since there are basically no internal charges for sending electronic mail in SKF. The marginal cost of a message is often zero, or close to zero, as the fixed connections in Telenet have excess capacity and since user charges on dial-up connections typically are low, especially when MEST messages are tagged onto other traffic. That stimulates spontaneous uses, satisfying communication needs otherwise not provided for. Two specific examples may serve to highlight the point.

The very large research and development department (approx. 250 people) in SKF's US bearing operations was spun off in 1984 and soon after discontinued. To avoid being left out in the cold, the remaining small product engineering and quality department in King of Prussia extensively use MEST. In that way, they can keep a tab on other (read: European) SKF research and development. Even in an environment of relatively limited MEST use, MEST has become an important instrument to keep up with the centers of activity.

An example of a totally unintended use is the clearing-house, or 'market' function arising at Intertrade in Brussels. Intertrade is the central warehouse for the African and Middle Eastern markets[116]. Its own warehousing operations and its good communications location led to internal trading in surplus stocks successively growing from the mid-1980s on. Excess quantities of bearings are now bought and sold by many different SKF

---

[116] Intertrade is a separate company within Bearing Services. There is also a Bearing Services sales subsidiary in Brussels.

companies through Intertrade[117]. Especially sales companies have benefitted from this possibility to adjust the composition and level of their local stocks. The bearings themselves may or may not pass through the warehouse. As of February, 1989, the function has been institutionalized by setting up a separate department within Intertrade, dubbed Global Bearing Trade. It reports to the logistics department of Bearing Services, but is a joint operation between Bearing Services and Bearing Industries. Global Bearing Trade has been given the additional task of developing sales also to external customers. Now, the central warehouse in Singapore is beginning to play a role similar to that of Intertrade, but confined to the Asia/Pacific region. SKF Latintrade in Florida can be expected to follow suit.

These examples can be multiplied. In fact, when supplementary or unstructured exchange of data is directly or indirectly referred to below, MEST is almost always the system used.

5.2.1.2 Reporting system

The Group Management System (GMS) is the oldest common system in SKF. It actually antedates the Group Telenet. In its earliest version, an external reporting system was implemented in 1978 using the GEIS network and computers[118]. Some 70 foreign subsidiaries transmitted their balance sheets and income statements to the head-office in this way. Reporting time was cut from twelve to eight calendar days after the end of the month[119], and the quality (e.g. internal consistency) dramatically improved. SKF was the first company in Sweden to use a computer-based reporting system internationally. GEIS later sold the system to other Swedish MNCs.

---

[117] Payments are handled through the Treasury Management System, see below subsection 5.2.1.3.

[118] For this very early development, see also Pousette (1983).

[119] See also Section 5.3.1.1 below.

An internal package was added 1980-1982. Operational information (such as production volumes, sales volumes, inventory levels and budget items) was included. By then, the external reporting was uniform. The internal reporting differed across divisions (and still does).

GMS was rather costly and a bit cumbersome to use at the local end. By 1985, the running cost for reporting only, reached SEK 1.5 million. Of approximately 80 companies reporting monthly, some 60 used telex to GEIS. More often than not, data had to be retrieved from the local computer, keyed in manually and cross-checked by the GEIS computer before it was released to the head-office for subsequent consolidation. There was little or no feed-back.

At the same time, Group Telenet was up and running. An on-line, interactive system for use on Telenet was developed by SKF. That took one year. The system was operational by January, 1986, and approximately 60 companies reported via Telenet at the end of the same year. That figure has now risen to around 100 (out of an estimated total of about 130 reporting companies). Subsidiaries in North and South America have been relatively slower to use the new system. Companies not connected to the Telenet still use telex, but now via MEST to GMS.

GMS is a foot-loose system in the sense that it readily can be managed from anywhere, given a connection to Telenet. The present GMS is still very simple, and is intended to be so. It is thus easy to use, and easy to adapt to changing reporting requirements. With some exceptions, there is still a manual interface between local systems and GMS[120]. It is not possible to 'lift' information automatically from the local systems. Conversely, that also makes it impossible for, say, head-office to 'peek over the shoulder' of a local company, viz. from a distance checking on particular items (as sometimes happens in other companies).

[120] For qualifications to this statement, see further Section 5.2.2.1 on material flow systems.

The flexibility as to changing data input and principles for consolidation was put to the test during the latest major organizational reshuffle of divisions, when the bearing operations left area-based divisions and were reconfigured along a mix of customer and product lines. During 1977, reporting followed both the old and the new organizations in parallel. From 1988 and on, only the new lines of reporting have been used. Some historical data were, in addition, 'reconstructed' according to the new reporting principles to permit being able to make time-series comparisons predating the new organization. The exercise was repeated in 1989/1990 below the divisional level when the time came to continue the reorganization within the standard bearing business (cf. Section 3.3 above).

In short, GMS is a system for reporting, consolidation and analysis. The input data for an external monthly report consists of a balance sheet (2 pages, 54 lines per page), an income statement (35 lines), and one page (total of 75 lines) for ustructured comments. The company's own data are combined with centrally given figures, such as inflation and exchange rates. There are automatic consistency controls of the data fed into the system. For instance, the system checks that local production, sales and net change in inventory add up. It also checks across reports, e.g. that internal deliveries are consistently reported. MEST is commonly used as a supporting system for additional comments, queries etc.

GMS is strictly hierarchical. The consolidation tree goes by country for external reporting and by product or customer group for internal purposes (according to the business organization, cf. Section 3.3 above). Country consolidation across divisions is basically only done implicitly and for bearings in the standard procedure. An exception has been made for Sweden, Singapore, and the US, which also explicitly report as single bearing operations to corporate management.

As data are checked, and cross-checked, they are 'released' successively to the higher level. However, all data make the journey to the head-office, so that data per company is available centrally. Consolidated reports are sent back to the subsidiaries. Apart from that, each company can only access its 'own' data.

All the information is stored and available for special reports and analyses. A "Management Information Package" offers a menu of cross-sectional and time-series comparisons that can be made. Creativity is, however, largely only limited by the existing data and user profile, viz. the level on the consolidation tree determines which data are accessible to a particular user. The interest in extracting information for special purposes is growing, much as a function of the reporting data base building up. As of 1988, an extensive database on macro-economic data covering 67 countries has been integrated into the system. It is continously updated. The data base is managed by an independent consultancy firm in Gothenburg but is available on-line through GMS for all users of the system. This new, conveniently accessed source of information has, in turn, also stimulated special analyses within GMS, notably by individual subsidiaries.

One might expect that subsidiaries could resist being drawn into such a hierarchical system as GMS. More complete and quicker information available centrally can reduce the 'degrees of freedom' afforded local subsidiary managers. Common flow-on effects for local subsidiaries are aligning the local reporting system to the corporate one and tighter over-all reporting discipline. The fact that GMS has the widest coverage of all SKF systems and that it generally is the first to be brought in when companies are acquired, demonstrate the importance given to GMS by corporate management. As a related example highlighting the same thing, recall the separate link from the Bearing Services Brazilian subsidiary to Telenet; a link exclusively motivated by the need to use GMS (and MEST).

However, there appears to be little such resistance by SKF subsidiaries to using GMS. Quite the contrary, subsidiaries with no link to Telenet, or with a poor connection, very often express keenness to become better integrated into the system. Apart from the improvements already mentioned, feed-back has become better. A distant SKF company can more easily judge its relative position within the SKF Group from the consolidated reports, and get a better feel for what happens at the divisional and corporate head-offices. One illustrative point of view sums it up by stressing that there is no local resentment against any increased central control with reporting through Telenet, on the contrary, the great benefit is that the connection gives the subsidiary much improved possibilities "to keep an eye on what goes on in Gothenburg".

Moreover, some of the restrictions of access to information can be overcome informally. For instance, the main European bearing subsidiaries regularly exchange their reports by transmitting them to each other outside GMS, thus obtaining data that GMS formally denies them access to.

5.2.1.3 Financial management system

The Treasury Management System (TMS) is very much of a 'sister' to GMS, being similar in most respects. The development of TMS closely parallels that of GMS, except that TMS has a somewhat smaller geographical and organizational coverage.

TMS is directly linked to the centralization of the corporate treasury function. In turn, that was prompted by GFSS being implemented, resulting in dramatically increased intra-SKF product flows. First among Swedish companies, SKF established a unit for international factoring and netting, SKF International AB, in 1974. Initially, business was done over the telephone, backed up by confirmations sent by the regular postal service. Like GMS, the first version of TMS used GEIS in the late 1970s but it was successively transferred to SKF Group Telenet as the latter expanded. The system was updated, made to run on-line, and completely moved onto Telenet in 1985. Dependence on the system is now so great that a, say, 24-hour interruption in service would mean that SKF International basically ceased to function.

TMS is foot-loose and multifunctional, without being monolithic. It evolved to support the main activities of SKF International; netting and currency clearing, corporate financing, parent company liquidity management, and a Group treasury function. All of these activities were carried out from Gothenburg until mid-1989, when a subsidiary, SKF Capital S.A. (formally opened up in 1988 in Brussels) started taking over these functions;

SKF International thus de facto moving. That development came comparatively late in SKF[121], due to SKF heretofore having been able to offset profits from SKF International's activities against previously incurred operational losses and thus did not need to locate financial activities abroad for tax reasons. The move to Brussels was, however, greatly facilitated by the flexibility of TMS, and, of course, by the existence of SKF Group Telenet. Brussels was to function as a coordination center for cash management and as an in-house bank for SKF.

Quite remarkably, the move was reversed in mid-1990, SKF citing high local costs for keeping staff in Brussels as the reason. Only some limited financing activities and trading now remain in Brussels. Naturally, the return move was also made comparatively so much easier due to TMS and Telenet.

From the subsidiary point of view, the most important aspect of TMS is the management of intra-SKF international trade payments. The importing subsidiary pays in one currency only, its own, and the exporting subsidiary receives in its local currency. SKF International carries the whole exchange rate risk during the two months from fixing the rate for the sale until payment is collected. If desired, the SKF importer can get credit as a supplier's credit or a medium-term loan with up to five years' maturity. The SKF exporter always gets paid regularly. Both importer and exporter have only one, dependable counterpart for their international intra-SKF business, SKF International. Their cash management is thus simplified. Subsidiaries cannot have foreign currency exposure in the banking system. TMS keeps track of the approximately 500 forward currency contracts running at any given time. The individual subsidiaries can only check on their own invoices and payments through TMS.

TMS is not only used for standard products from all SKF companies, but also for invoiced services from, for instance, SKF Dataservice, SKF Reinsurance and SKF International. Equipment from LMT to other SKF companies and deliveries to the regional warehouses, e.g. Intertrade (see above), are of course covered by TMS. Steel

[121] See Åhlander (1990) for an investigation of recent developments in treasury management and reasons therefore related to Swedish MNCs.

sales from Ovako Steel to SKF companies are also included. It can be estimated (cf. Section 3.4) to amount to roughly 10-15 percent of Ovako Steel's sales. The link between Ovako Steel and its sales companies is no longer handled by SKF International, but Ovako Steel uses TMS for internal clearing for a fee.

The TMS-managed trade covers some 80 countries. For each country there is a national netting of payments, in principle covering all SKF subsidiaries in that country[122]. Approximately 60 percent of such internal trade is netted out, while the remaining 40 percent results in actual payments to and from SKF International. These payments are done through the banking system, using their data communications networks. There is no direct communications link between TMS and any system operated by a bank. The transactions are done manually, since very few instructions need to be entered in order to effectuate a payment.

Finally, it should perhaps be pointed out that TMS, and GMS, are limited financial management systems, and as such they are complemented by local systems for accounts, payroll, general ledger, sales, purchasing and the like at the individual subsidiary level. We will return briefly to these systems below, but first we turn to the level below the corporate one.

5.2.2 Divisional Systems

To talk of divisional systems is perhaps employing a misnomer. Few non-local systems are unproblematic by strictly following SKF's present divisional organization. There is commonly a significant overlap. To make matters worse, these systems are generally referred to as "common applications" in SKF parlance. Still, they are definitely not so 'common' as to be corporate, in that they are not used across all divisional lines. Neither

[122] A subsidiary, or smaller scale, regional coordination center for Asia/Pacific is evolving in Singapore. In TMS terms, Singapore will be the intermediary counterpart between local companies and SKF centrally.

are they local, in that the same system is used by many widely dispersed units and not restricted to one node or company[123]. Other 'divisional systems' present us with fewer problems, though. This smaller set of systems can readily be treated in the context of one division.

Most systems are in practice centered on Bearing Industries users, often also involving Bearing Services one way or another. For the other three divisions, the picture is more varied; sometimes these non-corporate, non-local systems are used by some companies in the division, sometimes they are not used at all. This blurred domain of some divisional level systems will hopefully become clear, when each system is discussed.

Another complication is that some "common applications" essentially are stand-alone systems. The data commmunications network is then basically only used for supporting the implementation and maintenance of the system. The case in point is the Factory Administration System (FAS), which is regarded as the first truly common application in SKF. FAS is nevertheless little more than an internally developed computer program handling the practical administration of a bearing plant. It provides some control over the manufacturing process by claiming inputs and booking production capacity per order fed into the system.

FAS is, however, poorly diffused in SKF, and cannot expect to gain in importance. SKF systems policy also favors systems installations by Telenet node, and breaking down manufacturing systems by product line, rather than installation and break-down by factory. That makes FAS redundant, at least for the core units ("product divisions") in the new product organization for the standard bearings business (cf. Section 3.3 above), and it will not be discussed further.

Instead, we first turn to the dominating set of divisional systems, which relate to the material flow in bearing production and sales. Second, technical systems and databases will be surveyed briefly. Lastly, a few divisional systems fitting neither of these categories

[123] Systems that are only used within a national network are here regarded as being local (see Section 5.2.3 below).

well will be addressed and the question of system standards touched upon. Underlying the topics of the last main section, there is an element of systems commonality, running from bearings, to tools and components, and to distributor sales, which is not accounted for in the two first sections. To reduce complexity, this spill-over across divisions is not highlighted.

5.2.2.1 Bearing material flow systems

Recall that rationalization of bearing production in Europe manifested in GFSS prompted the decision to build the SKF Group Telenet in the first place[124]. Responsibility for coordinating bearing production and supply was assigned to the Forecasting and Supply Office (FSO) in Brussels, established in 1973. A computer FSO System matched forecast external demand with internal SKF production and supply. Input data from the European producing subsidiaries were initially hand-delivered by courier (sic!), as were the resulting capacity bookings, production plans and delivery schedules back to the subsidiaries. With the advent of on-line data communications, one could do away with the physical transport of magnetic tapes. The location of FSO to Brussels was primarily a function of its good communications, with the anticipated data communications network already in mind.

Essentially moving from full-range batch production of bearings in each company to continuous production by specialized plants (see further Hagström, 1987b) meant longer lead-times in production. The FSO System was based on these lead-times, with the consequence that production had to start well before customer orders were received. In short, production had to be forecast-guided and customers were supplied from warehouses. While bearing production was rationalized, the sales organization was left largely intact[125].

---

[124] See Section 4.2.

[125] A modest GFSS/FSO-type system in the Tools division is described in Section 5.2.2.3 below.

Developments in production techniques allowing greater flexibility (see also below) and the opportunities to reduce the response time to customer orders by more effective use of data communications, laid the foundation for a further trimming of the internal material flow in the early 1980s. The strategy was expressed as attempting to link customer orders to production scheduling. This 'beefed-up GFSS' was named the New Material Flow Concept (NMFC).

The heart of NMFC is a set of elaborate, inter-communicating information systems along SKF's value-added chain from its suppliers to its customers. Hitherto local systems for production and sales at the individual subsidiary level are replaced by successively developed common systems, which are still being implemented. A schematic overview of the setup is provided in Figure 5.1 below. The boxed-in areas represent main activities as divided by type of information system used in NMFC.

There is an implicit dividing line between the first and second boxes. Logically, the first box relates to the sales organization for external customers, with each unit selling the whole SKF product range. The three other boxes reflect activities within the manufacturing organization, with each unit producing only its designated segment of the product range. Thus, an individual sales company buys bearings internally from all manufacturing subsidiaries and an individual manufacturing subsidiary sells to all sales subsidiaries. - That is the principle; the organizational reality is more complex, but it has been brought closer in line with the NMFC systems with the introduction of the new 'product organization' (cf. Section 3.3 above).

Consequently, the new key direct information link is between the sales systems and the supply systems.

Figure 5.1

SKF's New Material Flow Concept

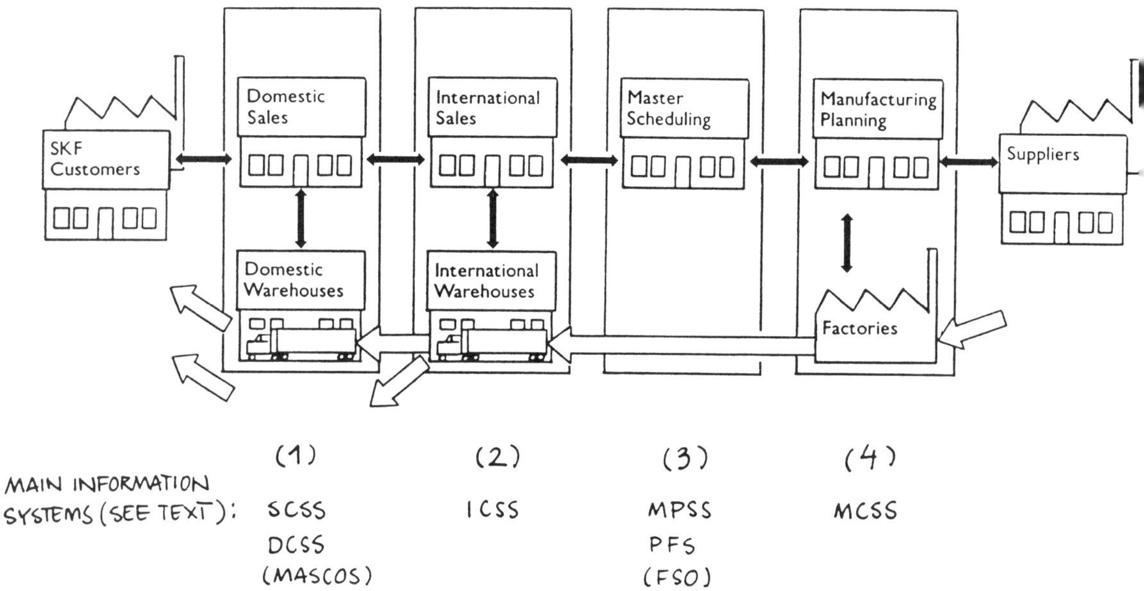

Source: Adapted from Bearing Bulletin, December, 1989.

In keeping with the logic of the NMFC, we start with the sales systems.

The Sales Company Service System (SCSS) is intended to encompass all administrative functions in a sales company, except salaries. It is made up of a whole host of subsystems, covering the main areas of marketing support, sales budget and support, customer order handling and invoicing, warehousing, and accounts and general ledger. The main function of SCSS is to allocate products to customers, and to mediate between external customers and the central warehouses associated with the manufacturing subsidiaries.

In practice, SCSS is typically installed at a sales subsidiary local computer, which also functions as a subsidiary or peripheral node in the data communications network. Distributors, agents and local sales offices can place orders, check on delivery status and make enquiries on line. SCSS will primarily seek to fill an order from the local Bearing Services stock. If need be, the search continues automatically to the stocks belonging to Bearing Industries warehouses. If still not available, the specialized manufacturing unit can reply when the required bearings will be produced and can be made available. In fact, the system is designed so it cannot answer 'no', it can only answer when the bearings can be delivered. Since transport schedules are included in SCSS, the exact delivery time can be fixed, irrespective of from where the required bearings are taken physically. Within seconds, a distributor or an SKF sales representative thus can have a specific order acknowledgement, an answer on availability and price of a particular bearing, or a status report on a particular delivery. Invoicing, shipping orders, stock replenishment and accounting are, of course, automatically adjusted accordingly.

SCSS is a fairly recent system. Development of the system began in 1983 and the first complete installation was made in Gothenburg in 1987. By the beginning of 1990, it had been implemented in all countries with main node national networks, and in the Netherlands, Austria and Hong Kong. The main development of the system was carried out in Sweden, with substantial input from Belgium (which was the pilot installation), South Africa, and later on the US. Several other subsidiaries in other countries contributed with IS resources and user competence as well, in particular Austria, the Netherlands, Switzerland and Latin American countries. The main responsibility for SCSS now rests with SKF Dataservice.

SCSS is essentially an updated and expanded version of the Modular Automated Sales COmpany System (MASCOS), at present in use in some 40 sales companies. MASCOS is used for sales of products from all SKF divisions, while SCSS is more ambitious requiring adaptations for non-bearing sales. The Tools and (now) Ovako divisions took part in the early development and have started to use SCSS. Component Systems sales subsidiaries have been slower to leave MASCOS (as have some Bearing Services subsidiaries[126]).

MASCOS is further a batch system, and each installation is dedicated for use by one company only, covering standard products quoted in the local currency. An SCSS, on the other hand, offers on-line access to several companies and sites, allowing for modified product designs and for up-to-date price information independently of in which currency the shipping price is quoted.

Since both systems are used by the organization, SCSS has been designed to interface automatically with MASCOS, thus upgrading the versatility of the existing MASCOS systems. Especially communications improve, as a local SCSS is directly linked to the manufacturing units.

Contrary to MASCOS, SCSS can be tailored to the specific needs of a sales subsidiary due to its modular functionality. This makes it easier to take account of local market and resource idiosyncracies. SCSS can also readily take in data from external databases, for instance for local marketing support.

This wider coverage of SCSS leads us to a very important role played by the system rather outside the NMFC. SCSS encapsulates the interface with the SKF data communications network, in the process becoming something of a single gateway into the network <u>and</u> the systems accessed through it. That includes both the already discussed GMS and TMS. Indeed, reports are generated and transmitted automatically as SCSS is used. The functioning of both GMS and TMS is enhanced as a result.

SCSS runs parallel with the <u>Domestic Customer Service System</u> (DCSS) in markets where bearings also are produced. The systems perform essentially the same functions as

---

[126] Some Bearing Services subsidiaries selling products from Tools and Component Systems in markets where the latter divisions lack their own sales subsidiaries are in a more complicated situation. They are likely to keep MASCOS, often in parallel with SCSS, waiting for wider internal diffusion of SCSS.

regards NMFC, wherefore they will not be repeated here. However, SCSS is a Bearing Services system for the aftermarket, while DCSS belongs to Bearing Industries and consequently serves sales to OEM-customers and to Bearing Services. In effect, SCSS and DCSS come together at the main national warehouse. That warehouse stocks the full range of bearings for the national market and is operated by Bearing Industries[127].

While SCSS is run on the smaller sales company computers, DCSS is a mainframe installation. The direct, non-aftermarket customer links discussed in Section 4.3 above feed into DCSS. Typically, an OEM-customer transmits its delivery schedule directly from its own system to DCSS, which fixes the delivery timetable[128]. Deliveries are allocated by DCSS between, on the one hand, the national stock and, on the other hand, claims on future production in the relevant manufacturing units. Orders from Bearing Services are handled similarly. Stock replenishment to the national warehouse (and from it to Bearing Services) is automatic.

Like SCSS, DCSS continuously generates reports also for divisional management and stores data for future reference.

DCSS is both older and newer than SCSS. What in effect are earlier versions of the system are installed in Luton and Schweinfurt. The present system was developed by Germany and France, with support from Sweden. The first installation was made in Clamart, operational in mid-1987. Gothenburg now also has DCSS.

The dividing line between the sales and manufacturing organizations in Figure 5.1 above is also the limit as to far into NMFC customers can come. Moving further upstream, we take the step into truly internal systems, viz. those directly related to production.

---

[127] For the sake of clarity, where there is no local production, the Bearing Services' stocks are in a sense the 'national' inventory. There is, however, some overlap in that smaller national markets geographically close to large producing units will draw on the national stocks of the latter. A good example is the Nordic countries, which all use the Swedish national main warehouse. The overall setup parallels that of the data communications network, with the stocking hierarchy closely following the division between national networks and SKF Group Telenet.

[128] Since many of the OEM-customers are motor vehicle manufacturers, DCSS is designed to accommodate the ODETTE standard (see Section 5.2.2.3 below).

The main national warehouse still haunts us, though. In practice located at the same site, but logically totally separate, we find the so called international warehouse. It stocks only the output of the local specialized production units for supply to all national warehouses. The international warehouse is managed by the International Customer Service System (ICSS). Perhaps it becomes clearer to exchange in one's mind 'international' for 'internal'.

ICSS constitutes the key interface between the sales and manufacturing organizations. ICSS is the system which finally and firmly books orders against internal supply not on hand in the domestic warehouses. The main functions of ICSS are order entry, delivery time fixing, pricing, order acknowledgement, 'goods out' and export documents creation (including allocation, packing, invoicing, package mix calculation etc.), data maintenance on orders, supply and basic categories (such as customers and products), and reports and statistics generation.

ICSS was the first system to be developed in the NMFC-chain of systems. Most development work was carried out in Gothenburg, except the warehousing subsystems, which were done in Clamart. The first installation came in Schweinfurt in 1982. By the first quarter in 1983, all the six main manufacturing companies in Europe had their own installations, serving their respective manufacturing units. The Spanish subsidiary's ICSS is an exception as it was installed in Gothenburg in 1988 to overcome local resource constraints but it is completely run from Spain. It is now in the process of being moved to Clamart. Overall responsibility for ICSS is now shared between Clamart, the Gothenburg manufacturing subsidiary and SKF Dataservice.

As the only material flow system so far to migrate outside the standard bearings business area, ICSS has been implemented for miniature bearings within the Specialty Bearings division. To this end, one ICSS installation has been made at the Thomery plant in France.

The greatest benefits to be derived from ICSS critically hinge on functioning communications. We have already touched on the on-line system-to-system interfaces with SCSS and DCSS. ICSS is, however, capable of interfacing with a large number of other systems and can also be accessed manually through the data communications network. Basically all organizational units with connection to SKF Group Telenet can use ICSS. There is, however, a qualitative gulf between having to manually key in inquiries and orders, and having a system-to-system link. Most of the sales organization units in Europe, North America, Panama, Argentina, South Africa, Singapore, Australia and New Zealand have at least a batch system-to-system link for transmission of orders, acknowledgements, packing specifications and invoices. ICSS use is thus well spread in SKF and the system manages the vast majority of international bearing shipments within SKF.

There is obviously significant overlap between DCSS and ICSS. Both are also very large systems requiring a mainframe computer, in practice the same one. DCSS is probably best seen as a temporary solution. Indeed, a new version of ICSS, ICSS+, is being developed and which will incorporate both the present systems. SCSS will then interface with ICSS+. The fact that installation of DCSS in Italy has been postponed and that North America still uses local systems indicate that ICSS+ is not too far off. Logically, the repercussions for warehouses should be that all national, full-range stock will pass onto Bearing Services and that only the international/internal inventory rests with Bearing Industries[129].

The market 'pull' through the stocks of finished bearings spills over into production via the automatic interface between ICSS and the Master Production Scheduling System (MPSS; see Figure 5.1 above). It is perhaps best characterized as a system for overall planning of production. To explain what MPSS really does, we need to briefly look at production planning prior to MPSS and - equally briefly - to consider the sequence of main activities in the production of bearings.

In the old GFSS/FSO scheme production was effectively planned per month since production orders were issued to the factories once per month. Factory capacity for different manufacturing activities was booked accordingly all through the manufacturing

---

[129] The status of warehousing and how to support the associated activities is discussed further in Section 5.2.3.3 below.

sequence, six months or more in advance of the finished bearing becoming available. Planning was further done by separate routines for a very narrow range (often one dimension) of bearings. This scheme optimizes continuous production of long series but is rather inflexible and gives long lead-times.

MPSS is designed to improve production flexibility without having to forego the efficiencies gained through production specialization. The overriding philosophy of MPSS is to plan successively by main activity while building on commonalities between products, thus avoiding excessive specification early in production. The capacity of each activity is defined and booked by product line (viz. by "product division" rather than by factory, cf. Section 3.3 above) to improve the flow from one activity to the next.

The idea can be illustrated by considering a stylized production sequence. Roughly, raw materials are ordered six months before final assembly takes place. The corresponding figures for booking turning and grinding are four and two months, respectively. The degree of planning aggregation possible decreases continuously, as do the margins for intervention, in what progressively becomes fine production planning.

MPSS draws up a rolling, over-all production plan, identifies resource requirements and checks them against available manpower and machine-capacity. Subsequently, a master production schedule covering all products is drawn up, taking constraints concerning lead-times and lot sizes into consideration. The actual production orders are then defined per day. In sum, MPSS can handle all products in a uniform way and attempts to keep the scope for possible intervention as wide as possible, as long as possible. ICSS can cut into the process approximately up to one month before assembly[130].

MPSS is not solely guided by demand information from ICSS, though. The Product Forecasting System (PFS) is the twin of MPSS, calculating product forecasts and safety stocks (based on forecast error). Here, the central FSO System also intervenes, giving

[130] Note however, that ICSS continuously feeds in term orders for OEM-customers and for stock replenishment, but which come in earlier in the planning process, typically not significantly altering the production scheduling at this stage.

forecasting input into PFS and checks on planning for all the MPSS installations in the aggregate. The different MPSSs are adjusted accordingly. Demand forecasting is in practice still overwhelmingly carried out centrally by FSO.

The overall responsibility for MPSS/PFS rests with FSO in Brussels, which thus retains some of its role as the hub of the product flow within SKF. Reporting to divisional management goes via FSO in this case, and not directly as for the other systems.

MPSS/PFS was developed by FSO with assistance from the Swedish and Italian nodes. It was installed in all the main European manufacturing companies during the period 1987-1989.

The last major system in the NMFC-family (see Figure 5.1 above) is the Manufacturing Customer Service System (MCSS). Here, we come to the shop floor, viz. the day-to-day running and costing of manufacturing.

MCSS is driven by MPSS. MCSS identifies the demand for components and raw materials, and issues purchasing orders, having checked inventories and outstanding orders. As has been noted above, data communications supplier links are still rather poorly developed. Of the few in place, only steel purchases from Ovako and orders for paper (for bearing cartons) from STORA in Sweden can go automatically from MCSS[131].

Further, MCSS continuously schedules operations, checks on capacity and work-load, monitors work in progress and resource consumption, records changes in inventories, compares actual with standard costs, and calculates new costs. The main improvements brought by MCSS are integrated on-line planning and control of manufacturing and inventories, and continuous database maintenance. MCSS regularly generates reports, which go on to the divisional head-office.

[131] With the new purchasing organization (cf. Section 3.3 above), a new supporting system is in the cards. In the meantime, other systems (e.g. MEST) are used.

MCSS was developed from a standard, off-the-shelf system. The adaptation to SKF was done jointly by Sweden, Italy and a London consultancy firm (cf. the temporary leased line in Section 4.3.2 above). Starting in 1986, the main European bearing producing companies now have it installed. Spain is a special case, as they are awaiting conversion of MCSS for use on a smaller mainframe computer. In practice, there is an MCSS per (bearing) main node, as there is for the other large material flow systems. The different factories then access the 'national' system for planning production in their lines. The material flow systems must be able to function separately on the national level in order to safeguard against interruptions in international data communications stopping production.

The company-wide responsibility for maintenance and support of MCSS has been assigned to the Turin node. Nine people at the node exclusively work with MCSS. They can exemplify the setup also for the support teams of the other systems. The MCSS team is functionally separate from the node IS staff, reporting to the international IS board (rather than the local one). Joint costs are distributed among using companies and direct support costs are invoiced.

Finally, after having covered the whole interlocking chain of material flow systems, we are forced to recognize that although they tell the main story, they do not tell the whole one. A host of other systems support the NMFC. They fall in two categories: technical systems interfacing with material flow systems, and special feature systems, akin to subsystems in the material flow systems. In the latter category, worth mentioning are: one system (FOCUS), which keeps a tab on large-volume orders from specific customers, so called priority items; one system, PROduction Delivery PERFormance system (PRODPERF), which monitors factory compliance with delivery schedules; and one system, CUSTomer SERVice system (CUSTSERV), which does the same for deliveries to external customers. CUSTSERV and PRODPERF (and PRODMAST, see below) are moreover the only systems connected to NMFC that have migrated across the Atlantic. The first one was installed in the US at the end of 1988, followed by PRODPERF in early 1989. Also, a simpler, PC-based version of PRODPERF is in use at the Latin American Bearing Industries subsidiaries since 1988.

Digressing somewhat from the physical flow of products, the roles of PRODPERF and CUSTSERV should also be seen in the context of the new product organization (cf. Section 3.3 above). PRODPERF monitors the performance along the whole production line, and CUSTSERV does the same for the sales organization's activities. Whereas the NMFC systems provide data on each step along the line (and, in some cases in parallel), PRODPERF and CUSTSERV thus supply divisional and corporate management with information on the over-all performance of the production and sales organizations respectively. That function of PRODPERF and CUSTSERV is furthermore most likely to have contributed to their relatively prompt migration outside Europe.

SKF's major technical systems are the subject of the next section, but one, the PRODuction MASTer file (PRODMAST) is especially important in the present context. It is the repository of product data and the vehicle for fast and reliable updating of such data for use by the material flow systems.

5.2.2.2 Technical systems and databases

Databases are typically an integral part of systems, as we have already seen from the corporate and material flow systems. However, technical databases are often maintained separately from the processing applications. One way of seeing the link between the two is to view the technical systems as how to do something, and to regard the databases as containing the 'what' to do it with.

Given the over-arching heading, some caveats are in order. The employed epithet 'technical' is far from unambiguous. Somewhat arbitrarily, we think of systems, where technical product or process specifications are part and parcel of the system's principal function.

Again, bearing-related systems make up the bulk of systems under the rubric of divisional-level technical applications. We will only identify those major systems and we will avoid going into detail unless warranted by their importance for overall operations. Strictly technical calculation systems will be discussed in generic terms, rather than in particular. We will also exclude shop-floor, factory automation systems, which only control a limited segment of the production process. For instance, the common systems that come with SKF machinery from LMT will not be considered.

Strictly speaking, most technical systems are not really dependent on data communications for their functioning, since there is no automatic interface between different installations. Specifically, the important CAD/CAM applications are stand-alone systems, but designated "common applications" by SKF. However, some of them are large installations requiring a lot of processing power and/or become more of a repository of technical knowledge. On both counts, they stimulate non-local usage via Telenet and are thus relevant, given our communications-oriented perspective. Moreover, maintenance and updating of "common" systems is commonly done in a uniform fashion via Telenet.

The existence and remote use of technical systems is a more salient feature for our purposes than the specific operations the systems perform. Recall that access to different systems in various locations figured prominently as a rationale for establishing the SKF data communications network (cf. the remote job entry facility). In practice, this use of the network has been slower to take off than the administrative and operational uses already discussed. We surmise that there are both Telenet- and systems-related explanations for this state of affairs.

On the Telenet side, transmission capacity and quality have put a restriction on dispersed use of technical systems. The sheer amount and the representations of technical data (consider, for instance, a CAD-drawing) both require dramatically higher transmission capacity, and are much more sensitive to transmission errors than administrative data. Since around the mid-1980s, it has in practice ceased to be a concern for leased lines, particularly when back-up lines are available. It continues to be a problem for most dial-up connections, especially long-distance packet-switched ones. Moreover, the early network architecture itself was a barrier. Many technical systems run on DEC computers and the interface with Telenet was very cumbersome, if it was available at all. New gateways and the establishment of a DEC-net 'within' Telenet, also in the mid-1980s, have removed many of these obstacles.

The technical systems have become more versatile as well over time. The area of application has widened, increasing the number of different potential users for an individual system. A related aspect is the internal diffusion of technical systems. It takes time for knowledge about a system's existence and capabilities to spread in the organization. That is a more important consideration for technical systems, since usage is more a function of need, than for administrative systems, which to a larger extent are diffused as a matter of SKF policy.

We choose to highlight SKF's Engineering and Research Centre (ERC) in the Netherlands as a host for technical systems with such wide appeal, reflecting its central role in research within SKF. Systems housed in other Telenet nodes are parallel cases, but on a smaller scale. ERC is also a focal point in a broader sense, in that it is also a center for training and for quality auditing in SKF.

With product development largely decentralized to the different manufacturing units, local application engineering departments frequently draw on the technical systems at ERC. This possibility is clearly seen by subsidiaries as adding muscle to their own technical capabilities. Systems that cannot be motivated for local installment because of cost or available computer processing capacity can be used via ERC. An added benefit is that through such usage, SKF standards for products and procedures get disseminated as such standards are embedded in the systems. The standards setting extends to production techniques and tooling, since ERC also carries out research in these areas.

A system that epitomizes remote systems usage is BEAring CONsultant (BEACON). It is available through Telenet. BEACON analyses customer bearing applications in terms of load, deflection, bearing life etc. The potential boost in technical capability for organizational units not having a similar system is evident, and for those that do, BEACON can be useful for comparison. In fact, there exists a whole host of locally developed programs performing similar functions, but for very specific application categories. BEACON is not a substitute for those systems, but rather a system with broader product coverage, explicitly for easy use by SKF application engineers world-wide to support the advising of customers.

There is an additional twist to remote usage of BEACON. It was originally developed by ERC, starting in 1986, but the physical installation was made in Gothenburg in 1988. However, the responsibility for program content still remained at ERC, meaning that requests for documentation, questions etc. should be directed to ERC.

In general, the smaller the subsidiary the greater is the value attached to the ERC link. Large manufacturing units, which could have motivated local technical systems and development in the absence of direct communication with ERC may now not be able to do so. An extreme case is the Bearing Industries R&D department in the US, which was discontinued in 1984. From having numbered some 250 people, it is now down to a tenth of that. The new department has changed name to "Product Engineering and Quality", signalling a shift in scope of activities. Although coinciding with the upgrading of the Telenet link, there were also other, more complex reasons for the change. However, data communications were far from unimportant, as evidenced by the present relatively high communications intensity (compared both to other units in SKF and to other US functional uses of Telenet) between King of Prussia and ERC. Further, there is less need for a complete set of US technical applications, since adaptation to US market product standards can now be handled by 'European' systems, or can be left to the last stages in the process, e.g. the development of a new bearing variant.

The converse of the above effects can also be illustrated. Schweinfurt has traditionally had a very strong position in technical development in SKF. Large local production, long experience, and a local skill pool are the chief explanations. From the Schweinfurt horizon, Telenet has brought a larger (internal) 'market' for its technical systems. Schweinfurt's de facto leading role in many system areas, notably CAD/CAM, is well recognized by other subsidiaries[132], although the overall responsibility for a system may formally rest with, commonly, Gothenburg or ERC.

In addition, some local, Schweinfurt developed systems have been enhanced in cooperation with ERC, and subsequently been copied for use at other sites. A good example is the PC-80 system (Production Concept for the 80s), which took over main elements from a local system (MAMMUT). PC-80 is a system for control of a continuously working production line, while mixing lot sizes and dimensions, requiring one-shift manning only (see further Hagström, 1990a). It is primarily intended for customers in the automotive and electrical industries. ERC has now developed a successor, PC-90. Specially designed machinery from LMT has been incorporated into the concept. Production flexibility is further enhanced by allowing shorter series and quicker change-overs within production runs. The scope for change has also been increased by the new machinery being more versatile, each line being able to handle a wider range of dimensions and types of bearings.

To illustrate the 'pull' effect of remote use of technical systems, consider the case of the Italian Specialty Bearings subsidiary for aerospace bearings, Avio. It calls much more frequently on ERC, and ERC systems, as a counterpart for improving production techniques than on its formally designated counterpart MRC, the SKF aerospace bearing product center. The better technical systems in terms of performance, and the wider knowledge of bearing properties in general embedded in the systems, make ERC the favored location by Avio. ERC in the Netherlands and MRC in the US are, of course, equidistant from Avio in data communications terms. Although unintended, this rather 'out-of-line' liaison is not stifled by SKF.

Usage of ERC-based systems is also stimulated by the first-hand experience gained by research engineers from other SKF-companies while on secondment to ERC. They normally stay for three years before returning, and at any given time there will be roughly

[132] The Schweinfurt node's strong competence in manufacturing systems meant that the local systems for a long time were the most advanced in SKF. Now, they are overtaken figuratively and literally by MCSS.

fifteen such engineers at ERC. The short courses offered by the SKF College of Engineering, located at the ERC, give much less familiarity with the systems, but reach a greater number of SKF employees from a greater number of, and also more varied, organizational units.

An interesting case of the latter, and of another use of Telenet, is a recent course program for application and sales engineers. In a bid to upgrade their technical capabilities in response to perceived increasing customer demands, a set of 2-4 week course modules have been developed. Between the sessions in situ, participants return to their ordinary jobs in SKF, carrying PC-based training sessions for individual study. Although at present intended to be self-contained, Telenet in general, and MEST in particular, are used for questions and the like arising out of this self-study. Since the communications network is already in place, this kind of distance-learning seems poised to increase and become more sophisticated. By way of extrapolation, it represents a way of formalizing the kind of learning now acquired through actual remote use of systems.

Another area set to change is quality control. Standard testing of products is carried out at the manufacturing site and at the product centers. Monthly quality reports are, however, sent to ERC[133]. Apart from control of adherence to standards and of product quality, a wide-ranging central data base on product performance (complementing ERC's own laboratory-like testing) is building up. That information can feed back both to local product design and to customer sales support.

Naturally, product databases already do exist. The earliest and most important one is the Bearing Engineering DAtabase (BEDA)[134]. The concept dates back to the early 1980s and the database has since successively grown in product coverage and volume of data given per item. BEDA is essentially an extensive bearing product catalogue with complete engineering specifications for finished bearings, bearing parts and bearing accessories.

---

[133] As an aside, most reports are actually still sent by telefacsimile (in part because of the way they are compiled and because they are short, but accompanied by graphs).

[134] An example of a more specialized database is the car database, containing technical information on bearings in current car models. It is primarily intended to be used in its PC-version.

Apart from bearings in regular production, bearings under development are included. The highly technical specifications are also complemented by general information, such as verbal descriptions of product characteristics.

BEDA is primarily intended for internal use, i.e. to help rationalize internal engineering work, but also to improve customer service. Meeting these objectives simultaneously requires a very differentiated approach to access. Product catalogue data is freely available, also to external parties. Additional technical product specifications (the so called "technical handbook") are released to all SKF engineers. Next, there is more production related data, which have further restrictions on internal release. Lastly, data on products under development are basically not released at all outside the location where they are being developed[135].

There is one BEDA at each main node, with the exception of Madrid and King of Prussia[136]. BEDA is too big for the Madrid computers and in the US interest in getting BEDA has so far been scant, to a large extent since product specifications are metric.

The evolution of BEDA is very much of a change from a straight-forward database to becoming an integrated member of the SKF 'family of systems'. Up until 1989, Gothenburg had the responsibility for maintaining and supporting BEDA, and units with no local access used the Gothenburg installation via Telenet. However, it proved difficult to keep BEDA current. In part that was a function of the sheer complexity of the database, in part the several parallel locations made it cumbersome to continuously adjust the different installations to each other. With production and product development decentralized, each BEDA installation easily took on a strong local flavor. Changes were entered for the local, specialized segment of the bearing product range. In practice, the Gothenburg BEDA-version was used as the primus inter pares, although updated with a considerable lag to take account of local developments.

---

135 Data on prototypes and on bearings in production are actually stored in two different parts of BEDA; PRE BEDA and MASTER BEDA, respectively. PRE BEDA data are stored locally only.

136 Naturally, the Ovako Steel nodes also do not have local BEDA installations.

Now, BEDA is in the hands of a broad-based board with SKF Dataservice as the support unit. The operation of BEDA is a concern for several, geographically dispersed working groups and task forces. Updating and content responsibility has been given to the specific product lines ("product divisions" in the new product organization, cf. Section 3.3 above) for products and to the product line coordination units ("product centers") for standard tolerances. The different BEDA installations then exchange the updated information every week. The Schweinfurt main node has taken over the function of access-point for subsidiaries lacking their own BEDA installation. Finally, BEDA interfaces with other systems have improved considerably. From having been extremely rudimentary, BEDA is now integrated with NMFC (specifically with MCSS and ProdMast), and readily compatible with related systems, such as BEACON and CAD applications.

Seen over the whole period, BEDA has been an important means for establishing SKF product standards for manufacturing units and a valuable source of detailed product information, not least for sales subsidiaries. These strengths underlie BEDA's new lease on life, which has meant a costly modernization of the database/system. The sheer size[137] and complexity of BEDA also make maintenance of it a significant drain on resources. Add to that the still rather cumbersome updating of the different installations, coupled with the value of continuous updating for users, and it seems very likely that BEDA will be concentrated. Non-released data (on products being developed) could remain locally for security reasons, while the rest of BEDA could become a single installation only. The drawback that local access can be denied due to interruptions in international data traffic has lessened with the improvements in the reliability of data communications links. Reductions in the storage/ /communications price ratio should add to the attractiveness of such an option.

A major application such as BEDA also tends to spawn offspring. It is one parent - internal CAD/CAM applications being the other - of an application aimed at customers, and embodying both technical systems and a database; the <u>CADalog</u>. Since 1986, customers have been able to get the SKF bearing product catalogue with some CAD

[137] BEDA contains some 20 000 products and can manage up to 1 200 entries per product.

features in computer-readable form. The CADalog was developed in Gothenburg and the main responsibility for the application rests with the Bearing Industries main Swedish subsidiary.

The CADalog performs three main tasks. First, the bearing selection subsystem assists in choosing the right bearing in a dialogue with the user. In an iterative process, the customer specifies his requirements and the subsystem suggests appropriate bearings from the SKF standard product catalogue. Second, the CADalog can produce CAD images of the selected bearing, giving all the relevant geometry for construction and design incorporating the bearing. Third, a bearing calculation program is available for advanced construction, identifying the correct bearings in machinery with up to five bearings on a shaft.

The CADalog is available on-line through Telenet. The first two features can also be had on diskette for use on a PC. A nominal fee is charged for the diskettes with updated versions sent out once a year. The sophisticated analysis program is not released to customers for competitive reasons. The customer has to run the application on SKF's computers. By the end of 1988, some 4 000 CADalogs had been distributed to external users, almost exclusively in Europe. It comes in eight different languages[138] and covers approximately 25 000 standard bearing types.

To our knowledge, the CADalog is the very first of its kind in the world. The key aspect is that the CADalog is not just a run-of-the-mill database, but that it is designed to interface with six different CAD systems. The customer can use it interactively with his own CAD applications, or, as in the case of a distributor (or an SKF sales subsidiary), with his customer's CAD applications. The customer thus gets instant access to bearing expertise, easily integrated into his own systems.

---

[138] By comparison, the traditional product catalogue is available in 16 languages and 500 000 copies have been printed. The very first SKF product catalog, from 1916, had a print run of 136 000 and six language versions.

Additional benefits to the customer include the CADalog attempting to find a standard bearing for a given need. For instance, a construction engineer of electrical motors is often unaware that a standard type of bearing already exists that satisfies the requirements of a particular motor. Instead, he specifies a much more expensive customized bearing in his design. The CADalog displays the nearest standard bearing from the whole SKF range and gives the product code. In consequence, ordering is also greatly facilitated. For customers with on-line access to Telenet, ordering etc. can be done automatically as the CADalog can feed data directly into SKF order entry systems (e.g. DCSS and SCSS).

For SKF, the obvious advantage lies in tying customers closer, in effect restricting their choice of bearing to SKF products. Further, by alerting the customer to the existence of some standard bearings, SKF expects to steer the customers toward buying a smaller range of bearings, bringing economies in production and distribution. Facilitated ordering should also make a customer less likely to work his way through a competitors' catalogue to find a corresponding product. Bearings almost always represent a minute fraction in the cost of the final product of which they are a part, wherefore a customer may be less sensitive to price than to other characteristics. Bearings are typically crucial for the functioning of the final product and the customer is likely to value knowing a bearing's performance in detail and knowing exactly that a bearing will be physically available for building into his products. The CADalog and simplified ordering routines are designed to cater for these customer needs, adding to SKF's competitive edge.

Not resting on its laurels, SKF has developed CADalog further. A training version for use by new customers and by universities was launched in 1989. That same year, a new feature building on the successful CAD-conversions was tried. The program provides for exchanging CAD-drawings between SKF and its customers, i.e. SKF will also be able to 'import' the customers' CAD-drawings into its own systems. By running these CAD-drawings internally, SKF can enhance its contribution to the customer's design. The CADalog application can respond to the customer with additional recommendations for efficient speed, lubrication, maintenance schedules etc. adapted to his chosen design. It is also possible to make customized modifications in the dimension of a bearing. So far, the new program is only available on magnetic tape, necessitating physical transport between the customer and SKF. At present, SKF UK is using the expanded CADalog in this way with four major customers (Ford, Austin-Rover, GKN and Eaton). This CAD interchange is planned to go on-line during 1990.

On the basis of the original CADalog, a version for linear motion products has recently been developed. Dubbed LinCAD, it performs CADalog's basic tasks for arrangements incorporating linear bearings and ball screws. It was launched in 1989. Although a logical complement to bearings (cf. circular and linear motion) and with many similarities in the underlying technology, linear motion products is a separate business within the Component Systems division. It is a small area, constituting 14 percent of divisional sales or only 1 1/2 percent of total SKF sales. The linear motion business clearly could not have supported development of a LinCAD from scratch. Further, the similarities with bearings is the most probable explanation for this first migration of the CADalog into a new area.

The Tools division has its own variation of the CADalog concept, also offering its product catalogue on diskette. The PC Product Database is primarily that, viz. a database. It is a simpler application than the CADalog, and more oriented toward finding a product and ordering it. To this end, the PC Product Database performs some different tasks. A tool, for instance, a drill, can be identified by size, by SKF alfanumeric code, by bar code, by application, and by user code. Moreover, the PC Product Database updates customer prices and create orders for transmission to the Sheffield mainframe. The information is filed in a database for subsequent analysis of ordering patterns.

The most innovative features are the possible searches by application and by user code. The application oriented tool selection has similarities with CADalog's bearing selection but the user has to specify the application unilaterally. Allowing the user to keep his own product code, which is automatically translated to the SKF code by the PC Product Database, greatly facilitates both his searches and subsequent ordering. The customer-oriented conversions reflect a common approach by the PC Product Database and CADalog (cf. the more advanced CAD-conversions).

Somewhat surprisingly, the PC Product Database was developed totally independently from the CADalog. In fact, the CADalog was still known by name only in Sheffield when the PC Product Database was launched in late 1988. This state of affairs further underscores the propensity of the Tools division to choose its own route when it comes to business-related use of data communications and systems.

Some reasons for this apparent independence on the part of the Tools division has been discussed above (cf. Section 4.3.2). To the separate history of the division and the need to forestall competitor moves, one can add specific industry characteristics which differ somewhat from those prevailing in the bearing industry.

Typically, as much as 90 percent of the products are sold through distributors and only 10 percent directly to end-users[139]. The distributors tend both to carry several suppliers' wares within the same product range and to have a much broader range of products than that manufactured by the SKF Tools division. Drills, taps, milling tools and other cutting tools are also consumables by function and commonly purchased in small lots. Consequently, there is no real need for sophisticated CAD-interfaces, but rather a need to adapt to the customers' (read: distributors') administrative routines for the products. The feature of access to the PC Product Database by bar code further illustrates the point, as it is primarily intended for a storeman to replenish a product stock simply by passing a bar code pen along the shelf label.

Since we are now slowly moving away from technical systems, we will continue this discussion in the next section, as we turn to other systems, and to the role of non-SKF standards for communication between systems.

[139] The third largest production unit in the Tools division, Prototyp-Werke in West Germany, is a special case with a 60/40 distribution. As given by the Annual Report 1989, the overall share of Tools sales going through distributors is 78 percent.

5.2.2.3 Other systems and standards

Almost all the major divisional level systems have already been identified. Some systems in the Tools and Bearing Services divisions warrant some further attention, though. Since those systems conclude our survey of divisional systems, the issue is raised of how divisions that are relatively poorly served by such systems manage. In turn, that prompts a brief discussion of the possibility for standards to function as a platform for integrating systems for related businesses. - But first we will continue the Tools story.

Orders based on the PC Product Database are readily usable for demand forecasting and subsequently for improving production scheduling. Experience from the links to the Sheffield mainframe, which eleven end-users and eleven distributors have been using for the past few years (see Section 4.3.2 above), indicates this to be the case. These customers have access to interactive order handling and to electronic mail (MEST) through their connections. Enquiries on Sheffield product availability, fixing of delivery dates, and order placement against stocks can be handled in this way.

A third, more advanced, category of systems concerns internal product flows. Since Sheffield was connected to the Telenet in 1984-1985, an on-line order inquiry and inventory status system has been in operation. Order entry is possible also for products not yet in stock. Orders can be given different priorities in a three-tier classification scheme. In countries where Tools lack sales representation, Bearing Services subsidiaries sell the Tools range[140]. The Sheffield systems then receive the information from the local MASCOS systems. At present, add-on features are being implemented that will allow Sheffield to directly control target stocks at the sales units and to intervene regarding order quantities. Within a few years, it is planned that data will be extracted directly from Sheffield from the local sales systems.

---

[140] However, on the large West German market the Tools sales subsidiary in Erkrath is complemented by the Component Systems sales subsidiary in Frankfurt also selling tools (see also below).

In parallel, there is some product exchange between the UK, Swedish, Italian and Brazilian manufacturing subsidiaries, which is administered through file transfers over Telenet[141]. So far, the biggest impact has been in coordination of product development, but the objective is to rationalize production similar to what has been done in bearing production. The Brazilian subsidiary has less specialized manufacturing due to Brazil's stringent import restrictions. However, coordination regarding supply on third markets is notable, and rapidly gaining in importance. It is especially relevant for the US market, which is almost exclusively supplied from Brazil and the UK. The historically important link with the US is thus assuming even greater significance.

The similarities with the bearing material flow systems may appear striking. However, the Tools version is, as we have seen, much less complex and far-reaching, and is carried out on a much smaller scale. There is no automatic connection between, on the one hand, systems for sales and distribution, and, on the other hand, systems for production. Even within each category, systems are not well integrated with one another.

Selling exclusively to the aftermarket, Bearing Services faces a set of customers very similar to that of the Tools division. Although backed up by the material flow (and technical) systems, Bearing Services has developed[142] a database, primarily supporting sales to distributors. The CROss rEference SyStem (CROESUS) is available for installation on local sales subsidiary computers since late 1988. It is updated through Telenet (and can, of course, be accessed this way as well if not installed locally). CROESUS supplements existing aftermarket bearing catalogues, among other things containing more extensive and up-to-date technical information. Like printed aftermarket catalogues, CROESUS is organized by application area (e.g. vehicle aftermarket). The rather different feature here, however, is that CROESUS lists the SKF equivalents of

---

[141] The only remaining Tools manufacturing subsidiaries are Prototyp-Werke in West Germany, Cofler & C in Italy and the Titex locations. Except the first one, they were acquired as late as in 1990, and thus too recent to be considered here. Prototyp-Werke has so far been excluded from production exchange by virtue of it manufacturing a somewhat different range of tools (primarily special taps) than the other Tools units. Recall also that Prototyp-Werke is a fairly late acquisition (1986), and that it has a very modest data communications status (cf. Section 4.2.2.2 above).

[142] The systems development was jointly carried out by Bearing Services, SKF Dataservice, and the Bearing Industries subsidiary in the Netherlands.

competitors' product designations as well. With this information on hand, for instance, a distributor can more easily replace a competitor's bearing on his own shelf and more easily offer an SKF alternative to his customers. That the opposite may occur, viz. the replacement of SKF products, appears to be a calculated risk but the additional services, of course, do not extend to competitors' wares and coverage of the latter is not complete.

Bearing Services explicitly intends to go further down this road, using the data communications links for closer cooperation with distributors. The existing links will especially be exploited more for promotional activities supporting sales. In turn, that could well entail upgrading the data communications links with distributors.

The (end-)user category among Bearing Services' customers is particularly receptive to a high service component with the product since, typically, a limited number of bearings are critical parts in their own production equipment. Bearing Services also offers a comprehensive package of ancillary services (and products) related to product performance in such diverse areas as training, mounting, lubrication, shaft levelling, maintenance, and condition monitoring. The two last items are of special interest for our purposes.

First, Bearing Services supplies equipment which can alert the customer on-line that a bearing needs replacement. Second, a computer program for maintenance management, Analyses, Planning and Information (API), is sold[143]. Among other things, API schedules standard replacement orders for bearings; orders which can go on automatically to Bearing Services if the customer has a commensurate connection with SKF. Monitoring equipment and API can be used separately, but can also operate in tandem, automatically ordering from SKF when a bearing shows signs of wearing out (which may not coincide with the predicted time). The next logical step is when the on-line monitoring system is connected directly to SKF. Such a setup began being tested on machine grinding spindles at the Luton Bearing Industries subsidiary in 1990 and it will most likely come to be offered to external customers as well. - In this context, it is also

[143] API has been developed by Bearing Services' Danish subsidiary.

worth pointing out that plants belonging to Bearing Industries are high-priority customers in the "user" segment.

Bearing Services also sells products from Component Systems in geographical markets, where the latter has no local presence[144]. However, this sales volume is rather limited, amounting to less than one-tenth of Component Systems sales. The division's own sales subsidiaries in eight European countries and one subsidiary in the US contribute some 20 percent of divisional sales. In order to handle the mix of sales representation MASCOS is used in virtually all these cases. The sales organization is too small to motivate the development of tailored systems and the need to communicate also with non-dedicated sales subsidiaries have meant that MASCOS has become something of an SKF, in-house, standard solution.

This state of affairs is set to change for two main reasons. First, MASCOS is on the way out, with Bearing Services, the prime user, busily implementing the strongly bearing-related SCSS. Second, potential competition makes it imperative to reconsider the presently poor data communications links with OEM-customers. The problem of the inability of Component Systems to bear the costs of developing dedicated systems remains, however, especially as the seven businesses have little in common on the product side. Moreover, the division has grown from acquisitions, with a resultant plethora of different local systems in place in the various companies.

SKF's solution has been to search for some standard system interface to function in a clearing-house fashion between very different internal organizational units and vis-à-vis external customers. The natural choice, now available, is the standard set by the Organization for Data Exchange by TeleTransmission in Europe (ODETTE). In essence, the ODETTE standard defines how electronic data interchange (EDI) can be accomplished between systems in different companies for paper-less administration of product flows between the same companies. As it stands now, the ODETTE standard can be thought of as a blueprint for a de facto giant ordering system.

---

[144] For reference, see Table 4.1 above. The one exception is Spain, where the Tools subsidiary represents Component Systems.

Frustrated by the slow progress of the UN sponsored, much grander EDIFACT standard (Electronic Data Interchange For Administration of Commerce and Trade), the European automotive industry initiated ODETTE, making it a joint development project also involving its suppliers. The considerable progress of ODETTE, making it the leading operational standard at present, has prompted companies outside the automotive sector (primarily in engineering and machine-building industries) to adopt it as well[145]. For instance, starting in 1990, SKF now uses ODETTE vis-à-vis one of Electrolux's divisions in Sweden.

Confidence in the viability of the EDIFACT standard has, however, grown considerably during the last couple of years and an ODETTE decision from December, 1989, holds that ODETTE-standard messages are to be converted to EDIFACT in 1993[146].

SKF's involvement with ODETTE dates right back to the inception of the organization itself in May, 1984. Naturally, SKF could ill afford to risk jeopardizing its relationships with some of its main customers. ODETTE has, however, significantly taxed SKF's IS capabilities since it has come late relative to SKF's own systems development, and since SKF has little leverage relative to the large motor vehicle manufacturers (cf. Hagström, 1987b). At first, the required adaptation was handled to a great extent on a local, case-by-case basis. That approach is reflected in the great variety of data communications links to car manufacturers in the national networks (cf. Section 4.3 above). Now, the ODETTE standard is incorporated into DCSS.

SKF's experience in accommodating the ODETTE standard and the wide adoption of the standard make it the 'natural' choice, alluded to above, for Component Systems. Its customers are beginning to follow ODETTE, and the cost of systems adaptation can be shared with other SKF divisions. Though for all its virtues, it should be noted that the

[145] Other industries are following the ODETTE example, starting to cooperate around EDI standards. Examples are CEFIC for the chemical industry, EDIFICE for the electronic industry, and DISH&SHIPNET for the shipping industry.

[146] For a comprehensive overview of recent developments, see Tele (1990, No. 2). No doubt, simple bridges between EDIFACT and ODETTE will also be common in due course.

ODETTE standard implies systems integration to a significantly lesser extent than that discussed for SKF's divisional level systems[147]. But 'internalizing' ODETTE can bring at least some systems integration, hitherto sorely lacking within the Component Systems division. The bottom line is the ODETTE standard improving distribution of Component System products to new and existing customers, both inside and outside SKF. Moreover, it may open the way for some rationalization of production within the different Component Systems businesses.

Finally, a related example of standard-setting, and tying into the Tools discussion above, is a cooperative system involving the Tools division and that may well come to serve as a model in SKF. So far, it is a local, Swedish application (and should therefore logically be left for the next section) but it is interesting in the present context as it is used primarily toward small customers.

BASCET AB is a company, dating back to 1985-1986. It merged with Infolink AB in 1987 to form BASCET-Infolink AB[148]. Without going into detail, BASCET is a system offering fairly simple order entry and inquiry on-line. Infolink has batch file transfer functions, allowing more sophisticated order handling, delivery and other information. The systems interconnect although BASCET uses a proprietary standard, while Infolink uses EDIFACT as it becomes operational. As of the beginning of 1989, ODETTE can be used for communications with both systems. Some 50 suppliers, and about 700 wholesalers and retailers in the hardware and building trades[149] are connected to BASCET-Infolink. Users are located in Sweden and Norway.

---

[147] ODETTE is at present working on extending the standard to include some CAD transfers. That extension (and others that now can be anticipated) does not alter the assessment of degree of systems integration.

[148] BASCET derives its name from six of its owners: Bacho Verktyg, Atlas Copco, SKF Tools, Sandvik Coromant, Esab, and Tibnor (Slip Naxos and Essve Produkter have also come in as owners). Infolink AB is owned by Ferro AB, in turn also owner of Sweden's largest chain of hardware stores.

[149] Tingströms in Gothenburg is one of these customers. Tingströms is also the main supplier of tools to the shop floor in Bearing Industries' Swedish subsidiary using a separate communications link (as described in the accompanying case study Hagström, 1987b, and in Hagström, 1990a).

Through BASCET-Infolink, Tools has got new access also to very small customers (although it may be routed via wholesalers). In addition, BASCET-Infolink is a cooperative venture within important customer-industries and a venture where Tools has a strong position. Apart from being part-owner, Tools has the right to veto new suppliers being connected to the systems. As could be expected, there is little competition from other suppliers in the Tools range of products. Complementing supplies instead alleviate the drawback of being a supplier of only a small part of the range carried by, say, a distributor. At the same time, the cost of customer connections and systems development can be shared with other, largely non-competing companies.

A last point is that through participation, SKF can influence the choice of standards, thereby simplifying the connection to internal systems. Bringing in the ODETTE standard suits SKF well, and goes to show that it is not limited to relationships between OEMs and their suppliers.

5.2.3 Local Systems

We choose 'local systems' as the term to describe systems that in principle are not used outside national networks. In the extreme, they are stand-alone systems for a particular site only.

Local systems can both substitute for and complement non-local, or common, SKF systems. The former is most common for systems stemming from a time before SKF systems standards were enforced in a given location. The existence of local substitutes can moreover be a function not only of a subsidiary not having a link to SKF Group Telenet, but of having a link of insufficient capacity or quality.

The most obvious complementing systems are those covering activities for which no common systems exist. Personnel-related systems have already been mentioned as fitting that description. Other systems are motivated on the grounds of local idiosyncracies. The main reasons here are legal restrictions, and externally imposed systems (such as third-party network systems and some dedicated, often stand-alone, customer connections). Still other complementing systems are more of adjuncts to common systems. For instance, a factory lay-out planning system, or an expanded database on local customer characteristics, enhance the function of common material flow systems. Also, a very specific technical application may only have local relevance.

The described raisons-d'être for local systems are not mutually exclusive.

The responsibility for all systems installed on a local computer rests with the local IS manager. It includes development, implementation, maintenance, interfaces and the costs associated therewith. Local installations of common systems are, however, supported by the designated center for that system but services rendered are invoiced. If and when such an installation, or remote access to a major non-local system, should be done is decided by consensus between the local subsidiary and the IS-staff concerned, be it at corporate level, divisional level or at another location (e.g. ERC). The local degrees of freedom will vary, though. For instance, it is inconceivable that a major Bearing Industries subsidiary in Europe could opt out of the material flow systems (and also that they would want to). On the other hand, the Brazilian Bearing Industries subsidiary could unilaterally decide that the costs outweighed the benefits for on-line remote access to ICSS, instead settling for only the centrally required GMS and TMS access.

It is a central IS policy concern to phase out local 'competing' systems where feasible and to enforce SKF systems standards. That is a tortuous process, given the complexities involved as will be illustrated by briefly looking at the situation from the vantage point of a few Telenet nodes, proceeding by major functional area.

5.2.3.1 Financial and administrative systems

The wide diffusion of GMS and TMS make most local financial applications very specific complements to those systems. Many of these systems are also old, often antedating SKF Group Telenet. The reason is that financial and administrative activities in general were the first to lend themselves to computerization by virtue of being fairly simple aggregating and filing applications[150]. As a rule, the larger and the earlier computers were used, the more commonly are local systems used in this area. SKF sales subsidiaries, being small, have naturally been more ready to replace old systems, or to start at all, with common systems, notably MASCOS.

Local (viz. non-international) accounts receivable and payable, general ledger, and payroll systems typify these oldish, idiosyncratic applications. The systems are tailored to meet national legal requirements and are, by now, very familiar to use. Only in exceptional cases can they communicate with other SKF systems, which accounts for the standard manual interface with GMS and TMS already noted.

There are, however, some significant variations in systems use. In Europe, different sites belonging to the same subsidiary company are likely to have very local, often PC-based, systems. They are then backed up by systems at the main site, a node in Telenet. An interesting example from Bearing Industries is a financial package (MMS), originally from GE. It is primarily an aggregating system but it also has analytical features such as cost allocations by geographical area, by function etc. It is only used nationally but it has spread to most subsidiaries in spite of not being an official 'common' system. Although accounting categories are similar to SKF 'standard', the system cannot interface with SKF systems.

In the US, financial applications are heavily centralized. All financial systems are handled by the King of Prussia main node, with remote access via terminal for the outlying units.

---

[150] For a discussion, see Hagström (1990a).

The one exception is payroll cum personnel records, which are standardized, but run on local PCs. Reporting systems were until a few years ago so nationally centered that subsidiaries from all bearing divisions could only send reports to King of Prussia and not, for instance, also to Specialty Bearings divisional head-office, or to Gothenburg.

Brazil offers an extreme example of local adaptation. The subsidiaries subscribe to local payroll and general ledger systems with monthly updating. Even a company of the Bearing Industries subsidiary's size cannot keep up with the legal changes affecting these areas.

For other financial and administrative applications, different systems are used on a per subsidiary basis.

5.2.3.2 Manufacturing and technical systems

By way of generalization, local manufacturing and technical applications are very specific, reflecting the fact that integrated systems in this area are a rather recent phenomenon overall. When general systems nevertheless were available, these older systems were 'general' in the extreme, as judged with hindsight.

Early manufacturing systems were aimed either more closely at the shop floor activities, or at the administration of a whole factory at a highly aggregate level. FAS is a good example from SKF of such a more general system. The specific systems would control only a particular activity or even a type of machine on a stand-alone basis. Many of these limited systems are still around in SKF.

In Bearing Industries most manufacturing systems will, or have been, superseded especially by MCSS, which controls manufacturing more as a continuous process. In this sense, MCSS both links and costs hitherto separate activities, and does so on-line. Some special systems remain local, though. Ancillary activities (such as quality control, machine tool control, tool design, and machine maintenance scheduling) are still run on local systems but are shared among more than one site over the national network. Recall also that purchasing systems are local but that purchase orders from such systems often be transferred directly, notably to Ovako Steel. Finally, systems specifically tied to running a particular machine are, of course, singularly local, although they may be common in SKF (such as for machinery from LMT).

In other divisions manufacturing systems largely remain a local concern, although they are upgraded with newer off-the-shelf, but company stand-alone, systems. That also goes for peripheral Bearing Industries subsidiaries/nodes. However, FAS is used in Latin America, in Brazil's case with a single installation for the two plants.

In the US, an all-embracing manufacturing control system was installed as early as 1979-1981. It was first run on local processors but has now been centralized to King of Prussia. The system architecture is common for all plants, including Specialty Bearings plants, but some local options screens are available. There is a single manufacturing database for all plants. For reference, this manufacturing control system in principle covers both MCSS and MPSS tasks.

Technical and engineering applications have evolved similarly to those in manufacturing. However, the technical and engineering staff in SKF have traditionally run their systems separately, in the larger companies on separate (often DEC) computers as well. With the concentration of basic research to ERC and of product development to designated manufacturing units the situation changed. The establishment of a DECNET 'within' Telenet and of associated gateways further propelled the increased remote use of technical applications (cf. the discussion in Section 5.2.2.2 above).

Simply put, the previous full-range set of technical support systems for local needs has largely been supplanted by three categories of systems. First, there are the 'common' remote access systems in different locations, as already described. Second, some applications were de facto transferred to the realm of manufacturing and those systems.

Third, there are supportive systems run locally but often on a work-station- or PC-basis. The latter would also include some CAD-applications and the CADalog.

Sales engineers have become more keen users of the technical systems in the process. They can access distant systems nationally and internationally, but much more commonly benefit from the PC-based supportive systems. The situation is similar for geographically outlying manufacturing units, where locally availability of sophisticated technical applications is scant.

5.2.3.3 Systems for distribution and sales

The reason for treating distribution and sales separately from manufacturing is that the related systems are not effectively linked. The exception, of course, is the bearing material flow systems. In general, local systems for distribution and sales 'start' at the national finished goods store, and the information they generate is used as an input in manufacturing planning, but without automatically interfacing with the manufacturing systems.

Sales subsidiaries can conveniently be divided into two main categories; distant ones with little, or no, substantial links to local manufacturing and those which are geographically close to a manufacturing subsidiary. The former have very rudimentary local systems or use a common SKF application, notably MASCOS. Distant sales subsidiaries are typically small operations, with computerization for local needs coming relatively late. With limited local capabilities, they have been, and are, easily converted to SKF standard applications. Irrespective of having a local system or MASCOS, these sales subsidiaries in principle order from manufacturing units such as external customers but they do so internationally through Telenet. For bearings, SCSS changes that role, making all sales subsidiaries more integrated with international distribution and with manufacturing.

Local systems for sales and distribution are more common in places with extensive national data communications networks, in practice markets where there is local manufacturing. Sales units can here draw on greater local resources for information systems in general and their activities are more closely integrated with the manufacturing operations. Only for Bearing Services is selling carried out outside the manufacturing subsidiary. Recall that this change is fairly recent, dating back to late 1986.

Further, internal sales and distribution were amenable to early computerization, following on the heels of the first financial and administrative applications. Having once settled in, local systems are not that readily phased out.

Again, the US represents the extreme case within SKF. The 'homegrown' AdvanCed CustomEr Service System (ACCESS) serves all bearing sales in the US market. It is a centralized order handling, pricing and inventory control system. Implementation started in 1983 and by 1988 MRC was also included in ACCESS. In parallel, order entry and customer service activities have been centralized to the main Allentown warehouse, which meant that the sales staff was reduced and that these activities now are carried out through, or by, the Allentown staff. Whereas a sales office previously would handle a customer order directly and request delivery from wherever the required bearing was produced or stocked, the request is now relayed to Allentown, from where delivery is fixed and monitored, credit checked, and invoices sent out. ACCESS is most similar to DCSS, but it also covers SCSS for US sales.

ACCESS is complemented by the Integrated Inventory Database, which is a single system for all finished goods inventories, and by the Customer Information Control System, which is a similar database on customers.

Even in the large Bearing Industries subsidiaries in Europe there are local systems running parallel to standard SKF systems. As exemplified in Italy, there is a locally developed distribution control system (SISCO), predating the common systems; a local system for the small, regional warehouse (DCS-CSS); and a system for physical handling of goods in the national warehouse. These systems are still used, in spite of DCSS/SCSS having been installed.

In fact, especially local warehousing systems, commonly covering administration, goods handling, picking, bar code reading etc., are more the rule than the exception in Europe. This relative prevalence of local systems reflects the SCSS/DCSS/ICSS not being too well suited for the nitty-gritty of warehousing activities. New systems are being developed to cope with that, though. SCSS has a recent add-on subsystem developed by the Dutch and Belgian bearing subsidiaries, and ICSS+ may come to incorporate these activities as well. In the meantime, considerable effort has been expended in adapting local systems to interface smoothly with the NMFC systems.

Apart from the warehousing systems, the systems mentioned in this subsection have been substituting systems. Other, complementing local systems are common for customer interfaces. Both network characteristics and local customer preferences motivate their existence. These systems have been discussed indirectly in the context of the five national networks surveyed, wherefore we choose the additional West German example when briefly returning to these issues here.

Ford has a dedicated switched line, and 17 other OEMs have dial-up links to the Schweinfurt node. Although similar in functional terms (information and order entry services), the former has demanded more adaptation of the DCSS interface, while the latter connections are handled automatically by the system. Bearing Services also operate out of the Schweinfurt node, with 64 distributors, and 14 (out of 17) sales and engineering offices having dial-up connections. The distributors have been tied successively since 1984 into a local system offering enquiry, order entry and order acknowledgement from a PC. This interface is idiosyncratic to the SKF systems. Many of the sales and engineering offices are skeleton operations, since sales engineers have started to operate from home, only occasionally calling into the office. They 'carry their office access' with them, using the public circuit-switched data communications network to connect primarily to local sales support systems from their PCs. Another significant local systems adaptation stems from the linking of about 50 distributors via public

Videotext (Bildschirmtext) during 1989. They will get services similar to the original 64 distributors but via a wider standard type of access. - All these illustrations reiterate the need to complement SKF standard systems because of local market conditions.

Finally, it is worth noticing that other sales and distribution systems not mentioned here need not be substituting systems. For instance, the Bearing Industries and Bearing Services subsidiaries jointly use BRASCOS (BRASil Customer Order System), which has borrowed its main features from MASCOS. The Tools division has similarly borrowed from MASCOS in its applications, when tying into distribution from manufacturing sites. Component Systems manufacturing units have their own, varied systems, since standard solutions are largely unavailable.

5.3 Systems Revisited

Having proceeded largely on a system-by-system basis, higher-level impact of the surveyed systems has eluded identification. Here, we wish to provide some such additional information, complementing the discussions on system-specific effects, which are interspersed in the preceding text.

If we lamented the lack of unequivocal data when taking a bird's-eye view of the SKF data communications network (cf. especially Section 4.4 above), the situation here is even worse. When considering investments in IS, it is general practice to calculate communications and systems at cost and then to attempt to isolate some benefits, which at best can be estimated[151]. Not only are the quantified benefits commonly beset by a high degree of uncertainty, they frequently are outweighed by the associated 'known'

[151] Companies are also likely to start with IS investments for cost-cutting purposes, to a great extent because such benefits are relatively easily measured and forecast. Profit-generating IS investments will tend to come later, in part since they are more difficult to motivate economically ex ante. (For the fuller argument, see Hagström, 1987a and 1990a).

costs. Consequently, investments are very often decided on the basis of qualitative judgments of elusive benefits.

We have already found (in Section 4.4) that the cost data, as a rule, are not released by companies. By the same logic, neither is information on the identified benefits. From the firm's vantage point, the argument is even more powerful for withholding information on the perceived qualitative advantages, since they are widely held to have great competitive potential[152]. A large measure of secretiveness is therefore quite understandable.

SKF is, of course, no exception to the above.

Again, we have to rely on circumstantial evidence, most of it indirect and qualitative. Moreover, whatever additional information on more general effects of information systems use in SKF that we are able to unearth, it is not possible to separate beyond dispute the impact of IS from other causes (cf. Hagström, 1987b). With these reservations in mind, it is reasonable to follow SKF's own blueprint when concluding this chapter on systems with something of an overview of information systems in SKF.

The main company objectives that the use of information systems are to support have been formulated by SKF[153] as:

- reduced administrative costs;
- reduced investment in stocks;
- increased customer service; and
- differentiation and product enhancement.

To these ends, the information systems strategy assigns priority to:

- common systems;

---

[152] Arguably the most pervasive tradition in management-oriented IS research makes this strategic evaluation of information technology the key issue (cf. McFarlan and McKenney, 1983; McFarlan, 1984b; Rockart and Scott Morton, 1984; Porter and Millar, 1985; Wiseman, 1985; and Earl, 1988; see also the main text).

[153] These, and the following, are publicly stated objectives and priorities. Here, they appear as taken from presentations given by Håkan Landahl, Director, Group Information Systems and Managing Director of SKF Dataservice AB, November 29, 1988, and by Mauritz Sahlin, Group Chief Executive, AB SKF, October 30, 1989.

- communications; and
- integration.

There is no implied order of importance in this enumeration.

Our aim is not to provide a thorough evaluation of the propositions above. Rather, this section is simply structured as to discuss information systems first in relation to the professed objectives, then to priorities.

Finally, uncertainty also pertains to identifying points of reference. We will therefore supplement the comparisons of SKF's IS capabilities vis-à-vis its customers and suppliers with a very brief look at the competition.

5.3.1 Information Systems and Objectives

In spite of dividing the discussion according to professed objectives, the objectives are clearly interrelated. Pursuing one objective at times has negative effects for another. Perhaps surprisingly, information systems use may, however, reduce such prima facie conflicts. That line of reasoning will recur in the following three sections.

We have seen how the earliest use in SKF of information systems both internationally and nationally has come in financial management and administrative areas. We shall concentrate on the latter but first pausing for a note on the former in the first section. Inventory reduction, on the one hand, and improved customer service and product enhancement, on the other, will each be afforded separate treatments.

5.3.1.1 Administrative costs

Financial management, and in particular treasury management, is fraught with legal and other intricacies making it meaningless to construct even an illustrative proxy for the administration of financial assets. Balance sheet machinations cannot be disentangled from actual financial gains and losses in published accounts. It is, however, clear that SKF's level of activity in this area has increased dramatically. For instance, reported interest income has risen from about one-fourth to one-third of interest expense in the mid-1970s to roughly balance in the late 1980s, even when allowing for exchange rate gains and losses. Over the last decade or so SKF has become an actor in its own right in the international money and capital markets. To illustrate, SKF takes foreign exchange and interest rate positions, and issues its own commercial papers. The increased activity is, in turn, contingent on the use of information systems. Indeed, it can be argued that exploiting the mentioned intricacies of financial management was the very purpose for introducing these systems, especially when linking financial activities to the underlying international business operations (cf. also Section 5.2.1.3 above).

Turning instead to trade accounts, the objective in its most straight-forward form is to pay late and receive early. If SKF has been more successful, in a very broad sense, in managing these accounts than its customers and suppliers, payables would tend to increase and receivables to decrease over time as a share of sales. These rough indicators are shown in Figure 5.2 below. The chosen time period is contingent on these data not being published prior to 1976. Changes in accounting practices have been minor during the time period, and appear not to significantly influence the series. Trade accounts receivable are calculated net of allowances for doubtful accounts.

If any trends can be discerned, they are weak. Seen over the whole period, accounts payable as a share of sales fell by some 5 percentage points, while accounts receivable rose only marginally. A small consolation is that the changes are in the desired direction.

Figure 5.2

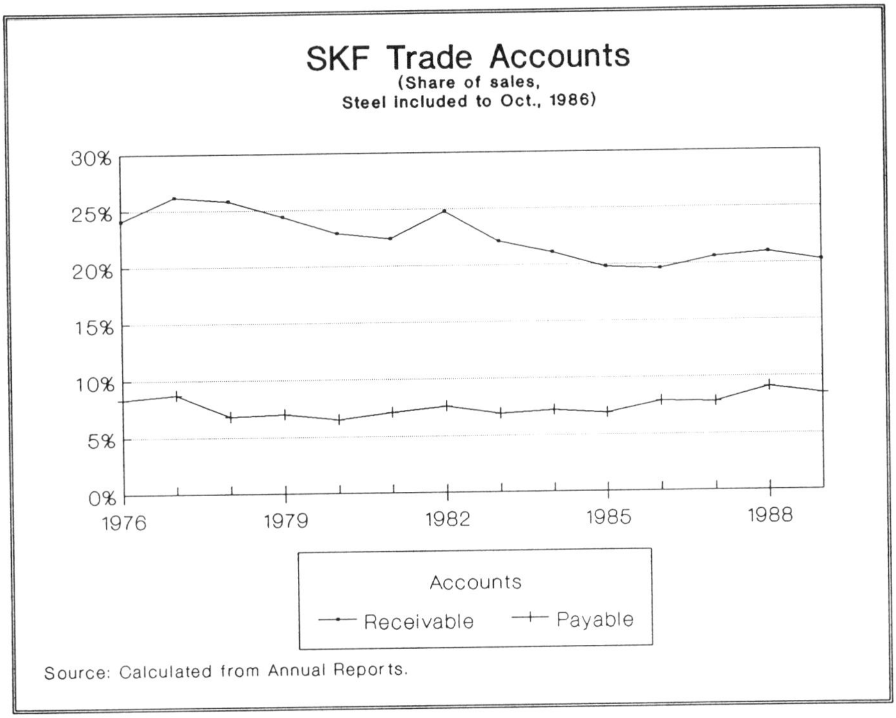

Regarding payables, recall that the steel industry dominates among SKF's suppliers, and that SKF's steel division was divested in 1986. The very minor changes registered thus dissolve as they primarily refer to the post-1986 period. However, steel is generally purchased on long-term contracts with set payment conditions, wherefore SKF's possible superior account management would not have much effect on the payables series.

The much more important receivables series is also more interesting. Here, SKF has been able to successively reduce its outstanding stock of receivables in relation to sales, which is notable, given that well over 50 percent of sales go to OEM industries. For standard bearings, just over half of sales are effectuated by Bearing Industries directly to

OEMs[154]. Since these customers in general are powerful in relation to SKF, one would expect it to be difficult for SKF to hold its ground. Relative to distributors, SKF is a stronger party, although overcapacity in bearing production and stiff competition during almost the whole period has limited SKF's room for manoeuvre. Offering favorable payments conditions is also a competitive weapon.

Of course, we cannot ascribe the fall in the receivables series to SKF's superior financial management systems. But we do know that SKF started using information systems in this area earlier than most of its OEM customers. Any advantage SKF may have had here would, however, have been eroded by the mid-1980s, with the OEMs catching up in information systems use (notably automotive manufacturers). Comparing with distributors, SKF is the more accomplished user as a rule.

The data in Figure 5.2 at least do not contradict the picture painted and that SKF may have derived some benefits from earlier and more sophisticated information systems for financial management than its customers. In addition, it should be noted that trade accounts refer to external sales and that payments for internally managed sales are excluded. The directly relevant information systems are thus the ordering and local accounts systems. Recall also from the previous discussions that SKF's purchasing systems are rather poorly developed, while the sales administration systems (and to some extent the local accounts applications) are rather sophisticated by most standards.

However, good communications links and systems interfaces can allow for a reduction in the payments float; something customers and suppliers jointly benefit from at the expense of financial intermediaries. For trade accounts, the potential float refers only to payments mediation, though. This effect would thus be very slight for straight-forward bills collection, and much less important than the by-passing, of banks primarily, for management of firm internal financial flows and for external financing and hedging.

---

[154] In 1989, Bearing Industries' external sales were SEK 10.0 billion, with the corresponding figure for Bearing Services reaching SEK 9.6 billion (SKF Annual Report, 1989).

Another significant processing cost can, loosely speaking, be designated as the 'administrative float'. It concerns the resources required to perform a given administrative task and the time it takes do it. On both accounts, reduction of the 'float' is a prime objective of information systems use.

In terms of time, one possible indication is the speed with which reports travel in the organization. Improvements in this respect within SKF are straight-forward, connected to the successive upgrading of GMS (cf. Section 5.2.1.2 above). We can, however, add that the basic internal figures for the monthly reports are now in as early as a couple of days after the close of the month.

Another, indirect way of approaching the issue is to look at the external release of reports. That should be a relatively unbiased indicator, since stock exchange regulations require companies to divulge such information to the market as it becomes available and one can assume that once in, companies would to a similar extent have the information 'lying around' before release. The main difference would consequently stem from the time at which companies get the data in.

As a rule, SKF is the very first of the companies listed on the Stockholm Stock Exchange to issue its quarterly reports and by a good margin, in spite of being a relatively very complex company with many reporting subsidiaries[155]. Quarterly reports are kept internally for two-three weeks for additional quality control before they are released. That means that figures for external purposes are complete at headquarters after about two weeks. In general, SKF is regarded by its peers as having a very fast and reliable reporting system, which also lives up to high standards concerning coverage of reporting items.

---

[155] For comparison, SKF published its half-year results August 9, 1990. The second company to do so was the much less complex Korsnäs AB (a forestry products company with yearly sales of SEK 3.9 billion and more than three-quarters of its employees in Sweden; according to the Annual Report, 1989) five days later. - Larger Swedish MNCs published their results considerably later than SKF; AGA - August 20, Sandvik - August 21, Electrolux - August 22, Atlas Copco - August 23, Ericsson - August 23, Asea (the Swedish half-owner of ABB) - August 29, Alfa-Laval - August 30, and Esselte - August 30, with others coming later still.

In terms of resources, the Bearing Industries subsidiary in West Germany attempted to estimate the number of additional local administrative staff that would be required in the hypothetical absence of computers and Telenet. At a similar level of ambition (but without considering processing time), conservatively, at least another 500 people were said to have been needed, corresponding to 7 percent of total subsidiary employees.

On the aggregate level, SKF's administrative costs are only given publicly together with costs of external sales. That series is shown in Figure 5.3 below, in relation to total SKF sales. The figures are comparable for the whole period, except that external sales of steel are included up to 1986.

Rather than decreasing, sales and administration costs increase considerably over the period. This rise appears to run contrary to SKF's professed objective. However, the picture warrants some qualification.

First, the series depicts two fairly distinct periods, with the values hovering around the 15 percent mark 1966-1975, and around 19 percent 1977-1989. This division tallies well with the implementation of GFSS, which, among other things, cut production and capital costs on the one hand, and demanded more administration of the resultant more complex internal flows, primarily of products, on the other. On both counts, viz. residually and increased work-load, sales and administration costs will be jacked up.

Second, the very early 1980s was characterized by a broad strategic shift, in that SKF has since been striving to add value to the final product, differentiating it by also improving customer service. With more final product value attributed to post-production activities, sales and administration costs would naturally rise.

Figure 5.3 then reflects the dominant bearing business going from local sales of locally produced undifferentiated products, via a transition period with high demands on administration, to sales of internationally produced, more differentiated products.

Figure 5.3

The problem when considering information systems in this context is that the relevant comparison is what the sales and administration series would have looked like without these systems being used. Arguably, the values would have been higher (if the present customer-orientation had been possible to pursue at all). Some weak support for that contention can be had from the fact that the sales and administration costs have tended to fall during the 1980s, in spite of customer service simultaneously having improved. Indeed, customer service, in a broad sense, now critically hinges on the use of information systems by SKF, and we will return to this issue below. Moreover, the fall is sustained even when the steel division is excluded from the series from 1986 and on.

The steel business has about half the sales and administration costs in relation to sales, compared to SKF present figures[156].

5.3.1.2 Inventories

The themes prompted by Figure 5.3 recur when looking at inventory levels. In a narrow sense, both production and sales are, of course, best served by maintaining as large inventories as possible. Subject to that constraint, reduction of costly inventories is a long-standing objective. Figure 5.4 plots SKF inventories; again against sales. The chosen time period reflects availability of comparable data. The reporting principles regarding stocks held changed substantially as of 1977, and the break-down on different inventory categories is only available from then on[157]. A smaller change in inventory valuation was effectuated in 1987 and has been incorporated in the graph[158]. The residual, making up total inventory, is raw materials and supplies (see also Figure 5.5 below). Only the main categories "finished goods" and "work in progress" inventories are displayed in Figure 5.4 below in order to avoid cluttering.

Inventories have clearly been reduced, with total inventories as a proportion of sales having roughly been halved in the two latest decades. The same goes for finished goods and work in progress. The reduction has been fairly continuous during the whole period, the beginning of which coincides with GFSS taking effect. The kink in the two top curves for 1982 is an exceptional business cycle phenomenon. That particular year saw a singular, 10 percent drop in demand for bearings; the biggest such fall by far since the first oil-price rise in the early 1970s.

---

[156] Ovako Steel reported sales and administration costs, also <u>including</u> research and development costs, as standing at 10.1 percent of total sales in 1988 (Annual Report, 1988).

[157] The figure for total inventory for 1976 was given ex-post according to the new reporting principles.

[158] Inventories are valued according to the first-in-first-out principle. Up until 1987, some subsidiaries used last-in-first-out. Applied to 1985 and 1986, first-in-first-out valuation would have given "total inventory" as 39.3 percent and 41.5 percent of sales respectively (as opposed to 36.9 percent for 1985 and 39.1 percent for 1986 as shown in Figure 5.4).

Figure 5.4

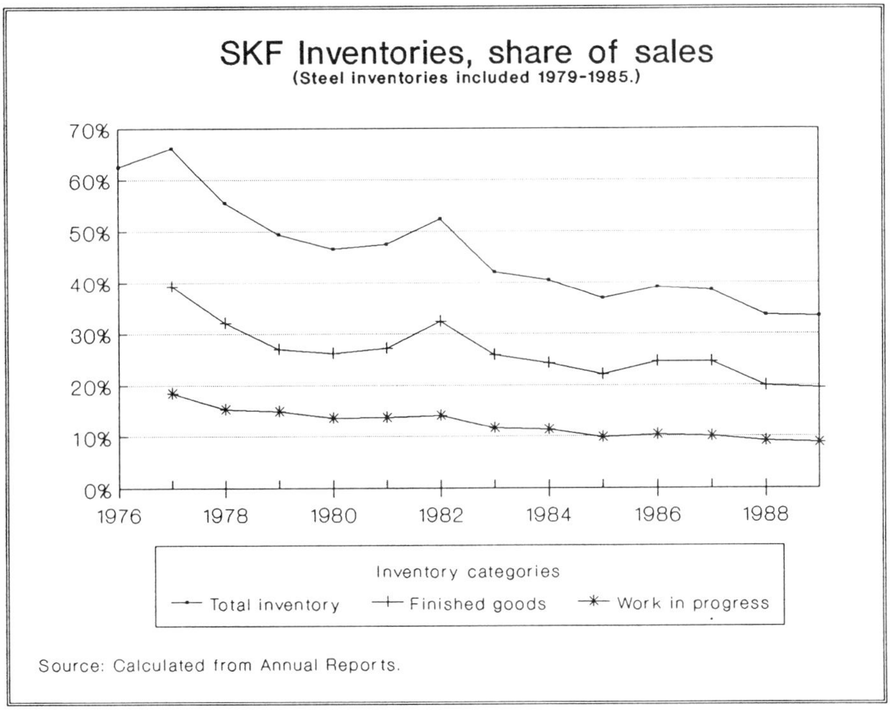

Impressive as they may be, the series in Figure 5.4 understate the reductions in inventory levels. First, the divestment of the steel division jacks up the inventory share (cf. the change from 1985 to 1986 in Figure 5.4), since the steel industry holds lower inventories than does SKF. Second, the displayed total inventory figures for 1987-1989 have been inflated by a couple of percentage points, due to some subsidiaries' inventories being revalued in accordance with corporate, more conservative, principles (see Footnote 7, above). Acquisitions in the latter half of the 1980s (notably the Spanish Bearing Industries subsidiary in 1985, MRC in 1986, and Steyr in 1988) also raised SKF inventory levels, but only to a minor extent compared to what they would have been otherwise.

The apparent uniformity in inventory reduction across different categories of inventories is better detailed in Figure 5.5 below. (The same caveats apply as to Figure 5.4.).

Figure 5.5

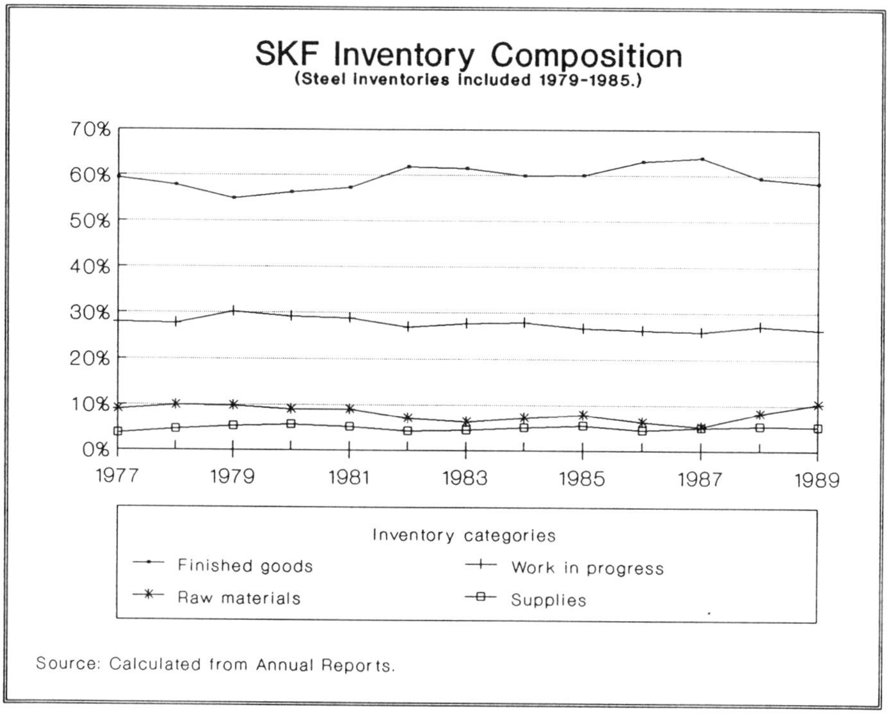

Relative changes between inventory categories are small. However, work in progress displays a rather more consistent, and a somewhat greater (compare also with Figure 5.4), fall than do other categories seen over the whole period. That observation at least does not contradict the emphasis placed on a continuously improved material flow in bearing production, first from specialization, then from NMFC.

The relatively quicker decline for finished goods during the few initial and final years likewise tallies with the expected effects of GFSS and later of NMFC. Recall that GFSS quickly cut inventories not only by specialization, but also by more than halving the product range (cf. Hagström, 1987b). The improved integration between production and sales is especially a feature of the later 1980s.

Overall, reducing work in progress is more of a humdrum exercise, while finished goods stocks presents a much less clear variable, also being more susceptible to the vagaries of external demand. The raw materials category is fraught with influences of hedging, which is one likely reason for its relative instability in Figure 5.5. "Supplies" is too heterogeneous (anything from tools to typing paper) and too small a category to warrant much comment. It does, however, constitute something of a more stable baseline over time, slightly increasing its relative share when other categories contract faster and vice versa.

At best, the support for the interpretation of Figure 5.5 is weak. Bearings have naturally dominated the discussion as they do in SKF activities, and indeed in information systems use. Ideally, we would like to isolate the SCSS/DCSS/ICSS/FSO system-managed distribution of finished products. Hard data on such effects are not released by SKF for reasons already discussed. Some circumstantial evidence is available, though.

GFSS is commonly credited by SKF itself for roughly halving the inventories of finished bearings (compared to what they would have been otherwise) during one decade or so; approximately from the mid-1970s to the mid-1980s. That claim exceeds the aggregate stock reductions as displayed in Figure 5.4. However, in a very general presentation of NMFC[159] it is shown that stock coverages of "FSO-items" have declined from six "periods" in 1976 to three "periods" in 1985. Actually, three "periods" is attained in 1981, but stock coverages increase during 1982-1983, reaching above three-and-a-half "periods". For 1987, slightly less than two-and-a-half "periods" are recorded.

The reduction from six to three "periods" 1976-1985 does lend credence to the alleged inventory reduction. "FSO items" refer to those bearings that enter into the FSO-system, viz. standard bearings. What constitutes a "period" is shrouded in secrecy, but a month does not seem to be too far-fetched a guess. Six months stock coverage of the large volume items in 1976 does not seem too much at odds with a reported total SKF

---

159 In Bearing Bulletin, June, 1988.

inventory of finished goods valued at about 40 percent of yearly sales that same year (cf. Figure 5.4).

We can then qualify our previous discussion on inventory reductions. Broadly, stocks of finished standard bearings appear to have declined significantly faster than of other SKF finished products. Information systems have played an important role in trimming inventories in general, and the reduction is most evident precisely for standard bearings, where information systems use is the most pronounced.

Moreover, the general scenario of early, strong GFSS/FSO effects beefed up by the new NMFC during the last few years that tentatively emerged from Figures 5.4 and 5.5, fits well with the reductions in "periods" of stock coverages for "FSO items". The correspondence goes so far as up to the recorded 'humps' in the series circa 1982, as discussed[160].

Reducing inventories (of finished goods) is, however, not only a question of reducing stock levels for each item at existing sites. The number of sites may be reduced and the stock composition adjusted.

Aggregate data on the number of stocking points used are not available. It has clearly been cut, though (see also Hagström, 1987b). The two countries with the largest SKF bearing operations (West Germany and Italy[161]) provide examples of the fact that this pruning can be quite dramatic. In Italy the number of national stocking points have decreased from 17 to 4 (Airasca, Bari, Bologna, and Milan) since the mid-1980s. In West

---

[160] More limited figures on recorded lead-times also closely follow the development seen for the aggregate figures. Taken from the same general presentation (see the previous footnote), the lead-time in the FSO system has gone from slightly below six "periods" in 1983 to three-and-a-half "periods" in 1987; a reduction by more than 40 percent. Given that a purpose of displaying these figures is to extol the virtues of NMFC, the brief interval chosen is likely to show an 'impressive' fall. However, it is noteworthy that this time period corresponds to the implementation and subsequent operation of ICSS, which was designed to bridge orders and production (cf. Section 5.2.2.1 above).

[161] Size of operations is approximated by number of employees. West Germany recorded 7 840 employees in the Bearing Industries and Bearing Services subsidiaries combined (8 495 incl. Specialty Bearings) in 1989. Corresponding figures for Italy were 5 388 (5 861). [Figures calculated from the Annual Report, 1989.]

Germany, a single warehouse (Schweinfurt) has replaced the 25 warehouses operated in the earlier 1980s.

Making the net of stocking locations much less fine-meshed naturally hinges on improved transportation both to the warehouses and from there on to customers. Specialization of production further underlines this need. In parallel, SKF has increasingly come to rely on outside transport providers. This shift is particularly noteworthy regarding transports of bearings from plants to warehouses and among warehouses. Shipping bearings was previously a less important, but more complex, activity largely carried out in-house. Logistics and control of bearing shipments are now largely handled through automatic data interchange between the systems of the production and sales organizations, while the actual transport has been externalized to specialists (viz. trucking companies) running a given transport capacity on a given schedule. These transport times have also roughly been halved in Europe during the second half of the 1980s.

The way improved logistics and stock reductions benefit internal relationships, they can benefit external ones as well. Reducing the 'float' of finished products brings gains to both parties at no third party's expense. The good information system linkages between Bearing Industries units and many OEMs make the latter in this respect akin to Bearing Services units. The same goes for the major customers on the aftermarket; the large distributors.

The question of how much stock should be held is, however, more controversial regarding the aftermarket than for OEMs or internal 'customers'. From SKF's vantage point, high distributor stock levels mean good availability for end-users. That translates into higher sales and to distributors 'taking over' some inventories of finished goods from SKF. Distributors naturally will resist holding too much expensive inventory. The smaller, and the more dependent on SKF as a supplier, a distributor is, the lesser his bargaining power vis-à-vis SKF. The use of improved communications links and information systems alleviate this conflict of interest, though. A relationship with a hypothetical small distributor can serve to demonstrate our point.

First, better administration of orders can be singled out as a mutual interest. An illustrative example from Sweden is how the standard sequence of ordering and mailing, registering at SKF, processing the order acknowledgement and mailing, and receiving the order acknowledgement at the customer's and mailing the order confirmation typically takes 4-12 working days. With direct access to SKF's systems, or with file transfer capability, the sequence can be collapsed to become instantaneous (or a couple of days if, for instance, over-night batch transmission is used). Shorter order lead-times lead to joint inventory reductions and less manual processing to higher delivery reliability.

Second, better and more timely information made available to the distributor (order inquiry, delivery schedules, current prices, product data etc.) will tend to improve the accuracy and timeliness of his ordering, thereby allowing further stock reductions for both parties.

Third, with customer order histories accumulating as adjuncts to SCSS (and similar systems) and thus becoming easily accessible, SKF can better anticipate a small distributor's ordering. Both stock levels and stock composition can then be adjusted to correspond more closely to actual demand. More accurate knowledge of ordering patterns translates into smaller buffers being required.

Fourth, SKF can make selected information available to the distributor, over and above information directly connected to ordering. By combining the accumulated information on the particular distributor (and indirectly on his customers) with aggregate customer order histories and with aggregate forecast demand, SKF can advise the individual distributor on ordering procedures, stock levels and stock mix. Better inventory management by the small distributor improves his customer service and thus can increase SKF sales at a given level of inventory (i.e. a lower inventory/sales ratio for SKF).

The first, second and third points are standard in SKF-distributor relationships. The fourth is perhaps best characterized as both prevalent and burgeoning. Individual customer order histories are supplied, usually annually, to customers as a basis for their order planning. With access to Telenet, these customers can trace and analyze their order patterns in detail. Adding aggregate information and more actively advising, say, a distributor on inventory management is in practice contingent on a functioning SCSS/DCSS/ICSS link being in place[162]. The more extensive advisory services provided by SKF are still in their infancy. In a more modest form, the Tools division also offers some advisory services regarding customer stock management. Customers connected to the Sheffield mainframe routinely get their order histories with some analyses but the latter are based on the individual account only (see also Section 5.2.2.3 above).

The case of the small distributor highlights how information systems related to inventories of finished goods are used by SKF in external relationships and thus complements the discussion of the observed inventory reductions in Figures 5.4 and 5.5. Similar considerations hold for OEM customers and large distributors as well but to a lesser degree. Larger customers often can perform the described functions themselves or jointly with SKF.

5.3.1.3 Customer service and product enhancement

By dwelling on the small distributor, we have, in a somewhat roundabout way, brought in the objectives of increased customer service and product enhancement. Information systems use regarding administration and inventories work on the bottom line by reducing costs, while better service and product upgrading[163] typically add to costs. The latter are, of course, intended to be more than offset by associated larger sales volumes and/or higher prices.

---

[162] Recall, however, also the indirect 'advising' on technical matters through the use of, for instance, the CADalog (see Section 5.2.2.2 above) and CROESUS (see Section 5.2.2.3 above).

[163] Product differentiation and enhancement are here viewed in the context of information systems, viz. adding different information services to the product. For a wider product perspective, including, for instance, offering an integrated hub unit for automobiles instead of only wheel bearings, see Hagström (1987b).

It is not possible for us to corroborate beyond dispute that SKF's use of information systems brings more business. Any such figures do not, to our knowledge, exist, even within SKF. It is more than likely to be the case, though. First, it is generally held in the bearing industry that SKF's use of information systems vis-à-vis customers, in a general sense, significantly affects at least sales volumes positively (e.g. Wolf, 1985; and International Management, 1986). The reasonably positive development of the SKF market share over the last few years does not contradict this contention (see also Section 5.3.3 below).

Second, the subsidiary representatives interviewed[164], without exception, confirmed that customer communications links, coupled with internal SKF systems related to distribution and sales support, provided a key competitive advantage in the respective national markets, allowing higher sales and prices than otherwise would have been the case. The most vehement arguments were put forth in the UK and in Italy. In the UK, large OEM contracts were said to have been won, critically as a result of IS-administered service, and SKF's strong position in the aftermarket was put down in no small part to its early commitment to providing service to distributors by way of data communications links. In Italy, SKF actually introduced computers at more than 50 bearing distributors, and then proceeded to link them to the national network, in the mid-1980s. In the process, SKF incurred some considerable start-up costs. The subsequently achieved rationalization of the aftermarket distribution in Italy (cf. above) was unequivocally held to ultimately depend on this move.

The increased ambition in providing customer service, as has been demonstrated throughout this treatise, does take its toll in terms of non-production costs. Although information systems have made substantial cost reductions possible, some gains are offset by increasing costs for improved customer service; much of which, in turn, has been made possible at all through the advent of information systems.

[164] See the References, Section 7.4.

The point can perhaps be made clearer by thinking of some effects at the subsidiary level. In practice, rather than firing people made redundant in sales and administration functions, new hiring is restricted and people are broadly transferred from administrative to sales support activities. As the new, higher level of customer service is maintained more efficiently, sales staff starts to decrease. The process is supported by the very information systems making the change possible at all. The sequence is modelled on the experience in Europe, and specifically describes the change at the West German Bearing Industries and Bearing Services subsidiaries. A typical example from the US shows some differences. The Bearing Industries subsidiary more than halved its order entry/customer service staff in 1987 in one stroke, axing some 50 jobs, by replacing local units with a single unit in Allentown with on-line access to the other sites[165].

This reasoning casts additional light on the sales and administration costs as seen in Figure 5.3 above. Recall that the reluctance of those costs to contract in relation to sales follows on the strategic shift pinpointed to the very early 1980s, when downstream activities were given more weight. From the subsidiary perspective, we see that there is a case for expecting a lag of a few years before benefits become noticeable. That observation is concurrent with the slight accelerating tendency of the series to fall towards the end of the period displayed in Figure 5.3.

Lastly, customer service improvements are, however, not only a question of level of ambition in terms of performing additional activities. A given level can be attained more efficiently simply by reducing processing time. Customer service in the more narrow sense of availability, or delivery performance, is a case in point. Without involving much more than quicker processing of essentially the same data as before, information systems can make it easier to match internal supply with customer demand.

Returning to the FSO-covered products, delivery performance from the finished goods inventories has improved considerably during the 1980s. That is the picture that emerges

[165] Only exceptionally are SKF subsidiaries able to quantify such personnel reductions, since the figures are not calculated other than possibly as ex ante estimates, and are not recorded.

from reported customer service performance[166]. From a little over 60 percent coming into the 1980s, 80 percent of from stock orders could be filled in 1981. The period 1982-1984 represents a hiatus with no change. In 1985, the corresponding figure was approximately 85 percent, rising further to 90 and 92 percent in 1986 and 1987, respectively.

This raised delivery performance was achieved at the same time as aggregate stock levels were reduced (cf. Section 5.1.3.2 above). The same information systems instrumental in cutting inventories, simultaneously helped SKF increase stock coverage relative to customer orders. The latter improvement can primarily be put down to better stock mix, more accurate forecasts, more reliable orders (viz. fewer errors), and reduced 'administrative float'. The traditional trade-off between low inventory and high availability could thus be shifted onto a more favorable scale. So, when starting to pursue both objectives simultaneously, the traditional conflict is mitigated, at least temporarily.

5.3.2 Information Systems Priorities

The SKF IS policy priorities of common systems, communications, and integration are actually two means and one end. By implementing common systems within a corporate-wide data communications network, SKF strives to attain a higher level of integration for the company. Our interpretation does prompt several qualifications, primarily as regards integration. That tack will be followed throughout this section.

The degree of commonness of systems and the reach of the communications network has already been discussed extensively. A recurring theme is how communications and systems use vary in SKF. IS policy priorities are not applied with the same fervor throughout the organization. Consequently, IS-induced integration is also a matter of varying degree.

---

166 See Bearing Bulletin, June, 1988.

So far, the 'push' of central IS policy out in the organization has taken the center stage in this study. The 'pull' from dispersed users has entered more haphazardly, tied specifically to aspects of communications network status or of local systems use. A more comprehensive and qualitative view of IS priorities from the field is still lacking. Much of the ensuing discussion is then based on the subsidiary interviews (cf. Section 7.4 below). When talking about 'users' we think of an organizational unit, unless otherwise specified.

At present, access to the SKF data communications network is generally perceived as much more pressing by dispersed users than by Group Telenet administrators either centrally or at the main nodes. As a rule, those organizational units lacking a connection are keen to establish one and those without connections of a quality comparable to a leased line are keen to upgrade their links. Internal demand for links thus outstrips the corresponding supply, which is constrained by considerations of technical feasibility and of cost.

The wish for access is also rather uniform within the outlying organizational units. It is not only a concern for the managing director and the IS department. Other departments, or the like, tend to view communications access as an opportunity; a way to be able to enhance local capabilities.

Users well served regarding communications commonly express a wish to take on greater responsibilities locally, viz. to be a host for systems with remote access. For general management and the IS department this means higher status in SKF and that greater local IS capabilities can be motivated. For other parts of the local organization, the reason is more one of having particular applications 'close to home' so as to make any 'required' (as perceived) adaptations easier.

Usage of common (at whatever level) systems follows the same broad pattern, with the exception of applications deemed inferior to already used local ones. That resistance typically applies to the large computer centers and to rather limited systems such as a specific warehousing system or a homegrown technical database with non-standard product specifications. The perceived superiority of a local system does not, however, need to be factual; familiarity with the local system can cloud the assessment of a common SKF replacement.

The view from the horizon of the US main node can illustrate some of the above points. Access to Telenet and to SKF systems is seen as exceptionally valuable. Usage is a slightly different matter, though, in that the relatively long-lasting isolation of SKF's US bearing operations (cf. the consent-decree) has meant that an extensive family of local systems has become well established. Also, the US has remained separate from GFSS-related product specialization. Still, the question of bearing material flow systems migrating across the Atlantic is one of 'when' rather than 'if'. At present, remote access to ICSS for managing international bearing shipments is seen as sufficient, with local systems managing the national production and distribution.

Some peculiarities of the US scene also bring out the 'Europeanness' (for lack of a better word) of the SKF communications network and common systems. The combination of the higher technical sophistication of the local market for IS-related products and services (including a bias for large systems), and of the management style in the US has put a premium on national centralization of IS resources and capabilities. With connection to Telenet, a somewhat different approach became apparent to SKF's US users. The knowledge-sharing through remote access to dispersed and varied technical applications was an immediate benefit, as was the perceived greater 'closeness' to the rest of SKF. The greater stress on training and user-friendliness also made its impact. The tolerance, and appreciation, of local flexibility in communications and systems increased.

The Spanish node typifies, in some ways, the opposite experience. The greatest benefits subsequent to Telenet connection was felt to be becoming party to more sophisticated communications and systems, bringing with it better discipline and a more 'efficient' culture. A case in point was the immediate implementation of GMS and TMS, which quickly raised the standard of local financial management and prompted improvements in reporting procedures. Regarding bearing material flow systems, inclusion in the European product exchange through ICSS opened a bigger market for locally manufactured bearings. The Spanish Bearing Industries subsidiary produces a much wider range of bearings than its European counterparts in SKF and can now easily be called upon in times of supply-shortages for particular bearing types.

Looking further afield, outlying organizational units will tend to stress the benefits of international back-up of IS capabilities, in a wide sense, even more. Local short-comings can be alleviated and IS resources vastly in excess of what can be locally motivated are made available. One often overlooked, but important, aspect of improved communications in this context is that the outliers can keep a better tab on what 'is going on' in the company.

Witness the keenness of the Brazilian Bearing Industries, Tools and Component Systems subsidiaries to become connected to SKF Group Telenet. In all cases, the lack of sufficient connections was strongly lamented with specific reference to the present difficulties, relative to other units, in keeping up with developments in SKF in all areas. We have already touched on this aspect for general management (Section 5.2.1.2) and IS activities (Section 4.3.5) but it extends further. There was a well-articulated need for continuous exchange with other SKF units of concepts and of 'how to do things', especially in production, quality assurance, and product development.

Indeed, from the interviews and other SKF material there emerges a common appreciation at subsidiaries that information dissemination has successively changed in character with the advent of Telenet and the evolution of common systems. With a stylized description, subsidiaries have moved from only being a sender of information on local activities and a recipient of orders and aggregate information to more of a hub of information exchange. It has become easier to seek out information elsewhere and information is more often sought by others.

Getting information from repositories at central units (such as divisional headquarters or ERC) has clearly been facilitated, and central units are better able and willing to respond to the need for disaggregated information (such as comparative performance figures for sister subsidiaries or suggested quality assurance procedures for a specific local range of products). These effects are largely a function of more, and more disaggregated, information being available at central locations.

The greatest change as perceived at the subsidiaries is, however, that communication and information retrieval are less and less confined to dyadic relationships with various central units. Sister subsidiaries are increasingly the direct source of as well as the direct 'requestor' of information. Remote usage of a specific technical system or of a database (as discussed in Section 5.2.2.2) falls in this category. But so does unstructured exchange of information on the maintenance of a particular piece of machinery between two sister subsidiaries. These types of more 'lateral' information exchange are the prime source of the changed character of information dissemination in SKF. And 'information', as used here, goes back to the reasons for establishing a telecommunications network, viz. access to distant processing power, systems, and data (cf. Section 4.1).

In fact, a striking unanimity was found among subsidiaries concerning the data communications network and the common systems having contributed to more internal cooperation and coordination across the board and across borders. However, the degree to which this integration is achieved, of course, varies considerably. Not surprisingly, the variation across activities, geographical location, main subsidiary task, and type of business closely follows the network configuration and the existence of relevant common systems. On the other hand, a difference was found among subsidiaries in that the more such integration, the more importance was attached to 'pull', or spontaneous, use of information systems[167]. Highlighting opposites, say, in financial reporting in a European manufacturing Bearing Industries subsidiary the spontaneous use of information systems was judged much more important than in marketing in a distant Component Systems subsidiary.

As a general assessment, subsidiaries voiced a conviction that information systems are going to continue to merit increasing attention by management. An indication supporting this claim can be found at the country level. There is little or no formal coordination

[167] The argument on spontaneous use of the information systems infrastructure is developed more fully in Hagström (1991).

between SKF subsidiaries belonging to different divisions in a particular geographic market. However, there is a long-standing tradition in SKF that subsidiary managers in a country meet a few times a year. Typically, the discussions cover the local market outlook, customers, national institutional changes, and corporate developments. Information systems have been added to this select list of topics. Inclusion on the agenda tends to coincide with connection to Telenet and the attention afforded the subject tends to increase over time. Information systems are now also discussed in these circumstances in Brazil, although not all subsidiaries are linked to Telenet (see Section 4.3.5).

The different node managers also meet nationally at varying intervals. Here, the division of authority is clear, though, in keeping with the hierarchical structure of network management.

In spite of the expanding role of information systems in SKF as a whole, they are not immune to cost pressures. In this light, the priorities of communications and common systems have tended to reduce duplication of effort in the area of information systems in SKF and systems management has become easier. These trends are confirmed and welcomed by field and center alike.

In addition, as the external market for information systems products and services becomes more sophisticated, the use of purchased, standard solutions increases. For communications services, recall that this tendency shows up as denting the SKF policy of not subscribing to public, third-party communications services. More important, in the present context, is the growing role of externally developed systems in SKF. There is less of a need to develop costly idiosyncratic systems if a reasonably similar system can be bought off the shelf.

Better systems available on the open market actually reflect the dual developments of the market 'catching up' with SKF expertise in the area and of newer systems being more versatile. In practice, an externally purchased system has to be substantially adapted to fit SKF's requirements, but that still is a far cry from the costs incurred with the traditional own systems development. Older systems like MEST and the FSO-system are totally tailored to SKF, while, for instance, the newer MCSS is a modification of a standard manufacturing control system.

The improved efficiency effects of these external developments and of SKF information systems priorities are not uniform throughout the organization. Rather, the repercussions vary for different types of nodes. Also, the officially embraced intention to decentralize information systems responsibilities in SKF out to different nodes is not mirrored in discussions with local information systems managers.

Broadly, SKF main nodes and peripheral nodes now face a pressure to reduce their activities as the need for local support and development decreases. European main nodes have also lost (or are in the process of losing) the administration of Bearing Services applications with the splitting up the area based bearing divisions. Bearing Services main locations are being set up as subsidiary nodes. Other divisional subsidiary nodes display a weak tendency to expand operations, plainly as a result of greater usage at all of information systems and the administration associated therewith.

New responsibilities are taken on, particularly by main nodes, in connection with some systems moving from being run per site to being run per node (e.g. MPSS replacing factory systems). There is a similar trend for outlying units in relation to subsidiary (and main) nodes (e.g. field sales offices for bearings more and more relying on remote access to SCSS/DCSS). Sites without node status thus unambiguously lose in importance.

The net effect so far is generally a reduction of effort for IS departments at main nodes, peripheral nodes, and SKF end-points (sites). Subsidiary nodes tend to gain in importance.

In terms of total corporate IS staff, a continued expansion has been halted and there appears to have been a slight reduction in numbers in the last few years[168]. Main

[168] The inferred staff reductions are judged exclusive of changes at acquired companies. When integrated into SKF, they tend to get their IS department reduced if they have one, and to get one if they do not.

European SKF nodes have typically cut staff by some 10 percent in traditional activities over the last two to three years. The US main node is an exception as it has continued to add staff. It is a function of national centralization of IS management (including the MRC acquisition) and an upgrading of local capabilities to European main node level. All systems development has been centralized with only a skeleton staff remaining at other sites, handling the minor local adaptations in iteration with King of Prussia. At the other extreme, the Spanish main node, which is by far the smallest, is in the process of more than halving its IS department during 1989-1992. The Sheffield node has remained more or less stable.

In total, the main nodes (including Gothenburg) employ more than half of SKF's some 1 000 IS staff[169]. SKF Dataservice in Gothenburg accounts for about 10 percent of the total. Its staff numbers have been published since 1981. In Figure 5.6 below it is shown how the SKF Dataservice employees have grown both in absolute numbers and relative to the company as a whole.

The levelling-off in Figure 5.6 of both series 1987-1989 represents a milder reining-in than that of the larger main nodes. The prior expansion during the 1980s also outstrip that experienced by the other main nodes, save possibly the King of Prussia node. It seems like SKF has strengthened the relative position of its central node, when comparing with other main and peripheral nodes. By all accounts from the field available to us, this trend is set to continue, and possibly even to accelerate.

[169] The absolute total number of IS staff is unclear (probably also to SKF). It is estimated by SKF at some 1 000 people, which corresponds to about 2 percent of total SKF employees.

Figure 5.6

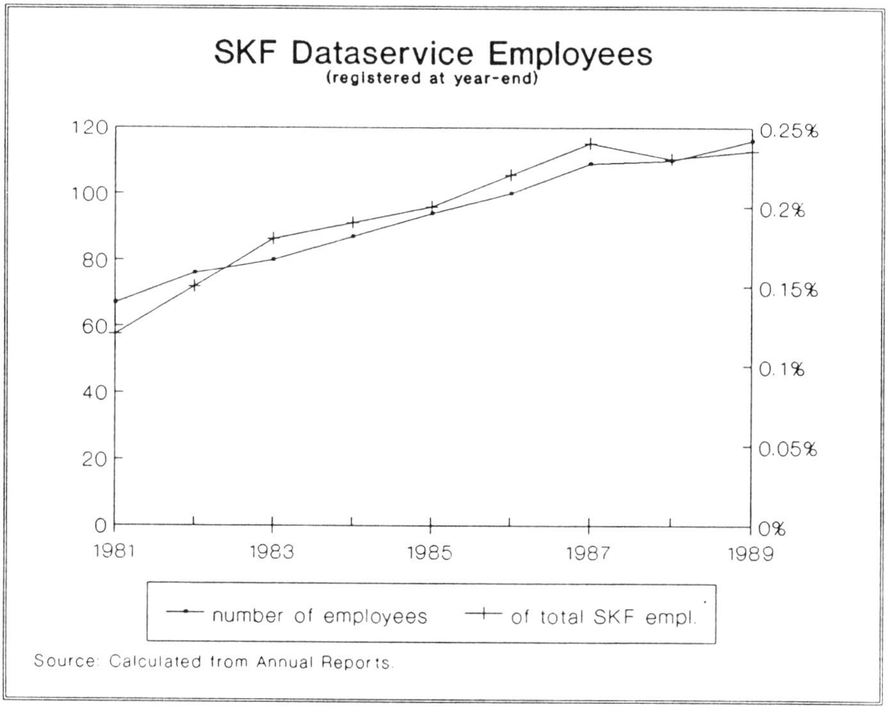

The share of systems development taking place under the auspices of the central node appears to be increasing. Joint development involving several dispersed IS departments is still very common, but there are clear tendencies, as identified by node managers, of a buttressed 'primus inter pares'-role for the Gothenburg node. The trend is much weaker for technical than other systems. Although later used widely, specific technical systems are developed under the leadership of the center of relevant competence. Clearly, LMT maintains control of systems associated with its machinery, for instance. More general technical applications, like CADalog and BEDA, on the other hand, tend to fall within the purview of Gothenburg.

The more run-of-the-mill activities, maintenance and support of common systems, do, however, open an avenue for nodes to mitigate pressures for the slimming-down of operations. For instance, the Turin node winning that function SKF-wide for MCSS meant that the planned IS staff reductions largely could be counterbalanced. In addition, specific local conditions can be exploited. The King of Prussia and Luton nodes fill an informal function in SKF as a scouts, keeping an eye on developments in the most advanced IS markets. The Luton main node has also managed to maintain a position as a center of expertise regarding customer connections[170] while slipping in over-all IS operations..

The somewhat bleak picture emerging from the discussion on IS staff developments may seem at odds with the earlier contention of expanding information system usage in SKF. In fact, the contradiction is illusory.

Apart from the already mentioned different types of productivity gains in information systems area, the domain of the IS function is encroached upon by users. More experienced users are more actively involved. This involvement takes various forms. Specific instances surfacing during the interviews with IS staff can be categorized into:

- non-IS staff shouldering a greater share of systems development work by being able to more succinctly state system requirements;
- outright purchase of specific systems by functional departments; and
- systems support increasingly being sought from fellow-users rather than from the local IS department.

In practice, the systems bought are often simple add-ons. The systems support referred to tends to be limited to post-implementation 'how-to-use-it' questions, but which can be very time-consuming to respond to. The functional areas said to be most adept at these activities were financial management, production engineering and sales.

---

170) Recall the early linking of distributors and the present trials of a new CADalog interface with four major customers (see Sections 4.3.2 and 5.2.2.2).

Although in some way undermining the supremacy of IS staff, no strong resentment by IS departments was voiced. On the contrary, assistance in systems development and support was generally welcomed as it was seen to facilitate the department's work. Bringing in 'own' applications met a more mixed reaction, but the IS department can always exercise its right of veto when common hardware or system interfaces are required.

A corollary of having common systems and communications as priorities is enforced standardization of systems and interfaces, which in turn means that once those restrictions are complied with, particular demands can be acceded to. Good communications naturally widens the geographical space across which users can share experiences, thus also supporting users' more active involvement. From this user perspective then, SKF's intention to decentralize information systems responsibilities takes on real meaning.

However, the diffusion of the information systems function clearly does not stop at the organizational boundary. It extends to external parties. Although to a lesser degree than, and somewhat differently from, what happens internally, non-SKF units share in information systems management[171]. Relying on discussions in previous sections, it is convenient to distinguish between three types of such sharing, namely:

- usage of others' networks and/or systems;
- cooperation in development; and
- joint systems support.

Also from previous sections, it follows that the external parties primarily refer to customers, and to a small extent other players in the same or related industries, with direct competitors and suppliers being of negligeable import in this context[172].

---

[171] Here, we exclude purchased, distinct services, such as usage of third-party value-added communications networks or assistance by consultants in systems development.

[172] As noted before, Ovako Steel is a special case among suppliers. It assumes management responsibility for its nodes but is otherwise a passive user of SKF information systems. On the other hand, when, and if, the purchasing function is upgraded in terms of information systems, a more participative and active position for Ovako Steel can be envisaged.

To exemplify, multi-branch distributors often have a communications network of sorts, thereby limiting the SKF interface to one point but automatically affording SKF a means of communicating with other branches as well. Large OEM customers often insist on using their systems. Good internal systems cohesion in SKF makes such interfaces more manageable, and subsequently SKF can often follow in the customer's own systems upgrading. This can also take the form of cooperative systems development (e.g. as with Ford in the UK). ODETTE and BASCET-Infolink represent clear cooperative efforts, involving competitors as well. The more limited joint systems support is akin to its internal counterpart. Depending on capability, external parties can help SKF users out informally after, say, SCSS or a file transfer has been installed. - Although the magnitude of shared information systems effort in the examples may make some points tenuous, the principle of diffusion remains.

In conclusion, emphasizing communications and common systems does support and create conditions for greater integration, also over and above from what follows from sheer usage. Some conditions extend to outsiders, too[173]. With the distinction between IS staff and users increasingly blurred, a higher level of ambition regarding the role played by information systems in SKF can be maintained, in spite of a possibly dwindling formal IS effort within the company proper.

5.3.3 Competitors' Information System Use

So far, information systems usage by SKF's competitors has only been touched upon en passant. The purpose of the final part of our overview of information systems in SKF is to remedy that (intentional) oversight by giving a summary assessment. We will not attempt to give a exhaustive survey of the competitors' standing in this area, but rather to highlight any challenges to SKF stemming from relative proficiency in information systems use by the competition.

---

[173] See also a similar line of argument in Hagström (1990a).

Recall first that SKF has been judged to, at present, be well ahead of its suppliers and customers in aggregate information systems use, save some OEM customers (notably automotive manufacturers). This lead does not manifest itself in similarly superior specific applications. Except for CADalog, more advanced systems can be found in SKF's business environment on a system-by-system comparison. On the other hand, SKF's data communications network has few rivals, at least in manufacturing industry.

SKF's singularly strong position becomes even more pronounced if the comparison is limited to competitors. That assessment holds for SKF as a whole.

Although the Tools and Component Systems divisions are laggards internally, no evidence of any significant competitor superiority regarding information systems has been found. The Tools and Component Systems divisions operate in very fragmented industries where information systems are poorly diffused. Another explanation is the possibility for these divisions to 'piggyback' on SKF's communications and systems. No major competitor has a similar advantage. Moreover, the Tools division has by all accounts achieved a very high degree of sophistication in its own right within its product areas regarding information systems usage.

SKF's mainstay business requires more elaboration, however. There is no need to modify previous statements on SKF's overall relative strength in the area of information systems when scrutinizing the bearing industry. However, through interviews and search of external sources, three noteworthy exceptions to SKF's superiority have been found. They are:

- CAD links in West Germany;
- customer connections in the US market; and
- production control systems in use by Japanese competitors.

These three challenges will briefly be discussed in turn.

SKF and FAG are the major suppliers on the West German bearings market, each with an approximate 30 percent share. Another local competitor, Ina, commands a rather smaller share. Still, Ina is the most innovative company when it comes to sophisticated customer links. It outperforms SKF's 18 larger customer connections both in number and quality of service in West Germany.

Most importantly, Ina has on-line interchange of CAD drawings with its customers, where SKF essentially only can offer information and order entry services. The main advantage derives from Ina being able to store and distribute CAD drawings in dialogue with its customers. Customization of bearings thus becomes easier. At present, SKF cannot offer anything similar. Recall that the CADalog (with some 100 installations in West Germany in 1989) is restricted to standard bearings and mainly a tool for application engineering. However, the CADalog can bridge several CAD systems, where Ina's applications are individually tied to specific systems. That could make it cumbersome for Ina to go beyond its present customer relationships.

SKF's competitive relationship with Ina appears to be rather benign. Both companies buy and sell each other's bearings, to a limited extent supplementing its respective product ranges on the local market. Testifying to the innovativeness, or cheekiness, of Ina is the fact that Ina has placed a stand-alone terminal at the SKF marketing department for the administration of this product interchange. It is the only such competitor connection in SKF known to us. There are no other data communications links between SKF and Ina.

FAG is a different kettle of fish altogether. In fact, FAG is SKF's traditional arch-rival in the bearings industry. FAG is older than SKF (founded in 1883), and its head-office is located back-to-back with SKF's single largest subsidiary (since 1929, when SKF acquired Fichtel & Sachs A. G. in Schweinfurt). FAG is still the biggest competitor on the West European market and is considered to be a technically very advanced bearing company. That expertise does not extend to information systems, though. Here, development is relatively poor and competence low. FAG has largely failed with its customer connections. One main reason is an early piecemeal approach to information systems. When customer links could not be put off anymore for competitive reasons in the first half of the 1980s, FAG could not accommodate the required integration. After years of effort the existing Honeywell, Nixdorf, and Siemens computers all had to be replaced by IBM. So far, FAG has suffered less from these troubles than could be expected, since the company's activities are strongly concentrated to its single European production site in Schweinfurt. Plain physical proximity thus compensates to some extent for shortcomings in data communications.

Moving on to the US, SKF's main local competitors are Timken and Torrington (the latter a division within the Ingersoll Rand Corporation). SKF and Torrington both claim approximately 12 percent of the local market, with Timken reaching a slightly higher, about 15 percent, share. Timken and Torrington play different competitive roles. Timken is a volume producer of some special bearings, but with a limited product range (mainly conical, taper bearings). Torrington attempts to seek out high margin customer segments with bearings of a high technical standard. A common feature of both companies is that they are comparatively better than SKF in connecting their US customers.

Neither Timken nor Torrington are particularly advanced in information systems usage by any standard. Both have, however, concentrated their efforts on customer linkages that feed into their production planning. More specifically, Timken and Torrington are, at present, better equipped to respond to customer demands, mainly from OEMs, of invoice-less payments systems and smooth flows from factory to user than is SKF. The competitors are further much more adept at using EDI, also via third parties. SKF at present lacks viable data communications links with OEM customers and has rather poor third-party connections (cf. Section 4.3.2 above). SKF's ACCESS (see Section 5.2.3.3) is surprisingly internally oriented and consequently relatively cumbersome and rigid for any external user. The bottom line is simply that, on the whole, Timken and Torrington have local customer data communications linkages, while SKF does not[174].

In Japan, SKF is the source of virtually all imports but reaches only a dismal, 1/2 percent market share. The three main actors NSK, NTN and Koyo Seiko are known for having very efficient production and logistics, competing mainly on price. In terms of information systems, the Japanese relative strength lies in automated production and good logistics.

---

[174] The major exceptions are the fixed links with TRW and Bearings Inc. (cf. Section 4.3.4).

By all accounts, the three are very similar in these respects. We choose to single out NSK for two reasons. NSK is reckoned by SKF to be the slightly more advanced user of information systems and it has clearly emerged as SKF's prime competitor with the recent acquisition of UPI of the UK. It is also worth noting that NSK has a cooperation agreement with Torrington[175].

NSK started its computerization in the late 1960s with the concept of a large, integrated database built around products[176]. It has grown to become a dominant information system for the company, the MArketing, desiGn and MAnufacturing (MAGMA) system. It encompasses diverse information, like sales, customer orders, product information, CAD drawings, production plans and budgets. The later (1980s) thrusts have come in factory automation, where NSK is a forerunner in Japanese industry. NSK has possibly the most automated factories in the bearing industry. They are, in turn, linked to MAGMA, which takes in customer orders and information from customers on design requirements. NSK's data communication network connects its 9 factories in Japan with the head-office via leased lines. They share a common inventory control system. The foreign subsidiaries[177] and some of the major suppliers have dial-up links for a limited interface with MAGMA.

The picture that emerges is one of NSK as a tight-knit, efficient, primarily domestic, and strongly production-oriented company. It is noteworthy that NSK reports an inventory level of less than half that of SKF[178]. An important explanation can found in NSK's very strong reliance on OEM relationships, essentially with a small number of local

---

[175] SKF has a limited liaison agreement with Koyo Seiko dating back to 1985. The agreement is basically a license for Koyo Seiko to manufacture gearboxes and sell them in the Far East.

[176] Independent sources on the Japanese manufacturers are hard to come by. The main secondary sources used here are Wennersten and Holmberg (1987), Affärsvärlden (August 10, 1988, The Economist (August 19, 1989), and The Financial Times (January 18, 1990).

[177] Excluding UPI, NSK has about a dozen foreign subsidiaries, four of which are manufacturing (in South Korea, Brazil, the US and the UK).

[178] According to NSK's Annual Report 1988, inventories stood at a remarkable 15 percent of sales in 1987. The corresponding figure for SKF was 39 percent. The business mixes are different, but NSK derives some 60 percent of its sales from bearings (the rest being machinery and automotive components).

automotive manufacturers. Its own sales network (and corresponding stocking requirements) is consequently thin, especially overseas.

The bias toward production is also reflected in that NSK does not have any data communications links with customers. The information derived from MAGMA is transmitted via telefacsimile to customers. The exception is payments routines, which use a national, third-party value-added network. Moreover, there is no electronic mail system at NSK. MAGMA is not targeted for further development and efforts in the information systems area are, at present, directed at production[179]. In fact, NSK's very good reputation regarding information systems use is probably more a reflection of the local standard than of exceptional proficiency in an international context.

In conclusion, we can see that none of the identified challenges by competitors in the information systems area is an international application. Although being only minor back-yard challenges, they originate one each in the three largest country markets for bearings; the US, Japan, and West Germany. Still, it appears very exaggerated to deduce any imminent serious threat to SKF's competitive position emanating from competitors' use of information systems. On the contrary, SKF's leading position here seems quite secure.

On the very bottom line, SKF has also consistently been more profitable than its main competitors (with the exception of Torrington in the last few years).

---

[179] Actually, only some of the Japanese factories had leased-line links to the head-office in mid-1987.

6. CONCLUSIONS

The usage of international data communications and the attendant computerized systems in SKF is deeply embedded in SKF's over-all operations; its strategy and structure. Our attempts at identifying and disentangling various types of information systems usage have left us with an array of different systems and usage patterns. The established dichotomy of network and systems, and subsequent subdivisions, has, however, enabled us to give due weight to the function of (data) communications in information systems usage. In turn, that has permitted a clearer discussion in each case - be it the network status of a company unit or the functioning of a system - of the contextual relationship with SKF activities.

International data communications-cum-systems emerge as a means for SKF strategy implementation and structural design. Old things can be done differently and new opportunities can be exploited. Learning makes this a continuous process. The combined versatility of this means and the generality of its application to many activities, make for information systems playing a rather complex role in an organization. That has also been shown in the preceding chapters to hold for SKF on a case-by-case basis.

Some, more comprehensive interpretations of the rationale for, and effects of, information systems usage in SKF can, however, be found interspersed in the text above. Notably Sections 4.3 and 5.3 look first at the resource cost of information systems and then at performance relative to professed objectives and priorities.

The present chapter is intended to complement the descriptions and interpretations already given by structuring the discussion differently from what has been done in the preceding chapters. Here, we by and large follow the more general arguments in Hagström (1990a, 1990b, and 1991). Consequently, this chapter is not meant to be a summary, although some repetition and overlap cannot be avoided.

First, the pattern of information systems usage in SKF as it has changed over time, and as it varies across the organization, are reviewed. The second main section turns to the role of information systems as it pertains to performing and organizing of activities in SKF. In the final section, we take a look at the whole study: some basic tenets are questioned, some types of information systems usage not found are identified, and, lastly, some salient, general characteristics of SKF as an accomplished user of information systems are suggested.

6.1 Evolution of IS Use in SKF

If we distance ourselves from the empirical quagmire, reservations and nuances recede into the background. With this perspective, both an unevenness and a shifting emphasis concerning where in SKF the services of information systems are employed with most fervor appear. The latter is all the more interesting, given that SKF's competitive environment, its scope of operations, and its IS policy have remained remarkably stable since the mid-1970s and the beginning of computer-based information systems reaching outside particular sites.

6.1.1 Temporal Overview

Broadly, three cumulative phases can be discerned in terms of IS usage in SKF. The emphasis has shifted from cost-cutting, via revenue generation, to integration[180].

High hopes were attached to the potential of information systems in the early-to-mid-1970s. The early ambitions fed off a strong technical culture in SKF, wide-spread technical optimism concerning IS, and the already envisaged major role for IS in the

[180] The phases are labelled 'defensive', 'offensive', and 'integrative' respectively in Hagström (1990a), which also contains a commensurate general argument on the sequence of information systems usage.

running of GFSS, the operational backbone of the new restructured SKF. IS was a high-ranking staff unit. A mammoth totally integrated computer system was just around the corner. However, STICS failed and communications links did not reach required standard (if, indeed they could be established at all). IS disappeared as a corporate staff unit and some key people were changed. However, even with more modest ambitions, SKF became a trail-blazer in building an international proprietary data communications network.

The underlying reason for pushing SKF into the role of an international pioneer was that implementing GFSS was seen as a question of survival for SKF, given the competitive challenge at the time. In the area of IS, purely technical applications had to stand back for the need to achieve a better functioning of the GFSS administration. In keeping with broad SKF tradition, a technical or, rather, a product focus also remained as the dominating FSO-system allocated production capacity and issued shipping schedules for finished products, in accordance with forecast demand. This bias is noticeable to this day.

Given the priority assigned to product-related systems and the delays suffered in establishing Telenet, international reporting and the first financial applications were externalized (cf. GMS and TMS).

Hard-nosed <u>cost-cutting and rationalization</u> of operations were the name of the game. This trimming of the organization meant increased specialization (particularly of production) and, consequently, increased interdependence manifest in complex intra-company product flows. On the sales side, a smaller number of sales and stocking points served the same customers with the full product range coming in each case from a larger number of (internal) suppliers.

Growth in international IS usage in SKF from the latter half of the 1970s to the mid-1980s thus followed two main paths; a widening of data communications and a deepening of existing applications. The continued geographical expansion of data communications, notably through Telenet, was very much motivated by a wish to improve control of company operations in general. Developments in systems were primarily related to the efficient coordination of the product flow interdependence. That these concerns still hold can be illustrated with the experience of the Spanish Bearing Industries subsidiary. In practice virgin territory in terms of IS capabilities when connected in 1985, first GMS/TMS, then the ICSS/FSO-systems, then other applications came to be used.

Some developments surfacing in the early-to-mid-1980s betray a second shift in emphasis in the broad approach to IS usage in SKF. Rationalization efforts continued but the relative rigidity of optimization with rather long planning cycles began to give way to more flexible adjustment as regards the internal product flow. Increased external input through taking better account of actual customer orders was part of the change. New bearing material flow systems were developed (cf. NMFC), with ICSS emerging as the linchpin and the link with the past FSO-driven coordination. Customer connections to Telenet began to proliferate.

A prerequisite for the improved internal flexibility and customer orientation was the high degree of internal standardization achieved with common systems and a cohesive communications network in place. Adding revenue-increase to the cost-reduction motive, better customer service could be reflected in the prices charged and the business gained (or kept). Apart from order-related IS services, product offerings were enhanced by making technical knowledge more readily available to customers. Such customer access to technical knowledge comes directly via Telenet connections or indirectly through similarly upgraded capabilities of SKF's own sales organization. The CADalog is but one example, but it highlights the combined improvements in order and technical services offered by SKF and also the IS mode of delivery (see also Section 6.2.1 below).

Accommodating customer connections is clearly not limited to having external parties using SKF systems like a member of the SKF family, although that often is the case vis-à-vis distributors. Externally determined standards for system interfaces and systems can be quite widely applicable (as ODETTE and EDIFACT, or standards imposed by third-party, value-added networks) but can also be idiosyncratic, since some customers are in a position to insist on using standards of their own choosing (notably large OEM-customers). The point here is that in addition to being an initial requirement, internal standardization gets a second boost from continued efforts at adaptation to external parties. In turn, this heralds a third shift in emphasis in SKF information systems usage.

The infrastructural qualities of IS are becoming relatively more important at this juncture. From the late 1980s and on, integration internally, but also extending outside SKF proper, is increasingly becoming a hallmark of information systems usage. Put differently, the demand side of IS, external as well as internal, is strengthened relative to the previously dominating supply side.

One significant factor aiding this development is that, in general, systems are more versatile and 'open' than before. Another decisive factor is that SKF has kept its own systems simple, and they have proven to be quite robust. The fact that SKF has not 'got carried away' and kept developing increasingly sophisticated systems is worth stressing. Given SKF's track record, the potential for hubris has been present throughout but kept in check (save the early days of STICS). Broadly, information systems are still run by computer personnel but user interests are coming more to the forefront, both formally in systems development, and through actual usage. - We will return below to this evolving, and therefore less than distinct, function of IS.

6.1.2 Differential Use

Before turning to current issues, the underlying differential information systems usage of the previous section needs to be spelled out. Painting with broad strokes, three implicit aspects of variation in information systems usage emerge from the discussion so far: type of activity, geographic location, and business. They will be considered briefly in turn.

Activity determinants of application of IS have been afforded the best coverage in the previous section. Reporting, (short term) financial management, and product flow from manufacturing to customer are outstanding in terms of to what degree they can be judged to be supported by IS. Product development and manufacturing processes make up the second, lower ranked, broad category of activities. Marketing, service and research follow third. Quality assurance and purchasing strangely enough come further down the (not exhaustive) list. Strange, since both functions are relatively amenable to computerization, and since they are a purported corporate priority and a logical extension of the product flow, respectively[181]. Human resources (save local personnel administration) are a function largely void of IS support, apart from some very limited computer-assisted distance training. The same goes for the corporate staff functions of legal and public affairs. Strategic (and long-term financial, e.g. large investments) decision-making is a separate issue, since it basically envelops the enumerated activities.

Geographically, Western Europe is comparatively best served with Telenet connections and common systems. Usage is also most intensive in Western Europe. That is not surprising given the relative concentration of SKF operations to Western Europe. The geographical distribution of the Telenet main nodes obviously reflect the same thing. However, the first five main nodes[182] still form an inner circle of sorts, now with back-up leased lines having been established. In addition, the 'old national' network centered on the Gothenburg node (cf. Section 4.2.2.1) should be included in this select group. SKF units also without high node status in the Nordic countries and in Belgium and the Netherlands are consequently comparatively very well catered for in terms of IS. The differentiation within Europe of access to communications and systems services is consequently still more determined more by historical developments than by straight size of local operations, which is the official SKF criterion. Therefore, we find, for instance, better services for the small sales subsidiary in Oslo than for the Spanish main node. The conclusion stands, although the initial five main nodes, of course, were the biggest SKF locations in Europe.

---

[181] There are no good, unequivocal explanations for this state of affairs. However, the early emphasis on products (R&D, manufacturing and sales) for competitive reasons may have led to other areas having been somewhat neglected. In addition, purchasing has, on the one hand, traditionally been very much of a local responsibility in SKF, and, on the other hand, purchases of the main input from SKF/Ovako Steel have been supported by IS. The stress on quality has furthermore moved more clearly to the forefront during the latter half of the 1980s.

[182] Gothenburg, Sweden; Schweinfurt, Germany; Turin, Italy; Clamart, France; and Luton, UK (cf. Section 4.2.2.1 above).

That size alone is a doubtful indicator is also evident from SKF's large US operations. Although the US units are relatively well supported by IS, the King of Prussia main node is not quite up to 'inner circle' European node standards. That is further noteworthy in view of the strong centralization of computer processing in the US national network.

Moreover, the US is less well integrated within the common information systems using more local applications. Extensive IS use in the US also came later than in Europe and is still strongly geared towards cost-cutting (cf. Section 6.1 above). The much smaller Singapore operations are better integrated in, and in tune with, over-all SKF IS use. That goes for their respective regional communications and systems responsibilities as well. Among other things, it means that, for instance, the newer Taiwanese sales subsidiary is 'closer' in terms of IS than the older Peruvian one. This difference is exacerbated by the relative technical and regulatory difficulties in establishing links at all.

Completing the picture, sizeable stand-alone operations (of the type found in India and South Africa) are only to a rudimentary extent integrated into the SKF IS structure.

Linking external parties, in practice customers[183], follows the same main pattern. A given customer is more likely to be offered SKF IS services if located in Western Europe than in the US, and so on. An upshot of this differential likelihood is that many customers in Europe are better served with IS services by SKF than are its own geographically distant subsidiaries.

The probability of a given subsidiary being linked to the data communications network is furthermore strongly influenced by its <u>product business</u>. The propensity of becoming connected, as well as the number and sophistication of applications, is obviously the highest for the standard bearing business, as has been repeatedly pointed out in this study. Specialty Bearings is considerably less integrated into SKF's IS structure, with Component Systems even further out in the periphery. For Component Systems the IS status will also vary across the separate businesses, with the greatest degree of integration

[183] Ovako Steel is a special case, see Chapter 4 above.

for the businesses that are the closest to bearings, viz. those that use the sales organization of, or supply to the manufacturing of, standard bearings (seals being a case in point). In general, it is the corporate, and to a very small extent some technical, applications that are relevant for Component Systems units.

The Tools business is more difficult to rank, specifically vis-à-vis IS usage in Specialty Bearings. The latter scores well because of its important US sites being firmly integrated in the US national network and attendant applications, because of many of its other sites being located at main Telenet nodes, and because of remote usage of some technical applications (notably at ERC). However, there is no real divisional level commonality of systems. Tools exhibits much more divisional commonality, but is far less integrated in the dominant standard bearings driven systems, notably by not really using any such technical applications.

The Tools division instead shows more similarities with the standard bearings business concerning IS support of product flows. Exploitation of IS has, however, come later and is still much less developed for the tools than the bearing business. Partly because of the smaller scale of operations, but also by policy, the Tools approach to IS is more centralized and interventionist. Sheffield's preeminent status as a coordination center within the division comes across clearly, it being the hub of (data) communications, business-related systems, and coordination of distribution. The Tools division also differs in that small sales subsidiaries have been become users of the divisional systems even before relatively big tools plants. Some customers have received similar preferential treatment, particularly locally in the UK.

It is unlikely that the Tools report card on IS will change much with the formation of CTT. If anything, progress will probably be slowed down as both SKF corporate systems and divisional systems need to be introduced to Titex. With the relative strengthening of continental European activities, and the relocation of divisional headquarters, the hitherto undisputed leading role of Sheffield would be undermined. Especially concerning information systems, the change from Tools to CTT presents an opportunity for bold new initiatives as rationalization and integration are sought.

The rather loose terminology in this section is a reflection of the elusiveness of the concept of IS integration. A final observation bringing some of the identified variability together is that data communications linkage (and through that systems access) appears to be a good proxy for closeness to the core of SKF operations, or, for relative strategic importance. The advantage of looking at the quality of connections is that it can constitute a more than trivial, ready measure for an inherently qualitative issue. One drawback is some lack of precision in that the measure refers to sites, rather than to specific activities. But instead of reiterating much of the discussion in Chapter 4 above, we only illustrate the approach here.

Obvious candidates for inclusion in a 'core SKF' are the sites with high capacity back-up leased lines, viz. Gothenburg, Schweinfurt, Turin, Luton, and Brussels (FSO). The quality boost of the DECNET overlay adds Nieuwegein (ERC) and Lidköping (LMT) to the group. Other units would then be successively more peripheral. Moreover, this principle does not only operate in a cumulative fashion, it also has current implications as can be seen from the varying degree of urgency with which different acquisitions are connected (e.g. as in the cases of Steyr and MRC). These indicative results tally well with what could be deduced from the rather more lengthy discussion in Chapter 3, where SKF operations were reviewed in a more traditional manner.

A converse illustration would be one of exceptionally poor quality connections. Two less than obvious examples from the US are the foundry products and needle bearings plant in Indiana and a foundry products plant in Missouri. The former has an uncharacteristically simple dial-up connection and the latter had its leased-line link similarly downgraded. In these cases it was tantamount to hanging out the 'for sale' sign; something that became widely known much later.

By the same token, not only some Component Systems businesses but, indeed, the whole Tools division (now CTT) would be the most likely candidates for divestment, were the going to get really tough for SKF. That more speculative conclusion does, however, receive additional support from the fact that these businesses are still being less subject to efforts of information systems integration than are peripheral/distant bearing-related units.

6.2 The Role of IS in SKF

Concluding that SKF possesses leading edge capabilities in information systems usage compared to its competitors and, indeed, to industrial MNCs in general, is a circular reasoning, since that was among our case selection criteria. But, with no unpleasant surprises surfacing in the course of the investigation, the study allows us to reaffirm SKF's prominent position with so much more conviction.

It is also clear that SKF's lead is continuously being eroded by the wider diffusion of communications standards and the improved markets for communications services and for systems. Internal IS competence is becoming less of a prerequisite for establishing data communications networks and bringing in computer systems. A corollary point is that straight-forward IS capabilities are becoming less firm idiosyncratic.

SKF still derives some advantage in relation to competitors from its size as there are some economies of scale, notably in systems development and maintenance. However, we have seen that SKF's relative prominence does not rest on having outstanding systems at its disposal. No particular application is extraordinary in any significant respect, except the CADalog. Instead, SKF earns its laurels from the first-rate handling of international data communications and the accomplished integration of various systems.

Due to its pioneering efforts, SKF today has unrivalled experience in IS usage, an asset which is much more difficult for competitors to emulate than a particular type of application. The early and extensive adoption of IS in SKF has mean that IS has had time to permeate the whole organization. In turn, that has profound implications for the what, how and when of SKF activities. With maturity, the role for international data communications and systems in firm strategy and structure becomes more complex.

6.2.1 Performing Activities

The degree to which the use of information systems supports company objectives, as they are defined by SKF, is reviewed in some detail in Section 5.3.1 above. Here, we choose a slightly different perspective, looking more at the generic use of IS within the broader strategic orientation of SKF. To a large extent we thus transcend the distinctions already made in Section 6.1.

Arguably, the basic tenets of SKF's strategy are rationalizing internal operations and adding value to the end product. The latter spells differentiation, but tied to existing products.

At this high level of aggregation, the strategy has remained intact during the last quarter of a century. Growth has been achieved within existing product areas but the center of gravity in SKF's operations has moved downstream. IS has been a critical tool for changing the internal division of labor and the scope of company activities. We start by considering the former.

Rationalization largely translates into increasing internal specialization. Activities have been broken up and shifted around in the company. For the most part, performance of activities have been concentrated to avoid duplication of effort and to exploit economies of scale. Clear-cut examples are many aspects of financial management, basic research and, indeed, (tele)communications. These activities are concentrated across the company to one location. The implementation thereof is contingent on functioning data communications[184].

The most obvious instances of such fragmentation and concentration are, however, found in manufacturing and logistics. The dominating standard bearings business is a case in point but also the tools business has elements of it. Specializing by narrowly defined

[184] Quality assurance and purchasing have, belatedly, started to take the same route.

product, SKF can benefit from cheek-by-jowl location of product development and production. This deep specialization is commensurate with a geographical dispersion of the functions of manufacturing and product development.

The over-all logistics of production planning and hand-over of products to sales is separated out and in part concentrated to one coordinating location (FSO), in part embodied in the interlocking bearing material flow systems (cf. Section 5.2.2.1 above). In the first case, coordination between geographically dispersed, specialized manufacturing and likewise geographically dispersed but full-range sales is achieved with the support of IS. In the second case the decision rules are incorporated into the systems, which adjust to each other over the data communications network.

Much sales support has been concentrated similarly; by product and/or by application. Geographically dispersed, specialized support activities have, however, prompted a more elusive kind of dispersion of activities. In no small measure due to communications and systems access, the dispersed sales function has been upgraded. We have, for instance, seen how customer application capabilities in the local sales organization have been enhanced by remote access to pockets of specialized knowledge residing in particular computer applications and/or in specific organizational units (cf. Sections 5.2.2 and 5.3.1 above).

A related tendency is evolving concerning commonalities in the technical grey zone between research and product development, leading to upgrading of local knowledge. The difference from local sales support is that research and product development are concentrated activities, and upgrading comes more through sharing than through one-way transfer (cf. Section 5.2.2 above). One important reason for the delayed development in this area is directly due to data communications short-comings, since the transmission of CAD drawings places higher demands on minimization of errors than many telecommunications carriers can live up to.

Closely linked to specialization is the question of scope of activities performed. Old activities have been externalized and new activities internalized, again directly or indirectly contingent on SKF's IS capabilities.

The single most important externalization move by SKF was that of divesting itself of its steel-making business. There is no reason to question SKF's official motives for forming Ovako Steel (cf. Section 3.4 above) but we surmise that the option was made all the more palatable to SKF by Ovako Steel remaining within the SKF information systems structure (cf. Hagström 1987b and 1990a). Loss of control from loss of ownership could, in part, be compensated for by maintained control through IS.

Externalization is, however, neither only a question of degree of vertical integration, nor does it only involve the two extreme points of a firm's value-chain as commonly assumed.

A counter example is the physical transport of bearings. A critical activity in 'the middle' of the value-chain has been externalized by SKF (cf. Section 5.2.2.1 above). The activity is controlled through the NMFC family of systems.

An example having little to do with degree of vertical integration, as commonly perceived, is externalizing part of environmental scanning, notably by using external databases (cf. Sections 4.2.1 and 5.2.1.3). Here, a support activity is externalized.

Systems development also defies simple 'value-chain' terminology. Again, a support activity is externalized, in part by buying systems off the shelf and, more commonly, by soliciting external help in development. Far from all systems development is externalized, however (cf. Section 5.2). Systems development is customarily concentrated to dispersed locations, be it adaptation of a purchased system or an in-house development. Frequently, development work is run as a project involving several organizational units and outside consultants (cf. the example of MCSS in Section 5.2.2.1). The point in this context is that systems development is both externalized and internally concentrated, but with the degree of the former and the location(s) of the latter being dynamically adjusted. This flexibility is contingent on international data communications linking participating parties.

Clear cases of the converse, viz. internalizing activities, are many aspects of financial management previously handled by financial intermediaries and of telecommunications earlier left to carriers. More subtle instances are activities adding value to the end-product, where new services have been developed, and are offered, with the help of data communications.

In particular, IS supports differentiation towards customers. Different service packages in this vein are discussed at some length in Section 5.3.1.3 above. Suffice it here to point to the fact that internalization and differentiation go hand-in-hand. Many of the order- and inventory-related services offered by SKF essentially entail SKF taking over activities from the buyer, as highlighted by delivery and inventory planning for customers. Payments routines managed by SKF similarly imply internalizing activities earlier left to intermediaries (or to customers).

This selective internalization at the customer end is a key to resolving the potential, higher-order conflict between the strategies of rationalization and differentiation. Typically, the former implies minimizing diversity while the latter adds to diversity through striving for customization. The conflict is real, however, when diversity is taken to mean product diversity, and in an integrated firm.

In SKF, the opposing demands can be said to have been reconciled very broadly in two ways. In businesses where product diversity is required over-all integration has been sacrificed and production broken up into small businesses defined by competence to solve particular customer category requirements (cf. Specialty Bearings). In the main bearing business, product diversity has been sacrificed and differentiation has instead been achieved through add-on services. In both cases IS plays a pivotal role. For the small businesses, IS is relatively most important for supporting the specific technical competencies and the intensive customer relationships. For the integrated bearing business, the commensurate role of IS is administration of the bridging logistics and being a means for differentiated service provision[185].

---

[185] Tools conforms in principle to the standard bearings case, and Component Systems to Specialty Bearings, in this context. The salient characteristics are, however, much less distinct.

The strategy supporting role of IS in customer linkages warrants some further comments, not least since it is an issue that has received an inordinate amount of attention in IS-related research[186]. While addressing some additional aspects of the same issue, we do not, however, adhere very closely to that mainstream approach (see also Section 6.1.1).

First, we have seen how SKF pursues different lines of action in connecting customers depending on its relative bargaining position, the country market for information services, competitors' possible moves, and local SKF IS capabilities[187]. However, this approach has meant excessive external adaptation on the part of SKF (large OEM-customers, third-party value-added networks, and even special-purpose links unconnected to the internal network; cf. Section 4.3). The collective cost of this external flexibility now appears to be reaching a limit as evidenced by SKF promoting more 'open' system interfaces with customers. Examples here are the budding use of the ODETTE-standard with distributors and of public Videotext applications (e.g. in Germany). It is noteworthy as it runs contrary to official SKF policy, and seemingly means foregoing an existing competitive advantage.

Second, there is, however, more to tying customers than just establishing a data communications link. The services offered is another source of competitive advantage. More or less tailored service packages for particular customer categories have already been mentioned but external adaptation is an issue here as well. The CADalog (cf. Section 5.2.2.2) epitomizes both points, being an integral part of the service offering and by being exceptionally versatile concerning system interfaces. In those respects it also highlights some of SKF's key comparative advantages where strong and focussed internal IS capabilities permits relatively very high degree of integration of services and flexibility towards customers.

---

[186] Especially widely quoted writings include McFarlan and McKenney (1983), McFarlan (1984b), Rockart and Scott Morton (1984), Porter and Millar (1985), Wiseman (1985), and Keen (1986). Our approach is wider, however (for discussions on this context, see Hagström, 1988, 1990a, and 1991a and also the main text; recall also the earlier arguments on vertical integration in the present section).

[187] Compare, for instance, the very different situation on these scores for SKF's Spanish and US national networks (cf. Sections 4.3.3 and 4.3.4, respectively).

Third, the extent of access allowed external parties is an issue that hides a trade-off between providing customers with good service and safeguarding sensitive internal information. SKF has taken a comparatively very 'open' attitude; an option which, in practice, is open only to accomplished IS users. The CADalog is again a good example, where the on-line back-up bearing calculation program lets customers share SKF expertise, while withholding the competitively sensitive 'how to' technical information.

Fourth, the possibilities for tailoring services even closer to individual fit grow with time as particular customer case histories and aggregate customer databases build up (e.g. DCSS/SCSS and the Tools' PC Product Database in Sections 5.2.2.1 and 5.2.2.2, respectively). SKF is beginning to exploit these opportunities (cf. Section 5.3.1.3), which ties in with the advantage accruing to having experience in IS usage (cf. Section 6.2). One example, taking this one step further, is the current efforts at designing sales promotion activities according to the characteristics of particular customers, even of small distributors.

Finally and on a different tack, no discussion on the strategic role of IS, however brief, would be complete without recognizing the strategic impact of better reporting[188]. Improved reliability, timeliness and detail of reporting data reduce company response time and increase response accuracy insofar as strategic response relies on reporting information. - The control-related issues of reporting fall in the domain of organizational design.

[188] For fuller arguments on this issue, see Hagström (1988, 1990a, and 1991).

6.2.2 Organizing Activities

If the over-all strategy of SKF, as well as the industry environment, can be said to have been relatively stable over time[189], the same is not true for the organization. It is better characterized by repeated change and increasing complexity (cf. Hagström, 1987b, and Section 3.4 above). Neither is the growing complexity mirrored within SKF's portfolio of products.

Most organizational principles can be traced in SKF's present formal organization. At the divisional level, there are global product divisions (Tools, Component Systems, and Specialty Bearings), a customer-based division (Bearing Services), and a division combining the two (Bearing Industries). Important functional units with world-wide responsibilities fall outside the divisional organization (e.g. SKF International and ERC), as does direct reporting in the mother-daughter fashion (LMT and SKF USA Inc.). More traditional 'daughters' with cross-divisional operations exist on some country markets (e.g. SKF in India and South Africa). Separate units with regional such responsibilities also hide in the formal organization (Business Area East for Eastern Europe and SKF South East Asia in Singapore).

The different divisions exhibit different organizational patterns, in spite of SKF's seemingly uniform "business organization" into 27 global businesses (cf. Table 3.2). The small Tools division conforms best to a mother-daughter structure (but with Sheffield, so far[190], as the de facto 'mother'). In Specialty Bearings, type of technology is a better guide to subdivisions than is global product responsibility. The latter is most prevalent in Component Systems and to the extreme of the division resembling a holding company. In fact, interaction is more intense with Bearing Services than across the Component Systems businesses (seals being a case in point).

---

189 The view of a stable general strategy in SKF finds support in Collis (1991), but who emphasizes the significant shift in favor of Japanese and against US producers in the industry.

190 The organizational repercussions of the formation of CTT are still unclear.

The complicated, interlocking "new product organization" of Bearing Industries and Bearing Services (discussed at some length in Section 3.3 above, see also Section 3.4) in itself incorporates most organizational principles. Organizational units with ostensibly global responsibilities exist for functions (e.g. the service units, but also FSO and Global Bearing Trade), products, and customer segments. In particular, the "product line" organization typifies the daunting complexity involved, each line encompassing only parts of existing subsidiaries, and even sites, in several countries (cf. Table 3.3 above).

SKF's mixed organization reflects a need for adaptation to particular external conditions (e.g. government regulations or customer characteristics) and a wish for coordination of activities across several dimensions simultaneously. No orthodox, uniform organizational models can fulfil these requirements, which clearly also go beyond what any traditional (two-dimensional) matrix arrangement can accommodate.

We surmise that the chosen organizational complexity would have been an impossibility were it not for SKF's accomplished use of international data communications and computer systems. Put differently, SKF demonstrates how IS raises the threshold of organizational complexity that can be efficiently managed.

Much operational coordination is handled 'automatically' through IS (the bearing material flow systems being a case in point). A coordinating organizational unit that does not really 'exist' is Global Bearing Trade, which primarily is an internal electronic marketplace. Internal specialization of activities reflected in the organization is typically linked to a particular system (e.g. TMS and coordination of international payments by SKF International). IS is a prerequisite for maintaining traditional links between now organizationally separated activities (the separation of 'R' from 'D' has already been mentioned; a local example is the separation of sales from distribution in Germany, where the sales force has been spread wide and thin while distribution has been concentrated). The demands on the formal reporting in terms of speed, reliability and detail can only be met by using IS. Monitoring complex interdependencies depends on IS, as is amply illustrated by how the performance in the exceptionally complicated multi-unit, cross-divisional "new product organization" is checked by two straight-forward systems: PRODPERF for the production chain, and CUSTSERV for distribution and sales (cf. Sections 3.3 and 5.2.2.1).

The point we wish to make is that the exemplified important control and coordinating functions carried out through use of IS make SKF's organization viable at all. Of course, other control and coordination mechanisms are also employed, but they cannot substitute for the use of IS in SKF. Often other mechanisms are supported by IS use, such as project teams (e.g. for systems development, cf. Section 5.3.2), steering committees and informal personal networks (use of MEST, cf. Hagström, 1987b and Section 5.2.1.1), and training (distance-teaching by SKF College of Engineering, cf. Section 5.2.2.2). Indeed, it was the perceived need to improve control and coordination that originally motivated SKF's early build-up of its IS capabilities. Recall that GMS/TMS and the FSO-system were the first to be implemented. Recall also that these systems still tend to be the first ones used when a new unit is connected to Telenet (cf. the example of the Spanish subsidiary in Section 6.1.1 above).

Implicit in the observation that IS has accommodated greater organizational complexity in SKF, is the role of IS in also facilitating organizational change.

Reorganization has become more frequent (cf. Hagström, 1987b) but also less dramatic in SKF. IS plays a significant part in making organizational adjustments less cumbersome. For instance, during the latest divisional realignment of the bearing divisions in 1986, the old and the new reporting lines ran in parallel in GMS, smoothening the changeover (cf. Section 5.2.1.2). During the recent reorganization of the standard bearing business (cf. Section 3.3), the underlying information systems have remained intact, providing an element of stability both during the organizational upheaval and in relation to the resultant somewhat ambiguous responsibilities assigned to different entities. In addition, traditional conflicts between different parts of the organization may be mitigated by IS. A very concrete example is the concentration of finished-goods stocks, which is commonly resisted by the local sales organizations on the grounds that reductions in stocking points lead to deterioration of customer availability (cf. Section 5.3.1.). However, the concomitant more efficient stock management through intensive IS application meant that smaller total stocks could be combined with better availability, thus reducing resistance to the change.

Moreover, the continuous spawning of small, specialized units, often with global reach, is another example of organizational adjustment (as opposed to major reorganization). In some cases they have come to take over traditional SKF headquarter functions (e.g. FSO, ERC, SKF Capital, and, to some extent, global customer coordination as in Autech) in the process. The successive dispersion of headquarter functions has, however, primarily meant a transfer of responsibilities to the divisions, also when that head-office is located abroad (as Specialty Bearings, and now CTT as well). In the latter case IS has not been directly instrumental in making it happen but the improved control possibilities brought by IS make it all the more palatable to corporate management.

A consequence of SKF's complex and changing organization is that the archetypal subsidiary with responsibility for all country activities has all but disappeared. New, highly specialized, not uncommonly small subsidiaries, often with global reach, have come in their stead. Their raison-d'être can be traced to any of various dimensions (function, product, technology, customer-segment or geographical area). The resultant mix of very idiosyncratic subsidiaries is a good explanation for why classic, detailed organizational charts do not exist in SKF. It is even easier to understand when also considering that any given set-up, or even individual subsidiary, is highly prone to change. As we have seen above, this change of subsidiary roles has been closely tied to the use of IS in SKF.

6.2.3 Integration

Increasing internal specialization and more intimate linkages with external parties, notably customers, (cf. Section 6.2.1) are centrifugal forces, as manifest in the fine-meshed mixed organization (cf. Section 6.2.2), thus begging the question of internal cohesion. The identified present emphasis on IS integration (cf. Section 6.1.1) foreshadows a discussion on the integrative role of IS.

But first, stressing information systems integration in SKF in practice mainly means giving high priority to two things:

first,	the development and internal diffusion of common systems; and,
second,	to the improvement of the communications reach through extending Telenet and the use of standard systems interfaces, in both cases internally as well as externally (cf. Section 5.3.2).

These priorities reflect intentional integration; of systems and of SKF activities. But, we need to widen the perspective to explicitly also take account of more unintended or, at least, unarticulated integrative effects of IS usage, as observed in SKF[191].

Many of the examples of IS supporting organizational change (cf. Section 6.2.2) are a function of using IS as an administrative tool but without really considering its integrative role as such. The same can be said about the implicit policy regarding the varying propensity to connect different organizational units (cf. Section 6.1.2). In the present context we can take the latter argument one step further: we can deduce (see also Section 4.2.2.2) that SKF uses IS as one significant means of integrating new acquisitions but, again, without perceiving it as such.

If SKF does not appear to fully recognize the importance of the integrating role of IS, subsidiaries do. A clear indication of that is the interest expressed especially by peripheral units to be connected, or to have connections upgraded, to the SKF data communications network (e.g. as in the case of the Brazilian subsidiaries, cf. Section 4.3.5). A particularly pertinent example is when a subsidiary view has it that the greatest advantage of being included in GMS, a powerful headquarters instrument of control, is that it provides the subsidiary (sic!) with much improved possibilities "to keep an eye on what goes on in Gothenburg" (cf. Section 5.2.1.2).

---

[191] A more extensive, and general, argument on spontaneous internal use of IS is found in Hagström (1991) and in the main text.

The unintended integrative effects of IS exemplified above thus spring from two different ways of using IS. In the first case, viz. applying IS as a tool, originally conceived uses have unintended flow-on integrative effects. In the second case, integration stems more from the enabling characteristic of IS, from just having a well-developed international data communications network with wide access to a range of common systems. This infrastructural aspect of IS is further abetted in SKF by the relative simplicity of SKF's common systems and by the concomitant high degree of imposed standardization of communications and systems interfaces.

The IS infrastructure opens for unintended uses, which are driven by local users (rather than pushed from central management). Local 'pull' has become successively more important as regards the integrating role of IS in SKF.

Admittedly, many technical systems and databases (cf. Section 5.2.2.2) 'invite' demand by remote access. So far, we have stressed their function for upgrading local capabilities but there is more to it in terms of fostering integration.

First, this upgrading need not take the designated route, with the user instead seeking out the best source. For instance, Avio de facto maintains a closer computer-mediated liaison with ERC on technical matters than with MRC, the organizationally determined counterpart (cf. Section 5.2.2.2). Second, there is a significant flow-on effect of standardization that goes beyond products or calculation techniques to include approaches to problem-solving and practical 'how-to-do' knowledge. The Avio relationship above was very important for adjusting the local manufacturing techniques and improving tooling. Third, demand-driven upgrading of capabilities through remote access also involves another kind of internal diffusion of 'best-practice' via internal marketing of skills. Schweinfurt has found a larger internal market for its technical capabilities through queries and requests emanating from remote users of its technical applications. In addition to diffusion, 'best-practice' may be advanced further in the process.

Even more spectacular examples of spontaneous, integrative use of the IS infrastructure are the emergence of internal electronic markets and the informal exchange of reporting information among subsidiaries. So far, the electronic trading of surplus stocks of standard bearings (cf. Section 5.2.1.1) is the only fully-fledged such market in SKF but it has stimulated followers, not least since divisional management(s) decided to institutionalize the naturally unfolding phenomenon. In the case of the major European Bearing Industries subsidiaries transmitting their reports not only up the line to headquarters but also 'across lines' to their peers (cf. Section 5.2.1.2), the activity is tolerated, rather than encouraged, by central management. The subsidiaries in question gain access to information formally denied them by the corporate access rules and they can more independently adjust their activities to changing internal conditions.

The last few examples force us to qualify the integrative role of IS. 'Integration' of activities here takes place at 'lower' levels in the organization and tends to weaken the higher level prerogative of guidance. Somewhat paradoxically, the function of IS as permitting central control and coordination of an increasingly fragmented organization motivate establishing an elaborate IS infrastructure, which, in turn, unleashes more independent coordination among lower level units. Given information flows can be channeled in new directions and significant new flows can appear, also encompassing external parties.

To sum up, it appears as if SKF, on the one hand, underestimates many integrative effects of the intended uses of IS and, on the other, is largely unaware of the different type of integration emanating from unintended use of IS. The latter, more organic, integration involve coordination of activities between internal units, and with external parties, not necessarily commensurate with head-office wishes.

However, a possible lack of insight or of articulation need not imply a frustrated wish to counteract these tendencies. On the contrary, 'organic coordination' is often strikingly effective, arising as it does out of a real need, previously not catered for. At least three circumstances speak in favor of such an interpretation. Obviously, the symptoms of a more automatic adjustment among subsidiaries and with external parties are tolerated (even if the mechanisms are not recognized). Also, the greatly improved possibilities to monitor complex and dispersed activities brought by accomplished IS use constitute an 'early warning system' were things to get out of hand. Lastly, central management has other means at their disposal for securing internal cohesion, notably informal means of coordination and control[192].

6.3 Re-view

Notwithstanding the present chapter already suffering from some overlap, a couple of issues have fallen by the wayside. In the last main section we wish to pick up some of these loose ends.

First, we will consider if IS is not just a red herring. Following Yin (1981 and 1984), the most plausible interpretations conflicting with our conclusions are discussed. Second, we return to our findings and attempt to identify some aspects of IS use in SKF that were <u>not</u> encountered, although one could have expected them to appear. At the very end, we extrapolate...

6.3.1 Alternative Interpretations

Three broad challenges to critical steps in our reasoning seem particularly patent.

Recall first SKF's very early, and thus costly, foray into proprietary data communications and the rationale for doing so. Is it not likely that the initial rationalization (GFSS) of production could have been achieved <u>without an elaborate international data communications network</u>? Perhaps that is true also of successive rounds of production

192 See Hagström (1990a and 1991) for extensions of these arguments.

specialization. After all, SKF's product offerings are relatively uncomplicated. There is neither any complex assembly of widely sourced components, nor are there any systems sales. At most, SKF supplies a collected mix of finished products, just-in-time to the customer.

The argument is true, initially, since GFSS clearly was operational before direct communications had been established. However, the FSO-system was implemented earlier, but unsupported by data communications. According to the above argument, the continued struggle by SKF to build an international data communications network would then simply have been overkill. But it was precisely the expensive experience of not having supporting communications that prompted the forced, pioneering efforts leading to the establishment of SKF Group Telenet (when STICS had failed). Moreover, if that decision were to be conceded as having been erroneous, successive heavy investments in IS (notably the FSO-related NMFC systems) must be termed sheer madness on the part of SKF. That does not stand to reason.

Second, it could well be argued that there simply is <u>no measurable effect of IS</u> in SKF.

True, we have only found weak support for such effects from circumstantial evidence (Section 5.3, e.g. inventory reductions). On the other hand, where hard data on the aggregate level have failed us, qualitative data (and isolated instances of micro-level quantitative data) have more than made up for any shortfall in the present study. Indeed, it is the requirement for corroborating evidence that motivates this study being so lengthy and detailed.

Actually, early, one-shot cost-reductions resulting from trimming the organization with the help of IS are quite readily calculated in each instance but these figures are not released by SKF. The evaluation of being able to do new things (e.g. customer service), or to more radically alter the way in which things are done (e.g. logistics), is more difficult. In addition, IS use has qualities of a firm-internal public good, and is thus inherently impracticable to appraise. What is the exact value of faster strategic response or of the quicker internal dissemination of a superior technical application? In fact, we also strongly suspect that these kinds of estimates of benefits simply are not available within SKF[193].

However, SKF's sustained commitment to IS development at least indicates the company's conviction of it giving a positive contribution to the bottom line. We have reviewed some different benefits accruing to SKF in the present chapter (especially in Sections 6.2.1 and 6.2.2) and even surmised that there are further, unrecognized benefits as well (cf. Section 6.2.3). Positive, dynamic learning effects may well become the most important as usage matures.

A third challenge is that building advanced IS capabilities in SKF perhaps is important in retrospect only. It could have been done by mistake or by default. Consequently, one could argue that IS is neither a strategic nor an organizational design issue, or that it has, at least, not been perceived as such.

Either conclusion is directly belied by the explicitly strategic part assigned to IS when GFSS was conceived, i.e. even before international data communications or the FSO-system existed. Subsequent decisions have confirmed the integral role of IS in implementing strategy and supporting organizational change in SKF. The resources devoted to IS over time and the continued central placement of the IS function lend further credence to the view that IS has remained a key corporate concern.

However, it should also be made clear that both as a tool and in its enabling capacity, IS has been found to be a necessary, but not sufficient, condition for successfully pursuing some strategies and for achieving some types of organizational change in SKF.

---

[193]) Very understandably, it seems as if the proportion of an IS investment that exceeds identifiable cost-savings and/or does not attract local (subsidiary) funding (cf. Section 5.3.2) is judged more on a strategic ad-hoc-basis in SKF.

6.3.2 IS Uses Not Realized

Much effort in the present study has been devoted to describing, and tracing the implications of, SKF's actual use of IS since its first applications to the present. Given the identified capabilities of SKF in this area, some uses seem to have been shunned all together or left less well exploited. We do not intend to redress the imbalance between actual and potential usage of IS in SKF, but rather only to itemize some additional uses of IS not encountered (and indicate underutilization), but which arguably would fit with SKF's pattern of IS usage. Despite SKF's premier position, there may be some room for improvement.

The brief entries below appear under headings drawn from the evolutionary sequence outlined in Section 6.1.1 above. There is no implied order of importance.

Rationalization and control of existing resources.

- System for career tracking combined with reporting information. With more detailed information on company or department performance incentives can be made more varied and manning improved. No computerized career tracking system is in use in SKF.

- On-line manuals which would allow continuous updating. At present, even the IS manual can only be had printed on loose sheets.

- On-line remote monitoring, e.g. of the performance of critical production equipment, for central or, for instance, LMT use[194].

[194] To illustrate, Toyota Motors monitors the body-assembly lines at the Kentucky plant in real-time from the head-office in Japan (Financial Times, September 10, 1990).

- Ad-hoc follow-up, e.g. specifically follow new products through manufacturing and sales. This would involve having a 'channel' open for such on-going developments.

- Corporate applications library to avoid duplication of effort in divisions. For instance, the Tools PC Product Database was developed independently of the existing CADalog. (The subsequent development of LinCad illustrates the benefits of cross-divisional application.)

- Internal 'advertisement' database for miscellaneous products and services. The point is to tap local capabilities more efficiently also for non-core activities. For instance, SKF UK produces particularly good advertising and other promotional materials and SKF Singapore has an exceptionally wide range of SKF Gifts; in both cases little is known about it in the organization.

Product enhancement and external connections.

- Systems for purchasing. The purchasing function could clearly be better synchronized (for developments under way see Section 3.3), particularly by implementing better supplier connections and by moving away from the high dependence on very local suppliers. It should also be fairly simple to organize internal electronic markets for surplus input goods.

- More links to competitors and external service providers in order to possibly externalize more activities. More buying in can range from traditional products (e.g. less critical components like balls, and even bearings from competitors - private label, making up for a shortage, supplementing own range etc.) to services (e.g. systems development, technical running of Telenet keeping only the strategic functions, and specific miscellaneous services, such as travel management, general information and scanning services).

- Better utilization of IS to improve exploitation of market and customer similarities. Customer databases are now local, making it difficult to identify small customer segments/profiles. Particular, locally developed, packages of products and services could perhaps be sold more widely.

- Improvement of IS-managed 'packaging' and sales coordination. The range of products-cum-services combinations could conceivably be enlarged, also involving more contributions from other divisions and outside suppliers. The Bearing Services' extensive sales organization could also probably sell more Component Systems and Tools products with better IS back-up, cutting across divisional lines. The attitude of SKF that there is very little synergy across businesses (cf. Section 3.2) betrays a lingering production orientation to the detriment of exploiting synergies on the customer side.

- Upgrading of customer connections and more common support for such links. The present 10 percent share of customer links that can handle file transfer would need to be raised in line with the above. Further, customer connections are perhaps too much of a local concern, limiting exploitation of economies of scale and resulting in little over-all knowledge about such connections (i.e. not knowing how many and exactly which they are).

- Improved links 'short-circuiting' the value-chain. For instance, a structured 'reporting system' from sales and service units to central research and development entities could promote more focussed research on what the customer needs (as opposed to what can be done)[195].

---

[195] von Hippel's (1976) conclusion that the interface with customers is perhaps the major source of innovation for a company suggests that improved feed-back from the field can be very beneficial.

Integration and spontaneous uses

- Support internal electronic markets also for equipment and services.

- 'Trouble-shooting' systems, for instance of a bulletin-board type. Particular problems encountered in one location can be billed for soliciting solutions from other units.

- System for informal exchange of information, e.g. a conference system with on-going 'conferences' for SCSS users, heat treatment questions, new product/service ideas for the automotive sector etc. External parties could also be admitted on a selective basis.

- Broad- and narrowcasting. A better electronic mail type of a system seems needed, as MEST is rather old-fashioned and primitive. A new or upgraded MEST could distribute information about recent developments (e.g. reporting an acquisition before employees get to read about it in the press), new product information (e.g. to selected engineers and distributors), policy announcements (general or targeted to specific employee subsets) and the like. The better user profiles are specified, the easier it becomes to tailor the information dissemination. This kind of 'casting' could be used very selectively, and only as a complement to other, more traditional media.

The reasons for the above uses not having materialized in SKF could be that they have been discarded on good grounds, lack of resources, or that they simply have been overlooked. Whatever the particular reasons, they clearly do not invalidate our discussion so far, they merely indicate that the existing potential of IS may be greater than SKF has had the opportunity to exploit. The exercise does, however, feed off the suspicion that SKF underestimates the comparatively favorable and receptive climate for IS use in the organization, especially in peripheral units.

6.3.3 The 'wired' SKF

Most authors passing judgement on SKF 'post-GFSS' tend to stress the highly integrated structure and the relatively strong centralization of decision-making. Poole (1976) sees SKF as a strong, centralized federation of subsidiaries, a view indirectly echoed later by Wolf (1985). Leksell (1981) points to the less common combination of a rather high degree of formalization and a pattern of high communication intensity (in general terms), giving SKF a high score of integration of activities when compared with other Swedish MNCs. Antonelli (1981) is the only writer to specifically address the impact of international data communications. He concludes that SKF has undergone a dramatic centralization of decision-making and loss of subsidiary autonomy but his observations are limited to the vantage point of SKF's main Italian subsidiary (the present Bearing Industries and Bearing Services subsidiaries combined).

One exceptional view (Porter, 1990:57), en passant, finds SKF having quite autonomous subsidiaries. Another contemporary opinion is that of Collis (1991), who, after a detailed study of the bearings industry, argues for SKF having become a globally managed company with production on a three-region basis but with global coordination across other functions. The change is judged to have come with the ultimate abandonment of country management as manifest in the introduction of the customer-oriented divisions in 1987.

We have found a surprisingly complex and flexible SKF, not readily reducible to any simple category. Surprising, since a 'simple' company like SKF 'should not' need to be so messy according to the received wisdom. Our contention is also that SKF would not be quite so messy either, were it not for its sophisticated information systems infrastructure. As we leave the more well-charted waters of history and explicit policy, the hall-mark characteristics of complexity and flexibility can be expected to become even more pronounced.

The improved capacity for temporal adjustment of activities through IS use makes for a more foot-loose SKF in more senses than one. Very dynamic shifting of activities between locations in response to changing conditions is already noticeable, particularly regarding activities most closely tied to IS use (broadly administrative activities and financial management). Quick moves can be effectuated by 'unplugging' and then 'replugging' into the network at a new location (e.g as in the cases of SKF International, cf. Section 5.2.1.3, and the Latin American warehouse, cf. Section 4.3.4). It can be done by more easily adjusting the scope of operations at a particular location (e.g. expansion/contraction of overlapping production, cf. Spain's role in Section 4.3.3). Upgrading of local capabilities and overcoming local resource bottle-necks (cf. the quick upgrading of the Spanish IS function by remote support, Section 4.3.3, and the surmounting of local restrictions on IS activities in Brazil, Section 4.3.5) are other aspects of a more flexible response to changing external conditions. Adjusting by dynamically externalizing and internalizing activities is also likely to become more prevalent (some indication of this already happening can be had from the fluid division of labor in SKF's customer connections).

The supple MNC requires various and shifting roles for different organizational units. Roles are both assigned and assumed; responsibilities are both diffused and concentrated (cf. Sections 6.2.2 and 6.2.3). The loci of decision-making, also on strategic issues, become less readily identifiable. The set of organizational units making up the MNC at any given time will tend to comprise a growing range of types and increasingly idiosyncratic individual units.

A very good illustration of the multi-faceted trend towards increased complexity is the fate of the traditional subsidiary (an idealized picture of which is given in Figure 3.7 above) in SKF. Broken up, stripped of some activities transferred to specialist units, and having gained some responsibilities but which reside in parts of the subsidiary, the legal subsidiary becomes a platform, or home, for a changing set of activities subject to different coordination mechanisms, which also extend outside the legal subsidiary.

The capability for readaptation of the organization, reconfiguration of activities, in response to changing competitive conditions is the decisive factor for long-term corporate survival. To do so continuously (rather than in costly, discrete leaps) is destined to become a source, not unlikely the source of competitive advantage. In turn, this capability is inexorably linked to 'mature' exploitation of IS.

We have seen how SKF is moving down this route, pursuing a more organic adjustment of its activities; an unthinkable proposition without a sophisticated IS infrastructure. The resultant complexity leaves less room for direct, 'hands-on' management of activities. More 'spontaneous' coordination, often at lower levels in the organization, can more easily be 'tolerated' by corporate (and divisional) management because of the increased control possibilities brought by IS. The threat of accelerating disintegration is real, though, and there is a concomitant need for compensating, greater reliance on informal means of coordination. IS can play a supportive role also in this respect (cf. Section 6.3.2 above).

A final twist is that IS in itself is a carrier of an integrating culture as evidenced by the experience in the US and Spain, where connection in the former case softened the local, mechanically hierarchical approach, and in the latter brought 'order' (cf. Sections 4.3.4 and 4.3.3 respectively).

7. REFERENCES

The sources consulted have been divided into four categories in order to give a more comprehensive overview of the material. The secondary references are split into bibliographic sources, newspaper and magazine articles, and publications issued by SKF companies. Most of the interviews conducted specifically for this study are listed last. (The numerous telephone conversations and correspondence are not recorded. Many of those contacts concern people not listed as interviewees.) Only the sources directly providing material for the present study are referenced below.

7.1 Bibliography

Adrianson, L. and Söderström, R. (1983/1985), "Meddelanden att läsa: Datorbaserade textkommunikationssystem på sex svenska företag" ["Messages for Reading: Computer-Based Text Communication Systems in Six Swedish Firms"], Rapport nr. 4, **Teldok**, Stockholm.

Åhlander, K. (1990), **Aspects of Modern Treasury Management: Organization and External Financial Activities in Swedish MNCs**. Stockholm: Institute of International Business, Stockholm School of Economics.

Allen, B. (1987), "Make Information Services Pay Its Way", **Harvard Business Review**, Vol. 65, No. 1, pp. 57-63.

Antonelli, C. (1981), "Transborder Data Flows and International Business - A Pilot Study", **Directorate for Science, Technology and Industry**, Working Party on Information, Computer and Communications Policy, Expert Group on Transborder Data Flows, DSTI/ICCP/81.16. Paris: OECD.

Argyris, C. and Schön, D. A. (1978), **Organization Learning**. Reading, Mass.: Addison-Wesley.

Aronson, J. D. and Cowhey, P. F. (1988), **When Countries Talk: International Trade in Telecommunications Services**. Cambridge, Mass.: Ballinger Publishing Company.

Bar, F. and Borrus, M. with Coriat, B. (1989), "Information Networks and Competitive Advantages: The Issues for Government Policy and Corporate Strategy: Final Report" in OECD-BRIE, "Information Networks and Business Strategies: An OECD-BRIE Project on Competitiveness and Telecommunications Policy", BRIE Working Paper 38, **Berkeley Roundtable on the International Economy**, University of California, Berkeley, pp. 1-47.

Beckholmen, K. et al. (1982), **Vi på kulan: SKFs verkstadsklubb 1907-82** ["Us on the Ball: The Blue-Collar Trade Union at SKF 1907-82"]. Göteborg: SKFs verkstadsklubb.

Collis, D. J. (1991), "A Resource-Based Analysis of Global Competition: The Case of the Bearings Industry", **Strategic Management Journal**, Vol. 12, Special Issue, pp. 49-68.

Cleevely, D. and Cawdell, R. (1986), "A Telecommunications Taxonomy", **Telecommunications Policy**, Vol. 10, No. 2, pp. 107-119.

Danielsson, K. and Synnerstad, K. (1990), "Swedes, Locals or Third-Country Nationals?" (final undergraduate student essay in International Business), **Stockholm School of Economics**, Stockholm (mimeo, January 16).

Doll, D. R. (1978), **Data Communications: Facilities, Networks, and Systems Design**. New York, N. Y.: John Wiley & Sons.

Duncan, R. B. (1979), "Qualitative Reasearch Methods in Strategic Management" in Schendel, D. E. and Hofer, C. W., eds., **Strategic Management**. Boston, Mass.: Little, Brown and Company.

Earl, M. J. (1988), "IT and Strategic Advantage: A Framework of Frameworks" in Earl, M. J., ed., **Information Management: The Strategic Dimension**. Oxford: Clarendon Press, pp. 33-53.

Eaton, J. and Smithers, J. (1982), **This Is It**. Oxford: Philip Allan Publishers.

Fredriksson, O. (1988), "BASCET Infolink AB", **Stockholm School of Economics**, Stockholm (mimeo, December 16).

Fredriksson, O. (1990), "Information Technology and Product Delivery: One Swedish Example of EDI" in Holmlöv, P. G., ed., **Telecommunications Use and Users - Economic and Behavioral Aspects**. Stockholm: Stockholm School of Economics and Teldok, pp. 103-115.

Fredriksson, O., Holmlöv, P. G. and Julander, C.-R. (1987), "Distribution av varor och tjänster i informationssamhället" ["Distribution of Goods and Services in the Information Society"], MA Rapport, **Economic Research Institute**, Stockholm School of Economics, Stockholm.

Granstrand O. and Fernlund, I. (1978), "Coordination of Multinational R&D: A Swedish Case Study", **R&D Management**, Vol. 9, No. 1, pp. 1-7.

Hägg, I. and Hedlund, G. (1979), "'Case Studies' in Accounting Research", **Accounting, Organizations and Society**, Vol. 4, No. 1/2, pp. 135-143.

Hagström, P. (1987a), "New Information Systems and the Changing Structure of MNCs", paper presented at the conference on "Management of the MNC" at the **European Institute for Advanced Studies in Management** in Brussels, June 9-10 (mimeo).

Hagström, P. (1987b), "Linking New Information Systems to Corporate Strategy and Structure: The SKF Experience", Research Paper 87/11, **Institute of International Business**, Stockholm School of Economics, Stockholm.

Hagström, P. (1988), "New Information Systems in MNCs: Outline of a Research Project", Research Paper 88/3, **Institute of International Business**, Stockholm School of Economics, Stockholm.

Hagström, P. (1989), "The Rôle of International Data Communications in the Structure of Multinational Corporations: A Conceptual Framework", Information Technology & Management Working Paper 1989:14, **Institute for Management of Innovation and Technology**, Gothenburg.

Hagström, P. (1990a), "New Information Systems and the Changing Structure of MNCs" in Bartlett, C. A., Doz, Y. and Hedlund, G., eds., **Managing the Global Firm**. London: Routledge, pp. 164-185.

Hagström, P. (1990b), "Unshackling Corporate Geography", **Geografiska Annaler**, Series B, Human Geography, Vol. 72 B, No. 1, pp. 3-12 [Reprinted here as Appendix 2].

Hagström, P. (1991), "Inside the 'Wired' MNC" in Antonelli, C., ed., **The Economics of Information Networks**. Amsterdam: North Holland/Elsevier Science Publishers, (provisionally) pp. 305-325.

Håkanson, L. and Zander, U. (1986), **Managing International Research & Development**. Stockholm: Sveriges Mekanförbund.

Hammarkvist, K.-O. (1986), "Distribution i förändring" ["Changing Distribution"], **Fonden för Handels- och Distributionsforskning vid EFI**, Stockholm School of Economics, Stockholm.

Hippel, E. von (1976), "The Dominant Role of Users in the Scientific Instrument Innovation Process", **Research Policy**, Vol. 5, No. 3, pp. 212-239.

Hobday, M. (1990), **Telecommunications in the Developing Countries: The Challenge from Brazil**. London: Routledge.

International Organization for Standardization (1986), "Open Systems Interconnection", **Advance Technology Alert System (ATAS) Bulletin**, Centre for Science and Technology for Development, United Nations Secretariat, New York, Issue 3, June, pp. 33-34.

Keen, P. G. W. (1986), **Competing in Time: Using Telecommunications for Competitive Advantage**. Cambridge, Mass.: Ballinger Publishing Company.

Leksell, L. (1981), **Headquarter-Subsidiary Relationships in Multinational Corporations**. Stockholm: Institute of International Business and the Economic Research Institute, Stockholm School of Economics.

Lindskog, F. (1976), **Att leda ett internationellt företag** ["Managing an International Corporation"]. Avesta: Askild & Kärnekull.

Lundgren, K. (1990),"Vertical Integration, Transaction Costs and 'Learning by Using'" in Aoki, M., Gustafsson, B. and Williamson, O. E., eds., **The Firm as a Nexus of Treaties**. London: Sage Publications, pp. 112-132.

McFarlan, F. W., ed. (1984a), **The Information Systems Research Challenge**. Boston, Mass.: Harvard Business School Press.

McFarlan, F. W. (1984b), "Information Technology Changes the Way You Compete", **Harvard Business Review**, Vol. 62, No. 3, pp. 98-103.

McFarlan, F. W. and McKenney, J. L. (1983), **Corporate Information Systems Management: The Issues Facing Senior Executives**. Homewood, Ill.: Richard D. Irwin.

Martin, J. (1981), **Computer Networks and Distributed Processing**. Englewood Cliffs, N. J.: Prentice-Hall.

OECD (1980), **Policy Implications of Data Network Developments in the OECD Area** (No. 3 in the "Information, Computer and Communications Policy" Series). Paris: OECD.

OECD (1983a),"Preliminary Interpretations of a OECD/BIAC Survey", **Directorate for Science, Technology and Industry**, Committee for Information, Computer and Communications Policy, DSTI/ICCP/83.19, Paris.

OECD (1983b),"Transborder Data Flows in International Enterprises: Based on Results of a Joint BIAC/OECD Survey and Interviews with Firms" (Note by the Secretariat), **Directorate for Science,**

Technology and Industry, Committee for Information, Computer and Communications Policy, DSTI/ICCP/83.23, Paris.

OECD (1987), **Trends of Change in Telecommunications Policy** (No. 13 in the "Information, Computer and Communications Policy" Series). Paris: OECD.

OECD-BRIE (1989), "Information Networks and Business Strategies: An OECD-BRIE Project on Competitiveness and Telecommunications Policy", BRIE Working Paper 38, **Berkeley Roundtable on the International Economy**, University of California, Berkeley (mimeo, 573pp.).

Poole, J. (1976), "SKF Reintegrates Internationally", **Multinational Business**, No. 4, pp. 1-7.

Porter, M. E. (1990), **The Competitive Advantage of Nations**. New York, N.Y.: The Free Press.

Porter, M. E. and Millar, V. E. (1985), "How Information Gives You Competitive Advantage", **Harvard Business Review**, Vol. 63, No. 4, pp. 149-160.

Pousette, T. (1983), "Datakommunikation i företag" ["Data Communications in Firms"], Rapport nr. 9, **Teldok**, Stockholm, and Forskningsrapport nr. 24, **Industriens Utredningsinstitut**, Stockholm.

RDF (1984), "Datakommunikation i 80-talets centrum" ["Data Communications in Focus in the '80s"], Rapport nr. 19, **Riksdataförbundet**, Stockholm.

Rockart, J. F. and Scott Morton, M. F. (1984), "Implications of Changes in Information Technology for Corporate Strategy", **Interfaces**, Vol. 14, No. 1, pp. 84-95.

Seitz, N. B. (1980), "Data Communication and Data Processing: A Basis for Definition", **Telecommunications Policy**, Vol. 4, No. 1, pp. 49-62.

Sigvardsson, B. (1985), "The Marketing and Sales Environment of the 1990s", MTC 26, **Marketing Techniques Center**, Stockholm School of Economics, Stockholm.

Sigvardsson, B. (1986), "Konkurrensfördelar med informationsteknologi" ["Competitive Advantage with Information Technology"], presentation given at Business Videotex Service Seminar, **IBM**, Kista, Stockholm, September 18.

Steckzén, B. (1957a), **Hofors Bruks historia** ["The History of the Hofors Mill"]. Göteborg: SKF.

Steckzén, B. (1957b), **Svenska Kullagerfabriken: En svensk exportindustris historia 1907-1957** ["SKF: The History of a Swedish Export Industry (Firm)"]. Göteborg: SKF.

Tanenbaum, A. S. (1989), **Computer Networks**. Englewood Cliffs, N. J.: Prentice-Hall International.

Televerket (1989), **Idébok Affärsutveckling med Tele- och Datakommunikation** ["Book of Ideas: Developing Your Business with Telecommunications and Data Communications"]. Farsta: Televerket, Marknadsavdelningen.

Thorngren, B. (1990), "The Swedish Road to Liberalization", **Telecommunications Policy**, Vol. 14, No. 2, pp. 94-98.

Trauth, E. M. (1986), "An Integrative Approach to Information Policy Research", **Telecommunications Policy**, Vol. 10, No. 1, pp. 41-50.

United Nations (1982), "Transnational Corporations and Transborder Data Flows: A Technical Paper", **United Nations Centre on Transnational Corporations**, ST/CTC/23, New York.

United Nations (1983), "Transborder Data Flows and Brazil: Brazilian Case Study", **United Nations Centre on Transnational Corporations**, ST/CTC, New York.

United Nations (1988), "Transnational Corporations in World Development", **United Nations Centre on Transnational Corporations**, ST/CTC/89, New York.

Ungerer, H. with Costello, N. P. (1988), "Telecommunications in Europe", **European Perspectives Series**, Commission of the European Communities, Brussels/Luxemburg.

Wennersten, B. G. and Holmberg, S. (1987), "Kontorens informationssystem: Verkligheten bakom visionerna i Europa, USA och Japan" ["Office Information Systems: The Reality behind the Visions in Europe, USA and Japan"], Rapport nr. 31, **Teldok**, Stockholm.

Wiseman, C. (1985), **Strategy and Computers: Information Systems as Competitive Weapons**. Homewood, Ill.: Dow Jones-Irwin.

Wolf, B. M. (1985), "The Bearing Industry: Rationalization in Europe" in Casson, M., ed., **Multinationals and World Trade**. London: Allen & Unwin, pp. 175-195.

Yin, R. K. (1981), "The Case Study Crisis: Some Answers", **Administrative Science Quarterly**, Vol. 28, No. 1, pp. 58-65.

Yin, R. K. (1984), **Case Study Research: Design and Methods**. Beverly Hills, Calif.: Sage Publications.

7.2 Newspaper/Magazine Articles

Affärsutveckling med tele- och datakommunikation (en tidning producerad av Televerket i samverkan med Näringslivets Telekommité), Televerkets Marknadsavdelning, 1989.

Affärsvärlden, No. 20, 1978, No. 51/52, 1980, January 8, January 28, April 15, August 19, and November 4, 1987, March 2, May 26, June 2, August 10, August 24, September 7, November 2, December 7, and December 14, 1988, March 8, August 16, November 1, 1989, March 28, June 7, August 15, and September 12, 1990.

Business Week, January 27, August 4, 1986, and May 14, 1990.

Dagens Industri, February 17, 1977, March 15, August 31, September 1, December 17, December 22, 1988, March 29, April 12, June 7, August 14, September 14, 1989, January 19, February 22, February 28, April 10, July 6, and September 19, 1990.

Dagens Nyheter, November 25, December 20, 1986, February 2, December 22, 1987, December 22, 1988, May 17, 1989, and March 22, 1990.

Datavärlden, No. 50, December 3, 1987.

Economist, August 19, 1989.

The Financial Times, August 3, December 7, 1987, May 15, September 18, 1989, January 18, January 26, February 14, August 10, August 17, September 10, and September 18, 1990.

Fortune, April 28, and August 4, 1986.

Göteborgs-Posten, December 27, December 29, and December 30, 1986, January 3, January 9, January 14, and January 17, 1987.

International Management, June, 1986.

Ledarskap, No. 4, April, 1990.

MekanNytt, No. 1/2, February, 1987, No. 4, May-June, 1988, and No. 2, March, 1989.

Specialpublikation 1985 - Ekonomistyrning, "På SKF sätter ekonomistyrningen kunden i centrum", Bratt Publishing, Spring, 1985, Stockholm.

Svenska Dagbladet, May 18, 1985, December 22, 1988, March 22, and September 19, 1990.

Svensk Export, No. 2, 1989.

Teknik i Tiden, Styrelsen för teknisk utveckling, No. 2, 1988.

Tele: Televerkets Tekniska Tidskrift, No. 1, No. 3, 1989, and No. 2, 1990.

TeleJournalen Executive, No. 2, May, and No. 3, September, 1990.

Upp&Ner, No. 3, May, 1985.

Veckans Affärer, November 14, 1985, October 2, and November 20, 1986, February 19, February 26, April 9, June 4, and November 5, 1987, June 2, November 3, December 8, 1988, March 16, May 11, and August 17, 1989.

7.3 Main SKF Publications

(and Annual Reports; publications issued in Gothenburg, Sweden, unless specified)

Algumas pessoas têm problemas com rolamentos ..., SKF do Brasil Ltda., 1988.

Annual Reports, 1965-1989.

Annual Reports on Form 20-F (Annual Reports to Section 13 or 15(d) of the Securities Exchange Act of 1934 for the Securities and Exchange Commission, Washington, D.C., USA), 1987 and 1988, dated June 6, 1988, April 13, 1989, and May 15, 1990, respectively.

[**Annual Report**, 1988, NSK, Tokyo, Japan.]

[**Annual Reports**, 1988-1989, Ovako Steel AB, Danderyd, Sweden.]

[**Annual Report**, 1989, Korsnäs AB, Gävle, Sweden.]

Bearing Bulletin (SKF Bearing Industries News Worldwide), February, April, June, August, October, December, 1988, April, July, August, October, December, 1989, February, April/May, June/July, and August/September 1990.

CADalog, Publication No. 3733 S, April, 1986.

Hur ett SKF kullager kommer till, Publication No. 3302 II S, April, 1988.

Innerringen (SKF Sverige), No. 5/6, 1988.

Kullagertidningen 232, March, 1988.

Mini-ringen (SKF Sverige), Nos. 29, 31, 34, and 35, 1988.

Mu - The World of SKF, Publication No. 3277 E, March, 1982.

Nice Bearing Products, SKF Industries Inc., April, 1982.

Norlander, G., **CADalog - Framtidens konstruktörsverktyg**, April, 1986.

Produtos nacionais, Catálogo BR 850, SKF do Brasil Ltda., January, 1987.

Science Friction (A Presentation of SKF Norden), Publication No. 3115 E, November, 1981.

Service Initiative (A journal with ideas from the world of Bearing Services), November, 1989.

SkärJournalen, SKF Tools AB, Halmstad, Spring, 1988.

SKF - A Company in Motion (SKF Industries and the Bearing Business), SKF Industries Inc., September, 1986.

SKF & Dormer Tools (Katalog 86), SKF Tools AB, Halmstad, 1986.

SKF Component Systems (A Blend of Dynamic Technologies and Companies), Publication No. 3853 E, February, 1988.

SKF Steel 1984, Publication No. CP 34S05.85, SKF Steel AB, Danderyd, Sweden, 1985.

SKF i Sverige, Publication No. 3883, September, 1988.

SKF Press Releases, 1986 - August, 1989.

The Story of SKF, Publication No. 3276 E, May, 1982.

The Story of SKF Industries (Innovation), SKF Industries Inc.

Teknologi för Imorgon, Publication No. 3322S, SKF Engineering & Research Centre B.V., Netherlands, September, 1983.

We are building a more profitable Bearing Industries, Bearing Industries, 1989.

The World of SKF, Publication No. 3909 E, October, 1988.

The World of SKF Bearing Services, April, July, October, 1989, and July/August, 1990.

Ytterringen (En tidning om SKF i Sverige och världen), No. 1, March, No. 2, June, No. 3, October, No. 4, December, 1989, No. 1, March, No. 2, June, and No. 3, October, 1990.

7.4 Interviews

The interviews listed below were conducted by the author, face-to-face with the interviewees (with two exceptions, see footnotes below). The duration of the interviews ranged from one to five hours, with most interviews taking two to three hours. The author's interview notes were later sent to the respondents (except for in a handful of cases), giving them the opportunity to comment on the material. About half of the distributed interview notes solicited replies, in some cases also from people not present at the interviews (commonly superiors). The interviews outside Sweden were semi-structured, and in Sweden adapted to the special function of the respondent. The interview guides used in the semi-structured interviews are found in Appendix 1. Where applicable, the same questions were asked in Sweden.

Interviewee (by country)	**Position**	**Company**	**Date**
Brazil			
Maurice Costin	Managing Director	SKF Ferramentas S.A.	Aug. 8, 1988
Jorge Farsky	Export Sales Manager	SKF Ferramentas S.A.	Aug. 8, 1988
Gilberto Ribeiro de Martins	Manager of Systems and Information	SKF do Brasil Ltda.	Nov. 4, 1988
Atílio Silvestre Neto	Manufacturing Director	SKF do Brasil Ltda.	Nov. 4, 1988
Evaldo José Pessoa de Albuquerque	Managing Director	Seeger Reno Indústria e Comercio Ltda.	Nov. 3, 1988
Helmut Winder	Industrial Engineering Manager	SKF do Brasil Ltda.	Nov. 4, 1988
Italy			
Rossano Abrugiatti	Manager, Product Development & Design	SKF Avio	Apr. 18, 1989
Franco Avidano	Deputy Director, Information Systems	SKF Industrie S.p.A.	Apr. 18, 1989
Agostino Davoli	Manager, Quality & Laboratory	SKF Precision Bearings	Apr. 18, 1989
Mario Giacone-Griva	Information Systems Director	SKF Industrie S.p.A.	Apr. 18, 1989
Claudio Paliotti	Manager, Office & Technical Systems	SKF Industrie S.p.A.	Apr. 18, 1989
Alfredo Poletti	Manufacturing Deputy Manager	SKF Industrie S.p.A.	Apr. 18, 1989
Geofredo Russo	Quality Assurance Manager	SKF Precision Bearings	Apr. 18, 1989
Netherlands			
Henning Wittmeyer*	Head	SKF Engineering & Research Centre B.V.	Oct. 10, 1990
Spain			
Juan Arregui	Information Systems Manager	SKF Española S.A.	Apr. 20, 1989
Nils Miholic	Managing Director	SKF Española S.A.	Apr. 20, 1989
Sweden			
Toni Bergman	Manager of Communication Control	SKF Dataservice AB	Dec. 7, 1988
Hans-Georg Fornbäck	Group Treasurer and Managing Director	AB SKF and SKF International AB	Dec. 7, 1988
Ola Jönsson	Manager, Group Communication Coordination	AB SKF	Dec. 7, 1988
Håkan Landahl	Director, Group Information Systems and Managing Director	AB SKF and SKF Dataservice AB	Dec. 4, 1986 Nov. 29, 1988
Mauritz Sahlin**	Group Chief Executive	AB SKF	Oct. 30, 1989 Oct. 8, 1990
Claes Sturegård	Controller, Information Systems, Bearing Division	AB SKF	May 6, 1986
Göran Wannerskog	Company Controller	SKF Bearing Industries AB	Dec. 7, 1988 Dec. 8, 1988

Cont'd...

...cont'd

Interviewee (by country)	**Position**	**Company**	**Date**
UK			
Ulf Jemsby	Managing Director	SKF & Dormer Tools Ltd.	Feb. 7, 1989
Brian Seal	Systems Development Manager	SKF (U.K.) Ltd.	Feb. 8, 1989
John F. Vear	Director of Logistics	SKF & Dormer Tools Ltd.	Feb. 7, 1989
Bob Wiles	Operations Manager	SKF (U.K.) Ltd.	Feb. 8, 1989
USA			
C.J. Farrell	Director, Information Resources	SKF USA Inc.	Nov. 1, 1988
John W. Forrest	Manager of Engineering	Nice Specialty Bearings	Oct. 31, 1988
Peter S. Given	Vice President, Product Engineering & Quality	SKF Bearing Industries Co.	Nov. 1, 1988
Joseph G. Mastroianni	Group Leader, Data Communications	SKF USA Inc.	Nov. 1, 1988
Eugene T. Salter	Vice President and General Manager	Nice Specialty Bearings	Oct. 31, 1988
James A. Sortino	Applications Analyst	Nice Specialty Bearings	Oct. 31, 1988
David S. Young	Director, Manufacturing Engineering	SKF Bearing Industries Co.	Nov. 1, 1988
West Germany			
Harald Betsch***	Managing Director	SKF Linearsysteme GmbH.	Dec. 8, 1988
Lothar Erhardt	Information Systems Director	SKF GmbH.	Apr. 21, 1989
Herman Glöckner***	Head of Development and Quality	SKF Linearsysteme GmbH.	Dec. 8, 1988
Gudrun Otte	IS Manager	SKF Handel GmbH.	Apr. 21, 1989
Rudolf Schneider	Leiter Kommunikationsservice	SKF GmbH.	Apr. 21, 1989

* Interviewed by Robert Nobel and Udo Zander in the course of another research project at the Institute of International Business.

** Presentations (with opportunities for questions) given at the Stockholm School of Economics as a guest speaker in the International Business Course. On the latter occasion, this was complemented by a prior half-an-hour private conversation.

*** Interviewed by Robert Nobel and Udo Zander. Questions from the "SKF Interview Guide Outline" (see Appendix 1) were asked and the guideline submitted to the respondents.

APPENDIX 1:

INTERVIEW GUIDES

Two interview guides were used (cf. Section 7.4 above). The first, shorter list of questions ("SKF Interview Guide Outline") were sent to the interviewees prior to the interview. The second guide ("SKF Interview Guide") was brought by the author to the interview, and the relevant questions from that were posed.

Both guides are reproduced below.

SKF Interview Guide Outline
(International Data Communications)

A. Information infrastructure and systems

1. What types of links are used and how are they configured? With whom is it possible to communicate (both internally and externally; both nationally and internationally)?
2. Which specific systems are accessed and since when? Which systems are purely local?
3. What are their precise functions and how have those evolved over time?
4. What is the role of standards, manuals etc. in general and to what extent is this manifest in the systems you use?
5. Which activities are supported by international data communications (e.g. formal reporting and control, R&D)?
6. How have they changed in terms of
   - type and amount of information transmitted,
   - time allowed for information collection,
   - frequency of information transmission,
   - where sent to,
   - and type and speed of feedback?

B. Usage of international data communications

1. Do you have any quantitative measure of your company's international data communications usage? Costs?
2. With which units does your company communicate via international data communications and how intensively (frequently)?
3. How has this changed over time? Why, in your opinion?
4. Who initiated these changes?
5. When, how and by whom was it decided?
6. Which effects were intended and unintended respectively (incl. those which never materialized)?
7. Are any further changes imminent?

C. General assessment

1. Do you see any tendencies toward relocation of activities (geographically and organizationally) in the company that can be tied to international data communications?
2. In your view, what has been the major impact of international data communications on your work, on that of your unit, and on the company as a whole?

SKF Interview Guide

(General, to be used as a starting point for all interviews.)

I. Background

> Respondent
> Time
> Place
> Name of organizational unit
> Organizational location (formal)
> Performance measures
> Changes in the above during the last 20 years (with emphasis on the last five)

II. Questions

The core of the Interview Guide is a set of open-ended questions relating to different activities in the corporation. The respondent is supposed to provide information for the activities performed by his or her organizational unit. Unless specified, change over time refers to from when the unit was connected to international data communications up to the present.

A. General activities

1. Which are your main activities?
2. Who are your main competitors (also internally)?
3. Which are your main inputs and suppliers?
4. Which are your main outputs and customers? Have outputs been upgraded?
5. Has the set of activities performed changed during the last two decades?
   - additions, taken over from where or new?
   - removed activities, where to internally or externalized?
   - changes in content?
   - rationalizations (esp. new scale economies)?
6. How has the formal organization of your unit changed over the same time period?
7. What is the total number of employees and how has this changed?
8. What is the occupational distribution of your employees and how has it changed?

B. International data communications

1. Which activities are supported by international data communications?
2. With whom do you communicate via international data communications and how intensively (frequently)?
3. How has this changed over time? Why, in your opinion?
4. Who initiated these changes?
5. When, how and by whom was it decided?
6. Which effects were intended and unintended respectively (incl. those which never materialized)?
7. Are any further changes imminent?

C. Information infrastructure

1. Which specific systems are accessed?
2. What are their precise functions and how have those evolved over time?
3. How are the links configured? With whom is it possible to communicate?
4. Which external links do you maintain
   - suppliers (incl. suppliers of information only),
   - customers,
   - and competitors/"cooperators"?
5. How have these external links changed over time?

D. Reporting and control

1. What is the role of standards, manuals and to what extent is this manifest in the systems you use?
2. To whom do you report for each of the activities performed?
3. How is the formal reporting and control systems broadly organized and to what extent are they supported by international data communications?
4. How have they changed in terms of
   - type and amount of information transmitted,
   - time allowed for information collection,
   - frequency of information transmission,
   - where sent to,
   - and type and speed of feedback?

E. Organization

1. Which formal organizational changes have affected your activities especially?
2. Are you familiar with any organizational unit having been closed or merged? Did you maintain direct contact with that unit?
3. Do you know of any organizational units set up for a new, limited purpose. Are you in contact with that unit?
4. What is the evolution of temporary temporary organizational groupings, like task forces and committes, in the company, and which kind do you take part in?

F. Informal information

1. Irregular queries from elsewhere (esp. within the company), how have they changed?
2. Information disemination from elsewhere (esp. within the company), how has that changed?
3. Information disemination from you to internal units and external parties, how has that changed?
4. Your resort to irregular information gathering, how has that changed?

III. Concluding, General Evaluation

Has central control of activities increased or decreased? How? Why?
Has corporate coordination of actvities increased or decreased? How? Why?
How have your influence on and degree of autonomy in relation to company goals and policy changed?
Has the information exchange become more or less formalized? How? Why?
Do you see any tendencies toward relocation of activities (geographically and organizationally) in the company that can be tied to international data communications?
In your view, what has been the major impact of international data communications on your work, on that of your unit, and on the company as a whole?
What has been the attitude to these changes in your unit and in the company as a whole?

APPENDIX 2:

SUPPLEMENTARY FIGURES

The following seven diagrams supplement the discussion in Section 3. They are referred to in the text, but are presented here to avoid over-loading of the main text. Brief technical notes are provided in conjunction with each diagram where warranted, but are of a cumulative nature in that methodological information already given, is not repeated for each new figure.

Figure A.1

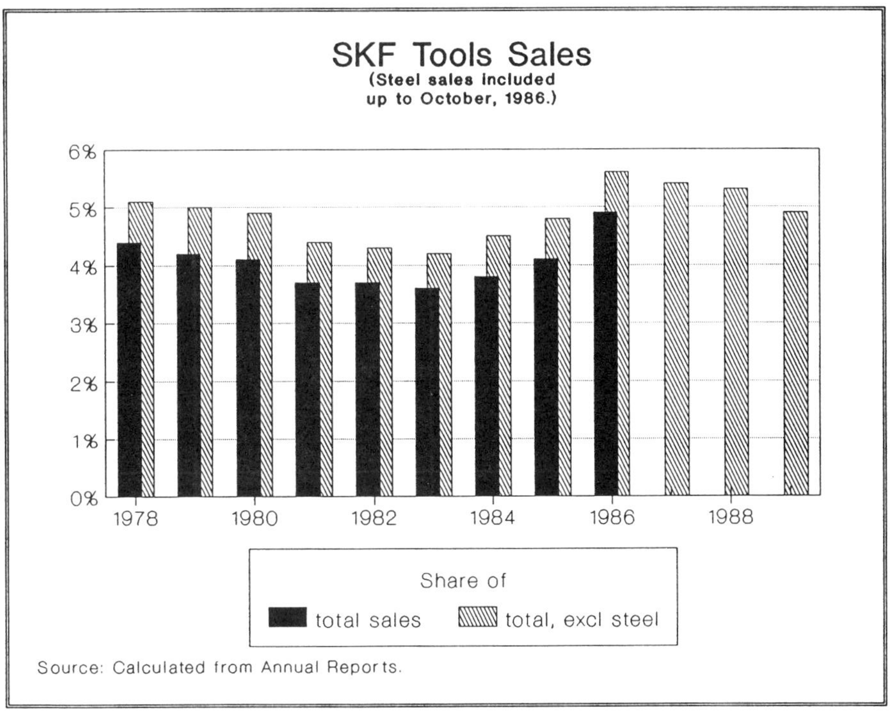

The share of SKF Group sales displayed above refers to gross sales, since no break-down of internal deliveries is available from SKF. Internal deliveries only very marginally influence the distribution of sales per product area.

> Internal deliveries were historically dominated by steel sales, have been readjusted substantially in response to organizational changes (and accounting procedures for inter-divisional settlements), and are relatively insignificant. Most dramatically, internal deliveries were officially reported to have dropped from 4.4 percent to 1.9 percent of gross sales (excl. steel) between 1984 and 1985 but without really affecting the distribution by major product group. For reference, internal deliveries stood at 2.1 percent of gross sales in 1989.

The figures displayed are comparable in that only minor revisions due to changing intra-SKF conditions have befallen the Tools division up to 1990 (the main posterior revision meant a downward adjustment of the Tools share from 3.73 percent to 3.66 percent on the 1982 figure).

It has been possible to reconstruct the series in Table A.1 exclusive of steel back to 1978 on the basis of figures given in successive Annual Reports (often from presented retrospective figures).

Much of what has been said about Table A.1 is relevant also for Table A.2 below. However, Component Systems has a shorter history as an independent division. Although not being extricated from the standard bearing business until 1984, the business can be traced back to 1982. Consequently, the series in Table A.2 is not affected by the already mentioned revision of data for 1982 (see also Table A.3 below). Furthermore, the figures are comparable in that some products (castings, some minor machine tools and car parts) that were transferred back to Bearing Industries in 1986 are excluded in Table A.2.

Figure A.2

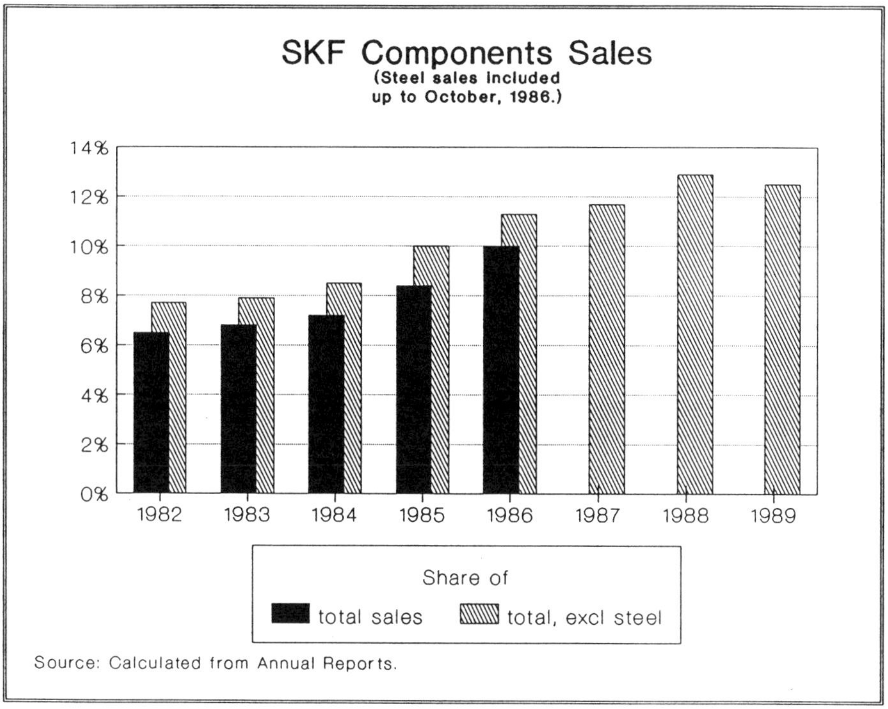

Figures on bearing sales prior to 1978 are not comparable with those shown in Table A.3 below. Changes in accounting principles in the late 1970s and our inability to exclude steel sales in a meaningful way have led us to restrict the time period considered to 1978-1989.

The latest available figures have been used throughout. However, the already referred to changes in the reported figures for 1982 do affect the bearing share, as they mainly concerned the distribution between bearings and components. Most importantly, the earlier figures exclude some 'other products' later brought in under bearings. In consequence, the series displayed below is 'jacked up' from 1982 onwards. The older series would have yielded a 68.1 percent share (vs. 74.6 percent as shown) and 80.6 percent (vs. 88.0 percent shown) for 1982, including and excluding steel sales, respectively.

Figure A.3

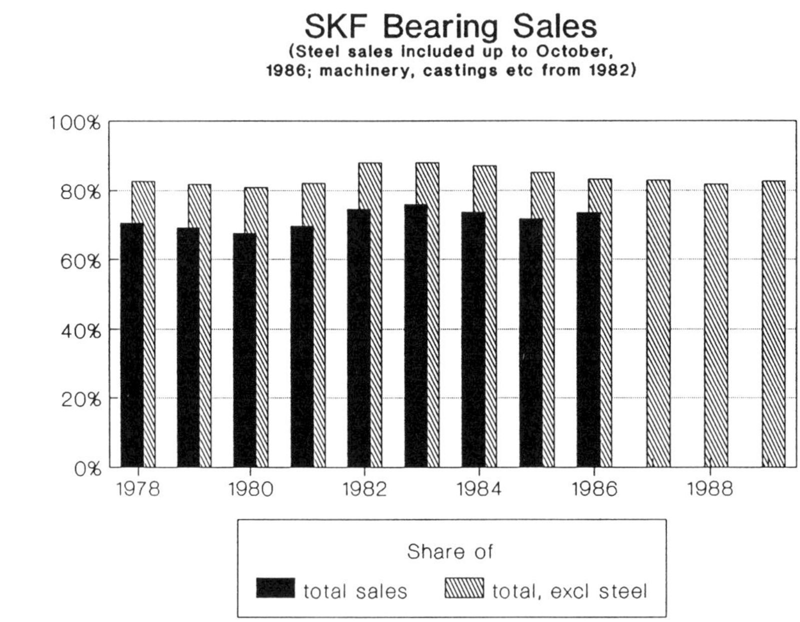

Source: Calculated from Annual Reports.

The following Tables A.4 - A.7 warrant no further remarks other than those already offered in this Appendix and in Section 3.2.3 above (cf. especially Footnotes 34 and 38 in Chapter 3).

Figure A.4

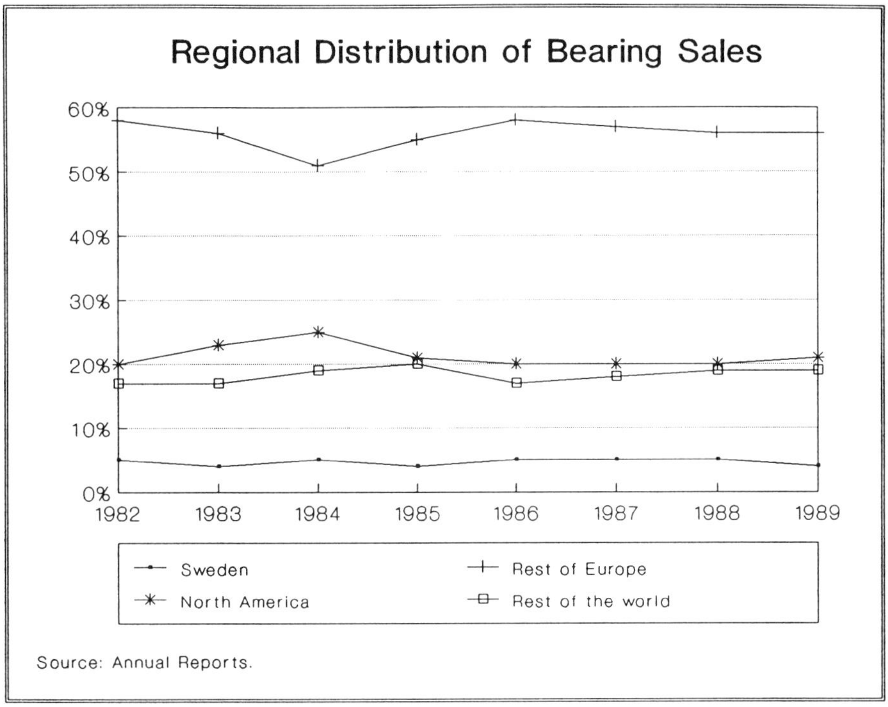

Figure A.5

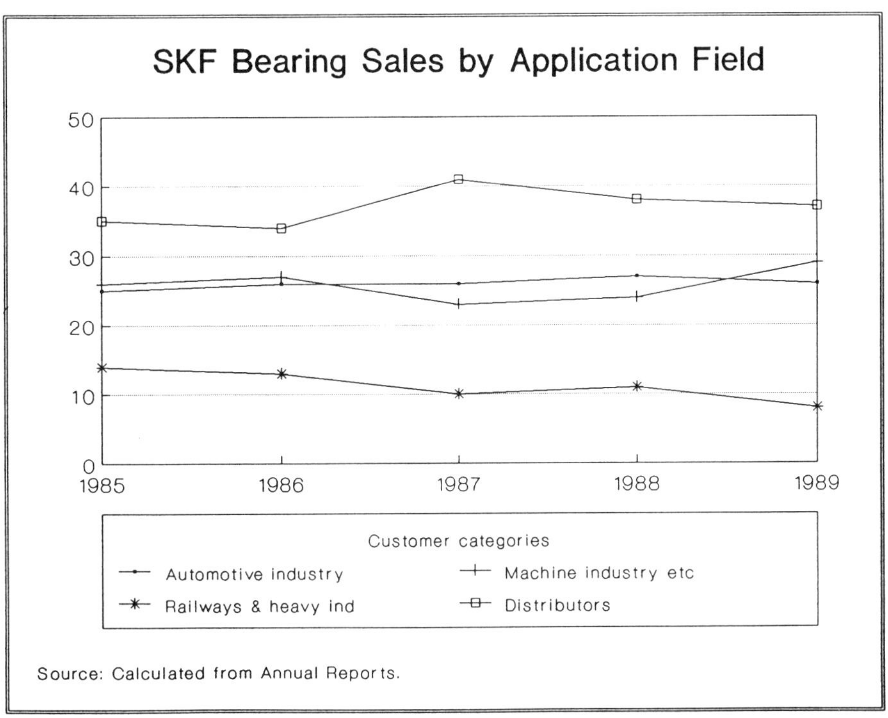

Figure A.6

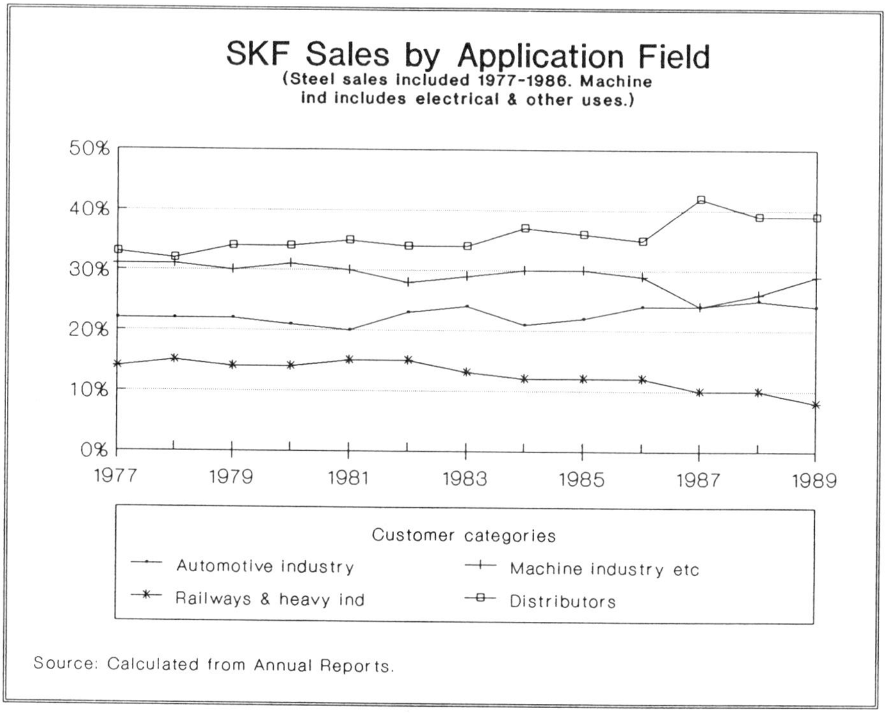

Figure A.7

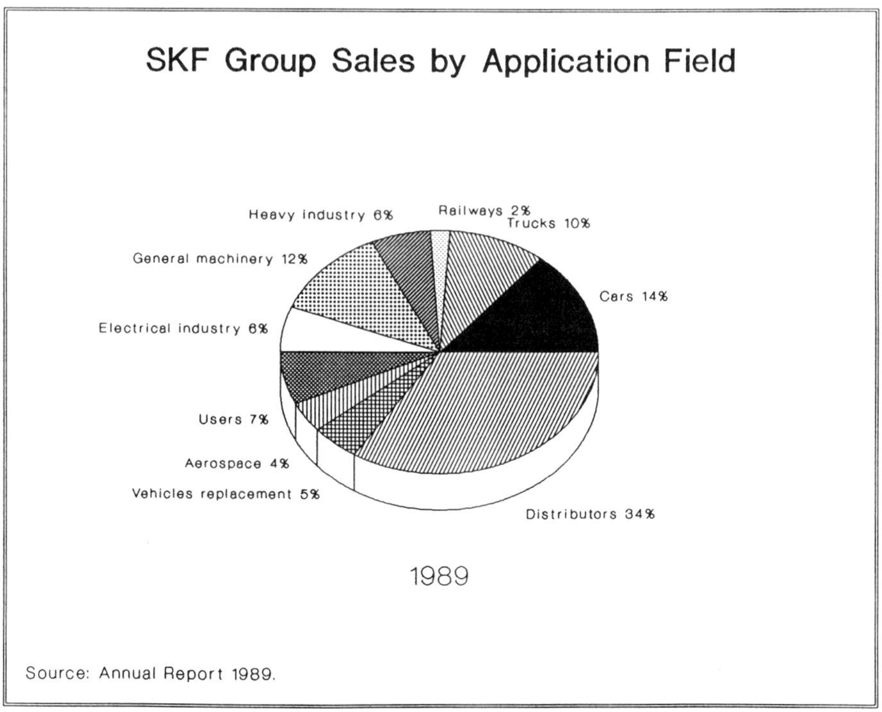

APPENDIX 3:

RECURRING ABBREVIATIONS USED IN THE TEXT

ACCESS	AdvanCed CustomEr Service System
API	Analyses Planning and Information
BEACON	BEAring CONsultant
BEDA	Bearing Engineering DAtabase
BRASCOS	BRASil Customer Order System
CAD	Computer-Aided Design
CAM	Computer-Aided Manufacturing
CCITT	Consultative Committee on International Telephone and Telegraph
CTT	Cutting Tools Technology
CR	Chicago Rawhide (Industries)
CROESUS	CROss rEference SyStem
CUSTSERV	CUSTomer SERVice system
DEC	Digital Equipment Corporation
DECNET	DEC NETwork
DCSS	Domestic Customer Service System
EDI	Electronic Data Interchange
EDIFACT	Electronic Data Interchange For Administration of Commerce and Trade
ERC	SKF Engineering and Research Centre B. V.
FAG	(Fischer A. G.) FAG Kugelfischer Georg Schaefer A. G.
FAS	Factory Administration System
FSO	SKF Forecasting and Supply Office
GE	General Electric
GEIS	GE Information Services Company
GFSS	Global Forecasting and Supply System
GM	General Motors
GMS	Group Management System

IBM	International Business Machines Corporation
ICSS	International Customer Service System
IS	Information Systems
ISDN	Integrated Services Digital Network
ISO	International Standards Organization
LAN	Local Area Network
LMT	Lidköping Machine Tools AB
MASCOS	Modular Automated Sales COmpany System
Mb	Megabit(s)
MCSS	Manufacturing Customer Service System
MEST	SKF Electronic Message Transmission
MNC	Multinational Corporation
MPSS	Master Production Scheduling System
MRC	MRC (formerly Marlin Rockwell Company)
NCB	National Coal Board
NMFC	New Material Flow Concept
NSK	Nippon Seiko Kogyo
NTN	NTN Toyo Bearing
ODETTE	Organization for Data Exchange by TeleTransmission in Europe
OEM	Original Equipment Manufacturer
OSI	Open Systems Interconnection
PC	Personal Computer
PC-80/-90	Production Concept for the 80s/90s
PFS	Product Forecasting System
PRODMAST	PRODuction MASTer file
PRODPERF	PROduction Delivery PERFormance system
PTT	(national) Post, Telegraph and Telephone authority
SCSS	Sales Company Service System
SKF	Aktiebolaget SKF (prior to 1976: Aktiebolaget Svenska Kullagerfabriken)
SNA	Systems Network Architecture
STI	Swedish Telecom International

STICS	SKF Totally Integrated Computer System
Telenet	SKF Group Telecommunications Network
TMS	Treasury Management System
TRW	TRW Inc.
UPI	United Precision Industries

APPENDIX 2

UNSHACKLING CORPORATE GEOGRAPHY

From:
Geografiska Annaler, Series B, Human Geography,
Volume 72 B, Number 1, pp. 3-12.
[Reprinted by permission of the publisher.]

UNSHACKLING CORPORATE GEOGRAPHY

ABSTRACT. The analysis of corporate spatial behavior appears to benefit from recognizing that the firm is a bundle of many different activities. They may be located together - prompting us to explicitly take account of firm-specific internal relationships - or separately - offering new possibilities for applying traditional location theory. Multinational corporations are especially well-poised to exploit location advantages, also as they vary over time for different activities. Dynamic adjustment as to where and to what extent activities are performed is becoming increasingly practicable. This largely conceptual argument is illustrated by specific examples from the use of data communications.

INTRODUCTION

In spite of the development of "corporate geography" or "geography of enterprise", the concept of the firm itself in spatial analysis remains rather undeveloped. Typically, the firm is taken as a given, indivisible starting point in industrial location theory, be it within the realms of traditional least-cost, behavioral, or structural approaches. Consequently, the implicit assumption is that substantial agglomeration advantages accrue automatically to very different economic activities when carried out within the same firm.

With internal relationships left outside the analysis, we can witness a remarkable preoccupation with external linkages in industrial location theory. This pervasive line of inquiry is probably a legacy of classical Weberian location theory. In the face of wide-spread disenchantment with the explanatory power of classical theory, a major last-ditch line of defense has been that the (least-cost) analysis needs to adequately take account of external agglomeration economies hitherto neglected (e.g. as in Smith, 1971 and 1981). Indeed, it has also been suggested that local external agglomeration economies are behavioral rather than monetary (Taylor, 1973). Going one step further, McDermott and Taylor (1982) make external linkages the linchpin when explaining locational patterns. More recent statements in the structuralist vein (notably Storper and Walker, 1989, and Walker, 1989) strongly favor analyses at the industry level and of territorial complexes, in the process explicitly militating against the importance of intra-firm linkages.

A directly related, distinguishing feature of industrial location theory in general is the heritage of <u>disjointed levels of analysis</u>. The watershed is between studying location behavior either in a defined region or of defined production entities. The intellectual challenge of attempting to unify the analyses has been more readily confronted in economic geography than in 'neighboring' disciplines, for instance, than in economics. Indeed, as early as when launching the very concept of "geography of the enterprise", McNee (1960) envisaged a natural evolution from studying individual corporate behavior to understanding the economic geography of specific industrial areas. Krumme (1984) illustrates the continued efforts at straddling the two basic perspectives[1]. The structuralist tradition tends to follow a slightly different, but related, tack. It basically steers clear of the problem by downplaying the relevance of individual firm activity and by assigning supremacy to larger scale social and economic processes. The issue is then typically framed in the macro-mould as one of the spatial division of labor (cf. Massey and Meegan, 1982; Meegan, 1984; Storper and Walker, 1989).

The reason for the keenness to join these levels of analysis may again be traced to the heritage from classical location theory. The basic propositions of non-homogeneous space and agglomeration economies external to the firm would, on the face of it, seem to hold promise in this respect. However, it is probably fair to say that economic location theory has, to some extent, become a prisoner of the dilemma of wanting to explain micro behavior of firms and regional location patterns with the same theory (and often at the same time). While one clearly always carries implications for the other, the two

---

[1] He concludes: "In this paper, yet another attempt has been made to contribute to the bridging of the gap between macro-analysis and micro-theory."(Krumme, 1984, p. 118).

perspectives have so far defied attempts to be coherently incorporated into the same theoretical statement.

Without rejecting any of the classical contributions, it is argued here that more mileage can be gained from existing geographical theory, simply by relaxing some implicit assumptions and by being more narrow in focus. We especially wish to promote the micro-level analysis of corporate spatial behavior, while also maintaining the perspective of the individual firm. A contention is that the individual firm is interesting per se in a geographic context.

Consequently, the purpose is not to attempt to explain regional or industrial spatial patterns in general. We will instead concentrate on what possible contribution can come out of a more detailed view of firm activities and their internal relationships. To what extent are these firm activities 'located'?

As befits a largely conceptual paper, we will borrow generously from the rich tradition in industrial location in general and from corporate geography in particular.

More specifically, the first section elaborates our view of the opportunity set for the location decision in the firm. Second, the theoretical concepts are illustrated. Examples highlight corporate activities being relocated as a result of international data communications bringing improved transportability of information-based services. By using the case of new communications possibilities, we can readily stress the dynamic nature and international scale of many location decisions. Lastly, some general conclusions are offered.

THE MULTI-FACETTED FIRM

A major contribution of corporate geography to location theory has been to shift the focus of attention from the 'factory' to the 'firm'. Successively extending the scope of inquiry, this line of research has increasingly come to devote itself to the very large firm and specifically to the multi-plant, multi-product, multi-functional, and, lately, also to the multi-national firm (cf. Hamilton, 1974; Lloyd and Dicken, 1977; Linge and Hamilton, 1981; Taylor and Thrift, 1982; Hayter and Watts, 1983; Dicken, 1986; Chapman and Walker, 1987).

However, the stress has continued to be placed on the 'multi-plant/multi-product' features, and, in turn, on manufacturing. In a direct line from Weber, it is the location of the production process per se that still commands the center stage, although the description and analysis often are very sophisticated (for a good example, see the extensive investigation by Clarke, 1985).

Admittedly, the concept of production in location theory can readily be extended to also include services. But rather than constituting a theoretical break-through, this extension reflects the similarity of service production to the traditional manufacture of goods, when the firm itself is perceived as essentially uni-functional. Consequently, basically the same analytical tools can be employed in the analysis. Perhaps it is most clearly demonstrated in studies emphasizing external linkages when interpreting firm location patterns (e.g. Steed, 1976). In this respect, say, printers may be no more different from iron-foundries than the latter from manufacturers of electronic equipment.

The Multi-Functional Firm

The 'multi-functional' aspect of the modern, large corporation is commonly recognized in the geographic literature (e.g. Hamilton, 1974, p. 5; Lloyd and Dicken, 1977, p. 368ff; Dicken, 1986, p. 191ff; Chapman and Walker, 1987, p. 105ff), but the subsequent discussion tends to either reduce the number of functions actually considered to a bare minimum, or to essentially lose the firm perspective.

The most common distinction between internal corporate activities is between control and production. Although different levels of control can be identified (cf. Törnquist, 1968), geographers have primarily dealt with the location of higher-order administrative functions or with the effects thereof for plant location. The former approach finds that both strategic and more routine decision-making tend to concentrate in information-rich locations, viz. especially corporate head-offices are located in major cities (Törnquist, 1970; Goddard, 1975). When the different activities are further subdivided, however, this approach takes the direction of analyzing the spatial distribution of occupational categories in general (e.g. Törnquist, 1973; Pred, 1973; Dicken and Lloyd, 1981; see also Storper and Walker, 1989), rather than studying the geography of the firm.

A similar leap from firm to regional perspectives is made by a strand of research concentrating on the effects of centralization of control functions (e.g. Westaway, 1974; Dicken, 1976). Here, the implications of external control for plant (re-)location in different regions are studied, but without going beyond the initial dichotomy of corporate functions. More comprehensive views will add functions like planning, research and development (R&D), and sales (e.g. McNee, 1974; Rees, 1972 and 1974), but that is done in the context of the firm growth process, in effect making specific location of firm activities less important than the overall process.

All the above perspectives have their merits, but there seems to be a need for reasserting the multi-functional aspect of the firm, also for our more limited objective of discussing location of corporate activities. An intuitive way to approach that issue is to think of the firm itself as a <u>bundle of activities</u>, performed with some permanence in time in order for the firm to meet its objectives.

A suggestive, but by no means exhaustive, list of different activities typically carried out in a firm is provided in the box (see Figure). It is the principle that is important, not the definitional questions of what exactly should constitute an 'activity'. However, it should be noted that, as used here, an activity is a distinctly different concept from that of decision-making, also when we consider non-production activities.

Figure

BOX: Standard Business Functions and Activities Performed in A Hypothetical Large Firm

Corporate Management
- Strategy formulation
- Strategy implementation ('structural strategy')
- Performance requirements/goals
- Acquisitions/divestments; agreements with external parties
- Large investments
- Operations in the aggregate

Finance
- Long term
  - Investments
  - R&D plan
  - Market investments
  - Finance and credit
  - International risks
  - Internal resource allocation
  - Portfolio strategies
- Short term
  - Budget
  - Cash flow analysis
  - Cost calculation
  - Tax calculation
  - Internal pricing
- Liquidity & payments
  - Invoicing, reinvoicing
  - Accounts receivable & payable
  - Tax payments
  - Cash management
  - Currency management
  - Interest management
- Control
  - Procedures and systems for reporting
  - Cost follow-up
  - Budget follow-up
  - Investment follow-up
  - Inventory control
  - Customer credits
  - Sales reporting
  - Accounting, consolidation and legal reporting

Research & Development
- Basic research
- External scanning
- Design
- Engineering
- Documentation
- Project administration
- Prototypes
- (Liaison)

Purchasing
- Plan
- Suppliers
- Goods/services purchased
- Logistics
- Quality control
- (Liaison)

Production
- Production cost calculation
- Investment in production facilities and machinery
- Production planning
- Maintenance of production facilities and machinery
- Production scheduling
- Manufacturing, plant operation
- Material flow
- Quality control
- Inventory control
- (Liaison)

Distribution
- Planning
- Scheduling
- Transport logistics
- Documentation
- Inventory
- (Liaison)

Marketing & Sales
- Sales forecasts
- Product strategies
- Competitor analysis
- Pricing
- Choice of channel
- New customer contacts
- Contacts, existing customers
- Product catalogue
- Order entry
- Delivery details
- After sales service and maintenance
  - Service strategy
  - Service contracts
  - Service calls
  - Administration of spares
- (Liaison)

Administration
- Personnel
- Payroll
- Training
- Legal, taxes
- Public relations
- Internal communications
- Computerized information systems
- Library, archives, databases

By recognizing that activities can be seen as separate, the insights gained in traditional, production-oriented location theory can be recycled. Location of an isolated activity is clearly a very similar issue to the classical one of location of production. One distinct advantage with a disaggregated view of the firm, however, is precisely that we can more closely approximate the classical assumption of the uni-functional firm. Rather than suppressing the influence of other firm activities, each activity can be considered separately and the many various locational influences more easily identified. Of course, many activities in a firm are commonly located together, but it is analytically helpful to make that explicit. Put differently, there is little need to assume 'automatic' internal agglomeration advantages.

To illustrate, first recall that Smith (1981, pp. 337-348) in a now classic investigation found that even a very sophisticated application of the variable-cost model failed to explain the locational pattern for production in a branch of the U.S. electronics industry. He then goes on to hypothesize that sites for the facilities could be chosen in order to exploit external agglomeration economies especially for research, instead of selecting a site for being the low cost location of production. Smith concludes that, in this case, these specific external agglomeration economies would need to be incorporated into the calculations.

With the terminology advocated here, the above conclusion would be somewhat rephrased to take account of the internal links between the identified two activities. Not only do the external agglomeration economies for the R&D function outweigh the least-cost considerations for location of just production, but so do also the internal benefits of locating the activities at the same site. Otherwise it would have been rational to locate only production at its least-cost location. The internal benefits probably stem from the short product life cycles in the electronics industry, and from the need for quick feedback from production to R&D putting a premium on short and effective links between the two activities.

Which activities physically can be located separately is largely a technical question[2], but which activities are/should be located separately is an issue for corporate geography.

[2] This pragmatic and somewhat atheoretic approach is inspired by transaction cost economics, where the 'transaction' is similarly defined (cf. Williamson, 1981, p. 1544). The similarities end there, however, as transaction cost analysis is primarily concerned with the changing boundary of the firm in general, and vertical integration in particular (for an application in economic geography, see Scott, 1986). Our focus is on the location of firm activities and the possible changes thereof (see below).

In modern corporate geography, the location decision has abdicated its classical position of primary importance to instead become an outcome of (all) other business decisions (cf. McNee, 1974; North, 1974). The focus of analysis becomes the spatial implications of business decisions. North (1974, p. 213) suggests that this requires not only studying the more commonly discussed relocation, branch and initial location decisions, but also extensions, closures and takeovers and mergers. For our purposes, it is convenient to classify these spatial adjustment alternatives according to whether they involve establishing a facility 'from scratch' or changing the extent of activity at an existing site. Reducing the number of categories considered, the former could be labelled a 'green-field' location (with a term inspired from management literature), and the latter group would consist both of existing firm sites and of acquisitions; i.e. a constrained set of possible locations.

Interestingly, North (1974) found in situ extension the most common type of expansion for a large number of different size companies, and, together with acquisitions, also the type to be the least sensitive to locational considerations. In other words, since the set of possible locations is so severely constrained, locational concerns are viewed as rendered largely unimportant in these cases.

How ever worded, North's (1974) conclusion was probably strongly influenced by two design characteristics of the investigation: first, it was limited to manufacturing activities (of manufacturing firms), and second, it did not extend to subsequent shifting around of activities. An example can demonstrate how these limitations could hamper an inquiry. Consider the case of an acquisition, where, for instance, the bulk of the R&D activities later on is shifted from the acquired company to a site of the acquiring company. Not only are non-manufacturing activities involved, the transfer itself could take some time to accomplish, therefore escaping detection. Moreover, the final site selection for the R&D activities could very well be determined by internal agglomeration advantages as the constrained set of possible locations are evaluated. Indeed, the acquired R&D function can be 'unbundled' and distributed among several existing sites of the acquiring company.

In the (most common) case of in situ extension, and where the firm has several alternative sites, the location of the expanding activities may well be similarly chosen. Firm-specific internal agglomeration advantages can determine both the (constrained) site selection and the range of activities carried out at a given site. Locational considerations are not only important for 'green-field' location decisions, but also for 'constrained' location of firm activities.

In essence, we are arguing here for little more than adding another level in the analysis in corporate geography. If the multi-functional firm is best seen as a bundle of different, internally linked activities, then that must be akin to a collection of uni-functional firms, but where the links are external. However, by setting the problem within one corporation, firm-specific locational considerations come into play. There is a qualitative difference between external links, which basically can be exploited by any firm, and internal links, which indeed are specific to a particular firm. Obviously, the constrained set of possible locations is firm-specific, but the argument carries even further.

The Multi-National Firm

The logical extension of spatial expansion by the firm is the multi-national corporation (MNC). In corporate geography, MNCs have also come to loom larger and larger in the analysis (cf. Linge and Hamilton, 1981; Taylor and Thrift, 1982; Dicken, 1986). This largely empirically based development has primarily drawn its inspiration from theories of corporate growth. Existing theories with clear locational implications have been appended, covering first a primarily national scale (McNee, 1974; Taylor, 1975), but then explicitly spilling over the borders of the home country (Håkanson, 1979; Watts, 1980). The sequential expansion into international markets goes from exports and sales agents, via sales subsidiaries to foreign country production (see Håkanson, 1979).

An important contribution coming out of this line of research is that a locational pattern observed at any given time only can be a snap-shot of an ongoing process. It must apply à fortiori to the spatial distribution of activities within an individual firm. However, there has been little commensurate attention paid to the internal activities of the firm itself. In the context of sequential expansion, only the location of sales (agents and subsidiaries), corporate management (head-office) and production (manufacturing and assembly) activities tend to be considered, and in rather general terms (e.g. Håkanson, 1979; Dicken, 1986). By being more generous as to the number of activities taken into account, more activity-specific location factors can be brought to the fore.

Locational influences also operate at different levels of aggregation. Perhaps the clearest statement of this principle of a spatial scale is found in Townroe (1976), who classifies location factors according to whether their influence is on site, community, or regional levels respectively. In view of our discussion in the preceding paragraph, the scale should be amended to include the national level and another one covering a group of countries. The latter category may be less obvious, but it appears to become increasingly relevant for the increasingly international MNCs.

Supranational location factors could be either institutional or physical in character. Institutional factors are, for instance, policies and regulations for the whole of the European Economic Community. Transport logistics are more physical, requiring, say, establishing a facility somewhere in Latin America. Many MNCs are apparently convinced of the advantages of coordinating activities at the supranational level, since they often are organized in geographic area divisions, or use that as one dimension in a matrix organization. A division then comprises a part of the world or several countries.

One important element is still missing in our construct and that relates to the 'fluid content', in a geographic sense, of corporate organization. We have mentioned that activities should be carried out with some permanence in time, but that does not have to extend to simultaneous permanence in space. The idea is simply that of MNCs being foot-loose. The locational process is not only a growth process, but also a process of continuous adjustment. This aspect is not recognized in corporate geography and we have to look further afield for inspiration.

Taking his cue from portfolio theory in financial economics, Kogut (1983) points to the sequential, network advantages accruing to an already internationally dispersed firm. One such advantage is the operating flexibility of an MNC, which can exploit opportunities for a form of arbitrage by shifting production among its existing network of production units in response to, for example, major exchange rate movements or changes in the local skill composition of labor.

If we transfer this notion into a specifically spatial setting, the adjustment would repeatedly influence the size and scope of operations at a particular site, but without involving either new investment or physical extension of a facility. In terms of our overall argument, the continuous adjustment can further be accomplished at other than the implied national level and it can include also non-production activities.

FIRM INTERNAL LOCATIONAL CHANGE IN PRACTICE

Isard and Isard (1945) argued that the dynamic influence of transport technology clearly alters geographic resistance to movement of people and goods, and, by implication, new transport technology then provides a good opportunity for tracing such changes. They analyzed the broad effects of aircraft; we translate the approach to consider both the general case of improved transportability of services, and the specific, novel ways of transporting information-based services. The reason for the latter is twofold, in that we want to emphasize non-production activities and to investigate the most recent technological change lessening resistance to spatial separation of activities. Indeed, it is the improved communications possibilities, in a wide sense, that make uni-functional views of the firm increasingly untenable.

In practice, we consider the new opportunities offered by improved telecommunications, notably data communications[3]. The purpose here is to illustrate, rather than verify, the concepts introduced in the previous section. More extensive case studies on the use of telecommunications in individual firms can be found in Marshall (1984) and Bakis (1987). However, those studies have a focus different from ours, both being largely descriptive and rather general regarding location factors.

Location of Separable Activities

The advantage of being explicit about the degree of aggregation can indirectly be demonstrated by drawing on Marshall's (1984) rich discussion of how information technology supports centralization of office work at Ford UK and decentralization at Unilever. Rather than following Marshall's explanation and putting it all down to the different prevailing corporate structures, it can be surmised that, instead, more activity-specific influences showed up at Ford than at Unilever since Marshall studied only the accounting function[4] at Ford, but all non-manufacturing activities collectively at Unilever. Actually, our interpretation gets some further indirect support from Marshall himself when he, en passant, compares only the same higher level management functions in both organizations. Then he also indicates finding the same tendencies - in this case toward centralization - in both instances.

A much more specific illustration is how SKF, the Swedish[5] world leader in roller

---

[3] The advent of effective (in terms of cost and performance) data communications makes it feasible to subdivide - or fragment - activities, to recombine activities, and to link activities in new ways. Standardization gives the system unprecedented capacity, but also imposes constraints. For instance, information is transported more as packed in containers than as general cargo in the new communications networks. - For a discussion of these underlying possibilities and restrictions, see Hagström (1990).

[4] Accounting is indeed commonly regarded to be a prime candidate for concentration using information technology (e.g. Hagström, 1990).

[5] Most of the examples given are based on research done on Swedish MNCs. An important advantage, for our purposes, is the very much higher dependence on foreign markets (both for sales and production) in small home country MNCs than in large home country MNCs. For instance, SKF has more than 95 %

bearings, sends virtually all its international telex messages from Gothenburg in Sweden by first routing them through its own, private data communications network. Thus, the approximately 150 subsidiaries around the world can benefit from the lower Swedish telex rates.

The example highlights that geographic location can be an important consideration also for an extremely limited activity. Moreover, transmission of telexes is clearly a stand-alone activity, and its location neatly fits with traditional, Weberian least-cost theory. A similarly isolated activity is warehousing of finished products, which frequently is located according to the Weberian minimum transport cost principle. More often than not, highly concentrated warehousing is contingent on a sophisticated data communications system. A good example is ESAB's warehouse in Holland, to which all its European plants deliver, and from which practically all its European customers are supplied with welding equipment and consumables.

Rather than undermining the relevance of traditional location theories, as is sometimes suggested (e.g. Hepworth, 1986), widespread usage of new information technology can open new fields of application for 'old' theories. As the examples of disaggregated firm activities show, there is even great scope for the much maligned least-cost location theory. Some indirect support for this contention can be found in a rare defense of Weberian principles. Dicken (1977) argues that least-cost location theory does have some explanatory power on an international, large firm scale, but he only considers aggregated activities. He is mainly concerned with manufacturing, but suspects it may be so also for headquarters and office functions (if allowing for external, information-related agglomeration advantages of the kind discussed in the previous section)[6].

However, recall that separating out activities often brings out the existence of internal agglomeration advantages. We can illustrate this with an example from Ericsson, manufacturer of telecommunications equipment. Stand-by servicing of the software

---

of its sales, and almost 90 % of its employees, abroad.

[6] A more extensive version of this line of argument can be found in Dicken (1986).

(which is the major part of value added) in an AXE telephone exchange is in principle carried out from Stockholm, irrespective of where in the world a malfunction appears. The software block is "lifted" from the exchange, transmitted via the telephone network, and then "replaced" when corrected. The location of the concentrated service unit was influenced both by low cost/skill availability, and by internal agglomeration factors. Highly skilled engineers are available relatively cheaply and abundantly in Sweden, and physical proximity to AXE 'product' development was deemed by the company to be extremely valuable.

Locational Opportunity Set

We do not wish to imply that external agglomeration advantages are without importance or that firm-specific location factors only are 'attractors'. Just consider the 'green-field' location of SKF's main, corporate R&D facility. Since 1972, it is situated in Nieuwegein, Holland - a place where SKF has no other activities. The carefully chosen site capitalizes on proximity to relevant technical knowledge (in the Eindhoven-Utrecht area), and is distant from SKF's head-office and major producing subsidiaries[7]. The reason for locating the R&D center <u>away</u> from SKF's most powerful subsidiaries, is to avoid any single unit to dominate the research activities to the detriment of over-all corporate objectives. Still, the center needs to be receptive to local production needs. Hence, a location close to the head-office was also rejected.

The increased relative freedom in locating activities enjoyed by SKF is contingent on excellent internal communications, in practice the SKF proprietary data communications network. These improved possibilities extend to 'constrained' location as well. Continuing our example, 'R' and 'D' have to a great extent been separated in SKF. The data communications network provides the '&', linking research with development and both with other activities in the company. Basic research is carried out in Holland, while

[7] The closest major subsidiaries are in Luton, UK, Clamart, France, and Schweinfurt, West Germany.

product development has been shared among producing subsidiaries around the world. Subsidiaries now have corporate product development responsibilities in accordance with their global product responsibilities. Hereby SKF can reap benefits from cheek-by-jowl production and product development without having to forego the economies of scale in basic research. Internal and external agglomeration advantages thus exert different locational influences for the R&D function, and in this case, the locational repercussions are clear.

The locational opportunity set is widening, accompanied by a tendency for the upper end of the locational scale to gain in weight. Site factors are losing in relative importance to national and also to supranational factors. Additional prominent considerations for locating the SKF research center were the comparatively low Dutch taxes for expatriates and the envisaged relative ease of labor mobility within the EC; also seemingly lending support to the approach of classical location theory. Although important, these higher-order external factors did not determine the final locational choice. As we have seen, that decision cannot be adequately understood if the more important firm-specific internal location factors are excluded from the analysis.

Other very good illustrations of expanding opportunities can be found in the finance area, where activities are especially amenable to use of international data communications. Local subsidiaries in large MNCs are often stripped of many of their financial activities, which are subsequently concentrated and located according to their specific locational needs. For instance, ASEA[8], the Swedish electro-mechanical equipment manufacturer, put its corporate trading and counter-trade unit in London, its international financing activities in Switzerland, and most of its portfolio management activities in New York.

An upshot of these examples is that fine-tuned spatial separation of activities is tantamount to being able to tailor activities in order to exploit very specific location advantages, be they external or internal to the firm.

---

[8] Now comprising half of the new Asea Brown Boveri.

Continuous Locational Adjustment

Increased locational freedom is also increased freedom to relocate and to dynamically adjust activities. Corporations become foot-loose as to where and to what extent corporate activities are performed.

Most corporate financial activities easily move in search of low taxes, good double taxation agreements, availability of financial expertise, ready links to financial partners, good communications and the like. The systems these activities are dependent on (e.g. for corporate cash management, invoicing-reinvoicing and debt monitoring) can normally be run from any place where one can 'plug into' the corporate communications network. Perhaps surprisingly, these conditions can extend also to more traditional activities. For instance, SKF transferred its Latin American regional warehouse smoothly and quickly to Miami, when the political situation worsened in Panama (the prior location). This relocation did not involve the physical shipments of stocks one could expect. The order, inventory and shipping systems could accommodate both the old and the brand new warehouses, shipping as much as possible from the former, while only filling up in the latter, until the transfer was complete. SKF's customers never really noticed any difference.

Some operational, or more day-to-day, locational adjustment of corporate activities is just around the corner. Again, SKF provides a good example. So far, SKF's production has been specialized by type and even dimension of bearing among its producing subsidiaries. However, recent changes in bearing production technology will permit shorter efficient production runs. Local production is likely to become an additional alternative to the present ones of production at the specialized plant or of taking from stock, when filling a customer order. Capacity utilization then improves in the corporate production and distribution network. But managing this set of options could conceivably lead a company like SKF to actively adjust production and inventories also to more temporary location factors, such as a skill shortage, exchange rate imbalances and interest rate changes. The notion of continuous locational adjustment is thus - within limits - relevant even for production, an activity commonly associated with locational inertia.

CONCLUSIONS

A firm is multi-functional, consisting of a large number of more or less loosely coupled activities. Firm activities are often located at the same site, but it is not uncommon that other location factors outweigh the influence of these internal agglomeration advantages. Indeed, the restrictions on the geographical location of corporate activities are continuously being undermined with improvements in transport and communications. Increased mobility of firm activities implies that dynamic locational adjustment becomes a feasible proposition and that the locational horizon widens for the firm.

We surmise that alertness to the existing possibilities for locating firm activities can significantly extend the reach of existing theory in economic geography, in particular in corporate geography. And location matters, but then things like firm-specific conditions, complex internal links and non-discrete locational choices also have to be brought into the analysis. Admittedly, there is a danger in making the concept of location so wide it becomes watered down, but in this case that is the price for relevance. However, although a full explanation cannot be reduced to any single cause, we have seen how even widely criticized classical location theory can provide very valuable insights in understanding the location of different firm activities, given a disaggregated level of analysis.

The policy implications for regional development are somewhat paradoxical. Broadly, site and community level location factors are losing in relative importance, while very specific local advantages or incentives may still successfully attract a new, specialized activity. Policy-makers at the regional level must be attentive to continuous locational adjustment at existing sites. Conversely, they also have to raise their sights, increasing their efforts at influencing policy at the national and supra-national levels.

Finally, the preceding discussion has deliberately been kept almost exclusively within even narrowly defined boundaries of economic geography. Since this has not been particularly restrictive for the argument, perhaps there is less need than commonly assumed to view economic geography as 'the poor relative from the country' among the social sciences. Consequently, there may even be a good case for reclaiming much of the analysis of the spatial aspect of economic activity from the heartland of other disciplines.

ACKNOWLEDGEMENTS. I wish to acknowledge Claes-Fredrik Claeson, Lars Håkanson, R. B. Le Heron, G. J. R. Linge, and an anonymous referee for comments on a previous version of this paper, while absolving them of any responsibility for its contents. Research funding has been provided by the Swedish Council for Research in the Humanities and Social Sciences (HSFR), and by the Information Technology Research Program of the Institute for Management of Innovation and Technology (IMIT).

REFERENCES

BAKIS, H. (1987): "Telecommunications and the global firm", pp. 130-160 in HAMILTON, F. E. I. (ed.): **Industrial Change in Advanced Economies**, Croom Helm Ltd., London.

CHAPMAN, K. and WALKER, D. (1987): **Industrial Location: Principles and Policies**. Basil Blackwell, Oxford.

CLARKE, I. M. (1985): **The Spatial Organization of Multinational Corporations**. Croom Helm Ltd., London.

DICKEN, P. (1976): "The multiplant business enterprise and geographical space: some issues in the study of external control and regional development", **Regional Studies** 10: 401-412.

DICKEN, P. (1977): "A note on location theory and the large business enterprise", **Area** 9: 138-143.

DICKEN, P. (1986): **Global Shift: Industrial Change in a Turbulent World**. Harper & Row Ltd., London.

DICKEN, P. and LLOYD, P. E. (1981): **Modern Western Society: A Geographical Perspective on Work, Home and Well-Being**. Harper & Row Ltd., London.

GODDARD, J. B. (1975): **Office Location in Urban and Regional Development**. Oxford University Press, London.

HAGSTRÖM, P. (1990): "New information systems and the changing structure of MNCs", pp. 164-185 in BARTLETT, C. A., DOZ, Y. and HEDLUND, G. (eds.): **Managing the Global Firm**, Routledge, London.

HÅKANSON, L. (1979): "Towards a theory of location and corporate growth", pp. 115-138 in HAMILTON, F. E. I. and LINGE, G. J. R. (eds.): **Spatial Analysis, Industry and the Industrial Environment; Volume I: Industrial Systems**, John Wiley & Sons Ltd., Chichester.

HAMILTON, F. E. I. (1974): "A view of spatial behaviour, industrial organizations and decision-making", pp. 3-43 in HAMILTON, F. E. I. (ed.): **Spatial Perspectives on Industrial Organization and Decision-making**, John Wiley & Sons Ltd., London.

HAYTER, R. and WATTS, H. D. (1983): "The geography of enterprise: a reappraisal", **Progress in Human Geography** 7: 157-181.

HEPWORTH, M. (1986): "The geography of technological change in the information economy", **Regional Studies** 20: 407-424.

ISARD, C. and ISARD, W. (1945): "Economic implications of aircraft", **Quarterly Journal of Economics** 59: 145-169.

KOGUT, B. (1983): "Foreign direct investment as a sequential process", pp. 38-56 in KINDLEBERGER, C. P. and AUDRETSCH, D. (eds.): **The Multinational Corporation in the 1980s**, The M.I.T. Press, Cambridge, Mass.

KRUMME, G. (1984): "Turbulent environments, corporate strategies and local employment perspectives", **GeoJournal** 9: 111-119.

LINGE, G. J. R. and HAMILTON, F. E. I. (1981): "International industrial systems", pp. 1-117 in HAMILTON, F. E. I. and LINGE, G. J. R. (eds.): **Spatial Analysis, Industry and the Industrial Environment; Volume II: International Industrial Systems**, John Wiley & Sons Ltd., Chichester.

LLOYD, P. E. and DICKEN, P. (1977): **Location in Space: A Theoretical Approach to Economic Geography (Second Edition)**. Harper & Row Ltd., London.

McDERMOTT, P. and TAYLOR, M. (1982): **Industrial Organization and Location**. Cambridge University Press, Cambridge.

McNEE, R. B. (1960): "Towards a more humanistic geography: the geography of enterprise", **Tijdschrift voor Economische en Sociale Geografie** 51: 201-206.

McNEE, R. B. (1974): "A systems approach of understanding the geographic behavior of organizations, especially large corporations", pp. 47-75 in HAMILTON, F. E. I. (ed.): **Spatial Perspectives on Industrial Organization and Decision-making**, John Wiley & Sons Ltd., London.

MARSHALL, J. N. (1984): "Information technology changes corporate office activity", **GeoJournal** 9: 171-178.

MASSEY, D. (1984): **Spatial Divisions of Labour: Social Structures and the Geography of Production**. Macmillan, London.

MASSEY, D. and MEEGAN, R. (1982): **The Anatomy of Job Loss**. Methuen, London.

NORTH, D. J. (1974): "The process of locational change in different manufacturing organizations", pp. 213-244 in HAMILTON, F. E. I. (ed.): **Spatial Perspectives on Industrial Organization and Decision-making**. John Wiley & Sons Ltd., London.

PRED, A. R. (1973): "The growth and development of systems of cities in advanced economies", in PRED, A. R. and TÖRNQVIST, G. E. (eds.): "Systems of cities and information flows: two essays", **Lund Studies in Geography, Ser. B Human Geography** 38: 7-82.

REES, J. (1972): "The industrial corporation and decision location analysis", **Area** 4: 199-205.

REES, J. (1974): "Decision-making, the growth of the firm and the business environment", pp. 189-211 in HAMILTON, F. E. I. (ed.): **Spatial Perspectives on Industrial Organization and Decision-making**, John Wiley & Sons Ltd., London.

SCOTT, A. J. (1986): "Industrial organization and location: division of labor, the firm, and spatial process", **Economic Geography** 62: 215-231.

SMITH, D. M. (1971): **Industrial Location: An Economic Geographical Analysis**. John Wiley & Sons, Inc., New York, N.Y.

SMITH, D. M. (1981): **Industrial Location: An Economic Geographical Analysis (Second Edition)**. John Wiley & Sons, Inc., New York, N.Y.

STEED, G. (1976): "Centrality and locational change: printing, publishing, and clothing in Montreal and Toronto", **Economic Geography** 52: 193-205.

STORPER, M. and WALKER, R. (1989): **The Capitalist Imperative: Territory, Technology, and Industrial Growth**. Basil Blackwell, Oxford.

TAYLOR, M. J. (1973): "Local linkage, external economies and the ironfoundry industry of the West Midlands and East Lancashire conurbations", **Regional Studies** 7: 387-400.

TAYLOR, M. J. (1975): "Organizational growth, spatial interaction and location decision-making", **Regional Studies** 9: 313-323.

TAYLOR, M. J. and THRIFT, N. J. (1982): "Models of corporate development and the multinational corporation", pp. 14-32 in TAYLOR, M. J. and THRIFT, N. J. (eds.): **The Geography of Multinationals**, Croom Helm Ltd., London.

TÖRNQVIST, G. E. (1968): "Flows of information and the location of economic activities", **Lund Studies in Geography, Ser. B Human Geography** 30.

TÖRNQVIST, G. E. (1970): "Contact systems and regional development", **Lund Studies in Geography, Ser. B Human Geography** 35.

TÖRNQVIST, G. E. (1973): "Contact requirements and travel facilities - contact models of Sweden and regional development alternatives in the future", in PRED, A. R. and TÖRNQVIST, G. E. (eds.): "Systems of cities and information flows: two essays", **Lund Studies in Geography, Ser. B Human Geography** 38, pp. 83-121.

TOWNROE, P. M. (1976): **Planning Industrial Location**. Leonard Hill Ltd., London.

WALKER, R. (1989): "A requiem for corporate geography: new directions in industrial organization, the production of place and the uneven development", **Geografiska Annaler**, 71 B: 43-68.

WATTS, H. D. (1980): **The Large Industrial Enterprise: Some Spatial Perspectives**. Croom Helm Ltd., London.

WESTAWAY, J. (1974): "The spatial hierarchy of business organizations and its implications for the British urban system", **Regional Studies** 8: 145-155.

WILLIAMSON, O. E. (1981): "The modern corporation: origins, evolution, attributes", **Journal of Economic Literature** XIX: 1537-1568.

LATEST IIB BOOKS

Lindquist, Maria: Infant Multinationals - The Internationalization of Young, Technology-based Swedish Firms. (Doctoral dissertation)
Stockholm: IIB, 1991.
SEK 400:-. ISBN 91-971005-87

Zander, Udo: Exploiting A Technological Edge - Voluntary and Involuntary Dissemination of Technology. (Doctoral dissertation)
Stockholm: IIB, 1991.
SEK 400:-. ISBN 91-971005-52

Berglöf, Erik: Corporate Control and Capital Structure - Essays on Property Rights and Financial Contracts. (Doctoral dissertation)
Stockholm: IIB, 1991.
SEK 400:-. ISBN 91-971005-60

Sölvell, Örjan, Zander, Ivo & Porter, Michael E.: Advantage Sweden.
Stockholm: Norstedts Juridikförlag, 1991.
SEK 370:-. ISBN 91-1-907522-7

Nordström, Kjell A.: The Internationalization Process of the Firm - Searching for New Patterns and Explanations. (Doctoral dissertation)
Stockholm: IIB, 1991.
SEK 400:-. ISBN 91-971005-79

Åhlander, Karl: Aspects of Modern Treasury Management - Organization and External Financial Activities in Swedish MNCs. (Doctoral dissertation)
Stockholm: IIB, 1990.
SEK 450:-. ISBN 91-971005-95

Ågren, Lars: Swedish Direct Investment in the U.S. (Doctoral dissertation)
Stockholm: IIB, 1990.
SEK 400:-. ISBN 91-971005-44

Bartlett, Christopher A., Doz, Yves & Hedlund, Gunnar (eds.): Managing the Global Firm.
London: Routledge, 1990.
ISBN 0-415-03711-5

Roos, Johan: Cooperative Venture Formation Processes: Characteristics and Impact on Performance. (Doctoral dissertation)
Stockholm: IIB, 1989. (Out of print)
ISBN 91-971005-3-6

Berglöf, Erik: Bilaga 12: Ägarna och kontrollen över företaget - en jämförande studie av sex länders finansiella system. SOU 1988:38 Ägande och inflytande i svenskt näringsliv.
Stockholm: Allmänna Förlaget, 1988.
ISBN 91-38-10199-8

Lorange, Peter & Roos, Johan (eds.): The Challenge of Cooperative Ventures.
Stockholm: IIB, 1989.
SEK 190:-. ISBN 91-971005-01

Hood, Neil & Vahlne, Jan-Erik (eds.): Strategies in Global Competition.
London: Croom Helm, 1988.
ISBN 0-7099-3796-2

Farhang, Manucher: Market Entry in the Middle East.
Stockholm: IIB, 1987.
SEK 250:-. ISBN 91-971005-02

Sölvell, Örjan: Entry barriers and foreign penetration - Emerging patterns of international competition in two electrical engineering industries. (Doctoral dissertation)
Stockholm: IIB, 1987.
SEK 350:-. ISBN 91-7810-999-X

Knutsson, Jan: Kinesiskt förhandlingsbeteende samt dess kulturella och institutionella grund.
Stockholm: IIB, 1986.
SEK 180:-. ISBN 91-7810-632-X

Håkanson, Lars (ed.): Effects of Industrial Investments in Developing Countries: The Mufindi Pulp and Paper Mill, Tanzania.
Stockholm & Dar es Salaam: EFI & IRA, 1986.
ISBN 91-7258-219-7

Håkanson, Lars & Zander, Udo: Managing International Research and Development.
Stockholm: Sveriges Mekanförbund, 1986.
ISBN 91-524-0843-4